MW01011872

MW01011872

The Post-Conviction Citebook

Joe Allan Bounds

INFINITY PUBLISHING

Cover Illustration by: Jane Eichwald of Ambler Document Processing

ISBN 978-0-7414-5373-0

Published by:

INFINITY PUBLISHING

Info@buybooksontheweb.com
www.buybooksontheweb.com
Toll-free (877) BUY BOOK
Local Phone (610) 941-9999
Fax (610) 941-9959

Printed in the United States of America

Published November 2012

Acknowledgements

Thanks to my late sister, Dorothy Bounds and to her son, Austin Bounds and Lora Tennison for their hard work and effort and Yusuf El-Amin. I want to say my special thanks to Jane Eichwald, my typist and cover designer with Ambler Document Processing for all of her hard work and consistent effort in making this book. Additionally, I thank Mr. and Mrs. W.A. McClure for their support and making the publication of this book possible.

GENERAL TOPICS

- **Ineffective Assistance of Counsel**

- **The Right to Counsel**

- **Ineffectiveness vs. Strategy Decisions**

- **Conflict of Interest**

- **Denial of Counsel**

- **Evidentiary Hearing**

- **Cause for Procedural Default**

- **Actual Innocence/Fundamental Miscarriage of Justice is an Exception to "Cause" for Procedural Default**

- **Factual Innocence Claims**

- **Legal Innocence Claims**

- **External Factors Can Constitute "Cause" For**

- **Procedural Default**

- **Novelty Issues of Constitutional Law**

- **Intervening Change in Law; or Retroactive**

- **Application of the Law**

- **The "Ends of Justice"**

- **Habeas Corpus Miscellaneous**

Introduction

The Post-Conviction Citebook is the ultimate shortcut quick reference for ineffective assistance of counsel claims. The book provides the user a 16 page Table of Contents with over 740 quick reference topics covering:

- Ineffective Assistance of Counsel
- Pretrial proceedings
- Motions
- Defenses
- Guilty Pleas
- Trials
- Jury Instructions
- Verdicts
- Sentencing
- Appellate proceedings
- Post-verdict
- Conflict of Interest
- Evidentiary Hearings
- Cause for Procedural Default
- Strickland
- Cronic
- Apprendi
- Blakely
- Booker
- Shepard

This is primarily a research reference book with favorable case law on almost any subject in the field of post-conviction remedies. The contents have been designed to assist the individual user in finding favorable case law by topic and in chronological order as a criminal trial or proceedings may unfold. This book is a valuable asset to any law library and will save the user countless hours in research.

The Federal court system has created an extremely narrow road in the field of post-conviction designed to prevent an individual from obtaining relief from a constitutional violation based on the procedural default rule. The pitfalls created by the procedural default rule require a criminal defendant to show "cause" for failure to raise the issue at trial or on direct appeal and actual prejudice resulting from the error. This book has been designed to assist the user in showing "cause" for procedural default.

INSTRUCTIONS ON USE OF BOOK (IMPORTANT)

The **TABLE OF CONTENTS** has been presented in chronological order as a criminal trial or proceedings may unfold which will assist the user of this book in finding case law by specific topic.

Ineffective assistance of counsel claims based on counsel's **FAILURE TO INVESTIGATE, TO LOCATE OR INTERVIEW WITNESSES and etc.**, covers an extremely wide range of various topics. In order to compact and prevent this book from being repetitive, we've placed the majority of the case law for **FAILURE TO INVESTIGATE, TO LOCATE OR INTERVIEW WITNESSES and etc., under the specific topics of the underlying proposition itself**. For example: Transcript related problems are listed under the Appellate Ineffectiveness Section because as a general rule, the transcripts are ordered during the appellate process. Therefore, it is extremely important to **read the TABLE OF CONTENTS** and locate the specific topic of the underlying claim itself.

TABLE OF CONTENTS

Table of Contents

Table of Contents

Table of Contents

Table of Contents

Table of Contents

Table of Contents

Table of Contents

Table of Contents

PRETRIAL INEFFECTIVENESS

PRETRIAL MOTIONS/FAILURE INEFFECTIVENESS

Arraignment Proceedings

Hamilton v. Alabama, 368 U.S. 52, 7 Led 2d 114, 82 S.Ct. 157 (1961)
> An arraignment is a critical stage in a criminal proceeding during which the accused, under federal constitutional law, is entitled to counsel and if the accused is without counsel at the arraignment, he may obtain relief from his conviction without showing that he suffered a disadvantage from such a denial. Also see *White v. Maryland, 373 U.S. 59, 10 Led 2d 193, 83 S.Ct. 1050 (1963)*

United States v. Hammonds, 425 F.2d 597 (D.C. Cir. 1990)
> Trial counsel's failure to appear at arraignment, compounded with other errors, may constitute ineffective assistance of counsel.

Preliminary Hearings

Arsenault v. Massachusetts, 393 U.S. 5, 21 L Ed. 2d 5, 89 S.Ct. 35 (1968)
> Defendant is entitled to counsel during preliminary hearing.

Coleman v. Alabama, 399 U.S. 1, 26 L.Ed.2d 387, 90 S.Ct. 1999 (1970)
> The Supreme Court found that a preliminary hearing is a "critical stage" of a criminal proceeding where the right to counsel attached. The guiding hand of counsel at the preliminary hearing is essential to protect the indigent accused against an erroneous or improper prosecution. First, the lawyer's skilled examination and cross-examination of witnesses may expose fatal weaknesses in the State's case that may lead the magistrate to refuse to bind the accused over. Second, in any event, the skilled interrogation of witnesses by an experienced lawyer can fashion a vital impeachment tool for use in cross-examination of the State's witnesses at the trial, or preserve testimony favorable to the accused of a witness who does not appear at the trial. Third, trained counsel can more effectively discover the case the State has against his client and make possible the preparation of a proper defense to meet that case at trial. Fourth, counsel can also be influential at the preliminary hearing in making effective arguments for the accused on such matters as the necessity for an early psychiatric examination or bail. [399U.S.9] Without counsel the indigent accused does not have the guiding hand.

Pretrial Motions

U.S. v. Matos, 905 F.2d 30 (2nd Cir. 1990)
> Trial counsel's willingness to accept the government's version of facts and failure to file any motions because he relied on the government's version of facts, and not based on his own reasonable investigation, calls counsel's representation into serious question of inadequacy.

Pretrial Ineffectiveness

United States v. Hammonds, 425 F.2d 597 (D.C. Cir. 1990)
    Trial counsel's failure to file any pretrial motions compounded with other errors constituted ineffective assistance of counsel.

Jemison v. Foltz, 672 F.Supp. 1002 (E.D. Mich. 1987)
    Trial counsel's failure to file pretrial motions and waiver of preliminary examination and other errors constituted ineffective assistance of counsel.

Rummel v. Estelle, 498 F.Supp. 793 (W.D. Tex 1980)
    Trial counsel's failure to file pretrial motions and a motion for a new trial compounded with other errors constitutes ineffective assistance of counsel.

Clark v. Blackburn, 619 F.2d 431 (5th Cir. 1980)
    Trial counsel's failure to file any pre-trial motions on defensive issues, to seek pre-trial discovery, or to obtain a transcript of testimony before the grand jury, warranted an evidentiary hearing to resolve the ineffectiveness of counsel claim.

Dismiss or Quash Indictment

United States v. Morris, 470 F.3d 596, 602-603 (6th Cir. 2006)
    Morris was constructively denied representation of counsel during state court proceeding. The investigation and prosecution of Morris was done under the Project Safe Neighborhoods, a joint effort between state and federal authorities. The State charged Morris with firearms and drug possession. Morris was assigned counsel shortly before he was taken to a pre-preliminary examination. Counsel only met with Morris on the day of the hearing and was forced to review Morris' "options" in a crowded and noisy "bull pen" with no privacy. She advised Morris the state prosecutor made a plea offer for: one to four years on the marijuana charge, plus two consecutive years for the felony firearms charge, or that the case would be transferred to federal court where he faced 62 to 68 months under the Federal Guidelines. After this meeting, Morris was taken into the pre-preliminary examination, where the prosecutor presented the same plea offer and required Morris to make an immediate decision. The Judge informed Morris that if he declined the state's plea offer, he would be referred to federal court to answer charges which could result in a more severe sentence. The Assistant United States Attorney informed Morris' counsel that Morris would face 62 to 68 months under the Federal Sentencing Guidelines, and counsel so advised Morris. Morris rejected the state's plea offer and the case was transferred to federal court. Subsequently, Morris filed a motion to dismiss the federal indictment because he was deprived of his right to effective assistance of counsel in the state court proceeding and sought to have the case remanded to state court. Morris asserted that he was not able to discuss his options privately with his attorney. His attorney did not have knowledge of the strength of the case; nor was she given time to investigate or interview witnesses. The Sixth Circuit concluded that the district court did not have the authority to remand the case back to state court, but concluded that the district court does have the authority to dismiss the federal indictment to remedy the constitutional violation. The Court remanded for further proceeding.

2

U.S. v. Hansel, 70 F.3d 6 (2nd Cir. 1995)
Trial counsel's failure to object to specific counts of the indictment which were barred by statute of limitations constituted ineffective assistance of counsel.

Rhoden v. Morgan, 846 F.Supp. 598 (M.D. Tenn. 1994)
Trial counsel's failure to move to dismiss a count of the indictment because of the State's failure to produce the alleged photographs at trial amounted to ineffective assistance of counsel.

Holsclaw v. Smith, 822 F.2d 1041 (11th Cir. 1987)
Trial counsel's failure to raise issue of insufficient evidence at the end of trial or move for dismissal based on insufficient evidence constituted ineffective assistance of counsel.

Hollines v. Estelle, 569 F.Supp. 146 (W.D. Tex. 1983)
Trial counsel's failure to file motions to quash indictment, motion for discovery, motion to produce exculpatory evidence under **Brady v. Maryland, 373 U.S. 83, 10 L.Ed.2d 215, 83 S.Ct. 1194 (1963)**, and a motion for speedy trial constituted ineffective assistance of counsel.

Multiplicitous Indictment

United States v. Weathers, 493 F.3d 229, 238-39 (D.C. Cir. 2007)
Counsel provided constitutionally ineffective assistance for failing to challenge that counts four and five were multiplicitous.

United States v. Jones, 403 F.3d 604, 607 (8th Cir. 2005)
Counsel was constitutionally ineffective by failing challenge the indictment as multiplicitous.

U.S. v. Weathers, 186 F.3d 948 (D.C. Cir. 1999)
Counsel's failure to object to an indictment that was improperly multiplicitous warranted an evidentiary hearing to resolve claim of ineffective assistance of counsel.

Superseding Indictment

U.S. v. Palomba, 31 F. 3d 1456 (9th Cir. 1994)
Counsel's failure to move to dismiss the two mail fraud counts introduced in the original complaint, but omitted from the original indictment and then charged three months later in a superseding indictment violated **18 U.S.C. §3161 (b)**, that requires any information charged must be filed by indictment within thirty days constituted ineffective assistance of counsel.

Untimely Indictment

Young v. Dretke, 356 F.3d 616, 624 (5th Cir. 2004)
Counsel was constitutionally ineffective by failing to move for dismissal of untimely indictment where dismissal would have served as a bar to reindictment under then-existing law.

Discovery

Brady v. Maryland, 373 U.S. 83., 87. (1963)
The Supreme Court held that due process requires the prosecution to disclose evidence favorable to an accused upon his request when such evidence is material to guilt or punishment. *Id. at 87.*

Pretrial Ineffectiveness

 United States v. Bagley, *473 U.S. 667 (1985)*

The Supreme Court held that evidence is material if there is a reasonable probability that disclosure of the evidence would have changed the outcome of the proceeding. Bagley filed a pretrial motion specifically requesting notice of any deals, promises, or inducements made to witness in exchange for their testimony. The government failed to disclose such agreements with its two principle witnesses. The Supreme Court remanded the case for determination of whether the disclosure of witness compensation was reasonably probable to have produced a different result. *Id. at 684.*

Jackson v. Brown, *513 F,3d 1057, 1070-1072 (9th Cir. 2008)*

The prosecution's failure to disclose its promises to McFarland for writing a letter recommending that McFarland be allowed to serve his California prison sentence in Arizona near his family in exchange for his testimony at trial violated **_Brady_**. The prosecution's failure to correct McFarland's false testimony concerning promises made to him in exchange for his testimony violated **_Napue_**. The state's promise of assistance to the two informants gave them both a incentive to lie concerning the most crucial points of their testimonies dealing with the special circumstances finding, and satisfied the materiality element of **_Brady_** and **_Napue_**.

Bell v. Bell, *460 F.3d 739, 753 (6th Cir. 2006)*

The state withheld impeachment material regarding favorable treatment of it's witness in murder prosecution, in violation of **_Brady_** warranting habeas relief.

United States v. Carter, *313 F.Supp. 2d 921, 930 (E.D. Wis. 2004)*

Disclosure of psychologist report during a competency evaluation of a cooperating co-defendant was required under **_Brady_** and **_Giglio_** where competency report contained impeachment material.

 Jaramillo v. Stewart, *340 F.3d 877, 883 (9th Cir. 2003):*

State's failure to disclose exculpatory **_Brady_** material, a witness' declaration that this victim initiated attack against petitioner with a shank and that petitioner wrestled murder weapon from victim, which would have established theory of self-defense.

United States v. Washington, *263 F.Supp. 2d 413, 421 (D. Conn. 2003):*

Government's suppression of witness' prior conviction for falsely reporting a crime was evidence favorable to the defendant under **_Brady_**, which would have cast doubt on witness' veracity or motivation for his statement in the **911** call requiring habeas relief.

Thomas v. Kuhlman, *255 F.Supp. 2d 99, 109-111 (E.D.N.Y. 2003)*

Counsel's failure to investigate crime scene, to read the police reports released by the State as **_Rosario_** material, which would have impeached Artis's testimony that she observed the defendant on the fire escape of the victim's building constituted ineffective assistance of counsel.

Fisher v. Gibson, *282 F.3d 1283, 1293 (10th Cir. 2002)*

Trial counsel failed to view the crime scene, to file any motions for discovery, and review the police reports in a capital murder trial compounded with other errors constituted ineffective assistance of counsel.

***Leka v. Portuondo*, 257 F.3d 89, 99-100 (2nd Cir. 2001)**
> The state's failure to disclose eyewitness evidence of an off-duty police officer who observed the incident from the second floor window of his apartment, constituted "suppression" of evidence for ***Brady*** purposes and required granting of the writ and ordering Leka's release, if the state failed to provide him a new trial within 90 days.

***Mitchell v. Ward*, 150 F.Supp. 2d 1194 (W.D. Okla. 1999)**
> The state's failure to disclose DNA evidence linking semen on victim's panties to another person to the defense and revealing that petitioner's DNA was not found on any of the samples tested violated ***Brady***. Habeas relief on rape and sodomy convictions were warranted based on failure to disclose ***Brady*** material.

***U.S. v. Mclaughlin*, 89 F.Supp.2d 617 (E.D. Pa. 2000)**
> Government's failure to disclose the defense witness's grand jury testimony and certain documents in government's possession violated ***Brady*** requiments which warranted a new trial.

***Tucker v. Prelesnik*, 181 F.3d 747 (6th Cir. 1999)**
> Defense counsel's failure to move for a continuance, to obtain medical records of assault victim, which would have impeached his ability to remember, to obtain and use evidence of earlier contradictory statements made by the victim which would have cast serious doubt about the victims credibility constitutes ineffective assistance of counsel.

***U. S. v. Mejia-Mesa*, 153 F.3d 925 (9th Cir. 1998)**
> Mejia-Mesa's allegations that the government withheld, suppressed or destroyed a page or pages from the defense, which would establish from the vessel M/V Eagle-I, log deck that the vessel was seized carrying cocaine outside the United States waters and constitutes a ***Brady*** violation. Thus, requiring an evidentiary hearing.

***Cheung v. Maddock*, 32 F.Supp. 2d 1150 (N.D. Cal. 1998)**
> Prosecutions failure to release evidence of victim's blood alcohol level which was both favorable and material to the defense and violated petitioner's due process rights to a fair trial under ***Brady.***

***Thomas v. Calderon*, 120 F.3d 1045 (9th Cir. 1997)**
> Defense counsel's failure to seek-discovery regarding informant, where two police agencies for whom he informed considered informant unreliable and his family considered him a pathological liar, amounted to ineffective assistance where evidence could have been used to impeach the informant's testimony.

***Williams v. Washington*, 59 F.3d 673 (7th Cir. 1995)**
> Trial counsel's failure to review letter written by victim and provided to counsel by state with discovery materials constitutes ineffective assistance. **See also *Hollines v. Estelle*, 569 F.Supp. 146 (W.D. Tex. 1983); *Pilchak v. Camper*, 741 F.Supp. 782 (W.D. Mo. 1990)**

***Mayo v. Henderson*, 13 F.3d 528 (2nd Cir. 1994)**
> Appellate counsel's failure to raise Rosario claim, for prosecution's failure to disclose police officer's memo, constitutes ineffective assistance of counsel. This case presents a clear evaluation of the prejudice prong of ***Strickland***.

Pretrial Ineffectiveness

Morrison v. Kimmelman, 650 F.Supp. 801 (D.N.J. 1986)
> Trial counsel's failure to pursue discovery, which would have made counsel aware of a bedsheet which had been illegally seized from Morrison's apartment amounted to ineffective assistance of counsel. The bedsheet contained stains that laboratory technicians testified were semen stains matching Morrison's blood type and head hairs matching the victim and Morrison. The police officer that took the bedsheet did not have a warrant, nor did he have Morrison's consent. The State conceded that the search and seizure in this case was unconstitutional. The Supreme Court remanded this case and the district court then held that counsel was ineffective.

Disclosure of Confidential Informant's Identity

Roviaro v. United States, 353 U.S. 53 (1957)
> The government must disclose an informant's identity where the informant is a material witness or the informant is crucial to the defense.

Gochicoa v. Johnson, 53 F.Supp.2d 943 (W.D. Tex. 1999)
> Failure to seek disclosure of the confidential informant's identify constitutes ineffective assistance of counsel.

Production of Exculpatory Evidence

Mitchell v. Gibson, 262 F.3d 1036, 1065 (10th Cir. 2001)
> The state withheld Ms. Gilchrist's notes of her conversation with agent Vick indicating her knowledge that DNA testing excluded Mr. Mitchell. Ms. Gilchrist's notes would have provided defense counsel effective ammunition to impeach Ms. Gilchrist's credibility and show her untruthfulness concerning the rape and sodomy of the victim, which required setting aside the death sentence because of the ***Brady*** violation.

Spicer v. Warden of Roxbury Correctional Institute, 31 F.Supp. 2d 509 (D.Md. 1998)
> The State's failure to disclose discrepancy between what witness' attorney told prosecutor witness would say and what witness actually told prosecutor was highly material and violated ***Brady*** by failing to disclose and warranted habeas relief.

Sparman v. Edwards, 26 F. Supp. 2d 450 (E.D.N.Y. 1997)
> Trial counsel's failure to discover exculpatory medical evidence and to cross-examine victims about inconsistencies in their statements to police and their trial testimony constituted ineffective assistance of counsel. See also ***Hollines v. Estelle, 569 F.Supp. 146 (W.D. Tex. 1983)***

U.S. v. Chandler, 950 F.Supp. 1545 (N.D. Ala. 1996)
> Evidentiary hearing warranted on habeas claim for government's failure to disclose results of witness's polygraph test.

Sims v. Livesay, 970 F.2d 1575 (6th Cir. 1992)
> Counsel's failure to investigate and present evidence consistent with defendant's claim that shooting was accidental and at close range, where there was powder residue on quilt with bullet holes, constitutes ineffective assistance of counsel.

U.S. v. Myers, 892 F.2d 642 (7th Cir. 1990)
  Trial counsel's failure to read and review documents disclosed by the government, which contained potentially exculpatory materials, constituted ineffective assistance of counsel.

Jencks Material

United States v. Hinton, 631 F.2d 769 (D.C. Cir. 1980)
  Trial counsel's failure to move for a continuance, after receiving a mass of Jencks material during the suppression hearing and the day of trial constituted ineffective assistance, and required a remand to determine the extent of prejudice.

Defensive Motions

McCoy v. Wainwright, 804 F.2d 1196, (11th Cir. 1986)
  Failure to investigate possible insanity defense, to move for a competency hearing, or to advise defendant of affirmative insanity defense required an evidentiary hearing.

Clark v. Blackburn, 619 F.2d 431 (5th Cir. 1980)
  Trial counsel's failure to file any pre-trial motions on defensive issues, to seek pre-trial discovery, to obtain a transcript of testimony before the grand jury warranted an evidentiary hearing to resolve the ineffectiveness of counsel claim.

Miranda Warning

Miranda v. Arizona, 384 U.S. 436, 16 L. Ed.2d 694, 86 S.Ct. 1602 (1966)
  The accused must be advised that he/she has a right to counsel before a custodial police interrogation.

Garner v. Mitchell, 502 F.3d 394, 414-416 (6th Cir.2007)
  Garner did not knowingly and intelligently waive his *Miranda* rights due to his mental disabilities as the expert's interpretation of the test result showed Garner's lack of full comprehension of the *Miranda* warning.

Brown v. Crosby, 249 F.Supp. 2d 1285, 1308-09 (S.D. Fla. 2003)
  Juvenile's waiver of his *Miranda* rights, prior to making a post-statement was not knowingly and intentionally made because waiver form was misleading and juvenile was mildly retarded.

Pirtle v. Lambert, 150 F.Supp.2d 1078 (E.D. Wash. 2001)
  The State's failure to disclose to defense defendant's statement to police that he knew why he was under arrest and you might as well shoot me now which was obtained in violation of the *Miranda* warning warranted habeas corpus relief.

Suppression of Evidence, etc.

Kimmelman v. Morrison, 477 U.S. 365, 91 L.Ed.2d 305, 106 S.Ct. 2574 (1986)
  A criminal defendant had raised a Fourth Amendment violation in a post-conviction proceeding under and through ineffective assistance of counsel for failure to raise or

7

properly litigate the claim. **See also** _Morrison v. Kimmelman, 650 F.Supp. 801 (D.N.J. 1986); U.S. Ex. Rel. Henderson v. Brierly, 300 F.Supp. 638 (E.D. Pa. 1969); Williams v. Arn, 654 F.Supp. 226 (N.D. Ohio 1986); United States v. Easter, 539 F.2d 663 (8th Cir. 1976); Hollines v. Estelle, 569 F.Supp. 146 (W.D. Tex. 1983)_

Ferguson v. City of Charleston, 532 U.S. 67 149 L.Ed.2d 205, 121 S.Ct. 1281 (2001)
The Supreme Court found that the State hospital's performance of urine tests to obtain evidence of maternity patient's cocaine use for law enforcement purposes was an unreasonable search, in violation of the Fourth Amendment, if patients did not consent to procedure.

Thomas v. Varner, 428 F.3d 491, 501-504 (3rd Cir. 2005)
Counsel's failure to move to suppress or object to an in-court identification by Fuller the prosecution key witness, after Fuller failed to identify Thomas during the pretrial hearing, his testimony concerning the photo arrays and lack of evidence other than Young's testimony linking Thomas to the shooting, required an evidentiary hearing to resolve ineffective assistance of counsel claim.

Owens v. United States, 387 F.3d 607, 610 (7th Cir. 2004)
Counsel was constitutionally ineffective for failing to have Owens admit that it was his residence that was searched and object to the admission of evidence because it was obtained in violation of the Fourth Amendment.

Koras v. Robinson, 257 F.Supp. 2d 941, 950-954 (E.D. Mich. 2003)
Appellate counsel's failure to raise trial counsel's deficient performance by failing to move to suppress petitioner's statement to police, after he had invoked his right to counsel under _Miranda_ and _Edwards_; petitioner's statement was the key evidence against petitioner that would have been suppressed, absent counsel's errors.

Northrop v. Trippett, 265 F.3d 372, 384 (6th Cir. 2001)
Counsel was constitutionally ineffective for failing to move to suppress cocaine drug evidence that was illegally seized by officers under the fruit of the poisonous tree doctrine.

Jones v. United States, 224 F.3d 1251, 1257-58 (11th Cir. 2000)
Counsel failed to move to suppress wiretap evidence based on sealing requirements of **18 USCS §2518(8) (a)**, where law was clear that unless government could offer a satisfactory explanation for the thirty-one (31) day delay in sealing Jones' tapes, all evidence derived from them must be suppressed. The Court of Appeals remanded for reconsideration of Jones' ineffective assistance of counsel claims.

U.S. v. Lozada-Rivera, 177 F.3d 98 (1st Cir. 1999)
Government agent's act of eliciting statements in violation of defendant's Constitutional right to counsel was not harmless where statement complained of contributed to the verdict obtained by the jury. **See also** _U.S. v. Covarrubias, 179 F.3d 1219 (9th Cir. 1999)_

U.S. v. Fleiz, 20 F. Supp.2d 97 (D. Mo. 1998)
Defendant's jailhouse statements were fruit of earlier violation of his Sixth amendment right to counsel and required suppression of statements.

Martin v. Maxey, 98 F.3d 844 (5th Cir. 1996)
> Ineffective assistance of counsel claim based on counsel's failure to adequately argue motion to suppress evidence obtained in violation of defendant's Fourth Amendment Rights was not procedurally barred, and required a remand for consideration on the merits of the claim.

Huynh v. King, 95 F.3d 1052 (11th Cir. 1996)
> Trial counsel's delay in filing a meritorious suppression motion in order to later obtain a more favorable federal habeas review was objectively unreasonable and required a remand for an evidentiary hearing to determine prejudice under <u>Strickland</u>. See also ***Duarte v. U.S., 81 F.3d 75 (7th Cir. 1996)***

U.S. v. Davenport, 986 F.2d 1047 (7th Cir. 1993)
> Trial counsel's failure to move to suppress confession may constitute "cause" under ineffective assistance of counsel for procedural default rule. **See also *ADCox v. O'Brien*, 899 F.2d 735 (8th Cir. 1990); *Application of Tomich*, 221 F.Supp. 500 (D. Mont. 1963) aff'd at 332 F.2d 987 (9th Cir. 1964); *Smith v. Dugger*, 911 F.2d 494 (11th Cir. 1990); <u>U.S. v. Matos</u>, 905 F.2d 30 (2nd Cir. 1990).**

Lofton v. Whitley, 905 F.2d 885 (5th Cir. 1990)
> Trial counsel's failure to move to suppress photograph of defendant that was illegally taken by police and used for identification purposes in photographic array constituted ineffective assistance.

Blackburn v. Foltz, 828 F.2d 1177 (6th Cir. 1987)
> Trial counsel's failure to move to suppress three prior armed robbery convictions constituted ineffective assistance.

Rice v. Marshall, 816 F.2d 1126 (6th Cir. 1987)
> Trial counsel's failure to move to suppress evidence, that charged defendant with rape and carrying a firearm when defendant had previously been acquitted on firearms charge based on "collateral estoppel" constituted ineffective assistance of counsel.

Streetman v. Lynaugh, 812 F.2d 950 (5th Cir. 1987)
> Trial counsel failed to press the motion to suppress defendant's confession to law enforcement that he committed the murder plus a series of thefts when authorities had threatened defendant and his family with physical violence. Authorities promised to release defendant and continue a supply of valium in exchange for defendant's cooperation against accomplice. Trial counsel failed to inform co-counsel of defendant's allegations. The defendant's confession was the State's main case at trial. The Fifth Circuit remanded for an evidentiary hearing.

Nell v. James, 811 F.2d 100 (2nd Cir. 1987)
> Trial counsel's failure to investigate, to consult with defendant about facts, and to move for suppression of identification testimony required an evidentiary hearing.

Kirkpatrick v. Blackburn, 777 F.2d 272 (5th Cir. 1985)
> Trial counsel's failure to move to suppress evidence obtained during illegal search of petitioner's residence required an evidentiary hearing to develop the record.

Pretrial Ineffectiveness

Smith v. Wainwright, 777 F.2d 609 (11th Cir. 1985)
Trial counsel's failure to move to suppress a confession constitutes ineffective assistance, where the confession is the primary evidence to support the state's case. **See also** *Goodwin v. Balkcom*, 684 F.2d 794 (11th Cir. 1982); *Lufkins v. Solem*, 716 F.2d 532 (8th Cir. 1983)

Allah v. LeFevere, 623 F.Supp. 987 (D.C. N.Y. 1985)
Trial counsel's failure to make motion for suppression of evidence of stolen property required an evidentiary hearing to resolve ineffective assistance of counsel claim.

Pinnell v. Cauthorn, 540 F.2d 938 (8th Cir. 1976)
Trial counsel's failure to move to suppress tape recordings, that discussed defendant's prior conviction and failed to object to the admission of the tapes into evidence amounted to ineffective assistance of counsel.

Severance Motions

Hernandez v. Cowan, 200 F.3d 995 (7th Cir. 2000)
Counsel's failure to attend suppression hearing where he would have learned the defendant had an antagonist defense and to move for a severance constituted ineffective assistance of counsel.

Williams v. Washington, 59 F.3d 673 (7th Cir. 1995)
Trial counsel's failure to move for a severance constituted ineffective assistance. See also *U.S. v. Myers*, 892 F.2d 642 (7th Cir. 1990)

U.S. v. Yizar, 956 F.2d 230 (11th Cir. 1992)
Counsel's failure to file a motion for severance warranted an evidentiary hearing to resolve the ineffective assistance of counsel claim. See also *Thames v. Dugger*, 848 F.2d 149 (11th Cir. 1988)

Hudson v. Lockhart, 679 F.Supp. 891 (E.D. Ark. 1986)
Trial counsel's failure to move for a severance and object to the State's surprise witness, or move for a continuance, to prepare for the surprise witness' testimony amounted to ineffective assistance of counsel.

Speedy Trial Motions

U.S. v. Mala, 7 F.3d 1058 (1st Cir. 1993)
Trial counsel's failure to litigate violation of speedy trial act may constitute ineffective assistance; however, this claim was raised on direct appeal and the Court of Appeals declined to address the merits of the issue. The Court of Appeals did indicate that if appellant filed a §2255 motion alleging ineffective assistance of counsel the district court should appoint counsel.

Nelson v. Hargett, 989 F.2d 847 (5th Cir. 1993)
Trial counsel's failure to pursue speedy trial claim has no strategic value. **See also** *Hollines v. Estelle*, 569 F.Supp. 146 (W.D. Tex. 1983)

Motions Contesting Violation of Interstate Agreement Act

Reed v. Farley, 512 U.S. 339, 129 L.Ed.2d 277, 114 S.Ct. 2291 (1994)
> A state prisoner is not entitled to federal habeas relief pursuant to **28 U. S.C. §2254**, based on a violation of the 120-day limit, in Article IV(c) of the Interstate Agreement on Detainers, where said claim did not result in "a fundamental defect which inherently results in a complete miscarriage of justice, [o]r an omission inconsistent with the rudimentary demands of fair procedure."

United States Ex. Rel. Holleman v. Duckworth, 652 F.Supp 82 (N.D. Ill. 1986)
> Trial counsel's failure to argue that the State violated the Interstate Agreement on Detainers Act constituted ineffective assistance of counsel and established "cause" for failure to raise the issue.

United States v. Williams, 615 F.2d 585 (3rd Cir. 1980)
> Trial counsel's failure to investigate the violation of the Interstate Agreement on Detainers Act, which would have warranted dismissal of the indictment, required an evidentiary hearing to resolve the ineffective assistance of counsel claim.

Investigate/Challenging Defendant's Competency

Burt v. Uchtman, 422 F.3d 557, 568-69 (7th Cir. 2005)
> Counsel's failure to request an competency hearing because Burt was taking multiple psychotropic medications, had mood swings, feared imaginary snakes, and wanted to plead guilty to capital murder so he could return to prison, and smoke cigarettes amounted ineffective assistance of counsel.

United States v. Collins, 430 F.3d 1260, 1265-1268 (10th Cir. 2005)
> Counsel's failure to represent Collins and introduce available evidence at the competency hearing because there was a breakdown in the attorney-client relationship constructively denied Collins his right to effective assistance of counsel and required a new trial.

Ellis v. Mullin, 326 F.3d 1122, 1128-1129 (10th Cir. 2003)
> Trial court's exclusion of pretrial psychiatric report, which diagnosed petitioner competency at time of fatal shooting violated petitioner's due process right to present evidence and a defense.

McGregor v. Gibson, 248 F.3d 946 (10th Cir. 2001)
> A criminal trial of an incompetent defendant violates due process and the appropriate remedy is to grant habeas relief.

Matheney v. Anderson, 253 F.3d 1025 (7th Cir. 2001)
> Defense counsel's failure to pursue petitioner's request for a hearing on his competency to stand trial prior to the commencement of trial required an evidentiary hearing to resolve ineffectiveness of counsel claim.

Pretrial Ineffectiveness

Appel v. Horn, 250 F.3d 203 (3rd Cir. 2001)
A constructive denial of counsel at hearing to determine defendant's competency to waive the right to counsel, rendered all subsequent proceedings against defendant void and required a new trial.

Hull v. Kyler, 190 F.3d 88 (3rd Cir. 1999)
Counsel's failure to cross-examine the government's single witness at competency hearing or present a large body of evidence supporting defendant's incompetency amounted to ineffective assistance of counsel.

U.S. v. Klat, 156 F.3d 1258 (D.C. Cir. 1998)
District court's failure to appoint a pro se defendant counsel for a competency hearing when the Court had found "reasonable cause" to believe that defendant was mentally incompetent to stand trial required a remand for an evidentiary hearing to determine whether the competency hearing would have had a different outcome.

Williams v. Calderon, 48 F.Supp. 2d 979 (C.D. Cal. 1998)
Evidentiary hearing was warranted where an issue of fact existed whether the defendant was competent to stand trial and whether counsel was ineffective in failing to present mitigating evidence. **See also *Becton v. Barnett*, 920 F.2d 1190 (4th Cir. 1990); *Barnett v. Hargett*, 174 F.3d 1128 (10th Cir. 1999)**

Williamson v. Ward, 110 F.3d 1509 (10th Cir. 1997)
Trial counsel's failure to investigate defendant's mental illness and to seek competency hearing constituted ineffective assistance of counsel. **See also *Hall v. Washington*, 106 F.3d 742 (7th Cir. 1997); *Parkus v. Delo*, 33 F.3d 933 (8th Cir. 1994); *Hill v. Lockhart*, 28 F.3d 832, 844-45 (8th Cir. 1994)**

Antwine v. Delo, 54 F.3d 1357 (8th Cir. 1995)
Counsel's failure to have a second mental examination conducted is inadequate trial preparation, rather than a strategic choice. **See also *Agan v. Dugger*, 835 F.2d 1337 (11th Cir. 1987)**

Ford v. Lockhart, 861 F.Supp. 1447 (E.D. Ark. 1994)
Trial counsel was ineffective in capital case, where counsel failed to investigate into defendant's past family history to learn that defendant's father had beaten the defendant frequently, beat defendant's mother and stayed drunk, which caused emotional harm to defendant and may have led jury to impose life sentence without parole instead of death sentence. **See also *Loyd v. Smith*, 899 F.2d 1416 (5th Cir. 1990); *Williamson v. Reynolds*, 904 F.Supp. 1529 (E.D. Okl. 1995)**

Loyd v. Whitley, 977 F.2d 149 (5th Cir. 1992)
Trial counsel's failure to secure independent psychological analysis of defendant and present evidence that defendant had a mental condition during the time he committed the crime constituted ineffective assistance. **See also *McCoy v. Wainwright*, 804 F.2d 1196, (11th Cir. 1986); *U.S. Ex. Rel. Rivera v. Frantzen*, 594 F.Supp. 198 (N.D. Ill. 1984); *U.S. v. Burrows*, 872 F.2d 915 (9th Cir. 1989)**

Deutscher v. Whitley, 884 F.2d 1152 (9th Cir. 1989)
Counsel's failure to investigate and present mitigating evidence, through a psychiatrist who examined defendant and would have testified that defendant's

history was consistent with mental disorder, characterized by episodes of uncontrollable violence, which testimony would have rebutted state's evidence, constituted ineffective assistance of counsel. See also *__Wilson v. Butler__, 813 F.2d 664 (5th Cir. 1987)*; *__Daniel v. Thigpen__, 742 F.Supp. 1535 (M.D. Ala. 1990)*; *__Thomas v. Lockhart__, 738 F.2d 304 (8th Cir. 1984)*

__Profitt v. Waldron__, 831 F.2d 1245 (5th Cir. 1987)

Defense counsel's failure to investigate and secure records from a mental institution, which would have shown a valid defense of insanity constituted ineffective assistance of counsel. **See also** *__Bouchillon v. Collins__, 907 F.2d 589 (5th Cir. 1990); __Hull v. Freeman__, 932 F.2d 159 (3rd Cir. 1991); __U.S. Ex. Rel. Rivera v. Frantzen__, 594 F.Supp. 198 (N.D. Ill. 1984)*

Motions for Funds

__Harris By and Through Ramseyer v. Wood__, 64 F.3d 1432 (9th Cir. 1995)

Trial counsel's failure to obtain an expert to prepare a social history amounted to ineffectiveness of counsel.

__Loyd v. Smith__, 899 F.2d 1416 (5th Cir. 1990)

Trial counsel's failure to retain independent psychiatrist in order to present evidence during sentencing phase constitutes ineffective assistance of counsel.

__Miller v. Wainwright__, 798 F.2d 426 (11th Cir. 1986)

Trial counsel's failure to secure expert on drug use, who would have cast serious doubt on the state's witnesses' credibility who had mental as well as drug-related problems, may constitute ineffective assistance of counsel.

__Miller v. Wainwright__, 798 F.2d 426 (11th Cir. 1986)

Trial counsel's failure to renew motion for appointment of private investigator constitutes ineffective assistance of counsel.

__United States v. Fessel__, 531 F.2d 1275 (5th Cir. 1976)

Trial counsel's failure to utilize Title 18, U.S.C. §3006(a) to obtain the funds for an expert at the government's expense constitutes ineffective assistance of counsel. Doctors who had examined Fessel indicated that he was incompetent. Nevertheless, trial counsel failed to investigate, or prepare to present an insanity defense, which deprived Fessel of a chance to present psychiatric testimony. **See also** *__Loyd v. Whitley__, 977 F.2d 149 (5th Cir. 1992)*

Motions for Continuance

__U.S. v. Santos__, 201 F.3d 953 (7th Cir. 2000)

The district court abused its discretion denying defendant's motion for continuance due to counsel scheduling conflict.

__Tucker v. Prelesnik__, 181 F.3d 747 (6th Cir. 1999)

Defense counsel's failure to move for a continuance to obtain medical records of assault victim, which would have impeached his ability to remember, to obtain and use evidence of earlier contradictory statements by victim, which would have cast serious doubt about the victims credibility constituted ineffective assistance of counsel. **See also** *Burley v. Cabana, 818 F.2d 414 (5th Cir. 1987)*

Tosh v. Lockhart, 879 F.2d 412 (8th Cir. 1989)
Counsel's failure to move the court for a continuance so that he could insure the presence of three alibi witnesses constituted ineffective assistance of counsel. **See also *U.S. Ex Rel Duncan v. O'Leary, 806 F.2d 1307 (7th Cir. 1986); Pilchak v. Camper, 741 F.Supp. 782 (W.D. Mo. 1990); VIA v. Superintendent, Powhatan Correctional Ctr., 643 F.2d 167 (4th Cir. 1981); Hudson v. Lockhart, 679 F.Supp. 891 (E.D. Ark. 1986); Stokes v. Peyton, 437 F.2d 131 (4th Cir. 1970); Code v. Montgomery, 799 F.2d 1481 (11th Cir. 1986)***

Walker v. Lockhart, 807 F.2d 136 (8th Cir. 1986)
Trial counsel's failure to obtain continuance for purpose of producing witnesses to substantiate defendant's claim that victim, with whom defendant had homosexual relationship, had given defendant permission to have victim's money constituted ineffective assistance of counsel.

United States v. Hinton, 631 F.2d 769 (D.C. Cir. 1980)
Trial counsel's failure to move for a continuance at suppression hearing on the day of trial after receiving a mass of Jencks material constituted ineffective assistance and required a remand to determine the extent of prejudice.

Pending Motions

ADCox v. O'Brien, 899 F.2d 735 (8th Cir. 1990)
Adcox pleaded guilty in state court to first-degree murder and was sentenced to life. Thereafter, Adcox filed a petition for writ of habeas corpus asserting that his guilty plea was neither knowing nor voluntary and that he had been denied effective assistance of counsel. Adcox argued that his guilty plea was involuntary by reason of ineffective assistance of counsel because his attorney failed to prepare for trial and because Adcox feared he would be sentenced to death should he be convicted and as a result he had no choice but to plead guilty.

Adcox's attorney failed to:

1. Take depositions of any witnesses;

2. File the proper pleadings in order to have a mental competency examination of Adcox;

3. Secure a copy of co-defendant Molitor's trial transcripts; and

4. Request rulings on pending motions to suppress Adcox's confession and to suppress physical evidence.

The Eighth Circuit found that Adcox's motion to suppress the confession alleged that his confession was not voluntary or knowing because it was made without the benefit of the Miranda warning and was given because of a result of coercion and duress. Adcox's confession and the seized evidence were the central focus of the government's case. A favorable ruling on those motions very easily would lead counsel to change his recommendation as to the guilty plea. The court remanded for further proceedings.

Non-existence Motion

Griffin v. U.S., *109 F.3d 1217 (7th Cir. 1997)*
Counsel filed a rule 35 (b) motion to reduce sentence, which is a non-existent motion for the defense under federal practice and constitutes deficient performance under *Strickland.*

Change of Venue

Nevers v. Killinger, *990 F. Supp. 844 (E.D.Mich. 1997)*
Trial court's refusal to grant a change of venue where prejudicial pretrial publicity and inflamed community atmosphere concerning white police officer killing black suspect deprived defendant of a fair trial and violated due process.

Harris v. Housewright, *697 F.2d 202 (8th Cir. 1982)*
Trial counsel accepted money from defendant's family for payment when he was court-appointed attorney and failed to properly handle change of venue issue which amounted to ineffective assistance of counsel.

Improper Venue

United States v. Cabrales, *524 U.S. 1 , 141 L.Ed.2d 1, 118 S.Ct. 1772 (1998)*
Missouri held improper venue for trial of money laundering charges under *18 USCS §§1956 (a) (1) (B) (ii) and 1957*, where money allegedly derived from illegal acts by others in Missouri, but where alleged money laundering by defendant occurred entirely in Florida.

PRETRIAL RESEARCH OR LEGAL ADVICE INEFFECTIVENESS

McGurk v. Stenberg, *163 F.3d 470 (8th Cir. 1998)*
Counsel's failure to advise defendant of his right to a jury trial as opposed to a bench trial constituted ineffective assistance of counsel.

U.S. v. Hansel, *70 F.3d 6 (2nd Cir. 1995)*
Counsel's failure to inform defendant that charges were barred by statute of limitations rendered the guilty plea involuntary.

Scarpa v. Dubois, *38 F.3d 1 (1st Cir. 1994)*
Defense counsel must understand the elements of the offenses with which client is charged in order to provide effective assistance of counsel.

Rhoden v. Morgan, *846 F.Supp. 598 (M.D. Tenn. 1994)*
Trial counsel's failure to research the law and recognize the change in law which would have shown that the Tennessee statute was unconstitutional constituted ineffective assistance of counsel and required an evidentiary hearing.

Morris v. State of Cal., 966 F.2d 448 (9th Cir. 1991)
Trial counsel's failure to be familiar with the law that being under the influence of methamphetamine was not illegal constituted ineffective assistance of counsel.

Martinez-Macias v. Collins, 810 F.Supp. 782 (W.D. Tex. 1991)
Trial counsel's failure to research the law, to call disinterested alibi witnesses that were available regardless of the risk of opening door to the presentation of extraneous criminal incident constituted ineffective assistance of counsel.

Pilchak v. Camper, 741 F.Supp. 782 (W.D. Mo. 1990)
Trial counsel's failure to give defendant pretrial advice or to enter into plea negotiations can constitute ineffective assistance of counsel. **See also *U.S. v. Rodriguez-Rodriguez, 929 F.2d 747 (1st Cir. 1991); Scott v. Wainwright, 698 F.2d 427, 429-30 (11th Cir. 1983)***

Stephens v. Kemp, 846 F.2d 642 (11th Cir. 1988)
Trial counsel has a duty to familiarize himself with regard to the specific scientific area in which an expert is needed; however, he need not become an expert himself, but he must conduct a minimal amount of background work in order that he may intelligently move the court for the need of an expert.

Hyman v. Aiken, 824 F.2d 1405 (4th Cir. 1987)
Trial counsel's failure to do basic legal research, to review the testimony of key witnesses, including his own client, and to be familiar with readily available documents necessary to understanding of their client's case constituted ineffective assistance of counsel.

Harich v. Wainwright, 813 F.2d 1082 (11th Cir. 1987)
Trial counsel's failure to research and understand the law based on Harich's intoxication defense required an evidentiary hearing. **See also *Young v. Zant, 677 F.2d 792, 798 (11th Cir. 1982)***

Martin v. Rose, 744 F.2d 1245 (6th Cir. 1984)
Trial counsel's actions in his refusal to participate in the trial because he erroneously believed that participation would either waive pretrial motions or render their denial harmless error constitutes ineffective assistance of counsel.

McQueen v. Swenson, 498 F.2d 207 (8th Cir. 1974)
Trial counsel's failure to investigate charge against defendant constitutes ineffective assistance under certain circumstances. **See also *United States v. Burton, 575 F. Supp. 1320 (E.D. Texas 1983)***

FAILED TO SECURE A TRANSLATOR

U.S. v. Anjum, 961 F. Supp. 883 (D.Md. 1997)
Trial counsel's failure to secure competent translator of defendant's native language constitutes deficient performance, but defendant failed to show that he was incapable of participating in his defense.

Flores v. U.S., *698 A.2d 474 (D.C.App. 1997)*
> Defendant's rights were impeded by admission of incorrect interpretation of witnesses testimony.

FAILED TO HAVE TAPE TRANSCRIBED

Cheung v. Maddock, *32 F.Supp. 2d 1150 (N.D. Cal. 1998)*
> Defense counsel's failure to have tape recorded statement of companion translated or transcribed and presented to jury constituted ineffective assistance of counsel.

FAILED TO OBTAIN EXTRADITION HEARING TRANSCRIPT

Fisher v. Gibson, *282 F.3d 1283, 1293 (10th Cir. 2002)*
> Trial counsel's failures to review or obtain the extradition hearing transcripts, which contained statements made by Fisher that could have been used to counter the otherwise inculpatory nature of the statements as presented by the prosecution constitutes ineffective assistance of counsel.

FAILED TO PREPARE FOR TRIAL

Turner v. Duncan, *158 F.3d 449 (9th Cir. 1998)*
> Trial counsel's failure to investigate and to adequately conduct a pretrial preparation was not a strategic decision and required a remand for an evidentiary hearing to determine whether a pretrial investigation would have produced a conviction of a lesser degree of homicide.

Capps v. Sullivan, *921 F.2d 260 (10th Cir. 1990)*
> Trial counsel's failure to interview or subpoena witnesses who would have substantially corroborated Capps' testimony material to his entrapment defense constituted ineffective assistance of counsel.

U.S. v. Myers, *892 F.2d 642 (7th Cir. 1990)*
> Trial counsel's failure to read and review documents disclosed which contained potentially exculpatory materials constituted ineffective assistance of counsel.

Kemp v. Leggett, *635 F.2d 453 (5th Cir. 1981)*
> Trial counsel's failure to prepare for trial, to interview a single witness, to call several character witnesses who were present in the courtroom, prepare a defense and proffer a written charge on voluntary manslaughter charge constituted ineffective assistance.

Cross v. United States, *392 F.2d 360 (8th Cir. 1968)*
> Trial counsel failed to subpoena any witnesses or prepare for trial because the defendant did not pay him all his money and claimed his own ineffectiveness in a motion for mistrial required an evidentiary hearing.

Moore v. United States, *432 F.2d 730 (3rd Cir. 1970)*
> Trial counsel's failure to prepare for trial, to locate witnesses who could not identify the defendant as the robber from a line-up warranted an evidentiary hearing to resolve the ineffectiveness of counsel claim. **See also *United States v. Fisher*, *477 F.2d 300 (4th Cir. 1973);***

United States v. DeCoster, 487 F.2d 1197 (D.C. Cir. 1973)
> Trial counsel's lack of pretrial preparations and investigation required a remand for a supplemental hearing on ineffective assistance of counsel claims. **See also** *Harris By and Through Ramseyer v. Wood, 64 F.3d 1432 (9th Cir. 1995); Goodwin v. Balkcom, 684 F.2d 794 (11th Cir. 1982); U.S. v. Mills, 760 F.2d 1116 (11th Cir. 1985); Pilchak v. Camper, 741 F.Supp. 782 (W.D. Mo. 1990); Harris v. Towers, 405 F.Supp 497 (D. Del 1974)*

FAILED TO INVESTIGATE, TO LOCATE OR INTERVIEW WITNESSES

Ramonez v. Berghuis, 490 F.3d 482, 489 (6th Cir. 2007)
> Counsel provided constitutionally ineffective assistance for failing to investigate and to call three witnesses to the crime, which counsel recognized could provide beneficial testimony to Ramonez, which would effectively defeat the essential elements of the State's breaking and entering of the home invasion crime.

Dando v. Yukins, 461 F.3d 791, 798-800 (6th Cir. 2006)
> Counsel was constitutionally ineffective for advising petitioner to plead no-contest without investigating the possibility of duress defense based on the Battered Woman's Syndrome.

Tenny v. Dretke, 416 F.3d 404, 408-409 (5th Cir. 2005)
> Counsel was constitutionally ineffective for failing to investigate, to call two monks and a nun as witnesses, and to elicit critical evidence from witnesses called that Mulvey was the aggressor which would have supported Tenny's self-defense theory.

Towns v. Smith, 395 F. 3d 251, 259 (6th Cir. 2005)
> Counsel's failure to investigate witness in a robbery and felony murder trial where witness was housed in county jail and counsel requested that witness be kept in the county jail so that counsel could interview witness constituted ineffective assistance of counsel.

Soffar v. Dretke, 368 F.3d 441, 471-72 (5th Cir. 2004)
> Counsel was constitutionally ineffective for failing to conduct a pretrial investigation; to contact and interview Greg Garner, or the police officer who interviewed and took Greg Garner's statement. Garner's statement contained significant exculpatory material that contradicted petitioner's confession and he was the only surviving victim.

United States Ex Rel. Hampton v. Leibach, 347 F.3d 219, 249-251 (7th Cir. 2003)
> Counsel's failure to investigate or call eyewitnesses whose names had been given to him, to make any effort on his own to locate occurrence witnesses; where there was at least one witness who would have testified that petitioner did not participate in the attacks amounted to ineffective assistance of counsel.

Steidl v. Walls, 267 F.Supp. 2d 919, 934-935 (C.D. Ill. 2003)
> Counsel was constitutionally ineffective by failing to investigate or call the supervisor of the government's eyewitness, who would have testified that this

eyewitness was at <u>work</u> during the <u>time</u> <u>frame</u> she claimed to have witnessed the acts leading up to the murders, which would have impeached the government's eyewitness.

Avila v. Galaza, 297 F.3d 911, 921-924 (9th Cir. 2002)
Counsel's failure to investigate and present evidence from about eight (8) different witnesses that petitioner's brother, <u>Ernesto</u>, was the shooter, not the petitioner constituted ineffective assistance of counsel.

Beltran v. Cockrell, 294 F.3d 730, 734-35 (5th Cir. 2002)
Trial counsel in a capital murder and robbery trial failed to investigate whether co-perpetrator, Rubin Plata, had a tattoo on his upper left arm and failed to introduce evidence that witnesses had tentatively identified Plata and that Plata had such a tattoo. The victim in this case was murdered with a derringer. Plata had committed an aggravated assault with a derringer four hours before the murder occurred in this case. The fact that Beltran's co-defendant had such a tattoo, and had been tentatively identified by witnesses, would have cast doubt in the jury's minds and established that counsel's omissions amounted to ineffective assistance of counsel.

Rios v. Rocha, 299 F.3d 796, 805-07 (9th Cir. 2002)
Trial counsel's failure to interview more than one witness, when there were 15 witnesses to the shooting, before deciding, prior to the preliminary hearing, to abandon a meritorious misidentification defense and present solely an unconscious defense amounted to ineffective assistance of counsel.

Pavel v. Hollins, 261 F.3d 210, 216-26 (2nd Cir. 2001)
Trial counsel's failure to investigate, prepare a defense, to call two important fact witnesses and present a medical expert witness to dispute the state's sexual abuse of a child case constituted ineffective assistance of counsel.

Stevens v. Delaware Correctional Center, 152 F.Supp.2d 561, 580 (D. Del. 2001)
Counsel was constitutionally ineffective for his failure to investigate and interview witnesses in a rape prosecution that left the jury to decide petitioner's fate with only the victims version of the events and required a new trial.

Coss v. Lackawanna County District Attorney, 204 F.3d 453 (3rd Cir. 2000)
Defense counsel's failure to subpoena certain witness and to interview those witness constituted ineffective assistance of counsel. **See also *Hollines v. Estelle, 569 F.Supp. 146 (W.D. Tex. 1983); U.S. v. Johnson, 995 F. Supp. 1259 (D. Kan. 1998); Demarest .v. Price, 905 F.Supp. 1432 (D.Col. 1995); Berryman v. Morton, 100 F.3d 1089 (3rd Cir. 1996)***

Lord v. Wood, 184 F.3d 1083 (9th Cir. 1999)
Counsel's failure to investigate evidence, which demonstrated his client's factual innocence, undermines the confidence in the verdict and constitutes ineffective assistance of counsel.

Hart v. Gomez, 174 F.3d 1067 (9th Cir. 1999)
Defense counsel's failure to investigate and present evidence corroborating witness' testimony that she accompanied defendant and his children to their ranch during time

the alleged molesting occurred constituted ineffective assistance where the evidence could have precluded conviction.

Holsomback v. White, *133 F.3d 1382 (11th Cir. 1998)*
Trial counsel's failure to conduct any pretrial investigation into the lack of medical evidence of sexual abuse in sodomy prosecution, where treating physician who performed rectal examination shortly after the last alleged incident revealed that victims claims of abuse were medically impossible constituted ineffective assistance of counsel.

Cheung v. Maddock, *32 F.Supp. 2d 1150 (N.D. Cal. 1998)*
Defense counsel's failure to investigate defense that companion, not petitioner, was shooter and to present companion's tape recorded statement for admission into evidence constituted ineffective assistance of counsel. **See also** *Sanders v. Ratelle*, *21 F.3d 1446 (9th Cir. 1994)*

Demarest v. Price, *130 F.3d 922 (10th Cir. 1997)*
Counsel's failure to adequately conduct pretrial investigation in regard to blood-splatter evidence, which would have uncovered strong scientific evidence that could have been used to challenge state witnesses constituted ineffective assistance. This case was remanded to determine whether petitioner's ineffective assistance of counsel claims were procedurally barred. **See also** *Maddox v. Lord*, *818 F.2d 1058 (2nd Cir. 1987)*

Johnson v. Baldwin, *114 F.3d 835 (9th Cir. 1997)*
Trial counsel failed to investigate or properly consult with defendant and discredit defendant's uncorroborated denial of presence at scene of alleged rape constituted ineffective assistance of counsel.

Jones v. Wood, *114 F.3d 1002 (9th Cir. 1997)*
Trial counsel's failure to investigate petitioner's daughter's boyfriend as suspect in petitioner's wife's murder constituted ineffective assistance of counsel.

Medina v. Barnes, *71 F.3d 363 (10th Cir. 1995)*
Trial counsel's failure to investigate criminal history of prosecution witness who identified defendant as the killer constituted ineffective assistance of counsel.

Harris By and Through Ramseyer v. Wood, *64 F.3d 1432 (9th Cir. 1995)*
Trial counsel's failure to investigate and prepare for trial amounted to ineffective assistance. **See also** *Stokes v. Peyton*, *437 F.2d 131 (4th Cir. 1970)*; *House v. Balkcom*, *725 F.2d 608 (11th Cir. 1984)*

Williams v. Washington, *59 F.3d 673 (7th Cir. 1995)*
Trial counsel's failure to investigate alleged victim's reputation for truthfulness amounted to ineffective assistance.

Bryant v. Scott, *28 F.3d 1411 (5th Cir. 1994)*
Trial counsel's failure to investigate and interview witnesses known to counsel three (3) days before trial, and to interview co-defendant who claimed defendant was not the second perpetrator of robbery charge constituted ineffective assistance of counsel.

Williamson v. Reynolds, 904 F.Supp. 1529 (E.D. Okl. 1995)
Trial counsel's failure to investigate and locate individual that last saw the victim constitutes ineffective assistance of counsel.

Siripongs v. Calderon, 35 F.3d 1308 (9th Cir. 1994)
Trial counsel's failure to investigate the existence of accomplices where there was evidence that other individuals were involved in the crime constituted ineffective assistance of counsel and required an evidentiary hearing.

U.S. v. Gray, 878 F.2d 702 (3rd Cir. 1989)
Trial counsel's failure to interview potential witnesses whose names had been provided to counsel by defendant amounted to ineffective assistance of counsel. **See also** *McQueen v. Swenson, 498 F.2d 207 (8th Cir. 1974)*

Montgomery v. Petersen, 846 F.2d 407 (7th Cir. 1988)
Trial counsel's failure to investigate and interview the only disinterested alibi witness, a store clerk Petitioner purchased a bicycle from on the same day of robbery, constituted ineffective assistance of counsel. **See also** *Grooms v. Solem, 923 F.2d 88 (8th Cir. 1991); Tosh v. Lockhart, 879 F.2d 412 (8th Cir. 1989); Code v. Montgomery, 799 F.2d 1481 (11th Cir. 1986); Hudson v. Lockhart, 679 F.Supp. 891 (E.D. Ark. 1986); U.S. v. Mills, 760 F.2d 1116 (11th Cir. 1985); Nelson v. Hargett, 989 F.2d 847 (5th Cir. 1993); Jemison v. Foltz, 672 F.Supp. 1002 (E.D. Mich. 1987)*

Sullivan v. Fairman, 819 F.2d 1382 (7th Cir. 1987)
Trial counsel's failure to locate and call five witnesses who had no apparent reason to help defendant where witnesses made statements to police that were exculpatory or inconsistent with prosecution witnesses' statements and there were significant reasons to conclude that their testimony would have been believed because they were eye-witnesses and their testimony was consistent in essential respects.

Wade v. Armontrout, 798 F.2d 304 (8th Cir. 1986)
Trial counsel's failure to conduct a pretrial investigation, or to interview prosecution's witnesses, constituted ineffective assistance of counsel and required an evidentiary hearing. **See also** *United States v. Tucker, 716 F.2d 576 (9th Cir. 1983)*

Nealy v. Cabana, 764 F.2d 1173 (5th Cir 1985)
Trial counsel's failure to investigate, locate and present potential witnesses' testimony, which could have affected jury's evaluation of truthfulness of prosecution witnesses amounted to ineffective assistance.

Alternative Suspect

Jones v. Wood, 207 F.3d 557 (9th Cir. 2000)
Defense counsel's failure to conduct a pretrial investigation of alternative suspect where evidence tended to connect alternative suspect to crime constituted ineffective assistance of counsel.

POLICE AND LABORATORY REPORTS – INEFFECTIVENESS

Harris v. Cotton, 365 F.3d 552, 555-57 (7th Cir. 2004)
> Counsel's failure to obtain toxicology report that showed victim was under the influence of cocaine and alcohol at time of the shooting, which would have supported defendant's testimony based on his self-defense theory constitutes ineffective assistance of counsel.

Thomas v. Kuhlman, 255 F.Supp. 2d 99, 109-111 (E.D.N.Y. 2003)
> Counsel's failure to investigate crime scene, to read the police reports released by the State as ***Rosario*** material, which would have impeached Artis's testimony that she observed the defendant on the fire escape of the victim's building constituted ineffective assistance of counsel.

Fisher v. Gibson, 282 F.3d 1283, 1293 (10th Cir. 2002)
> Trial counsel failed to view the crime scene, to file any motions for discovery, and review the police reports in a capital murder trial compounded with other errors constituted ineffective assistance of counsel.

✳ *Washington v. Smith, 219 F.3d 620, 633 (7th Cir. 2000)*
> Counsel was constitutionally ineffective for failing to read police report that would have led to evidence corroborating defense theory of case.

✳ *Washington v. Smith, 48 F.Supp. 2d 1149 (E.D. Wis. 1999)*
> Counsel's failure to investigate potentially exculpatory information contained in police report constitutes ineffective assistance of counsel.

✳ *Cheung v. Maddock, 32 F.Supp. 2d 1150 (N.D. Cal. 1998)*
> Defense counsel's failure to investigate victim's medical records constituted ineffective assistance of counsel under ***Strickland.***

Dorsey v. Kelly, 112 F.3d 50 (2nd Cir. 1997)
> Trial counsel's failure to introduce lab reports of scientific tests on semen found in complainant's underpants which suggested that semen could <u>not</u> have come exclusively from petitioner constituted ineffective assistance of counsel.

Hadley v. Groose, 97 F.2d 1131 (8th Cir. 1996)
> Counsel failure to investigate potential alibi evidence and handwritten additions to police report constitutes ineffective assistance.

Toro v. Fairman, 940 F.2d 1065 (7th Cir. 1991)
> Defense counsel's failure to review police and laboratory reports can constitute ineffective assistance of counsel, but defendant must establish that there exists a reasonable probability that result of proceeding would have been different.

Medical Records

Tucker v. Prelesnik, 181 F.3d 747 (6th Cir. 1999)
> Defense counsel's failure to move for a continuance to obtain medical records of assault victim which would have impeached his ability to remember, to obtain and use evidence of earlier contradictory statements by victim, which would have cast

serious doubt about the victims credibility constituted ineffective assistance of counsel.

Vick v. Lockhart, 952 F.2d 999 (8th Cir. 1991)
Trial counsel's failure to obtain medical reports of alleged rape victim constitutes ineffective assistance of counsel.

Victim's School/Counseling Records

Barkell v. Crouse, 468 F.3d 684, 692-693 (10th Cir. 2006)
Counsel failure to investigate victim's school records and counseling records, which indicated that victim had tendency to lie and failed to consult with child expert psychiatrist required an evidentiary hearing to resolve claim of ineffectiveness of counsel.

Drug Chemical Analysis

U.S. v. Bulter, 988 F.2d 537 (5th Cir. 1993)
Defendant has the right to have an independent chemical analysis performed on the alleged seized controlled substance.

United States v. Noel, 708 F. Supp. 177 (W.D. Tenn. 1989)
The court found that the defendant "...shall be provided an opportunity to test and analyze the alleged controlled substance by a qualified, independent expert selected by the defendant." Id. The Noel Court..."noting that the gravamen of the indictment against defendant rested upon the alleged drug being a narcotic within the provision of the U.S. Code, held that defendant was entitled to have an independent test performed on the alleged narcotic. Further, the district court admonished that defendant should not be limited to cross-examination of the government's expert on such pivotal determinative fact. "Id.

Plane Polarized Light Test/Optically Active Column Test

U.S. v. Patrick, 983 F.2d 206,208 (11th Cir. 1993)
The "plane polarized light" test or the "optically active column" test are used to distinguish the difference of D from L-Methamphetamine.

Mass-spectrometer And A Gas Chromatogram

United States v. Distler, 671 F.2d 954,960 (6th Cir. 1981)
The Sixth Circuit summarized the process of mass-spectrometer and a gas chromatogram scientific tests as follows: The methodology of oil matching involves the isolation of the molecular compounds associated with oil, particularly hydrocarbons and sulfur compounds. Instrumental in this process is the gas chromatography, which is essentially an extremely sensitive filtering machine. The particular sample to be tested is mixed with a liquid solvent. The mixture is heated until it forms a gas. The gas is then forced through a column, which is a glass tube filled with special filtration material. Each molecular compound will elute through a given column and temperature at the same rate. At the outgoing end of the column a detector is attached, which records the quantity and concentration of each particular molecular compound contained in the

sample. The <u>data</u> thus accumulated are converted into <u>electrical impulses</u> which are <u>recorded</u> in <u>graph fashion</u>, called <u>chromatogram</u>. Comparison of the <u>graphs</u> reveals whether the tested samples match. (emphasis added).

SUBPOENA WITNESS RELATED INEFFECTIVENESS

Luna v. Cambra, *306 F.3d 954, 962 (9th Cir. 2002)*
Counsel's failure to interview and subpoena Lopez an exonerating witness who had confessed to the crime in an out-of-court declaration constituted ineffective assistance of counsel.

Coss v. Lackawanna County District Attorney, *204 F.3d 453 (3rd Cir. 2000)*
Defense counsel's failure to subpoena certain witness and to interview those witness constituted ineffective assistance of counsel.

Ellerby v. U.S., *187 F.3d 257 (2nd Cir. 1998)*
Trial counsel's failure to subpoena alibi witnesses warranted an evidentiary hearing to resolve claim of ineffective assistance of counsel. **See also** *Washington v. Smith*, *48 F.Supp. 2d 1149 (E.D. Wis. 1999)*

Capps v. Sullivan, *921 F.2d 260 (10th Cir. 1990)*
Trial counsel's failure to adequately prepare his case by interviewing or subpoenaing the witness who would have substantially corroborated Capps' testimony material to entrapment defense constituted ineffective assistance of counsel.

Code v. Montgomery, *799 F.2d 1481 (11th Cir. 1986)*
Trial counsel's failure to conduct a pretrial investigation, interview or subpoena alibi witnesses and move for a continuance amounted to ineffective assistance of counsel and warranted a new trial.

Cross v. United States, *392 F.2d 360 (8th Cir. 1968)*
Trial counsel failed to subpoena any witnesses, or prepare for trial because the defendant did not pay him all his money and claimed his own ineffectiveness in a motion for mistrial required an evidentiary hearing.

Friedman v. United States, *588 F.2d 1010 (5th Cir. 1979)*
Trial counsel's failure to subpoena certain witnesses at government's expense on behalf of his indigent client required an evidentiary hearing to resolve the ineffectiveness of counsel claim. **See also** *Application of Tomich*, *221 F.Supp. 500 (D. Mont. 1963) aff'd at 332 F.2d 987 (9th Cir. 1964)*; *U.S. v. Gray*, *878 F.2d 702 (3rd Cir. 1989)*; *Eldridge v. Atkins*, *665 F.2d 228 (8th Cir. 1981)*; *Nealy v. Cabana*, *764 F.2d 1173 (5th Cir 1985)*

Matter of Klein, *776 F.2d 628 (7th Cir. 1985)*
A Grand Jury can serve subpoena's on an attorney and/or documents in the attorney's possession.

SCENE OF CRIME RELATED INEFFECTIVENESS

Thomas v. Kuhlman, 255 F.Supp. 2d 99, 109-111 (E.D.N.Y. 2003)
Counsel's failure to investigate crime scene, to read the police reports released by the State as **_Rosario_** material, which would have impeached Artis's testimony that she observed the defendant on the fire escape of the victim's building constituted ineffective assistance of counsel.

Berry v. Gramley, 74 F.Supp.2d 808 (N.D. Ill. 1999)
Counsel's failure to visit the crime scene or employ an investigator to locate and interview witnesses to corroborate defendant's testimony amounted to ineffective assistance of counsel.

Williams v. Washington, 59 F.3d 673 (7th Cir. 1995)
Trial counsel's failure to visit the defendant's home, where the alleged crime supposedly occurred which would have shown that due to relatively crowded conditions the alleged assault could not have taken place as claimed constituted ineffective assistance of counsel. See also **_Harris v. Reed, 894 F.2d 871 (7th Cir. 1990)_**

U.S. v. Gray, 878 F.2d 702 (3rd Cir. 1989)
Trial counsel's failure to conduct pretrial investigation by failing to go to the scene of the crime and locate potential witnesses amounted to ineffective assistance of counsel. **See also _House v. Balkcom, 725 F.2d 608 (11th Cir. 1984); Wade v. Armontrout, 798 F.2d 304 (8th Cir. 1986)_**

HIRE PRIVATE INVESTIGATOR

Berry v. Gramley, 74 F.Supp.2d 808 (N.D. Ill. 1999)
Counsel's failure to visit the crime scene or employ an investigator to locate and interview witnesses to corroborate defendant's testimony amounted to ineffective assistance of counsel. **See also _U.S. v. Gray, 878 F.2d 702 (3rd Cir. 1989)_**

Harris By and Through Ramseyer v. Wood, 64 F.3d 1432 (9th Cir. 1995)
Trial counsel's failure to retain an investigator to interview witnesses amounted to ineffective assistance. **See also _Demarest v. Price, 905 F.Supp. 1432 (D.Col. 1995)_**

Miller v. Wainwright, 798 F.2d 426 (11th Cir. 1986)
Trial counsel's failure to renew motion for appointment of private investigator constitutes ineffective assistance of counsel.

FACTS RELATED INEFFECTIVENESS

Williamson v. Reynolds, 904 F.Supp. 1529 (E.D. Okl. 1995)
Trial counsel's failure to investigate fact that defendant was on medication during which time he confessed to crime may constitute ineffective assistance of counsel.

U.S. v. Matos, 905 F.2d 30 (2nd Cir. 1990)
 Trial counsel's willingness to accept the government's version of facts and failed to file any motions because he relied on the government's version of facts, and not based on his own reasonable investigation, calls counsel's representation into serious question of inadequacy.

Streetman v. Lynaugh, 812 F.2d 950 (5th Cir. 1987)
 Trial counsel failed to press the motion to suppress defendant's confession to law enforcement that he committed the murder plus a series of thefts when authorities had threatened defendant and his family with physical violence. Authorities promised to release defendant and continue a supply of valium in exchange for defendant's cooperation against accomplice. Trial counsel failed to inform co-counsel of defendant's allegations. The defendant's confession was the State's main case at trial. The Fifth Circuit remanded for an evidentiary hearing.

Nell v. James, 811 F.2d 100 (2nd Cir. 1987)
 Trial counsel's failure to investigate, to consult with defendant about facts and to move for suppression of identification testimony constituted ineffective assistance and required an evidentiary hearing. **See also** *Application of Tomich, 221 F.Supp. 500 (D. Mont. 1963) aff'd at 332 F.2d 987 (9th Cir. 1964)*

Scott v. Wainwright, 698 F.2d 427, 429-30 (11th Cir. 1983)
 Trial counsel's failure to learn the facts and familiarize himself with the law in relation to the plea constitutes ineffective assistance and renders the guilty plea invalid. **See also** *House v. Balkcom, 725 F.2d 608 (11th Cir. 1984); Herring v. Estelle, 491 F.2d 125 (5th Cir. 1974)*

GRAND/PETIT JURIES INEFFECTIVENESS

Campbell v. Louisiana, 523 U.S. 392, 140 L.Ed.2d 551, 118 S.Ct. 1419 (1998)
 The Supreme Court held that: "A white criminal defendant has the requisite standing to raise equal protection and due process objections to discrimination against black persons in the selection of grand jurors."

Young v. Duckworth, 733 F.2d 482 (7th Cir. 1984)
 Defendant's constitutional right to counsel attached at initial hearing where there was sufficient evidence to present case to grand jury.

FAILED TO PUT "AGREEMENT IN WRITING"
OR ON THE RECORD

Houston v. Lockhart, 982 F.2d 1246 (8th Cir. 1993)
 Trial counsel's failure to put "agreement in writing" or on the record in the presence of the judge constituted ineffective assistance of counsel.

**Betancourt v. Willis**, 814 F.2d 1546 (11th Cir. 1987)

Trial counsel's failure to memorialize alleged sentence reduction, either by letter, affidavit or otherwise based on counsel's representation to defendant that judge had agreed to reduce defendant's sentence after plea constituted ineffective assistance.

FAILED TO APPEAR FOR ARRAIGNMENT

**United States v. Hammonds**, 425 F.2d 597 (D.C. Cir. 1970)

Trial counsel's failure to appear at arraignment compounded with other errors constitutes ineffective assistance of counsel.

COUNSEL APPOINTED ON DAY OF TRIAL

**Hunt v. Nitchell**, 261 F.3d 575, 583 (6th Cir. 2001)

Hunt was denied his right to counsel during pre-trial a "critical stage" where Hunt never consulted with counsel before the start of voir dire. Counsel moved for a ten minute continuance which was denied and had to proceed with voir dire without ever discussing the case with Hunt, and without conducting any discovery or independent investigation of the facts. Counsel was appointed to represent Hunt on the first day of trial which deprived Hunt of his Sixth Amendment right to counsel during pre-trial.

DEFENDANT'S RIGHT TO BE PRESENT

**Rogers v. United States**, 422 U.S. 35, 39, 45 L.Ed.2d 1, 6, 95 S.Ct. 2091 (1975)

Federal Rules of Criminal Procedure, Rule 43 guarantees to a defendant in a criminal trial the right to be present "at every stage of the trial including the impaneling of the jury and the return of the verdict." In this case, the jury sent a **note** to the trial judge inquiring whether the court would accept a verdict of "Guilty as charged with extreme mercy of the Court." The trial court's answer to the jury **note**, without informing the defense and without providing it with an opportunity to be heard required **reversal**.

**Fillippon v. Albion Vein Slate Co.**, 250 U.S. 76, 63 L.Ed. 853, 39 S.Ct. 435 (1919)

The Supreme Court observed "that the orderly conduct of trial by jury essential to the proper protection of the right to be heard, entitles the parties who attend for the purposes to be present in person, or by counsel, at all proceeding from the time the jury is impaneled until it is discharged after rendering the verdict." **Id., at 81, 63 L.Ed 893, 39 S.Ct. 435.** In applying that principle, the Court found that the trial judge had "erred in giving a supplementary instruction to the jury in the absence of the parties and without affording them an opportunity either to be present or to make timely objections to the instructions. **See also _Shields v. United States_, 273 U.S. 583, 71 L.Ed. 787, 47 S.Ct. 478 (1927).**

Bartone v. United States, *375 U.S. 52, 11 L.Ed.2d 11, 84 S.Ct. 21 (1963)*
> The district court enlargement of defendant's sentence in his absence violates **Federal Rules of Criminal Procedure, Rule 43**, and should have been dealt with by the Court of Appeals even though it had not been alleged as an error.

Campbell v. Rice, *302 F.3d 892, 898 (9th Cir. 2002)*
> The trial court violated defendant's due process right to be present when it excluded the defendant from a private in-chambers hearing in which defense counsel, prosecutor and judge discussed the conflict of interest because defense counsel was being prosecuted for a felony by the same district attorney's office that was prosecuting Campbell.

WAIVED DEFENDANT'S RIGHT TO JURY TRIAL

Miller v. Dormire, *310 F.3d 600, 603-604 (8th Cir. 2002):*
> Counsel was constitutionally ineffective by waiving defendant's right to a trial by jury. Prejudice was presumed under *Strickland*, because such misconduct is tantamount to a structural error. See *McGurk v. Stenberg*, **163 F.3d 470, 475 (8th Cir. 1998).**

WAIVED JURY TRIAL ALLOWING DEFENDANT TO BE TRIED BEFORE JUDGE WHO KNEW DEFENDANT'S CRIMINAL HISTORY

Jemison v. Foltz, *672 F.Supp. 1002 (E.D. Mich. 1987)*
> Trial counsel waived a jury trial and allowed defendant to be tried before a judge that was fully aware of defendant's long criminal history compounded with other errors constituted ineffective assistance of counsel.

CONSULTATION RELATED INEFFECTIVENESS

Escobedo v. Illinois, *378 U.S. 478, 12 Led 2d 977, 84 S.Ct. 1758 (1964)*
> Failure to allow accused to consult with counsel constitutes a denial of his right to counsel under the Sixth and Fourteenth Amendments and requires that the statements made by the accused to be suppressed.

Lewis v. Johnson, *359 F.3d 646, 660-662 (3rd Cir. 2004)*
> Counsel was constitutionally ineffective for failing to meet or consult with petitioner after the denial of his motion to withdraw guilty plea and sentencing.

Mitchell v. Mason, *257 F.3d 554, 566-74 (6th Cir. 2001)*
> Defense counsel's failure to consult, or visit with Mitchell, prior to trial and spent approximately six minutes with Mitchell prior to jury selection, spanning over three separate meetings in court bullpen, counsel was suspended from practice for one month immediately prior to trial and Mitchell sought new counsel for six months, amounted to a complete denial of counsel.

Nell v. James, 811 F.2d 100 (2nd Cir. 1987)
Trial counsel's failure to investigate, to consult with defendant about the facts, and move for suppression of identification testimony constitutes ineffective assistance and required an evidentiary hearing.

Douglas v. Wainwright, 739 F.2d 531 (11th Cir. 1984)
Trial counsel's failure to consult with defendant and inform him of option of taking stand and testifying in his own behalf compounded with other errors at sentencing amounted to ineffective assistance of counsel and required an evidentiary hearing.

United States v. Tucker, 716 F.2d 576 (9th Cir. 1983)
Trial counsel's failure to consult with defendant during trial due to the complexity of the case and defendant's knowledge of the documentary evidence and witnesses constitutes ineffective assistance. **See also** *Moore v. United States, 432 F.2d 730 (3rd Cir. 1970); Noland v. Dixon, 808 F.Supp. 485 (W.D.N.C. 1992)*

VOICE EXEMPLAR INEFFECTIVENESS

United States v. Baynes, 687 F.2d 659 (3rd Cir. 1982)
Trial counsel's failure to investigate possibilities of distinguishing the exemplar of defendant's voice from voice on intercepted tape recording, where intercepted tape recording was the only evidence against defendant amounted to ineffective assistance of counsel. **See also** *United States v. Baynes, 622 F.2d 66 (3rd Cir. 1980)*

PRISON-CIVILIAN CLOTHES RELATED INEFFECTIVENESS

Smith v. U.S., 182 F.3d 1023 (8th Cir. 1999)
Defense counsel's failure to object to defendant having to stand trial while in prison clothes, in violation of his right to a fair trial warranted an evidentiary hearing to resolve ineffective assistance of counsel claim.

Hernandez v. Beto, 443 F.2d 634 (5th Cir. 1971), cert. denied 404 U.S. 897 (1971)
Trial counsel's failure to object to defendant being tried in prison clothes was prejudicial and amounted to ineffective assistance of counsel.

Chalk v. Beto, 429 F.2d 225 (5th Cir. 1970)
The defendant requested for trial counsel to allow him to dress in his civilian clothes which were available, his attorney refused and he was forced to proceed to trial in prison clothing. The attorney also failed to object to the defendant being arrested without probable cause or a warrant. The attorney's actions in this case amounted to ineffective assistance of counsel.

FAILED TO ADVISE DEFENDANT OF RIGHT
TO TRIAL BY JURY

McGurk v. Stenberg, 163 F.3d 470 (8th Cir. 1998)
Counsel's failure to advise defendant of his right to a jury trial as opposed to a bench trial constituted ineffective assistance of counsel.

GUILTY PLEA INEFFECTIVENESS

EXPLANATION OF Hill v. Lockhart

The Supreme Court in *Hill v. Lockhart, 474 U.S. 52, 88 L.Ed.2d 203, 106 S.Ct. 366 (1985)*, held that the two part *Strickland v. Washington, 466 U.S. 668, 687-88, 694, 104 S.Ct. 2052, 2064-74, 80 L.Ed.2d 674 (1984)*, test applies to challenges to guilty pleas based on ineffective assistance of counsel. The *Hill* Court found in the plea bargaining context, a petitioner seeking to establish ineffective assistance of counsel must demonstrate that: (1) Counsel's advice and performance fell below an objective standard of reasonableness; and (2) The petitioner must show that there is a reasonable probability that, but for counsel's errors, he would not have pleaded guilty and would have insisted on going to trial. *Id. at [474 U.S. 59]* (emphasis added).

The *Hill* Court further explained that in many guilty plea cases, the "prejudice" inquiry would closely resemble the inquiry engaged in by courts reviewing ineffective assistance challenges to convictions obtained through a trial. For example, where the alleged error of counsel is a failure to investigate or discover potentially exculpatory evidence, the determination whether the error "prejudiced" the defendant by causing him to plead guilty rather than go to trial will depend on the likelihood that discovery of the evidence would have led counsel to change his recommendation as to the plea. This assessment, in turn, will depend in large part on a prediction whether the evidence likely would have changed the outcome of a trial. Similarly, where the alleged error of counsel is a failure to advise the defendant of a potential affirmative defense to the crime charged, the resolution of the "prejudice" inquiry will depend largely on whether the affirmative defense likely would have succeeded at trial. *Id.*

The Supreme Court rejected *Hill's* claim of error of counsel's erroneous advice as to eligibility for parole under the sentence agreed to in the plea bargain, because *Hill* failed to allege in his habeas petition that, had counsel correctly informed him about his parole eligibility date, he would have pleaded not guilty and insisted on going to trial. *Hill* alleged no special circumstances that might support the conclusion that he placed particular emphasis on his parole eligibility in deciding whether or not to plead guilty. Indeed, *Hill's* mistaken belief that he would become eligible for parole after serving one-third of his sentence would seem to have affected not only his calculation of the time he likely would serve if sentenced pursuant to the proposed plea agreement, but also his calculation of the time he likely would serve if he went to trial and were convicted.

Because *Hill* failed to allege the kind of "prejudice" necessary to satisfy the second half of *Strickland v. Washington* test, the Supreme Court concluded that the district court did not err in declining to hold a hearing on Hill's ineffective assistance of counsel claim and affirmed the judgment of the Court of Appeals.

———————————— * ————————————

"THE REMATCH OF HILL V. LOCKHART"

Hill filed a second petition for relief alleging he was denied effective assistance of counsel in pleading guilty due to counsel's failure to give accurate advice regarding probation. The United States District court for the Eastern District of Arkansas granted the petition. The director of Arkansas Department of Corrections appealed. The Eighth Circuit in *Hill v. Lockhart, 877 F.2d 698 (8th Cir. 1989)* held that: (1) habeas petition did not have to be dismissed as successive petition because there was no final determination on the merits of his first petition; and (2) erroneous parole eligibility advice given to petitioner was ineffective assistance of counsel rendering his guilty plea invalid. The Court of Appeals affirmed the district court order granting Hill's petition.

In short, the Eighth Circuit in *__Hill v. Lockhart, supra__*, found that Hill's lawyer was ineffective in failing to conduct a minimal research of the applicable statute governing parole eligibility for a second offender, plus counsel's failure to give accurate advice regarding parole eligibility, which was an integral factor in Hill's plea negotiations, constituted ineffective assistance of counsel rendering the guilty plea involuntarily. The *__Hill__* Court further found that *__Hill__* did *not* have to show that he would have been acquitted or given a shorter sentence at trial.

This case went en banc at *__Hill v. Lockhart, 894 F.2d 1009 (8th Cir. 1990) (en banc)__* where the Court reaffirmed, the district court's decision granting *__Hill__*'s petition.

FAILED TO RESEARCH OR INVESTIGATE

The Crime Charged

__U.S. v. Sanchez-Barreto, 93 F.3d 17 (1st Cir. 1996)__
Defense counsel coerced defendant's guilty plea in order to conceal his unpreparedness for trial,which constitutes ineffective assistance of counsel.

__Woodard v. Collins, 898 F.2d 1027 (5th Cir. 1990)__
The Court held that a remand was required to determine whether petitioner was prejudiced by his counsel's failure to investigate a crime to which, upon counsel's advice, petitioner pled guilty. Reversed and Remanded.

The *__Woodard__* court found that the first prong of *__Strickland__* had been satisfied but found that it could not ascertain from the record whether the second prong of *__Strickland__* has been met. First, a court generally must strongly presume that counsel has exercised reasonable professional conduct. *__Strickland, 466 U.S. at 690, 104 S.Ct. at 2065__*, and *__Samples, 897 F.2d at 196__*. No such presumption, however, is warranted when a lawyer advises his client to plea bargain to an offense, which the attorney has not investigated. Such conduct is always unreasonable. *__Id. at 1029__*. Second, the court must determine whether Woodard suffered prejudice. Woodard can show prejudice if "there is a reasonable probability that, but for, counsel's errors, he would not have pleaded guilty and would have insisted on going to trial." *__Hill, 474 U.S. at 59, 106 S.Ct. at 370__*. On remand, the district court must make findings to determine whether Woodard suffered prejudice. **REVERSED AND REMANDED. See also** *__McQueen v. Swenson, 498 F.2d 207 (8th Cir. 1974)__*

Law in Relation to the Plea

__Scott v. Wainwright, 698 F.2d 427, 429-30 (11th Cir. 1983)__
Trial counsel's failure to learn the facts and familiarize himself with the law in relation to the plea constitutes ineffective assistance and renders the guilty plea invalid. **See also** *__Herring v. Estelle, 491 F.2d 125 (5th Cir. 1974); Kennedy v. Maggio, 725 F.2d 269 (5th Cir. 1984)__*

Law and Facts of Case

Lambert v. Blodgett, 248 F.Supp.2d 988, 1000-1003 (E.D. Wash. 2003)

Counsel induced Lambert's guilty plea to aggravated first degree murder, which assured the most severe penalty available, without investigating Lambert's background; his alcohol exposure; the background of his codefendants who were to testify against him for impeachment material; discovery the enhanced tape recording of Lambert's taped statement; compare the tape recording to the transcript and discover the significant transcription error attributing a false admission of premeditation to Lambert; rendering Lambert's guilty plea not knowingly and intentionally entered as a result of counsel's ineffectiveness.

Trueblood v. Anderson, 156 F.Supp. 2d 1056 (N.D. Ind. 2001)

Counsel's failure to understand consequences of guilty plea to murder counts with respect to death penalty or to correctly advise petitioner that a guilty plea could be used as aggravating factor for death penalty in sentencing rendered guilty plea not voluntary or intelligently entered as a result of ineffective assistance of counsel.

Shafer v. Bowersox, 168 F.Supp. 2d 1055, 1079-80 (E.D. Mo. 2001)

The trial court's failure to advise Shafer, who waived counsel, during change of plea hearing of any possible defenses, such as diminished capacity or discuss the possibility of being convicted of a lesser included offense, which would produce a parolable sentence; evidence in the record did not demonstrate that Shafer understood the law in relation to the facts or the alternative course of action available to him rendering his guilty plea not knowingly, intelligently and voluntarily entered in violation of due process.

Esslinger v. Davis, 44 F.3d 1515 (11th Cir. 1995)

Defense counsel's failure to adequately investigate defendant's prior criminal history and recommended defendant to enter a blind guilty plea to a class A felony, which was subsequently enhanced under Alabama's Habitual Offender Act, constitutes ineffective assistance of counsel where there was a reasonable probability, that defendant would have proceeded to trial, absent counsel's errors.

United States v. Burton, 575 F. Supp. 1320 (E.D. Texas 1983)

Defense counsel must be familiar with the laws and facts of the case in order to provide effective assistance of counsel.

Colson v. Smith, 315 F.Supp. 179 (N.D. Georgia 1970)

Trial counsel's handling of 5,000 cases a year, failure to contact witness, consulted with defendant only a few minutes which placed fear in defendant, who maintained his innocence, to accept a guilty plea in capital case, constituted ineffective assistance and rendered guilty plea involuntarily entered.

Defendant's Legal Claims

Young v. Zant, 677 F.2d 792, 798 (11th Cir. 1982)

Trial counsel's failure to understand defendant's factual or legal claims fails to provide performance within the competency expected from criminal defense counsel.

Defendant's Competency

U.S. v. Kauffman, 109 F.3d 186 (3rd Cir. 1997)
Counsel's failure to pursue any investigation into insanity defense before advising defendant to plead guilty, after counsel saw a letter from defendant's psychiatrist stating that defendant was manic and psychotic when crime was committed constituted ineffective assistance of counsel and required the guilty plea to be set-aside. **See also _McCoy v. Wainwright_, 804 F.2d 1196, (11th Cir. 1986); _Bouchillon v. Collins_, 907 F.2d 589 (5th Cir. 1990)**

Weekly v. Jones, 56 F.3d 889 (8th Cir. 1995)
Counsel's failure to investigate defendant's medical evidence, coerced Weekly to withdraw his plea of insanity and plead not guilty, constitutes ineffective assistance of counsel.

Agan v. Singletary, 12 F.3d 1012 (11 Cir. 1994)
Trial counsel's failure to investigate defendant's competency, obtain prison or military medical files and make independent examination of facts prior to offering informed opinion that defendant should plead guilty constituted ineffective assistance. **See also _Loyd v. Smith_, 899 F.2d 1416 (5th Cir. 1990)**

Thomas v. Lockhart, 738 F.2d 304 (8th Cir. 1984)
Trial counsel's failure to investigate defendant's mental problems, to alert court and prosecutor of defendant's mental history a factor that may have affected plea negotiations and the sentence constituted ineffective assistance of counsel.

Defendant's Criminal History

United States v. Colon-Torres, 382 F.3d 76, 87 (1st Cir. 2004)
Counsel's failure to investigate Colon's criminal history category before inducing Colon's guilty plea required a remand for the district court to resolve factual disputes related to ineffective assistance of counsel claim.

Applicable Statute Governing Parole

Nolan v. Armontrout, 973 F.2d 615 (8th Cir. 1992)
Defense counsel's erroneous advice about parole eligibility may constitute ineffective assistance of counsel.

Hawkins v. Murray, 798 F.Supp. 330 (E.D. Va. 1992)
Trial counsel's failure to advise defendant that according to statute he would not be entitled to parole, prior to entering guilty plea constitutes ineffective assistance of counsel.

Hill v. Lockhart, 877 F.2d 698 (8th Cir. 1989)
Trial counsel's failure to research applicable statute governing parole eligibility for second offenders, where plea factor consisted of defendant's eligibility to make parole constitutes ineffective assistance of counsel.

21 U.S.C.§846 Congressional Amendment of Mandatory Minimums

Soto v. U.S., 37 F.3d 252, 254-56 (7th Cir. 1994) (per curiam)
> Trial counsel's failure to discourage Soto from pleading guilty due to counsel's failure to perceive that the government's theory that Soto engaged in a single long-term conspiracy was a mistake, which exposed Soto to the application of the Guidelines and a mandatory minimum sentence required an evidentiary hearing to determine the dates of the actual conspiracy that Soto was involved, and to resolve ineffective assistance of counsel claim.

Insufficient Evidence To Support Plea Under *Bailey*

Jones v. U.S., 153 F.3d 1305 (11th Cir. 1998)
> Jones plead guilty to using and carrying a firearm during and in relation to a drug trafficking offense. Jones filed a **28 U.S.C. §2255** motion contending that the evidence did not support the conviction and that his plea was not voluntary after the Supreme Court ruling in **Bailey** the district court denied the **§2255** motion without conducting an evidentiary hearing. Jones appealed claiming that the Supreme Court's decision in **Bousley v. United States, 118 S.Ct. 1604, 140 L.Ed.2d 828 (1998)**, required the case to be remanded for a hearing to determine whether Jones is actually innocent of the **18 U.S.C. §924 (c) (1),** charge and therefore can establish cause for procedural bar. The Eleventh Circuit **REMANDED for a hearing.**

Bouseley v. United States, 523 U.S. 614, 140 L. Ed. 2d 828, 118 S.Ct. 1604 (1998)
> The accused will be entitled to a hearing on the merits of his claim contesting validity of his guilty plea to firearms charge to permit him to attempt to make a showing of actual innocence to relieve his procedural default.

Insufficient Factual Basis For Guilty Plea

Coddington v. Langley, 202 F.Supp. 2d 687, 702 (E.D. Mich. 2002)
> Appellate counsel was constitutionally ineffective by failing to raise that there was insufficient factual basis for the guilty plea on direct appeal, where petitioner did not admit to touching his daughter for the purpose of sexual contact under Michigan law.

Obtain Discovery

Tate v. Wood, 963 F.2d 20 (2d Cir. 1992)
> Tate was entitled to evidentiary hearing on **Brady** claim concerning failure to disclose evidence that victim was initial aggressor. The test of materiality in the context of a guilty plea is whether there is a reasonable probability that, but for the failure to produce such information, the defendant would not have entered the plea but instead would have insisted on going to trial. The inquiry is an objective one that is resolved largely on the basis of the persuasiveness of the withheld evidence. **See, Miller v. Angliker, 848 F.2d 1312, 1322 (2nd Cir.), cert. denied, 488 U.S. 890, 109 S.Ct. 224, 102 L.Ed.2d 214 (1988).**

Stano v. Dugger, 889 F.2d 962 (11th Cir. 1989)
> Trial counsel advised the judge that he had not received full discovery from the state and he could not advise defendant of wisdom of whether state had sufficient evidence to

convict defendant or not. The trial judge accepted defendant's guilty plea anyway, which violated defendant's Sixth Amendment right to counsel.

FAILED TO ADVISE THE DEFENDANT OF . . .

Adequate Notice of the Offense

Henderson v. Morgan, 426 U.S. 637, 49 L.Ed.2d 108, 96 S.Ct. 2253 (1976)
The Supreme Court held that the judgment of conviction was entered without due process of law, since the defendant-petitioner's plea of guilty was involuntary in that he did not receive adequate notice of the offense.

Blalock v. Lockhart, 898 F.2d 1367 (8th Cir. 1990)
Defense counsel's failure to inform defendant of the accomplice corroboration rule constitutes ineffective assistance, combined with the trial court's failure to properly advise defendant of his rights to confront witnesses, remain silent and the nature of the charges, rendered the guilty plea not knowing or voluntarily entered and required an evidentiary hearing. See also *Jones v. Lockhart, 851 F.2d 1115 (8th Cir. 1988).*

Nevarez-Diaz v. U.S., 870 F.2d 417 (7th Cir. 1989)
Trial counsel's attempt to plead defendant guilty where it was apparent that defendant felt that he was guilty only because he was present at the time the acts occurred, constitutes ineffective assistance and rendered guilty plea involuntary.

Acceptance of Responsibility

United States v. Booth, 432 F.3d 542, 550 (3rd Cir. 2005)
Counsel's failure to inform Booth that he could plead guilty to an open plea to counts one and two and receive a reduction in sentence of 19 to 30 months for acceptance of responsibility, pursuant to **U.S.S.G. §3E1.1,** required an evidentiary hearing to resolve the ineffectiveness of counsel claim.

U.S. v. Clyburn, 368 F. Supp. 2d 545 (W.D. VA. 2005)
A sentence below the recommended Sentencing Guideline range was appropriate given the Court's entry of judgment of acquittal on the second weapons charge, and the finding that defendant would have likely plead guilty and received acceptance of responsibility, if that charge had not been brought by the government.

Accomplice Corroboration Rule

Blalock v. Lockhart, 898 F.2d 1367 (8th Cir. 1990)
Defense counsel's failure to inform defendant of the accomplice corroboration rule constitutes ineffective assistance, combined with the trial court's failure to properly advise defendant of his rights to confront witnesses, remain silent and the nature of the charges, rendered the guilty plea not knowing or voluntarily entered and required an evidentiary hearing.

Available Options and Possible Consequences

U.S. v. Stubbs, 279 F.3d 402, 412 (6th Cir. 2002)

The waiver of appeal in plea agreement was invalid where defendant's guilty plea was not voluntary or intelligently entered. Neither the defendant, his counsel, nor the district court was aware that defendant was not subject to a mandatory consecutive minimum 60-month sentence under 18 U.S.C. §924(o), and there is no evidence that defendant was aware of the true nature of the crime charged, and the statutory consequences of his guilty plea. Thus, rendering the guilty plea not voluntary or intelligently entered.

Haynes v. Burke, 115 F.Supp.2d 813 (E.D. Mich. 2000)

Defense counsel's failure to advise juvenile that any sentence imposed as a result of the guilty plea could be appealed by the prosecution, and could possibly result in a life sentence without parole constitutes ineffective assistance of counsel, and render the guilty plea involuntary or unintelligently entered.

Rogers v. U.S., 990 F.2d 1008 (8th Cir. 1993)

Appellate counsel's failure to raise the district court's failure to advise defendant that, if the district court refused to accept prosecutor's sentence recommendation, that the defendant had no right to withdraw guilty plea stated a sufficient claim of ineffective assistance of counsel and warranted an evidentiary hearing.

Brown v. Butler, 811 F.2d 938 (5th Cir. 1987)

Trial counsel's failure to advise defendant of available venue defense, prior to entering guilty plea rendered the plea involuntarily entered because the defendant was not able to make conscious decision of whether to plead guilty and constitutes ineffective assistance of counsel.

Hawkman v. Parratt, 661 F.2d 1161 (8th Cir. 1981)

Trial counsel's failure to interview witnesses, to adequately advise defendant of elements of the offense, potential defenses, to initiate plea bargaining negotiations before advising defendant to plead guilty constitutes ineffective assistance.

Beckan v. Wainwright, 639 F.2d 262 (5th Cir. 1981)

Trial counsel advised defendant to enter a guilty plea to a stipulated term of five-year sentence and defendant pleaded guilty based on counsel's advice. The attorney then advised defendant to withdraw his plea and go to trial based on the assumption he would only receive a five-year sentence if found guilty. Defendant followed counsel's advice and withdrew his plea and went to trial and was found guilty, and received a fifty-year (50) sentence. The court found that counsel's performance and advice was ineffective and granted the Petition for Writ of Habeas corpus filed by petitioner.

Charges Were Barred by Statute of Limitations

U.S. v. Hansel, 70 F.3d 6 (2nd Cir. 1995)

Counsel's failure to inform defendant that charges were barred by statute of limitations rendered the guilty plea involuntary.

Double Jeopardy Defense

Dickerson v. Vaughn, *90 F.3d 87 (3rd Cir. 1996)*
> Mispresentation of law applicable to double jeopardy issue rendered guilty plea invalid, and required state to grant petitioner's the right to file conditional appeals, nunc pro tunc on double jeopardy issue due to ineffectiveness of counsel.

Burgess v. Griffin, *585 F.Supp. 1564 (W.D. North Carolina 1984)*
> Trial counsel's failure to advise defendant of double jeopardy defense before entering guilty plea constitutes ineffective assistance of counsel.

Duress Defense-Battered Woman's Syndrome

Dando v. Yukins, *461 F.3d 791, 798-800 (6th Cir. 2006)*
> Counsel was constitutionally ineffective for advising petitioner to plead no-contest without investigating the possibility of duress defense based on the Battered Woman's Syndrome.

Defendant Could be Sentenced Under Guidelines

Risher v. U.S., *992 F.2d 982 (9th Cir. 1993)*
> Trial counsel's failure to inform defendant before entering guilty plea that sentence might be under the Sentencing Guidelines constitutes ineffective assistance.

Communicate Government's Plea Offer

Valentine v. United States, *488 F.3d 325, 332-333 (6th Cir. 2007)*
> Valentine was entitled to an evidentiary hearing to resolve the factual dispute, whether the government offered him a ten (10) year plea offer that his counsel prevented him from accepting.

Satterlee v. Wolfenbarger, *374 F.Supp.2d 562, 567-568 (E.D. Mich. 2005)*
> Counsel was constitutionally ineffective for failing to convey prosecution's plea offer of six to twenty years to defendant requiring reinstatement of the plea offer. **See also** *Satterlee v. Wolfenbarger*, **453 F.3d 362, 369-371 (6th Cir. 2006)** (habeas court has remedial authority to order conviction expunged).

Nunes v. Mueller, *350 F.3d 1045, 1053-1057 (9th Cir. 2003)*
> Counsel's failure to consult with petitioner and inform him of the state's plea offer to voluntary manslaughter constituted ineffective assistance of counsel. The appropriate remedy was to place petitioner back into the same position with an opportunity to accept or reject plea offer.

United States v. Leonti, *326 F.3d 1111, 1117 (9th Cir. 2003)*
> Counsel's failure to inform the defendant of plea bargain and advise him to take plea offer when it was in his best interest constitutes ineffective assistance of counsel.

Griffin v. United States, *330 F.3d 733, 739 (6th Cir. 2003)*
> Counsel failure to communicate government's five (5) year plea offer, and to advise petitioner that his codefendant's were planning on testifying against him required an

evidentiary hearing to determine whether petitioner was prejudiced by counsel's omissions.

Cullen v. U.S., 194 F.3d 401 (2nd Cir. 1999)
Defense counsel's failure to advise defendant of terms of plea bargain offer was deficient representation. **See also** *Wanatee v. Ault, 101 F.Supp.2d 1189 (N.D. Iowa 2000); U.S. v. McKinnon, 995 F. Supp. 1404 (M.D. Fla. 1998); U.S. v. Blaylock, 20 F.3d 1458 (9th Cir. 1994); Clanton v. Blair, 619 F.Supp. 1491 (D.C. Va. 1985); Williams v. Arn, 654 F.Supp. 226 (N.D. Ohio 1986); Teague v. Scott, 60 F.3d 1167 (5th Cir. 1995)*

Arredondo v. U.S., 178 F.3d 778 (6th Cir. 1999)
Defense counsel's failure to communicate to petitioner a plea agreement offer made by the government required an evidentiary hearing to resolve claim of ineffective assistance of counsel.

United States ex.rel. Caruso v. Zelinsky, 689 F.2d 435 (3rd Cir. 1982)
The defendant alleged that his counsel had failed to communicate to him a plea offer. The *Caruso* Court held that "[t]he decision to reject a plea bargain offer . . . is a decision for the accused to make . . . a failure of counsel to advise his client of a plea bargain . . . constitute[s] a gross deviation from accepted professional standards".

Johnson v. Duckworth, 793 F.2d 898 (7th Cir. 1986)
Counsel's failure to inform defendant of plea offer may constitute ineffective assistance, but its the decision of the defendant to accept or reject the plea offer, not counsel's. This case was affirmed because the Court found that counsel had presented the plea offer to defendant and discussed it with the defendant and his parents.

U.S. v. Busse, 814 F.2d 760 (E.D. Wis. 1993)
Trial counsel's failure to inform defendant of the impact of the Sentencing Guidelines and provide defendant with a copy of the United States' plea agreement constituted ineffective assistance of counsel.

U.S. v. Rodriguez-Rodriguez, 929 F.2d 747 (1st Cir. 1991)
Trial counsel's failure to inform defendant of plea offer as a result of a conflict of interest stated a Sixth Amendment claim warranting an evidentiary hearing.

Desirability of Accepting Plea Offer

Boria v. Keane, 83 F.3d 48 (2nd Cir. 1996)
Defense counsel's failure to advise defendant of the desirability of accepting plea bargain of 1 to 3 years, discuss the strength of the government's case and chances of acquittal constituted ineffective assistance of counsel. Thus, prejudice was established where the defendant received a 20 year sentence as opposed to the 1 to 3 years plea bargain offer. The court ordered the defendant's sentence be reduced to time served and discharged from prison. **See also** *Boria v. Keane, 99 F.3d 493 (2nd Cir. 1996)*

Elements of the Offense

Ivy v. Caspari, 173 F.3d 1136 (8th Cir. 1999)
Defense counsel's failure to advise 16 year old defendant that intent was element of second-degree murder charged rendered the guilty plea involuntarily and constitutes ineffective assistance.

Wanatee v. Auly , 39 F.Supp. 2d 1164 (N.D. Iowa 1999)

Defense counsel's failure to advise petitioner of applicable law on the aiding and abetting liability, or joint conduct liability during plea negotiations for second degree murder warranted an evidentiary hearing to resolve claim of ineffectiveness of counsel.

Miller v. Champion, 161 F.3d 1249 (10th Cir. 1998)

Defense counsel's failure to advise defendant prior to entering his guilty plea of "depraved mind" element of second-degree murder was sufficient to conduct an evidentiary hearing to resolve ineffectiveness of counsel claim.

Scarpa v. Dubois, 38 F.3d 1 (1st Cir. 1994)

Defense counsel must understand the elements of the offenses with which client is charged in order to provide effective assistance of counsel.

U.S. v. Bigman, 906 F.2d 392 (9th Cir. 1990)

Defense counsel's failure to apprise defendant of intent element of crime of second-degree murder constitutes ineffective assistance of counsel, and renders the guilty plea involuntary and not knowing.

Gaddy v. Linahan, 780 F.2d 935 (11th Cir. 1986)

Failure to explain the elements of the offense of malice murder renders the guilty plea involuntary and requires an evidentiary hearing.

Hawkman v. Parratt, 661 F.2d 1161 (8th Cir. 1981)

Trial counsel's failure to interview witnesses, to adequately advise defendant of elements of the offense, potential defenses, to initiate plea bargaining negotiations before advising defendant to plead guilty constitutes ineffective assistance.

Defendant's Conduct Did Not Impact Interstate Commerce

Ballinger v. U.S., 379 F. 3d 427, 429-30 (7th Cir. 2004)

Counsel's failure to advise Ballinger of the Supreme Court's decision in *Jones v. United States, 529 U.S. 848, 120 S.Ct. 1904, 146 L.Ed.2d 902 (2000)*, that his conduct did not sufficiently impact interstate commerce to warrant federal jurisdiction required an evidentiary hearing to determine whether Ballinger's plea was involuntary because he didn't understand the charges and whether his lawyer provided ineffective assistance of counsel.

Drug And §924(c) Weapon Offense Carries Consecutive Sentence

Fowler-Cornwell v. U.S., 159 F.Supp.2d 291 (N.D.W Va. 2001)

Defense counsel was ineffective in failing to advise petitioner that consecutive sentences were required on drug and firearm offenses, rendering the guilty plea involuntary and unintelligntly entered.

Impact of Sentencing Guidelines

Risher v. U.S., 992 F.2d 982 (9th Cir. 1993)

Trial counsel's failure to inform defendant before entering guilty plea that the sentence might be under the Sentencing Guidelines constitutes ineffective assistance.

U.S. v. Busse, 814 F.Supp. 760 (E.D. Wis. 1993)

Trial counsel's failure to inform defendant of the impact of the Sentencing Guidelines and provide defendant with a copy of the United States' plea agreement constituted ineffective assistance of counsel.

U.S. v. Day, 969 F.2d 39 (3rd Cir. 1992)

Trial counsel failed to explain to Day his possible career offender status and misadvised Day of the maximum sentence he could receive under the Guidelines, if Day proceeded to trial. Thereafter, based on counsel's advice, Day rejected the five (5) year plea offer by the government and was convicted at trial and received a twenty-two (22) year sentence. In this case, Day conceded that he was notified of the terms of the plea bargain; however, he alleged that the advice that he received was so incorrect and so insufficient that it undermined his ability to make an intelligent decision whether to accept the offer. The Third Circuit found that Day states a Sixth Amendment claim.

Insanity Defense

Ivy v. Caspari, 173 F.3d 1136 (8th Cir. 1999)

Defense counsel's failure to advise defendant of possible mental illness defense constituted ineffective assistance of counsel and rendered guilty plea involuntarily.

U.S. v. Kauffman, 109 F.3d 186 (3rd Cir. 1997)

Counsel's failure to pursue any investigation into insanity defense before advising defendant to plead guilty, after counsel having seen a letter from defendant's psychiatrist stating that defendant was manic and psychotic when crime was committed constituted ineffective assistance of counsel and required the guilty plea to be set-aside.

Mendenhall v. Hopper, 453 F.Supp 977 (S.D. Ga. 1978)

Trial counsel's failure to advise defendant of insanity defense rendered defendant's guilty plea involuntary and constituted ineffective assistance of counsel.

Judge's Intent to Impose a 30 Year Sentence

Harper v. Wainwright, 334 F.Supp. 1338 (M.D. Florida 1971)

Defense counsel's failure to inform defendant that judge intended to impose a 30-year term of imprisonment, if defendant changed his plea and defendant hoped at worst his sentence would be probation constitutes ineffective assistance.

Justification Defense For Posessions of Firearm

United States v. Mooney, 497 F.3d 397, 403-408 (4th Cir. 2007)

Counsel provided constitutionally ineffective assistance for advising Mooney to plead guilty because there was no justification defense for unlawful possession of a firearm. Mooney advised counsel that he acted in self-defense by taking the firearm away from his ex-wife who attacked him with the gun and took it and gave it to the police. Counsel's failure to recognize the justification defense in this case, which rendered the guilty plea not voluntary or intelligently entered and required setting aside the guilty plea.

Juvenile Sentence Could Be Appealed

Lyons v. Jackson, 299 F.3d 588 (6th Cir. 2002)
Defense counsel failed to advise a juvenile defendant that counsel recommended to plead guilty to first degree murder that the prosecution could appeal any juvenile sentence imposed, and resentence the juvenile to an adult life sentence without parole. Counsel's failure to advise the juvenile defendant of this crucial factor rendered the guilty plea involuntary in light of juvenile's testimony that he would have gone to trial had he known that the prosecution could appeal.

Miller v. Straub, 299 F.3d 570, 579-80 (6th Cir. 2002)
Defense counsel failed to advise a juvenile defendant that counsel recommended to plead guilty to first degree murder, that the prosecutor could appeal under Michigan law, with the possibility that the juvenile sentence would be overturned on appeal, and that he would be sentenced to a adult life sentence without parole.

Mere Presence Defense

Nevarez-Diaz v. U.S., 870 F.2d 417 (7th Cir. 1989)
Trial counsel's ineffectiveness constituted "cause" and the Court's failure, along with the prosecutor's failure to adequately inform defendant that mere presence at time crimes were committed did not constitute the elements of the offense amounted to a fundamental miscarriage of justice and required evidentiary hearing.

Mandatory Special Parole

Blair v. McCarthy, 881 F.2d 602 (9th Cir. 1985)
The State court's failure to inform defendant about mandatory parole term prior to guilty plea, and a showing that defendant would not have pled guilty had he been so advised warranted habeas relief.

Maximum Sentence/Penalty/Career Offender Status

Brady v. United States, 397 U.S. 742, 25 L.Ed.2d 747, 90 S.Ct. 1463 (1970)
Due process requires that before a court accepts a plea of guilty the defendant be fully advised with respect to the nature of the charges and the maximum possible penalty for the offense. **See also** _United States v. Wolak, 510 F.2d 164 (6th Cir. 1975)_

United States v. Grammas, 376 F.3d 433, 435-437 (5th Cir. 2004)
Counsel's erroneous advise to Grammas, who received 70 months that his maximum exposure would be 6 to 12 months constituted performance below an objective standard of reasonableness. Counsel's lack of understanding of Sentencing Guidelines and Grammas's decision not to plead guilty led to a longer term of

imprisonment, and required an evidentiary hearing to resolve ineffectiveness of counsel claim.

Magana v. Hofbauer, **263 F.3d 542, 549-50 (6th Cir. 2001)**
Trial counsel's erroneous legal advice that petitioner would only face ten (10) years on the three drug counts if he was convicted at trial, which caused petitioner to reject a state's plea bargain offer of 10 years due to counsel's complete ignorance of the relevant law under which petitioner was charged. Petitioner was denied his right to effective assistance of counsel when considering state's plea offer and remedy was to remand for a new plea hearing in state court.

United States v. Santos, **225 F.3d 92, 101 (1st Cir. 2000)**
A guilty plea is <u>involuntary</u> if based on advice that leads a defendant to erroneously believe that he is subject to a five (5) year mandatory minimum sentence when he is actually <u>subject</u> to a ten (10) year mandatory minimum sentence.

U.S. v. Gordon, **156 F.3d 376 (2nd Cir. 1998)**
Counsel's letter to defendant advising defendant that the maximum sentencing exposure was ten years where the actual maximum sentence was approximately **27 years** under the Guidelines constituted ineffective assistance of counsel and defendant was prejudicial where defendant stated he would have accepted whatever plea had been offered, absent counsel's erroneous advice.

U.S. v. Day, **969 F.2d 39 (3rd Cir. 1992)**
Trial counsel failed to explain to Day that he was possibly career offender status and misadvised him of the maximum sentence he could receive under the Guidelines if Day proceeded to trial. Based on counsel's advice, Day rejected the five (5) year plea offer by the government and was convicted at trial and received a twenty-two (22) year sentence. Day conceded that he was notified of the terms of the plea bargain; however, he alleged that the advice that he received was so incorrect and so insufficient that it undermined his ability to make an intelligent decision whether to accept the offer. The Third Circuit found that Day stated a Sixth Amendment claim.

Pitts v. United States, **763 F.2d 197 (6th Cir. 1985)**
Trial counsel's misrepresentation of the maximum penalty on counts of indictment, which defendant pled guilty constituted ineffective assistance of counsel and warranted an evidentiary hearing. **See also** *Teague v. Scott*, **60 F.3d 1167 (5th Cir. 1995)**

Beckan v. Wainwright, **639 F.2d 262 (5th Cir. 1981)**
Trial counsel advised defendant to enter a guilty plea to a stipulated term of five-year sentence and defendant pleaded guilty based on counsel's advice. The attorney then advised defendant to withdraw his plea and go to trial based on the assumption he would only receive a five-year sentence if found guilty. Defendant followed counsel's advice and withdrew his plea, went to trial and was found guilty and received a fifty-year (50) sentence. The court found that counsel's performance and advice was ineffective and granted the Petition for Writ of Habeas corpus filed by petitioner.

The Supreme Court's *McNally* Decision

U.S. v. Loughery, 908 F.2d 1014 (D.C. Cir. 1990)

Trial counsel's failure to advise defendant that the United States Supreme Court's decision in *McNally* had invalidated fraud counts rendered defendant's guilty plea involuntary and constituted ineffective assistance of counsel. Loughery was entitled to withdraw her guilty plea.

Serious Risk of Withdrawing Plea

Lewandowski v. Makel, 754 F.Supp. 1142 (W.D. Mich. 1990)

Counsel's failure to inform petitioner of significant risks of withdrawing guilty plea for second-degree murder because charges would be reinstated for first degree murder constituted ineffective assistance of counsel. The remedy was to reinstate the performance of the second degree murder plea.

Sentencing Guidelines

U.S. v. Wiener, 127 F.Supp.2d 645, 649 (M.D. Pa. 2001)

Trial counsel's failure to properly advise petitioner of the Sentencing Guidelines, which undermined petitioner's ability to make an informed decision about whether to enter into a plea agreement, required an evidentiary hearing to resolve the ineffectiveness of counsel claims.

Venue Defense

Brown v. Butler, 811 F.2d 938 (5th Cir. 1987)

Trial counsel's failure to advise defendant of available venue defense, prior to entering guilty plea rendered the plea involuntarily entered where the defendant was not able to make conscious decision of whether to plead guilty and constitutes ineffective assistance of counsel.

Second Weapon §924(c) Charge Carries Mandatory 25 Years Consecutive

United States v. White, 371 F.Supp.2d 378, 383 (W.D.N.Y. 2005)

Counsel was ineffective during plea negotiations because of his failure to advise White that if he proceeded to trial on the two-weapon charges that he faced a mandatory consecutive 25 year sentence on the second, **18 U.S.C. §924(c)** charge, and there exists more than a reasonable probability, that White would have accepted the proposed plea offer of 147 to 168 months.

Statute of Limitations

U.S. v. Hansel, 70 F.3d 6 (2nd Cir. 1995)

Counsel's failure to inform defendant that charges were barred by statute of limitations, rendered the guilty plea involuntary.

Viable Consent Defense

Jennings v. Purkett, *7 F.3d 779 (8th Cir. 1993)*
> Trial counsel's failure to advise rape defendant that defendant had a viable consent defense prior to pleading guilty amounted to ineffective assistance, especially where attorney had ties to victim's family.

INDUCED PLEA BASED ON . . .

Ambiguous Plea Agreement

U.S. v. Borders, *992 F.2d 563 (5th Cir. 1993)*
> Trial counsel who induced defendant to plead guilty to a plea agreement which was ambiguous amounted to ineffective assistance of counsel.

Appeal Denial of Speedy Trial Motion

Maples v. Stegall, *427 F.3d 1020, 1034 (6th Cir. 2005)*
> Counsel's erroneous advice to defendant that he could plead guilty and still file an appeal on his speedy-trial claim amounted ineffective assistance of counsel.

Coercion or Threats

U.S. v. Gonzalez, *113 F.3d 1026 (9th Cir. 1997)*
> Gonzalez plead guilty. Prior to sentencing he filed a motion for appointment of new counsel claiming that he was coerced and physically intimidated by his attorney to plead guilty. Gonzalez claimed that he originally refused to plead guilty and his attorney became very agitated, threatened to "smack [Gonzalez] between the eyes" and told Gonzalez to "take the plea." The Court at sentencing asked counsel, if the coercion was true and counsel denied it. Gonzalez claimed the coercion occurred in front of the probation officer. The district court created a conflict by inviting counsel to contradict his client and to undermine his veracity, which left Gonzalez without counsel. The Court abused its discretion in failing to conduct an evidentiary hearing.

U.S. v. Sanchez-Barreto, *93 F.3d 17 (1st Cir. 1996)*
> Defense counsel coerced defendant's guilty plea in order to conceal his unpreparedness for trial and constitutes ineffective assistance of counsel.

Lopez v. Scully, *58 F.3d 38 (2nd Cir. 1995)*
> Lopez in a pro se motion to withdraw his guilty plea asserted that counsel had coerced him into pleading guilty. At that point, counsel had a conflict of interest; to argue in favor of his client's motion would require admitting serious ethical violations and possibly subject him to liability for malpractice; on the other hand, "Any contention by counsel that defendant's allegations were not true would... contradict his client." The court remanded for resentencing with appointment of new counsel.

U.S. v. Shorter, *54 F.3d 1248 (7th Cir. 1995)*
> Defendant accused his attorney of forcing him to plead guilty. The attorney claimed that the defendant's statements were false which created a conflict of interest.

Moore v. U.S., *950 F.2d 656 (10th Cir. 1991)*

Coercion by trial counsel or the prosecutor to induce a guilty plea renders the plea involuntary.

U.S. v. Ellison, *798 F.2d 1102 (7th Cir. 1986)*

Ellison filed a motion to withdraw his guilty plea in the context of a letter form. Ellison claimed his guilty pleas were the result of psychological pressures of solitary confinement, the exclusion from family and friends, and the erroneous advice of his court-appointed attorney "that an immediate guilty plea would place [him] in better and more humane living conditions and renew [my] contact with family and friends" (emphasis added). The court conducted an evidentiary hearing on defendant's motion. Counsel testified against Ellison at the hearing. The court denied the motion to withdraw guilty plea. The Seventh Circuit reversed and remanded, holding that there was no doubt that a conflict of interest existed, where counsel testified against Ellison, but without counsel Ellison was deprived of his right to cross-examine counsel, in violation of the Sixth Amendment.

United States v. Sanderson, *595 F.2d 1021 (5th Cir. 1979)*

Trial counsel's misrepresentation of material facts, withheld information, and exerted pressure on defendant to induce a guilty plea and requires an evidentiary hearing to resolve claim of ineffective assistance of counsel.

Concealed Evidence and Pressured Defendant to Sign Plea Agreement

United States v. Segarra-Rivera, *473 F.3d 381, 386-387 (1st Cir. 2007)*

Segarra-Rivera was entitled to evidentiary hearing with conflict-free defense counsel on his motion to withdraw guilty plea where he asserted that counsel induced his guilty plea by concealing evidence and pressuring him to sign the plea agreement.

Judge's Threat of Maximum Penalty

U.S. v. Cruz, *977 F.2d 732 (2nd Cir. 1992)*

Trial judge's threat to impose maximum sentence if defendant went to trial without "good defense" required remand for resentencing in front of different judge.

FBI Threats

Marrow v. U.S., *772 F.2d 525 (9th Cir. 1985)*

Defendant's allegation that he informed trial counsel that the FBI had threatened to arrest defendant's female companion if defendant did not confess to crime. Counsel told defendant to plead guilty and tell the judge that plea was voluntary. Counsel's actions stated a claim of ineffective assistance of counsel.

Threats to Withdraw Bail Bond

Iaea v. Sunn, *800 F.2d 861 (9th Cir. 1986)*

Trial counsel threatened to withdraw and petitioner's brother threatened to withdraw bail if petitioner did not plead guilty which rendered the plea involuntary and required an evidentiary hearing to resolve the ineffective assistance of counsel claim.

Counsel Threatens to Withdraw

U.S. v. Estrada, 849 F.2d 1304 (10th Cir. 1988)

The Court held that: Defendant who alleged that prosecutor threatened to file unwarranted charges against him, that defense counsel coerced him to plead guilty by threatening to withdraw, and that both prosecutor and defense counsel promised him light sentence, was entitled to evidentiary hearing to determine voluntariness of plea.

Defendant's Failure To Pay Attorney Fee

Daniels v. U.S., 54 F.3d 290 (7th Cir. 1995)

Defense counsel induced guilty plea based on defendant's inability to pay counsel's fee, which created a conflict of interest and, required an evidentiary hearing.

Defendant Would Receive Probation

United States v. Unger, 665 F.2d 251 (8th Cir. 1981)

Defendant's assertion that counsel advised her that if she plead guilty to kidnapping charge she would be given probation, and that if she went to trial and was found guilty, that she would probably get the death penalty. These actions by counsel stated a valid claim of ineffective assistance of counsel and required an evidentiary hearing.

Erroneous/Faulty Legal Advice

Tollet v. Henderson, 411 U.S. 258, 93 S.Ct. 1602, 36 L.Ed.2d 235 (1973)

A criminal defendant can only attack the voluntary and intelligent character of guilty plea based on the advice he received from counsel.

U.S. v. Streater, 70 F.3d 1314 (D.C. Cir. 1995)

Defense counsel erroneously advised defendant that if the court denied his motion to suppress he should plead guilty because defendant could not claim privacy interest in automobile and claim he had no knowledge of drugs found in automobile at trial. Defendant's guilty plea was induced based on faulty legal advice and was not knowingly and intelligently entered due to ineffective assistance of counsel.

United States v. Rumery, 698 F.2d 764 (5th Cir. 1983)

Trial counsel induced defendant's guilty plea based on erroneous advice which renders the guilty plea itself involuntary and unintelligently entered and constitutes ineffective assistance.

Cooks v. United States, 461 F.2d 530, 532 (5th Cir. 1972)

Counsel erroneously induced defendant's guilty plea based on the fact that if he didn't plead guilty and proceeded to trial, that he would be subject to a sentence six times more severe than actually authorized by law, which rendered the guilty plea invalid and constitutes ineffective assistance of counsel.

Erroneous Advice About Cocaine Base

Rice v. U.S., 971 F. Supp. 1297 (D. Minn. 1997)

Counsel's erroneously advised petitioner that cocaine base was crack which caused petitioner to plead guilty entitled defendant to discovery on his ineffectiveness of counsel claim.

Erroneous Advice Used to Reject Plea Offer

United States v. Booze, 293 F.3d 516, 519 (D.C. Cir. 2002)

Trial counsel advised Booze to reject a 5 year plea offer that required Booze and each of his brothers to enter a guilty plea. Counsel allegedly advised Booze, that if he went to trial and was convicted he would be sentenced to less than five years. Booze proceeded to trial and was convicted, and sentenced to 17½ years. Such advice would constitute ineffective assistance of counsel, if such an offer was actually made, and required an evidentiary hearing to resolve the ineffective assistance of counsel claim.

TSE v. United States, 290 F.3d 463, 464-66 (1st Cir. 2002)

The government offered TSE a 97-month plea agreement on count 16. Defense counsel advised him that the "Government was prevented by law under the "doctrine of specialty" (dealing with extradition proceedings from Hong Kong) from prosecuting TSE on Counts 14 or 15, or any other count. Counsel advised TSE that the maximum sentence he could receive was 10 years on count 16. TSE, based on counsel's erroneous advice, proceeded to trial and was convicted on all three counts and sentenced to 188 months on each count. TSE claimed that he would have accepted the 97-month plea offer had it not been for counsel's erroneous legal advice. An evidentiary hearing was required to resolve the ineffective assistance of counsel claim.

United States v. Quiroz, 228 F.Supp. 2d 1259, 1264-66 (D. Kan. 2002)

Counsel's legal advice to petitioner that he faced a maximum penalty of ten (10) years, if found guilty at trial, or by accepting the government's plea offer he would get about a six (6) month break in sentencing, constituted ineffective assistance of counsel. Prejudice under *Strickland*, was shown because the government's plea offer called for approximately a 70 month sentence and petitioner received ten (10) years by going to trial based on counsel's advice.

Erroneous Good Time Credits to Induce Plea

Moore v. Bryant, 348 F.3d 238, 241-43 (7th Cir. 2003)

Counsel's incorrect legal advice to petitioner that by pleading guilty he would only have to serve 50% of the sentence, and by going to trial he would have to serve 85% of the sentence based on the soon to be good time credits constituted ineffective assistance of counsel. Counsel's advice was erroneous and counsel had not even read the statute or examined case law dealing with the retroactivity of the soon to be good time credits, rendering the guilty plea not voluntarily or intelligently entered.

Lying to Defendant

U.S. v. Giardino, 797 F.2d 30 (1st Cir. 1986)

Trial counsel lied to defendant to induce a guilty plea constitutes ineffective assistance and requires the plea to be set-aside.

Improper Legal Advice

Wanatee v. Ault, *259 F.3d 700, 704 (8th Cir. 2001)*
Counsel's improper legal advice during plea bargaining stage caused Wanatee to reject plea offer for second degree murder constituted ineffective assistance of counsel.

Illusionary Plea Agreement

Morse v. Trippett, *102 F.Supp. 2d 392, 406 (E.D. Mich. 2000)*
Defense counsel failed to correctly advise petitioner of the offense to which he was pleading guilty to and induced the plea to an illusionary plea agreement, wherein petitioner was threatened with being tried as a habitual offender fourth offense which carried a maximum life sentence, when petitioner actually only had (3) prior convictions that could be counted. Thus, rendering the plea both unintelligent and illusionary, as a direct result of inaccurate legal advice.

Defendant on Drugs During Plea

United States v. Howard, *381 F.3d 873, 881-883 (9th Cir. 2004)*
Counsel induced Howard to plead guilty knowing that he was on powerful narcotic painkiller Percocet/Percodan rendering him incompetent to make a judgment about whether to plead guilty, or to go to trial and required an evidentiary hearing to resolve claim of ineffectiveness of counsel claim.

Upshaw v. Singletary, *70 F.3d 576 (11th Cir. 1995)*
Ineffective assistance of counsel claim for instructing and persuading defendant to perjury himself to the court by denying that he was under the influence of drugs during the guilty plea colloquy warranted evidentiary hearing.

Misadvised Defendant About Sentencing Exposure

United States v. Herrera, *412 F.3d 577, 581-82 (5th Cir. 2005)*
Evidentiary hearing required to determine whether counsel misadvised Herrera about sentencing exposure because the attorney misunderstood the actual sentencing exposure under the Guidelines which caused Herrera to reject a 48 month plea offer and ended up with a 78 month sentence.

Misrepresentation of Death Penalty

Kennedy v. Maggio, *725 F.2d 269 (5th Cir. 1984)*
Defense counsel's misrepresentation of the death penalty available for aggravated rape, which was contrary to law rendered guilty plea involuntary and constitutes ineffective assistance.

United States v. Unger, *665 F.2d 251 (8th Cir. 1981)*
Defendant's assertion that counsel advised her that if she plead guilty to kidnapping charge she would be given probation, and that if she went to trial and was found guilty, that she would probably get the death penalty. Counsel's misadvice stated a valid claim of ineffective assistance of counsel and required an evidentiary hearing.

Specific Sentence

Ostrander v. Green, 46 F.3d 347 (4th Cir. 1995)

> Defense counsel induced guilt plea based on "misadvise" that defendant would plead to certain sexual offense and his sentence would be capped at 3 to 5 years and he would get work release real quick constituted ineffective assistance of counsel.

Hernandez-Hernandez v. U.S., 904 F.2d 758 (1st Cir. 1990)

> Trial counsel's inducement of a guilty plea by a specific sentence which petitioner did not receive constitutes ineffective assistance of counsel.

U.S. v. Espinoza, 866 F.2d 1067 (9th Cir. 1988)

> Trial counsel's promise that defendant would receive a specific sentence to induce guilty plea required an evidentiary hearing to resolve the claim of ineffectiveness of counsel.

Craver v. Procunier, 756 F.2d 1212 (5th Cir. 1985)

> Craver was charged with forgery by passing a $20 hot check, enhanced by prior convictions. Before the date set for his trial, Craver spoke several times with Keith Woodley, an experienced criminal lawyer. In one of these conversations, Craver and Woodley discussed briefly the district attorney's offer of a plea bargain for seven years. Craver expected the court to appoint Woodley as his lawyer and the court intended to do so; however, on the day of trial, Woodley was nowhere to be found. Jim Dudley, one of Woodley's partners who had little experience as a criminal lawyer represented Craver. After a maximum of a ten-minute conversation between Dudley and Craver, Craver pled guilty. The district attorney then recommended a twenty-year sentence. The trial court followed the district attorney's recommendation and sentenced Craver to twenty-year imprisonment. Craver filed a petition for writ of habeas corpus alleging ineffective assistance of counsel. The court granted relief.

McAleney v. United States, 539 F.2d 282 (1st Cir. 1976)

> Trial counsel's misrepresentation that government's attorney had agreed to recommend that defendant would receive a three (3) year sentence to induce guilty plea, where in reality no such agreement existed constituted ineffective assistance of counsel.

State and Federal Sentence be Served Concurrent

Finch v. Vaughn, 67 F.3d 909, 915-17 (11th Cir. 1995)

> Counsel induced Finch's state guilty plea based on the assumption that his state term of imprisonment would be served concurrently with the balance of his federal sentence, which was an incorrect application of the law and rendered his guilty plea not voluntary or intelligently entered as a result of ineffective assistance of counsel. See also *Warner v. U.S.*, 975 F.2d 1207 (6th Cir. 1992)

Racial Prejudice

Frazer v. U.S., 18 F.3d 778 (9th Cir. 1994)

> Trial counsel verbally assaulted defendant, used racial comments toward defendant and threatened to compromise defendant's rights in order to induce a guilty plea required an evidentiary hearing to resolve ineffective assistance of counsel claim.

Thomas v. Lockhart, 738 F.2d 304 (8th Cir. 1984)
Trial counsel informed defendant's family that defendant would have to prove his innocence and led defendant to believe trial would be futile due to racial prejudice rendered defendant's guilty plea involuntary and constituted ineffective assistance of counsel.

ERRONEOUSLY INFORMED DEFENDANT THAT . . .

He/She Would Not be Deported

United States v. Kwan, 407 F.3d 1005, 1015-17 (9th Cir. 2005)
Counsel misled Kwan that by pleading guilty to bank fraud he would not be deported and such advice was deficient performance. Counsel failure to inform the sentencing judge that a sentence <u>only</u> two days lighter would enable Kwan to avoid deportation and remain united with his family constitutes ineffective assistance of counsel and warranted granting the coram nobis petition.

United States v. Couto, 311 F.3d 179, 187-188 (2nd Cir. 2002)
Counsel was constitutionally ineffective because he misrepresented the deportation consequences in order to induce petitioner's guilty plea; erroneously advising the petitioner that there were many things that could be done to prevent her from being deported, where in reality the guilty plea meant virtually an automatic deportation and rendered the guilty plea not voluntarily or intelligently entered.

U.S. v. Corona-Maldonado, 46 F.Supp. 2d 1171 (D. Kan. 1999)
Counsel's failure to correctly inform defendant that he would be deported if convicted, when alien defendant specifically asked counsel constituted ineffective assistance of counsel.

U.S. v. Corona-Maldonado, 31 F.Supp. 2d 951 (D. Kan. 1998)
Defense counsel-induced defendant's guilty plea by advising defendant that he would not be deported if he pleads guilty. Such actions by counsel states a sufficient claim of ineffective assistance of counsel and required an evidentiary hearing to resolve claim.

U.S. v. Castro, 26 F.3d 557 (5th Cir. 1994)
Trial counsel's failure to seek judicial recommendation against deportation where defendant played only minor role in conspiracy had strong ties to the United States and judge's apparent leniency in sentencing constituted ineffective assistance of counsel.

Downs-Morgan v. U.S., 765 F.2d 1534 (11th Cir. 1985)
Trial counsel's misrepresentation that defendant would not be deported if he plead guilty where the Nicaraguan government may have executed or imprisoned defendant upon completion of deportation constituted ineffective assistance and renders plea involuntarily entered.

Erroneous Advised Defendant to Stipulate to Drug Quantity

United States v. Smack, 347 F.3d 533, 540 (3rd Cir. 2003)
> Counsel's advice to Smack to <u>stipulate</u> in plea agreement, to attempting to possess with intent to distribute approximately <u>ten (10) kilograms of cocaine</u>, where the actual delivery in this reverse sting operation was <u>only one kilogram of cocaine</u>, which deprived Smack of the opportunity to present arguments under **USSG §2D1.1**, Application Note 12, that controls the quantity used for Guidelines purposes in prosecutions arising out of reverse stings, and required an evidentiary hearing to determine whether Smack was prejudiced by counsel's deficient performance.

Prosecutor Threatened to File Additional Charges

U.S. v. Estrada, 849 F.2d 1304 (10th Cir. 1988)
> The Court held that: Defendant who alleged that prosecutor threatened to file unwarranted charges against him, that defense counsel coerced him to plead guilty by threatening to withdraw, and that both prosecutor and defense counsel promised him light sentence, was entitled to evidentiary hearing to determine voluntariness of plea.

Sentenced as a Career Offender

United States v. Colon-Torres, 382 F.3d 76, 89 (1st Cir. 2004)
> Counsel's failure to seek withdrawal of Colon's guilty plea after his career-offender status became clear at sentencing created a possible conflict of interest because counsel induced Colon's plea based on a much lower sentence, and required an evidentiary hearing to resolve the factual disputes.

U.S. v. McCoy, 215 F.3d 102 (D.C. Cir. 2000)
> Defense counsel failed to accurately apply the career offender provision of the guidelines when determining the sentencing range ***McCoy*** would face if he accepted the government's plea offer constitutes ineffective assistance. Counsel erroneously informed ***McCoy*** that if he pled guilty he would get a sentence between 188 to 235 months when he faced 262 to 327 months, which rendered the plea involuntary entered. McCoy demonstrated that a "reasonable probability" existed that he would have proceeded to trial had it not been for counsel's erroneous advice.

U.S. v. Gaviria, 116 F.3d 1498 (D.C. Cir. 1997)
> Defense counsel erroneously advised Gaviria that if he accepted the government's plea for conspiracy to distribute cocaine, criminal forfeiture count, and a charge unlawful re-entry into the U.S. following deportation that he would be sentenced as a career offender to 360 months to life. Defense counsel's advice was erroneous because in ***United States v. Price, 990 F.2d 1367, 1370 (D.C. Cir. 1993)***, the Court held that a defendant convicted of conspiracy could not be sentenced as a career offender because the statute under which the Guideline career offender provision was initially promulgated did not list conspiracy as a crime warranting career offender treatment. Gaviria proceeded to trial and was convicted, and, received a mandatory life. Had, Gaviria been correctly advised by counsel he would have accepted the government's plea offer and received a Guideline range of 188-262 months. The Court of Appeals remanded for an evidentiary hearing to resolve the ineffective assistance claim.

Defendant was Guilty Because of His Presence When Crime Occurred

Nevarez-Diaz v. U.S., 870 F.2d 417 (7th Cir. 1989)

Trial counsel's attempt to plead defendant guilty where it was apparent that defendant felt that he was guilty only because he was present at the time the acts occurred constitutes ineffective assistance and rendered guilty plea involuntary.

Defendant Would be Entitled to Parole

Hawkins v. Murray, 798 F.Supp. 330 (E.D. Va. 1992)

Trial counsel's failure to advise defendant that according to statute that defendant would not be entitled to parole, prior to entering guilty plea constitutes ineffective assistance of counsel.

Defendant to Plead to Whatever the Judge Said

Unger v. Cohen, 718 F.Supp. 185 (S.D. N.Y. 1989)

Unger characterized the criminal proceedings as "assembly-line justice" which certainly was correct. Unger was not allowed to contact the counsel of his choice. After spending a night in jail, a Legal Aid attorney met with him briefly at the courthouse, whose advice was to plead guilty to whatever the judge said. Counsel waived the reading of the charges, the reading of Unger's rights, and the allocution on the guilty plea. The record did not indicate an admission of factual guilt on Unger's part. Unger's counsel merely informed the court that her client intended to plead guilty. The court concluded that counsel's advice was not within the range of competence demanded of attorneys in criminal cases.

Reject a Two (2) Year Plea Offer

Turner v. State of Tenn., 858 F.2d 1201 (6th Cir. 1988)

Trial counsel's advice to defendant to reject a two (2) year plea offer for kidnapping constituted ineffective assistance where defendant received 40 years on the two counts and remedy was to preclude state from withdrawing its plea offer unless state made a showing that withdrawal was no vindictiveness. **See also *Turner v. State of Tenn., 664 F.Supp. 1113 (M.D. Tenn. 1987)***

Reject Plea to Argue Sentencing Entrapment

United States v. Day, 285 F.3d 1167, 1172 (9th Cir. 2002)

Trial counsel's erroneous advice to Day that he would only be allowed to argue that the government engaged in sentencing entrapment if he proceeded to trial, deprived Day of his opportunity to make an intelligent decision about pleading guilty and receiving a three-level reduction in his base offense level for acceptance of responsibility and established prejudiced under *Strickland*, which required vacating the sentence.

Reject Favorable Plea Offer

United States v. Rashad*, *331 F.3d 908, 911-912 (D.C. Cir. 2003)
> Counsel advised petitioner to reject the government's favorable plea offer. Counsel assured petitioner that the government's evidence could not support a conviction, and that he only faced 10 to 15 years if convicted at trial. An evidentiary hearing was required to determine whether counsel was ineffective, and if petitioner understood his sentencing exposure before rejecting the plea offer.

Reject Plea Offer Requiring State Not To Pursue Death Penalty

Hoffman v. Arave*, *455 F.3d 926, 939-941 (9th Cir. 2006)
> Counsel was constitutionally ineffective for advising Hoffman to reject the plea agreement to first-degree murder in exchange for an agreement that the State wouldn't pursue the Death Penalty during sentencing.

Parole Eligibility Advice/Date

Meyers v. Gillis*, *142 F.3d 664 (3rd Cir. 1998)
> Counsel erroneously advised defendant that if he pled guilty to second degree murder he would be "eligible for parole in seven years" when said offense carried a mandatory life sentence without parole eligibility, such advise resulted in prejudice to defendant because he would not have pled guilty, and absent counsel's erroneous legal advise defendant might have been convicted of lesser-include defense at trial.

James v. Cain*, *56 F.3d 662 (5th Cir. 1995)
> James claimed that he would not have plead guilty had counsel told him about Louisiana's two-step parole procedure. The Fifth Circuit reversed with instruction for a determination of whether James demonstrated prejudice.

Yordan v. Dugger*, *909 F.2d 474 (11th Cir. 1990)
> Trial counsel's misrepresentation that defendant would be eligible for parole after five to seven (5-7) years constituted ineffective assistance and renders plea involuntarily entered.

Hill v. Lockhart*, *877 F.2d 698 (8th Cir. 1989)
> Trial counsel's failure to research applicable statute governing parole eligibility for second offenders where plea factor consisted of defendant's eligibility to make parole constitutes ineffective assistance of counsel. **See also *Hill v. Lockhart*, *894 F.2d 1009 (8th Cir. 1990); Garmon v. Lockhart*, *938 F.2d 120 (8th Cir. 1991)***

Holmes v. U.S.*, *876 F.2d 1545 (11th Cir. 1989)
> Counsel's misadvice to petitioner concerning parole eligibility under plea agreement constitutes ineffective assistance of counsel. Petitioner sufficiently alleged that he would not have plead guilty and would have insisted on going to trial, absent counsel's erroneous advice which required an evidentiary hearing because the record did not conclusively show that petitioner was not entitled to relief.

Strader v. Garrison, 611 F.2d 61 (4th Cir. 1979)

> Trial counsel's misrepresentation about defendant's parole eligibility to induce guilty plea constituted ineffective assistance of counsel and rendered the plea involuntary. **See also** *Blair v. McCarthy*, 881 F.2d 602 (9th Cir. 1985); *Hawkins v. Murray*, 798 F.Supp. 330 (E.D. Va. 1992); *Carter v. McCarthy*, 806 F.2d 1373 (9th Cir. 1986); *Nolan v. Armontrout*, 973 F.2d 615 (8th Cir. 1992).

MISREPRESENTED . . .

Appellate Rights

Delgado v. Lewis, 223 F.3d 976, 980 (9th Cir. 2000)

> Counsel's absence from every important court proceeding except for the change of plea hearing, failed to pursue issues on appeal certified by state court as providing probable cause amounted to ineffective assistance of counsel and required setting aside the guilty plea.

Marrow v. U.S., 772 F.2d 525 (9th Cir. 1985)

> Trial counsel has a duty to advise defendant of right to appeal, if there is an error during the guilty plea proceedings.

Plea Agreement/Bargain

Trejo v. U.S., 66 F.Supp.2d 1274 (S.D Fla. 1999)

> Counsel's misrepresentation of the plea agreement that: (1) the cooperation of any defendant would ensure the benefit to all of them; (2) that this agreement need not be included in the plea agreement because it had been arranged with the prosecutor; (3) that based on their cooperation the defendants would receive a sentence as low as five years of imprisonment, but in any case not more than ten years, which required setting aside the guilty plea's based on ineffective assistance of counsel.

Warner v. U.S., 975 F.2d 1207 (6th Cir. 1992)

> Misrepresentations by trial counsel that plea bargain required state and federal sentences to be served concurrently constitutes ineffective assistance.

Holmes v. U.S., 876 F.2d 1545 (11th Cir. 1989)

> Defense counsel's misadvice to petitioner concerning parole eligibility under plea agreement constitutes ineffective assistance of counsel. Petitioner sufficiently alleged that he would not have plead guilty and would have insisted on going to trial, absent counsel's erroneous advice, which required an evidentiary hearing where record did not conclusively show that petitioner was not entitled to relief. **See also** *Tower v. Phillips*, 979 F.2d 807 (11th Cir. 1992)

Slicker v. Wainwright, 809 F.2d 768 (11th Cir. 1987)

> Trial counsel's misrepresentation that he had negotiated plea agreement which provided that defendant would not serve maximum penalty, constituted ineffective assistance and required an evidentiary hearing to allow defendant an opportunity to prove he would not have plead guilty, but would have proceeded to trial, absent counsel's misrepresentation of plea.

Defendant Must Prove His Innocence

Thomas v. Lockhart, 738 F.2d 304 (8th Cir. 1984)

Trial counsel informed defendant's family that defendant would have to prove his innocence and led defendant to believe trial would be futile due to racial prejudice rendered defendant's guilty plea involuntary and constituted ineffective assistance of counsel.

Life Sentence Without Parole

Sparks v. Sowders, 852 F.2d 882 (6th Cir. 1988)

Defendant's allegation that counsel misadvised him, if he did not plead guilty that he could get life without parole. Defendant would not have pleaded guilty without such misadvice which warranted an evidentiary hearing.

MISCELLANEOUS INEFFECTIVENESS

Counsel's Appearance on Speakerphone

Van Patten v. Deppisch, 434 F.3d 1038, 1044-1046 (7th Cir. 2006)

Counsel's appearance on speakerphone, rather than in person at plea hearing, violated defendant's Sixth Amendment right to counsel and was a structural error requiring reversal.

Refusing To Assist Cooperating Defendant

Pitcher v. United States, 371 F.Supp.2d 246, 264-265 (E.D.N.Y. 2005)

Counsel was constitutionally ineffective for providing inaccurate pretrial legal advice based on Pitcher's chances of acquittal, had Pitcher received reasonable advice as to the strength of the government case, he would have elected to cooperate and would have already served his sentence under the cooperation agreement. Thus, the appropriate remedy was to resentence to time served.

United States v. Leonti, 326 F.3d 1111, 1121-1122 (9th Cir. 2003)

Counsel failed to assist defendant cooperating with government in order to obtain a sentencing reduction pursuant to **U.S.S.G. §5K1.1** for substantial assistance to the government and failed to attend debriefing meeting with defendant, required an evidentiary hearing to resolve claim of ineffectiveness of counsel.

Trejo v. U.S., 66 F.Supp.2d 1274 (S.D. Fla. 1999)

Defense counsel who refused to represent his client, who decided to cooperate with the government and left co- defendant's attorney to handle his client cooperation agreement with the government created a conflict of interest which tainted all three of the defendant's convictions.

Prevented Defendant from Cooperating

U.S. v. Duran-Benitez, 110 F.Supp.2d 133, 153-156 (E.D. N.Y. 2000)
> Defense counsel dissuaded petitioner from cooperating with government to protect another client, who paid petitioner's legal bills. Counsel told petitioner stories about dangers of cooperating with the government to prevent him from cooperating because of a conflict of interest. The proper remedy was to restore circumstances that place petitioner in a situation where he could cooperate and secure a **U.S.S.G. §5K1.1** downward departure based on substantial assistance to the government.

Induced Mental Incompetent Defendant to Plead

Bouchillon v. Collins, 907 F.2d 589 (5th Cir. 1990)
> Trial counsel was ineffective for allowing Bouchillon to plead guilty when he was incompetent, the plea had to be set aside.

Agan v. Singletary, 12 F.3d 1012 (11 Cir. 1994)
> Trial counsel's failure to investigate defendant's competency, obtain prison or military medical files and make independent examination of facts prior to offering informed opinion that defendant should plead guilty constituted ineffective assistance.

Withdrawal of Guilty Plea

United States v. Segarra-Rivera, 473 F.3d 381, 383 (1st Cir. 2007)
> Evidentiary hearing warranted to determine whether counsel was burdened with a conflict of interest because the defendant accused counsel of failing to file his requested motion to withdraw guilty plea based on counsel concealing exculpatory evidence, manipulated defendant into signing plea agreement to avoid trial for which counsel failed to prepare, used improper means to obtain defendant's signature on plea.

United States v. Colon-Torres, 382 F.3d 76, 89 (1st Cir. 2004)
> Counsel's failure to seek withdrawal of Colon's guilty plea after his career-offender status became clear at sentencing created a possible conflict of interest because counsel induced Colon's plea based on a much lower sentence, and required an evidentiary hearing to resolve the factual disputes.

Lewis v. Johnson, 359 F.3d 646, 660-662 (3rd Cir. 2004)
> Counsel was constitutionally ineffective for failing to meet or consult with petitioner after the denial of his motion to withdraw guilty plea and sentencing.

Guzman v. Sabourin, 124 F.Supp. 2d 828 (S.D.N.Y. 2000)
> Conflict of interest arose between petitioner and counsel, during motion to withdraw guilty plea, when counsel testified against petitioner disputing petitioner's factual allegations concerning counsel coercing the guilty plea.

U.S. v. Burdeau, 168 F.3d 352 (9th Cir. 1999)
> Defense counsel induced defendant to withdraw a favorable guilty plea for ten (10) years based on misrepresentation of the law that defendant had a defense of voluntary intoxication to a robbery charge. The voluntary intoxication defense did not exist.

The Court of Appeals rejected defendant's ineffective assistance of counsel claims on direct appeal stating that claim is properly raised in a collateral proceeding not direct appeal. However, the Court of Appeals withheld its mandate for 60 days and urged the United States to move to dismiss the gun count, which would give the defendant the benefit of the plea agreement sentence. Although the Court rejected the ineffective assistance claim on direct appeal, there's clear indications that if the case comes back before the Court on the ineffectiveness of counsel claim that it would rule favorable.

U.S. v. Alvarez-Tautimez, 160 F.3d 573 (9th Cir. 1998)
Defense counsel's failure to file a motion to withdraw guilty plea, following the court's granting of co-defendant's motion to suppress and dismissal of the indictment, when the district court had not accepted defendant's plea and defendant had right to withdraw plea constituted ineffective assistance of counsel.

U.S. v. Garrett, 90 F.3d 210 (7th Cir. 1996)
The Court held that "defendant was entitled to three-level decrease in his sentencing score for acceptance of responsibility despite uncounseled motion to withdraw guilty plea." The defendant's first attorney died after he entered his plea and he did not have counsel when he filed his motion to withdraw guilty plea.

U.S. v. Ellison, 798 F.2d 1102 (7th Cir. 1986)
Ellison filed a motion to withdraw his guilty plea in the context of a letter form. Ellison claimed his guilty plea were the result of psychological pressures of solitary confinement, the exclusion from family and friends, and the erroneous advice of his court-appointed attorney "that an immediate guilty plea would place [him] in better and more humane living conditions and renew [my] contact with family and friends" (emphasis added). The court conducted an evidentiary hearing on defendant's motion. Counsel testified against Ellison at the hearing. The court denied the motion to withdraw guilty plea. The Seventh Circuit reversed and remanded, holding that there was no doubt that a conflict of interest existed, where counsel testified against Ellison, but without counsel Ellison was deprived of his right to cross-examine counsel, in violation of the Sixth Amendment.

Beckan v. Wainwright, 639 F.2d 262 (5th Cir. 1981)
Trial counsel's failure to advise defendant of consequences of withdrawing a negotiated guilty plea and stipulated sentence constitutes ineffective assistance of counsel.

WAIVER OF APPEAL/COLLATERAL ATTACK

DeRoo v. United States, 223 F.3d 919, 923 (8th Cir. 2000)
A plea agreement waiver of the right to seek post-conviction relief pursuant to **28 U.S.C. §2255**, does not waive defendant's right to challenge that his/her guilty plea was not knowingly and voluntarily entered because of ineffective assistance of counsel. See ***United States v. Henderson***, **72 F.3d 463, 465 (5th Cir. 1995);** ***United States v. Abarca***, **985 F.2d 1012, 1014 (9th Cir.), cert. denied, 508 U.S. 979, 113 S.Ct. 2980, 125 L.Ed.2d 677 (1993);** ***United States v. Craig***, **985 F.2d 175, 178 (4th Cir. 1983).**

Guilty Plea Ineffectiveness

United States v. Cockerham, **237 F.3d 1179, 1182 (l0th Cir. 2001)**
> A defendant's waiver in plea agreement of his right to bring habeas corpus challenge does not foreclose ineffective assistance of counsel claim related to the voluntariness or intelligence of the plea agreement or waiver.

U.S. v. Stubbs, **279 F.3d 402, 412 (6th Cir. 2002)**
> The waiver of appeal in plea agreement was invalid where defendant's guilty plea was not voluntary or intelligently entered. Neither the defendant, his counsel, nor the district court was aware that defendant was not subject to a mandatory consecutive minimum 60-month sentence under 18 U.S.C. §924(o), and there is no evidence that defendant was aware of the true nature of the crime charged, and the statutory consequences of his guilty plea. Thus, rendering the guilty plea not voluntary or intelligently entered.

Guilty Plea Does Not Waive Effective Assistance

U.S. v. Astacio, **14 F.Supp. 2d 816 (E.D. Va. 1998)**
> The defendant in his plea bargain agreement waived his right to challenge sentence through collateral relief. However this did not preclude a *28 U.S.C.§2255* motion arguing ineffective assistance of counsel. **See also** *Wiley v. Wainwright*, **793 F.2d 1190 (11th Cir. 1986)**

Guilty Plea Invalid Without Counsel

Brady v. United States, **397 U.S. 747, 25 Led.2d 747, 90 S.Ct. 1463 (1970)**
> A guilty plea to a felony entered without counsel and without a waiver of counsel is invalid. **See also** *Moore v. Michigan*, **355 U.S. 155, 2 Led 2d 167, 78 S.Ct. 191 (1957)**

Failed to Correct Prosecutor's Mistaken Belief on Violent Felon

Mask v. McGinnis, **233 F.3d 132, 141-142 (2nd Cir. 2000)**
> Counsel's failure to correct the prosecutor's mistaken belief that petitioner was a violent persistent felon under state law constituted ineffective assistance of counsel; petitioner would have been put in a better position for plea bargain negotiations, absent counsel's unprofessional errors and omissions.

Plea Negotiations Process

Paters v. U.S., **159 F.3d 1043 (7th Cir. 1998)**
> Counsel was ineffective in plea negotiation process and warranted an evidentiary hearing to determine whether petitioner would have accepted the Government's plea offer, which would have resulted in petitioner receiving a less harsh sentence.

U.S. v. Robertson, **29 F.Supp. 2d 567 (D. Minn. 1998)**
> Defense counsel's failure to advise petitioner to accept any of the plea offers made by the government, where the government had overwhelming evidence against petitioner and petitioner's "confession" to codefendant's, constituted ineffective assistance of counsel.

Mask v. McGinnis, 28 F. Supp. 2d 122 (S.D. N.Y. 1998)

Defense counsel's failed to recognize petitioner's status as second violent felony offender rather than persistent violent felony offender. Had counsel pointed this out to the prosecutor, there exists more than a reasonable probability that additional plea negotiations would have been pursued and prosecutor probably would have accepted some type of plea to offer a sentence lower than ten to life. Counsel's omissions constitutes ineffective assistance of counsel.

Failed to Explore Plea Agreement

U.S. v. Mohammad, 999 F. Supp. 1198 (N.D. Ill. 1998)

Trial counsel's failure to explore possibilities of plea agreement which would have probably resulted in at least a two (2) level adjustment in defendant's base offense level for acceptance of responsibility and possibly a different adjustment relating to the defendant's role in the offense constituted ineffective assistance of counsel.

Failed to Pursue Plea Negotiations Due to Conflict of Interest

Edens v. Hannigan, 87 F3d 1109 (10th Cir. 1996)

Counsel's failure to pursue favorable plea negotiations, motivated by a conflict of interest established ineffective assistance of counsel.

U.S. v. Magini, 973 F.2d 261 (4th Cir. 1992)

Trial counsel's failure to explore plea negotiation due to a conflict of interest required an evidentiary hearing.

Mannhalt v. Reed, 847 F.2d 576 (9th Cir. 1988)

Failure to explore possible plea bargain due to a conflict of interest deprives defendant of the right to effective assistance of counsel.

Failed to Provide Defendant with Copy of Plea Agreement

U.S. v. Busse, 814 F.Supp. 760 (E.D. Wis. 1993)

Trial counsel was ineffective during plea negotiations, where counsel failed to provide defendant with a copy of the plea agreement offered by the United States, and proper remedy was resentencing in accordance to the plea offer.

Failed to Memorialize Sentence Reduction

Betancourt v. Willis, 814 F.2d 1546 (11 Cir. 1987)

Trial counsel's failure to memorialize alleged sentence reduction, either by letter, affidavit or otherwise, based on counsel's representation to defendant that judge had agreed to reduce defendant's sentence after plea constituted ineffective assistance.

McAleney v. United States, 539 F.2d 282 (1st Cir. 1976)

Trial counsel's misrepresentation that government's attorney had agreed to recommend that defendant would receive a three (3) year sentence to induce guilty plea and in reality no such agreement existed constituted ineffective assistance.

Guilty Plea Ineffectiveness

Misrepresented Material Facts and Withheld Information

Ostrander v. Green, 46 F.3d 347 (4th Cir. 1995)
Defense counsel induced defendant's guilt plea based on "misadvise" that he would plead to certain sexual offense, his sentence would be capped at 3 to 5 years, and he would get work release real quick constituted ineffective assistance of counsel.

United States v. Sanderson, 595 F.2d 1021 (5th Cir. 1979)
Trial counsel's misrepresentation of material facts, withholding information, and exerted pressure on defendant to induce a guilty plea, constitutes ineffective assistance and requires an evidentiary hearing to resolve claim.

Failed to Prepare for Trial

U.S. v. Sanchez-Barreto, 93 F.3d 17 (1st Cir. 1996)
Defense counsel coerced defendant's guilty plea in order to conceal his unpreparedness for trial which constitutes ineffective assistance of counsel.

U.S. v. Hansel, 70 F.3d 6 (2nd Cir. 1995)
Counsel's failure to inform defendant that charges was barred by statute of limitations, rendered the guilty plea involuntary.

U.S. v. Magini, 973 F.2d 261 (4th Cir. 1992)
Trial counsel who was influenced by private pecuniary concerning, made private agreement with U.S. Attorney to exclude defendant's jewelry from forfeiture proceeding to collect attorney's fee; failed to prepare for trial and advised defendant to plead guilty because of a conflict of interest required an evidentiary hearing.

Prosecutorial Vindictiveness

Turner v. State of Tenn., 940 F.2d 1000 (6th Cir. 1991)
The Court concluded that presumption of prosecutorial vindictiveness occurred to the extent that defendant rejected plea offer due to ineffective assistance and prosecutor's plea offer after vacation of defendant's conviction was less favorable than original offer.

U.S. v. Estrada, 849 F.2d 1304 (10th Cir. 1988)
The Court held that: Defendant who alleged that prosecutor threatened to file unwarranted charges against him, that defense counsel coerced him to plead guilty by threatening to withdraw, and that both prosecutor and defense counsel promised him light sentence, was entitled to evidentiary hearing to determine voluntariness of plea.

Induced Plea Which Exposed Defendant to Greater Charges

U.S. Ex. Rel. Potts v. Chrans, 700 F.Supp. 1505 (N.D. Ill. 1988)
Trial counsel's advice to defendant to plead guilty to involuntary manslaughter charge in exchange for a 12-year plea agreement where evidence that defendant fired shots which caused the victim's death was not overwhelming and defendant could still face charge of murder, if the trial court found that the evidence did not support involuntary manslaughter charge in accordance to the plea agreement constituted ineffective assistance of counsel.

Failed to Seek Plea Agreement

U.S. v. Tatum, 943 F.2d 370 (4th Cir. 1991)
Trial counsel's failure to seek plea bargain agreement due to a conflict of interest constitutes ineffective assistance of counsel.

Pilchak v. Camper, 741 F.Supp. 782 (W.D. Mo. 1990)
Trial counsel's failure to give defendant pretrial advice or to enter into plea negotiations can constitute ineffective assistance of counsel.

Mannhalt v. Reed, 847 F.2d 576 (9th Cir. 1988)
Failure to explore possible plea bargain due to a conflict of interest deprives defendant of the right to effective assistance of counsel.

Induced Defendant to Change Plea of 'Not Guilty by Reason of Insanity' to 'Guilty'

Weekly v. Jones, 56 F.3d 889 (8th Cir. 1995)
Counsel's failure to investigate defendant's medical evidence, coerced Weekly to withdraw his plea of insanity and plead not guilty constitutes ineffective assistance of counsel. See also **_Weekley v. Jones_, 927 F.2d 382 (8th Cir. 1991)**

Failure to Object to Breach of Plea

U.S. v. Granados, 168 F.3d 343 (8th Cir. 1999)
Defense counsel's failure to challenge the prosecution's breach of plea agreement, in which the government agreed that defendant's **relevant conduct** would not exceed five kilograms of cocaine and counsel's unfamiliarity with the Sentencing Guidelines constitutes ineffective assistance of counsel.

U.S. v. De La Fuente, 8 F.3d 1333 (9th Cir. 1993)
Trial counsel's failure to contest the government breach of plea, where the government failed to move for a downward departure below the mandatory minimum pursuant to **_U.S.S.G. § 5K1.1_,** constitutes ineffective assistance and established cause for procedural default.

Voluntariness of Plea

Boykins v. Alabama, 295 U.S. 238, 23 L.Ed.2d 274, 89 S.Ct. 1709 (1969)
A plea of guilty shall not be accepted unless made voluntarily after proper advice and full understanding of the consequence of said plea.

Machibroda v. United States, 368 U.S. 487, 7 L.Ed.2d 473, 82 S.Ct. 510 (1962)
A plea of guilty, if induced by "promises" or threats, which deprive it of the character of a voluntary act "is void and open to collateral attack."

The Timmreck Test

United States v. Timmreck, 441 U.S. 780, 60 L.Ed.2d 634, 99 S.Ct. 2085 (1979)

The Supreme Court held that "a conviction based on a guilty plea is not subject to collateral attack under *28 U.S.C.S.§2255* solely on the basis that a formal violation of *Rule 11* occurred, such a violation being neither constitutional nor jurisdictional especially where no claim could reasonably be made that any error resulted in a complete miscarriage of justice or in a proceeding inconsistent with the rudimentary demands of fair procedure." *Id.*

United States v. Scott, 625 F.2d 623 (5th Cir. 1980)

A conviction on a guilty plea tendered solely as a result of faulty advice is a miscarriage of justice. *Scott* alleged that he would not have tendered a guilty plea had the district court advised him of the potential six-year sentence under the Youth corrections Act. The Fifth Circuit found that this allegation distinguishes *Scott's* pleading albeit slightly from those in *Timmreck*, where *Timmreck* never alleged that if he had been properly advised by the trial court he would not have pled guilty. *441 U.S. at 784, 99 S.Ct. at 2087.* *Scott's* pleadings sufficiently alleged prejudice, which, if proved, would afford a basis for collateral attack. *Scott, 625 F.2d at 625.*

Miscarriage of Justice

United States v. Scott, 625 F.2d 623 (5th Cir. 1981)

A conviction on a guilty plea that is entered solely as a result of faulty legal advice is a miscarriage of justice.

Self-Incriminations

Mitchell v. United States, 526 U.S. 314, 143 L.Ed.2d 424, 119 S.Ct. 1307 (1999)

Guilty plea in federal case held not to be waiver of right to invoke privilege against self-incriminations in sentencing phase; also, drawing by sentencer of adverse inference from accused failure to testify held to violate Fifth Amendment.

Counsel Absent During Plea Negotiations

Tyler v. U.S., 78 F.Supp.2d 626 (E.D. Mich. 1999)

Defense counsel who arranged a meeting between his client and government agents to discuss a plea agreement and then counsel was absent for the plea negotiations, where the defendant made incriminating statement which were used against him was per se prejudicial under *Cronic, 466 U.S. at 659, n.25, 104 S. Ct. 2039,* and amounted ineffective assistance of counsel.

TRIAL INEFFECTIVENESS

JURY SELECTION INEFFECTIVENESS

Baston Claim

Davis v. Secretary for the Dept. of Corrections*, *341 F.3d 1310, 1316-1318 (11th Cir. 2003)
Counsel was constitutionally ineffective for failure to preserve ***Baston*** claim for appellate purposes at the conclusion of voir dire and the end of trial, required granting a new trial or to afford petitioner an opportunity for an out-of-time appeal.

Riley v. Taylor*, *277 F.3d 261, 294 (3rd Cir. 2001)
The Court found the appropriate remedy under facts for ***Batson*** violation was to order a new trial, rather than remand federal evidentiary hearing.

Aki-Khuam v. Davis*, *203 F.Supp. 2d 1001, 1017, 1020 (N.D. Ill. 2002)
Defendant's Sixth Amendment right was violated by trial court setting procedures used for exercise of peremptory challenges, where court shifted burden of persuasion to defendant to prove that his motivation was not illegal discrimination.

Riley v. Taylor*, *277 F.3d 261, 294 (3rd Cir. 2001)
State court's failure to properly apply ***Batson*** analysis required granting habeas relief without prejudice.

Duarte v. U.S.*, *81 F.3d 75 (7th Cir. 1996)
Counsel's failure to raise Baston objection to peremptory challenge concerning a Spanish juror may constitute ineffective assistance. **See also** ***Weekley v. Jones*, *927 F.2d 382 (8th Cir. 1991)*; *Hollis v. Davis*, *912 F.2d 1343 (11th Cir. 1990)*; *Jackson v. Thigpen*, *752 F.Supp. 1551 (N.D. Ala. 1990)***

Government of Virgin Islands v. Forte*, *865 F.2d 59 (3rd Cir. 1989)
Trial counsel's failure to object to prosecutor's peremptory challenges to excuse white prospective jurors in prosecution of white man for rape of black female required an evidentiary hearing to resolve claim of ineffective assistance of counsel.

Strike Juror

Hughes v. United States*, *258 F.3d 453,463 (6th Cir. 2001)
Counsel was constitutionally ineffective for failing to strike juror who admitted bias. "The question of whether to seat a biased juror is not a discretionary or strategic decision. The seating of a biased juror who should have been dismissed for cause requires reversal of the conviction." **Id.**

Trial Ineffectiveness

Miller v. Webb, 385 F.3d 666, 677 (6th Cir. 2004)
> Counsel's failure to object to empaneling an actual biased jury was presumptively prejudicial constituting ineffective assistance.

Smith v. Gearinger, 888 F.2d 1334 (11th Cir. 1989)
> Trial counsel's failure to contest two prospective jurors that counsel knew were within the prohibited degree of consanguinity with victim or her mother required an evidentiary hearing to resolve claim of ineffective assistance of counsel.

Right to be Present Impaneling Jury

U.S. v. Gordon, 829 F.2d 119 (D.C. Cir. 1987)
> Trial counsel cannot waive defendant's right to be present during impaneling of jury.

Make Juror Incompetence Challenge

Edgemon v. Lockhart, 768 F.2d 252 (8th Cir. 1985)
> Trial counsel's failure to make juror incompetence challenge before the jury was empaneled required an evidentiary hearing to resolve ineffective assistance of counsel claim.

Exclude Jury During Dismissal of Rape Count

Marzullo v. State of MD., 561 F.2d 540 (1977)
> Trial counsel's failure to move to exclude the jury during a discussion to dismiss one count of a rape charge or to request a limiting jury instruction to disregard the prejudicial remarks of the first rape count amounted to ineffective assistance of counsel.

Removal of Recycled Jurors

Johnson v. Armontrout, 961 F.2d 748 (8th Cir. 1992)
> Trial counsel's failure to request removal of jurors who were recycled and had heard damaging testimony about the defendant in a prior trial constitutes ineffective assistance of counsel.

Strike Jurors Related to Prosecution's Team

Virgil v. Dretke, 446 F.3d 598, 612 (5th Cir. 2006)
> Counsel was constitutionally ineffective for failing to challenge two prospective jurors, who expressed that they were unable to serve as fair and impartial jurors because of their past association with law enforcement officers or to crime committed against family members, where those two jurors were seated on the petit jury that convicted petitioner and sentenced him to 30 years.

Harris v. Housewright, 697 F.2d 202 (8th Cir. 1982)
> Trial counsel's failure to strike jurors who apparently were related to the prosecutor's team and failure to use medical examiner's report to impeach medical examiner constituted ineffective assistance of counsel.

Judge Taints Jury

<u>*U.S. v. Iribe-Perez*</u>, *129 F.3d 1167 (10th Cir. 1997)*
> The defendant's right to a trial by impartial jury was violated where judge informed jury panel that defendant was going to plead guilty to very crime he was on trial for.

VOIR DIRE RELATED INEFFECTIVENESS

<u>*Mu'Min v. Virgina*</u>, *500 US 415, 114 L.Ed.2d 493, 111 S.Ct. 1899 (1991)*
> Voir dire enables court to select impartial jury and assists counsel in exercising peremptory challenges.

<u>*Gardner v. Barnett*</u>, *175 F.3d 580 (7th Cir. 1999)*
> The trial court's limits on voir dire regarding bias toward gangs violated the Sixth amendment and required a new trial.

<u>*Mach v. Stewart*</u>, *129 F.3d 495 (9th Cir. 1997)*
> Defendant's right to impartial jury was violated during voir dire of a potential jury when jury panel was exposed to potential juror's expert-like statements regarding veracity of children asserting claims of sexual abuse. Error rose to level of structural error thereby tainting the entire jury panel and mandating reversal.

<u>*Davidson v. U.S.*</u>, *951 F. Supp. 555 (W.D. Pa. 1996)*
> Trial counsel's failure to request voir dire of jury for juror misconduct constitutes ineffective assistance of counsel.

<u>*Harris By and Through Ramseyer v. Wood*</u>, *64 F.3d 1432 (9th Cir. 1995)*
> Trial counsel's failure to conduct proper voir dire amounts to ineffectiveness of counsel under the circumstance of this case. **See also** <u>*Pilchak v. Camper*</u>, *741 F.Supp. 782 (W.D. Mo. 1990);* <u>*United States v. Hammonds*</u>, *425 F.2d 597 (D.C. Cir. 1970)*

<u>*Government of Virgin Islands v. Weatherwax*</u>, *20 F.3d 572 (3rd Cir. 1994)*
> Trial counsel's failure to seek voir dire of jurors who were exposed to newspaper article which distorted defendant's trial testimony constitutes ineffective assistance of counsel and required an evidentiary hearing.

OPENING ARGUMENTS INEFFECTIVENESS

<u>*Seehan v. State of Iowa*</u>, *37 F.3d 389 (8th Cir. 1994)*
> Trial counsel's failure to object to highly prejudicial remarks made by the prosecutor during opening arguments deprived defendant of a fair trial and constitutes ineffective assistance of counsel.

<u>*Harris v. Reed*</u>, *894 F.2d 871 (7th Cir. 1990)*
> Trial counsel's failure to interview witness and call them to the stand after stating in opening arguments that he would put on several witnesses who would identify McWhorter as the murderer constituted ineffective assistance of counsel.

Anderson v. Butler, **858 F.2d 16 (1st Cir. 1988)**
> Trial counsel rendered ineffective assistance during opening arguments stating he would call expert witness during trial and failed to call said witness.

Reynolds v. Ellingsworth, **843 F.2d 712 (3rd Cir. 1988)**
> Appellate counsel's failure to raise prosecutor's improper remarks during opening arguments may constitute ineffective assistance of counsel.

Jemison v. Foltz, **672 F.Supp. 1002 (E.D. Mich. 1987)**
> Trial counsel's failure to make opening arguments and closing arguments to the jury in the defendant's behalf compounded with other errors constituted ineffective assistance of counsel. **See also** *United States v. Hammonds,* **425 F.2d 597 (D.C. Cir. 1970);** *Jones v. Jones,* **988 F.Supp. 1000 (E.D.La. 1997)**

Harris v. Towers, **405 F.Supp 497 (D. Del 1974)**
> Trial counsel's failure to present opening arguments and to utilize the non-motile sperm evidence, compounded with other errors and omissions, amounted to ineffective assistance of counsel.

Failed to Fulfill Promise to Jury

Hampton v. Leibach, **290 F.Supp.2d 905, 927-928 (N.D. Ill. 2001)**
> Counsel was constitutionally ineffective because of his failure to fulfill his promise made to the jury during opening statements, that the petitioner would testify that he was not a gang member.

United States Ex Rel. Hampton v. Leibach, **347 F.3d 219, 258-260 (7th Cir. 2003)**
> Counsel's failure to fulfill his promise to the jury in opening statement, that petitioner would testify and then failed to call petitioner as a witness, planted the seed in the jury's mind that petitioner reneged on his promise to testify, and tainted both the lawyers and petitioner's credibility with the jury, constituting ineffective assistance of counsel.

Ouber v. Guario, **293 F.3d 19, 33-35 (1st Cir. 2002)**
> Trial counsel's failure to call the defendant as a witness during trial when counsel repeatedly promised the jury that they would hear from the defendant during trial constituted ineffective assistance of counsel.

DEFENSE/EVIDENCE RELATED INEFFECTIVENESS

Accidental

Sims v. Livesay, **970 F.2d 1575 (6th Cir. 1992)**
> Counsel's failure to investigate and present evidence consistent with defendant's claim that shooting was accidental and at close range where there was powder residue on quilt with bullet holes constitutes ineffective assistance of counsel.

Admission of Gang-Related Evidence

Dawson v. Delaware, 503 U.S. 159, 117 L.Ed.2d 309, 112 S.Ct. 1093 (1992)
> The introduction of evidence of defendant's membership in the Aryan Brotherhood, a white racist gang, during capital sentencing violates the First Amendment where evidence had no relevance to issue before the court.

United States Ex. Rel. Clemons v. Walls, 202 F.Supp. 2d 767, 777 (N.D. Ill. 2002)
> Admission of gang-related evidence deprived petitioner of his due process right to a fundamentally fair trial where the evidence was introduced to pander jury's prejudice against gangs and gang members.

Advice of Counsel Defense

U.S. v. Taylor, 139 F.3d 924 (D.C. Cir. 1998)
> Trial counsel's failure to advise defendant of "advice of counsel" defense resulted from a conflict of interest amounting to ineffective assistance of counsel and required evidentiary hearing.

Alcoholic Evidence

Edgemon v. Lockhart, 768 F.2d 252 (8th Cir. 1985)
> Trial counsel's failure to object to questions related to defendant's marital affairs and drinking problems constituted performance below an objective standard of reasonableness.

Wood v. Zahradnick, 611 F.2d 1383 (4th Cir. 1980)
> Trial counsel's failure to present evidence that the defendant was an alcoholic and had drank too much, and failure to investigate an insanity defense which would have explained mental state of mind at the time of crime constituted ineffective assistance of counsel.

Alibi Defense

Clinkscale v. Carter, 375 F.3d 430,443-446 (6th Cir. 2004)
> Counsel's failure to file the alibi notice, under Florida Rule 12.1, which would have preserved Clinkscale's right to assert an alibi defense constituted ineffective assistance of counsel. The central focus of Clinkscale's trial was the identity of the perpetrator, the evidence essentially boiled down to a credibility contest between Williams and Clinkscale. Under these circumstances, Clinkscale's inability to provide supporting testimony for his strongest defense must be considered especially damaging and prejudicial.

Trial Ineffectiveness

Fisher v. Gibson, 282 F.3d 1283, 1295-96 (10th Cir. 2002)
Trial counsel failed to investigate, prepare, and present an alibi defense which could have shown that Fisher was in Coffeyville, Kansas, instead of Oklahoma City, when the murder occurred compounded with other errors constitutes ineffective assistance of counsel.

Bohan v. Kuhlmann, 234 F.Supp. 2d 231, 253-54 (S.D.N.Y. 2002)
Counsel was constitutionally ineffective for failing to provide notice of intent to pursue alibi defense, where there was a reasonable probability that had the jury heard Rodriquez's alibi testimony, that the outcome of the trial would have been different.

Hargrave-Thomas v. Yukins, 236 F.Supp. 2d 750, 770 (E.D. Mich. 2002)
Counsel was constitutionally ineffective by failing to investigate or interview potential witnesses whose testimony would have established a partial alibi defense, making the fact finder much less likely to decide beyond a reasonable doubt that petitioner committed the arson and murder.

Bruce v. U.S., 256 F.3d 592, 599 (7th Cir. 2001)
Defense counsel's failure to investigate and call two alibi witnesses, Thompson and Barton, where their testimony would have proved that **Bruce** was with them in Michigan during the time the armed bank robberies took place in Indiana, warranted an evidentiary hearing to resolve the ineffectiveness of counsel claim.

Koskela v. United States, 235 F.3d 1148, 1150 (8th Cir. 2001)
Counsel's failure to present alibi defense or call alibi witnesses required an evidentiary hearing to resolve claim of ineffectiveness of counsel.

Fargo v. Phillips, 129 F.Supp.2d 1075 (E.D. Mich. 2001)
Trial counsel's failure to conduct a competent pretrial investigation into petitioner's potential alibi defense where alibi witness would have placed petitioner with them at or near the time of the crime, amounted to ineffective assistance of counsel.

Moore v. Johnson, 194 F.3d 587 (5th Cir. 1999)
Trial counsel eliciting damaging evidence against Moore during cross-examination of the arresting officer, Autrey's testimony establishing the elements of the offense and defeated Moore's alibi's defense amounted to ineffective assistance.

Brown v. Myers, 137 F.3d 1154 (9th Cir. 1998)
Trial counsel's failure to investigate alibi defense or to present any alibi witnesses to corroborate petitioner's testimony undermined confidence in outcome of trial and constituted ineffective assistance of counsel.

U.S. v. Dawson, 857 F.2d 923 (3rd Cir. 1988)
Trial counsel's failure to interview and call alibi witness who put the defendant in another town at the time of the crime constituted performance below an objective standard of reasonableness. There existed a reasonable probability that the results of the trial would have been different absent trial counsel's unprofessional errors and omissions. **See also** *Wade v. Armontrout, 798 F.2d 304 (8th Cir. 1986); U.S. Ex. Rel. Patterson v. Neal, 678 F.Supp. 749 (N.D. Ill. 1988)*

Tosh v. Lockhart, 879 F.2d 412 (8th Cir. 1989)
> Trial counsel's failure to produce three alibi witnesses under the facts and circumstances of this case constituted ineffective assistance of counsel.

Montgomery v. Petersen, 846 F.2d 407 (7th Cir. 1988)
> Trial counsel's failure to investigate and interview the only disinterested alibi witness, a store clerk whom Petitioner purchased a bicycle from on the same day of robbery, constituted ineffective assistance of counsel.

Also see, Witnesses Alibi Section for more case law.

Alternative Defense

White v. Godinez, 301 F.3d 796, 801-804 (7th Cir. 2002)
> Counsel's failure to investigate alternative defense, supported by testimony of accomplice that petitioner and accomplice were asleep when Johnson and Walker stole their vehicle and guns, and committed the crimes charged constituted ineffective assistance of counsel.

Antagonist Defense

Hernandez v. Cowan, 200 F.3d 995 (7th Cir. 2000)
> Counsel's failure to attend suppression hearing where he would have learned the defendant had an antagonist defense and failure to move for a severance constitutes ineffective assistance of counsel.

Autopsy Evidence

Helton v. Singletary, 85 F.Supp.2d 1323 (S.D. Fla. 1999)
> Trial counsel's failure to investigate gastric evidence from autopsy of child- victim, where victim's stomach contents contained undigested food, indicating that murder occurred during defendant's absence amounted ineffective assistance of counsel.

Ballistic Test

Harris By and Through Ramseyer v. Wood, 64 F.3d 1432 (9th Cir. 1995)
> Counsel's failure to object to evidence of ballistic test constituted ineffective assistance of counsel.

Barbee v. Warden, Maryland Penitentiary, 331 F.2d 842,845 (4th Cir. 1964)
> Trial counsel's failure to request the results of police department ballistic and fingerprint test did not excuse prosecution's failure to inform defendant of such reports. Especially, where reports of ballistic and fingerprint test strongly tended to exculpate defendant and showed different weapon was used during assault with intent to kill and unauthorized use of automobile. The court reversed and remanded with instructions for issuance of a writ of habeas corpus unless state elected to try defendant within a reasonable amount of time. This case was not an ineffective assistance of counsel issue, but the proposition of the case supports such a finding.

Chain of Custody of Evidence

California v. Trombetta, 467 U.S. 479 (1984)
> The Supreme Court held that the Constitution requires the government to preserve evidence "That might be expected to play a significant role in the suspect's defense."

Johnson v. Norris, 999 F. Supp. 1256 (E.D. Ark. 1998)
> Defense counsel's failure to investigate circumstances of case and conducted inadequate cross-examination of key witness' whose testimony had several discrepancies regarding chain of custody of the cocaine, allegedly sold by defendant, where the key witness had medical problems, which included loss of memory, amounted to ineffective assistance.

Coercion or Duress

Bliss v. Lockhart, 891 F.2d 1335 (8th Cir. 1989)
> Trial counsel's failure to investigate, preserve evidence, and present petitioner's claim of coercion or duress by her husband whom counsel had jointly represented constituted ineffective assistance of counsel.

Streetman v. Lynaugh, 812 F.2d 950 (5th Cir. 1987)
> Trial counsel failed to press the motion to suppress defendant's confession to law enforcement that he committed the murder, plus a series of thefts when authorities had threatened defendant and his family with physical violence. Authorities promised to release defendant and continue a supply of Valium in exchange for defendant's cooperation against accomplice. Trial counsel failed to inform co-counsel of defendant's allegations. The defendant's confession was the State's main case at trial. The Fifth Circuit remanded for an evidentiary hearing.

Composite Sketch from Victim's Physical Description

Love v. McCray, 413 F.3d 192, 195 (2nd Cir. 2005)
> Counsel's failure to produce or make use of a composite sketch developed from the victim's physical description of the burglar that does not resemble Love stated a valid claim of ineffective assistance of counsel and warranted a COA.

Conceivable Insanity Defense

Brennan v. Blankenship, 472 F.Supp. 149 (W.D. Vir. 1979)
> Trial counsel's failure to present the defendant's only conceivable defense of insanity amounted to ineffective assistance of counsel.

Conspiracy Defense

Miller v. Senkowski, 268 F.Supp. 2d 296, 313-314 (E.D.N.Y. 2003)
> Counsel was constitutionally ineffective by failing to pursue the conspiracy defense, that petitioner was being forced into marriage, as promised during opening statements to the jury, and to present "evidence" supporting said defense compounded with other errors was prejudicial under *Strickland*.

Counsel Abandoned Defendant's Only Defense

De Luca v. Lord, 77 F.3d 578 (3rd Cir. 1996)
> Trial counsel abandoned defense of extreme emotional disturbance at early stage for no reason constituted ineffective assistance of counsel.

U.S. v. Swanson, 943 F.2d 1070 (9th Cir. 1991)
> Trial counsel's abandonment of Petitioner's only defense was inherently prejudicial where counsel conceded only factual issue in dispute in closing arguments which deprived Petitioner of effective assistance of counsel.

Corpus Delicti

Summit v. Blackburn, 795 F.2d 1237 (5th Cir. 1986)
> Trial counsel's failure to properly and timely raise the corpus delicit issue during trial base on lack of corroborating evidence amounted to ineffective assistance of counsel.

Digitally Enhanced Audio Tape Recording

U.S. v. Calderin-Rodriguez, 244 F.3d 977, 986 (8th Cir. 2001)
> Digitally enhanced audio tape recording of drug buy did not require a *Daubert* hearing because the operator had used software on approximately 50 occasions to enhance audio tape recordings.

Diminished Capacity

Jacobs v. Horns, 129 F.Supp. 2d 390, 411-12 (M.D. Pa. 2001)
> Trial counsel was ineffective for failing to investigate and present diminished capacity defense during capital murder trial.

U.S. v. Reveron Martinez, 836 F.2d 684 (1st Cir. 1988)
> Trial counsel's failure to raise defense of insanity or diminished capacity may constitute ineffective assistance of counsel.

Double Jeopardy

U.S. v. Sterba, 22 F. Supp. 2d 1146 (D. Or. 1998)
> The Court found that defendant's immunity from double jeopardy precluded another trial following mistrial prompted by prosecutorial misconduct.

Murphy v. Puckett, 893 F.2d 94 (5th Cir. 1990)
> Trial counsel's failure to raise valid issue of double jeopardy as defense in robbery case constituted ineffective assistance of counsel.

Rice v. Marshall, 816 F.2d 1126 (6th Cir. 1987)
> Trial counsel's failure to object at second trial to the introduction of the handgun into evidence constitutes ineffective assistance of counsel.

<u>**Trial Ineffectiveness**</u>

<u>*U.S. v. McDonald*</u>, *981 F.Supp. 942 (D, Md. 1997)*
> Counsel's failure to object to defendant being sentenced to bank robbery which was lesser included offense of armed robbery required the sentence to be vacated on the lesser included offense and constituted ineffective assistance.

<u>*Griffin v. U.S.*</u>, *598 A.2d 1174 (D.C. App. 1991)*
> Appellate counsel's failure to raise a double jeopardy claim on appeal constituted ineffective assistance of counsel, which warranted recalling the previously issued mandate.

Entrapment Defense

<u>*Capps v. Sullivan*</u>, *921 F.2d 260 (10th Cir. 1990)*
> Trial counsel's failure to interview or subpoena witnesses who would have substantially corroborated Capps' testimony material to entrapment defense constituted ineffective assistance of counsel.

Exclusion of Pretrial Psychiatric Report

<u>*Ellis v. Mullin*</u>, *326 F.3d 1122, 1128-1129 (10th Cir. 2003)*
> Trial court's exclusion of pretrial psychiatric report, which diagnosed petitioner competency at time of fatal shooting violated petitioner's due process right to present evidence and a defense.

Extreme Emotional Disturbance

<u>*De Luca v. Lord*</u>, *77 F.3d 578 (3rd Cir. 1996)*
> Trial counsel abandoned defense of extreme emotional disturbance at early stage for no reason constituted ineffective assistance of counsel.

<u>*Maddox v. Lord*</u>, *818 F.2d 1058 (2nd Cir. 1987)*
> Defense counsel's failure to present affirmative defense of extreme emotional disturbance in state murder case constitutes ineffective assistance of counsel.

Failed to Offer Evidence

<u>*Tucker v. Renico*</u>, *317 F.Supp. 2d 766, 774-75 (E.D. Mich. 2004)*
> Counsel was constitutionally ineffective because of his failure to introduce evidence at trial for sexual conduct and breaking and entering charges; that is, the petitioner and the victim had a long term spousal relationship; victim held herself out to be petitioner's wife and evidence would have been useful for impeachment purposes.

<u>*Vick v. Lockhart*</u>, *952 F.2d 999 (8th Cir. 1991)*
> Trial counsel's failure to present evidence that defendant's water had been turned off to his home at time the alleged rape where the victim claimed defendant forced her to take bath constituted ineffective assistance of counsel and required evidentiary hearing.

<u>*U.S. v. Cronic*</u>, *839 F.2d 1401 (10th Cir. 1988)*
> Trial counsel's failure to use evidence of security to cover overdrafts and object to improper testimony amounted to ineffective assistance.

<u>U.S. Ex. Rel. Potts v. Chrans</u>, 700 F.Supp. 1505 (N.D. Ill. 1988)
Trial counsel's failure in murder prosecution during bench trial to offer evidence, to make closing arguments on defendant's behalf amounted to failure to hold government to burden of proof and deprived defendant of the right to effective assistance of counsel.

Failed To Connect Evidence

<u>Odem v. Hopkins</u>, 192 F.3d 772 (8ᵗʰ Cir. 1999)
The Court of Appeals remanded to the district court to consider Odem's claims that counsel's failure to connect the two disclosures concerning the jacket belonging Odem's brother constituted ineffective assistance of counsel.

Failed To Introduce "Key" As Evidence

<u>McCoy v. Norris</u>, 958 F. Supp. 420 (E.D.Ark. 1996)
Trial counsel's failure to introduce into evidence key given to petitioner by alleged rape victim compounded with failure to call witnesses amounted to ineffective assistance of counsel.

Fingerprint Evidence

<u>Phoenix v. Matesanz</u>, 189 F.3d 20 (1st Cir. 1999)
Counsel's failure to call expert witness to rebut blood and fingerprint evidence which was basically the only state evidence linking the defendant to crime required a remand for reconsideration, where the district court failed to obtain the trial transcripts necessary to review defendant's claims.

<u>Atkins v. Attorney General of State of Ala.</u>, 932 F.2d 1430 (11th Cir. 1991)
Trial counsel's failure to object to admission into evidence fingerprint card which contained notation of petitioner's prior arrest that was not admissible, constituted ineffective assistance of counsel.

<u>Barbee v. Warden, Maryland Penitentiary</u>, 331 F.2d 842,845 (4th Cir. 1964)
Trial counsel's failure to request the results of police department's ballistic and fingerprint tests did not excuse prosecution's failure to inform defendant of such reports. Especially, where reports of ballistic and fingerprint test strongly tended to exculpate defendant and showed different weapon was used during assault with intent to kill and unauthorized use of automobile. The court reversed and remanded with instructions for issuance of a writ of habeas corpus unless state elected to try defendant within a reasonable amount of time. This case was not an ineffective assistance of counsel issue, but the proposition of the case supports such a finding.

<u>Beasley v. United States</u>, 491 F.2d 687 (6th Cir. 1974)
Trial counsel's failure to retain an independent fingerprint expert may constitute ineffective assistance of counsel.

Trial Ineffectiveness

Footprint Evidence

Hadley v. Groose, 97 F.3d 1131 (8th Cir. 1996)
> Trial counsel's failure to use police report to impeach police officer's testimony relating to footprints where counsel knew officer's testimony was contradicted by body of police report, constituted ineffective assistance of counsel.

Good Faith Defense

U.S. v. Cronic, 839 F.2d 1401 (10th Cir. 1988)
> Trial counsel's inexperience and failure to present a good faith defense constituted ineffective assistance.

Insanity Defense/Evidence

Genius v. Pepe,Jr., 50 F.3d 60 (1st Cir. 1995)
> Counsel's failure to pursue insanity defense after defendant was initially found incompetent to stand trial constituted ineffective assistance of counsel.

Noland v. Dixon, 808 F.Supp. 485 (W.D.N.C. 1992)
> Counsel's failure to call available witnesses in support of petitioner's insanity defense constitutes ineffective assistance of counsel.

Bouchillon v. Collins, 907 F.2d 589 (5th Cir. 1990)
> Trial counsel's failure to investigate or present insanity defense amounted to ineffective assistance. **See also** *U.S. v. Reveron Martinez, 836 F.2d 684 (1st Cir. 1988); Williamson v. Reynolds, 904 F.Supp. 1529 (E.D. Okl. 1995); Petty v. McCotter, 779 F.2d 299 (5th Cir. 1986); U.S. Ex. Rel. Rivera v. Frantzen, 594 F.Supp. 198 (N.D. Ill. 1984); Wood v. Zahradnick, 611 F.2d 1383 (4th Cir. 1980)*

U.S. v. Burrows, 872 F.2d 915 (9th Cir. 1989)
> Trial counsel's failure to investigate defendant's mental state and present evidence at trial, based on defendant's mental state, required an evidentiary hearing to resolve ineffective assistance of counsel claim.

U.S. v. Kauffman, 109 F.3d 186 (3rd Cir. 1997)
> Failure to investigate insanity defense where an investigation would have uncovered that the defendant had long history of bipolar syndrome and psychotic episodes leading to multiple psychiatric hospitalizations, and numerous doctors were willing to testify that defendant was hypomanic and psychotic had no strategic value and, constitutes ineffective assistance. **See also** *Weekly v. Jones, 56 F.3d 889 (8th Cir. 1995); Petty v. McCotter, 779 F.2d 299 (5th Cir. 1986)*

Profitt v. Waldron, 831 F.2d 1245 (5th Cir. 1987)
> Defense counsel's failure to investigate and secure records from a mental institution, which would have shown a valid defense of insanity constituted ineffective assistance of counsel. **See also** *Young v. Zant, 677 F.2d 792 (11th Cir. 1982)*

McCoy v. Wainwright, 804 F.2d 1196, (11th Cir. 1986)
>   Failure to investigate possible insanity defense, to move for a competency hearing, or to advise defendant of affirmative insanity defense constitutes ineffective assistance, and required an evidentiary hearing.

Impotency

Foster v. Lockhart, 9 F.3d 722 (8th Cir. 1993)
>   Defense counsel's failure to investigate, develop, and present the defense of impotency constituted ineffective assistance of counsel. See also *Foster v. Lockhart, 811 F.Supp. 1363 (E.D. Ark. 1992)*.

Harris v. Towers, 405 F.Supp 497 (D. Del 1974)
>   Trial counsel's failure to present opening arguments and to utilize the non-motile sperm evidence, compounded with other errors and omissions, amounted to ineffective assistance of counsel.

Identification

United States v. Wade, 388 U.S. 218, 18 Led.2d 1149 (1967)
>   An accused is entitled to the aid of counsel during lineup identification. Also see *Stovall v. Denno, 388 U.S. 293, 18 L.Ed.2d 1199, 87 S.Ct. 1967 (1967)*.

Berryman v. Morton, 100 F.3d 1089 (3rd Cir. 1996)
>   Counsel's failure to use victim's inconsistent identification testimony from an accomplice's previous trial constituted ineffective assistance.

Intoxication

Harich v. Wainwright, 813 F.2d 1082 (11th Cir. 1987)
>   Trial counsel's failure to object based on the prosecution's misstatement of the law based on Harich's intoxication defense amounts to ineffective assistance of counsel.

Wood v. Zahradnick, 611 F.2d 1383 (4th Cir. 1980)
>   Trial counsel's failure to present evidence that the defendant was an alcoholic and had drank too much and to investigate an insanity defense, which would have explained mental state of mind at the time of crime constituted ineffective assistance of counsel. See also *Ford v. Lockhart, 861 F.Supp. 1447 (E.D. Ark. 1994)*

Lack of Intent

U.S. v. Johnson, 995 F. Supp. 1259 (D. Kan. 1998)
>   Trial counsel's failure to pursue defense of lack of intent and withdrawal from conspiracy to distribute phenty-2-propanone required an evidentiary hearing to resolve ineffective assistance claim.

U.S. v. Wolf, 787 F.2d 1094 (7th Cir. 1986)
>   Trial counsel's failure to object to the jury instruction on intent or offer a dominant purpose jury instruction constituted ineffective assistance of counsel.

Trial Ineffectiveness

Rummel v. Estelle, 498 F.Supp. 793 (W.D. Tex 1980)

Trial counsel's failure to investigate the facts of the offense and pursue defense of lack of intent to write the hot check constituted ineffective assistance of counsel.

Improperly Handling Defendant's Confession

Moore v. Johnson, 194 F.3d 587 (5th Cir. 1999)

Defense counsel handling of defendant's confession by allowing the prosecution to exclude exculpatory language leaving only the state's version of the events, and failing to object to the state's breach of its pre- submission agreement not to rely upon the excluded portion of the confession amounted to ineffective assistance of counsel.

Lesser Included Charge

Young v. Zant, 677 F.2d 792 (11th Cir. 1982)

Trial counsel's failure to present a defense of lesser included charge of voluntary manslaughter based on a very strong argument that the killing occurred during the heat of passion, constituted ineffective assistance. See also *Chambers v. Armontrout, 907 F.2d 825 (8th Cir. 1990).*

Taylor v. Starnes, 650 F.2d 38 (4th Cir. 1981)

Trial counsel knew that the evidence presented at trial supported an instruction for a lesser included offense of assault and battery. However, he deliberately failed to request the instruction because the trial court and prosecution failed to provide the lesser included instruction. Counsel's intention was to create reversible error. This type of conduct on behalf of counsel constituted ineffective assistance of counsel.

Kemp v. Leggett, 635 F.2d 453 (5th Cir. 1981)

Trial counsel's failure to prepare for trial, to interview a single witness, to call several character witnesses who were present in the courtroom, to prepare a defense, and to proffer a written charge on voluntary manslaughter charge constituted ineffective assistance.

Marital Privilege

Edwards v. Lamarque, 439 F.3d 504, 516-517 (9th Cir. 2005)

Counsel eliciting testimony from petitioner sufficient to waive marital privilege constituted ineffective assistance of counsel.

Methamphetamine Defense

Morris v. State of Cal., 966 F.2d 448 (9th Cir. 1991)

Ms. Morris informed trial counsel that she was under the influence of methamphetamine and not cocaine at the time of her arrest. She was on trial for being under the influence of cocaine. Counsel advised her that methamphetamine use and cocaine uses were equally incriminating. This advice was below the objective standard of reasonableness. If Ms. Morris' counsel had been familiar with the law or had done his homework, he would have discovered that being under the influence of methamphetamine was not illegal. Therefore, there was a reasonable probability that the outcome of the trial would have been different.

Misidentification Defense

Henry v. Poole, 409 F.3d 48, 65 (2nd Cir. 2005)
Counsel was constitutionally ineffective because he created a false alibi, which constituted evidence of defendant's consciousness of guilt by producing an alibi for the wrong time and date. Henry was prejudiced because he had a strong defense of misidentification and suggestive lineup photograph showed that Henry was taller than the other participants.

Harris v. Senkowski, 298 F.Supp.2d 320, 327 (E.D.N.Y. 2004)
Counsel was constitutionally ineffective because of counsel's failure to confront robbery victim with her prior inconsistent statement describing the robbery victim as being eight inches shorter and 100 pounds lighter.

White v. Godinez, 143 F.3d 1049 (7th Cir. 1998)
Defense counsel's failure to pursue defense that defendant's brother hired hit men to kill victim and to call defendant and his girlfriend as witnesses to support defense constituted ineffective assistance of counsel.

Toney v. Gammon, 79 F.3d 693 (8th Cir. 1996)
Counsel's failure to pursue issue of mistaken identity defense required evidentiary hearing to resolve claim of ineffective assistance of counsel. **See also *Eldridge v. Atkins*, 665 F.2d 228 (8th Cir. 1981)**

Lawrence v. Armontrout, 900 F.2d 127 (8th Cir. 1990)
Failure of counsel to contact and investigate all potential alibi witnesses after defendant provided counsel with their names, which would have supported counsel's defense of misidentification constitutes ineffectiveness of counsel.

Non-Motile Sperm Evidence

Harris v. Towers, 405 F.Supp 497 (D. Del 1974)
Trial counsel's failure to present opening arguments and to utilize the non-motile sperm evidence amounted to ineffective assistance of counsel. See also ***Dorsey v. Kelly*, 112 F.3d 50 (2nd Cir. 1997)**.

Police Fabrication Defense

Tejeda v. Dubois, 142 F.3d 18 (1st Cir. 1998)
Trial counsel's failure to present a coherent argument to the judge and jury based on defense of police fabrication rendered defendant's trial fundamentally unfair, unreliable, and constituted ineffective assistance of counsel.

Polygraph Evidence

Rupe v. Wood, 93 F.3d 1434 (9th Cir. 1996)
The trial court excluded the results of polygraph test of state's witness in penalty phase which violated defendant's due process rights to have relevant, mitigating evidence surrounding the crime to present to the jury for deciding between penalty of

life or death; where issue of relative credibility and culpability between defendant and witness existed, without polygraph evidence, it allowed prosecutor to persuasively argue against defendant's credibility.

U.S. v. Chandler, 950 F.Supp. 1545 (N.D. Ala. 1996)
Evidentiary hearing warranted on habeas claim for government's failure to disclose results of witness' polygraph test.

Houston v. Lockhart, 982 F.2d 1246 (8th Cir. 1993)
Trial counsel's failure to have the parties stipulation that polygraph evidence could be admitted into evidence constitutes ineffective assistance of counsel. This claim required an evidentiary hearing.

Sanity Defense/Evidence

Greer v. Beto, 379 F.2d 923 (5th Cir. 1967)
Defense counsel's failure to present testimony on sanity issue at trial, after defendant had been found sane, along with the introduction of a jury verdict in the sanity trial stated a valid claim of ineffectiveness of counsel and warranted an evidentiary hearing.

Scientific Test

Demarest v. Price, 130 F.3d 922 (10th Cir. 1997)
Counsel's failure to adequately conduct pretrial investigation regarding blood-splatter evidence, which would have uncovered strong scientific evidence that could have been used to challenge state witnesses, constituted ineffective assistance. This case was remanded to determine whether petitioner's ineffective assistance of counsel claims were procedurally barred. **See also _Demarest v. Price, 905 F.Supp. 1432 (D.Col. 1995)_**.

Harris By and Through Ramseyer v. Wood, 64 F.3d 1432 (9th Cir. 1995)
Counsel's failure to object to evidence of ballistic test constituted ineffective assistance of counsel.

Stephens v. Kemp, 846 F.2d 642 (11th Cir. 1988)
Trial counsel has a duty to familiarize himself with regard to the specific scientific area in which an expert is needed; however, he need not become an expert himself, but he must conduct a minimal amount of background work in order that he may intelligently move the court for the need of an expert. **See also _Vick v. Lockhart, 952 F.2d 999 (8th Cir. 1991)_**

Miller v. Wainwright, 798 F.2d 426 (11th Cir. 1986)
Counsel's failure to obtain a forensic pathology expert to rebut the state's expert testimony that the alleged victim was alive when burned may constitute ineffective assistance of counsel.

House v. Balkcom, 725 F.2d 608 (11th Cir. 1984)
Trial counsel's failure to take advantage of state's own scientific test which provided exculpatory evidence constitutes ineffective assistance.

DNA Scientific Testing

Jones v. Wood, 114 F.3d 1002 (9th Cir. 1997)
Trial counsel's failure to test blood on petitioner's clothing or hairs found on his wife's hands and body constitutes ineffective assistance of counsel and required an evidentiary hearing.

Toney v. Gammon, 79 F.3d 693 (8th Cir. 1996)
Habeas petitioner was entitled through discovery to access to state's evidence to conduct DNA and other scientific testing; court's denial of discovery is an abuse of discretion if discovery is indispensable to a fair, rounded development of material facts.

Serology Evidence

Driscoll v. Delo, 71 F.3d 701 (8th Cir. 1995)
Trial counsel's failure to properly handle serology evidence constituted ineffective assistance.

Self-Defense

Smith v. Dretke, 417 F.3d 438, 442-444 (5th Cir. 2005)
Counsel was constitutionally ineffective for failing to call witnesses to testify about the victim's character for violence and aggressive behavior to support the defendant's self-defense theory.

Rolan v. Vaughn, 445 F.3d 671, 683 (3rd Cir. 2006)
Counsel's failure to investigate self-defense theory constituted ineffective assistance of counsel.

Paine v. Massie, 339 F.3d 1194, 1201-1204 (10th Cir. 2003)
Counsel failure to offer expert testimony based on battered woman syndrome (BWS) to support self-defense claim, for murder of abusive husband constituted ineffective assistance of counsel, where self-defense claim required expert witness' testimony that petitioner suffered from battered woman syndrome.

Currier v. U.S., 160 F.Supp. 2d 159, 166 (D. Mass. 2001)
Trial counsel's failure to investigate, prepare and present claim of self-defense which was the only realistic defense available constituted ineffective assistance of counsel.

King v. Kemna, 226 F.3d 981, 989 (9th Cir. 2000)
Counsel's failure to investigate King's mental condition; present evidence to the jury that King suffered from a gunshot wound to the brain with expert testimony regarding the consequences of that injury amounted to ineffective assistance of counsel. Had the jury heard such evidence it would have probably accepted King's self-defense testimony, that he did not knowingly cause or attempt to cause serious injury to his brother.

U.S. v. Span, 75 F.3d 1383 (9th Cir. 1996)
Trial counsel's failure to pursue an affirmative defense of self-defense and request a jury instruction on self-defense in this assault of a federal officer case constituted

ineffective assistance of counsel. **See also** *Weidner v. Wainwright, 708 F.2d 614 (11th Cir. 1983)*; *Gaines v. Hopper, 575 F.2d 1147 (5th Cir. 1978)*; *Chambers v. Armontrout, 885 F.2d 1318 (8th Cir. 1989)*

McConico v. State of Ala., 919 F.2d 1543 (11th Cir. 1990)

James McConico argued that an actual conflict existed where counsel simultaneously represented him in his criminal trial and Brenda McConico in her insurance claim. James McConico contended that counsel faced divided loyalties when he cross-examined his client Brenda McConico at James' trial especially as the matters were so closely related. The insurance policy contained an exclusion clause that denied payment if the policy holder died from "participation in, or as a result of having committing of an assault or felony." At trial, counsel argued that James shot in self-defense, and Morton was the aggressor in the incident that resulted in his death in order for counsel to preserve the insurance proceeds payable upon Morton's death to counsel's second client, Brenda McConico, and to avoid the exclusion clause of the policy. However, counsel was required to take the position in the insurance claim that Morton was not the aggressor in the incident. This position negated James' claim of self-defense. A vigorous defense of James' self-defense claim could have resulted in acquittal which would necessarily have made Morton the aggressor in the shooting incident. Counsel's conduct, by placing himself between two adverse parties and actively representing both, constituted a conflict of interest.

Chambers v. Armontrout, 907 F.2d 825 (8th Cir. 1990)

Trial counsel's failure to call or interview eyewitness whose testimony would corroborate Petitioner's self-defense claim, fell below an objective standard of reasonableness. The Court found prejudice because had counsel called Jones to testify, a self-defense instruction would have been submitted to the jury and counsel would have been permitted to argue self-defense. There was a reasonable probability that the jury might have acquitted Petitioner of capital murder, by either finding him guilty of a lesser charge or by finding that he acted in self-defense. Also, the jury could have credited Jones' testimony at sentencing, and it might not have sentenced Petitioner to death.

Semen Stains Evidence

Dorsey v. Kelly, 112 F.3d 50 (2nd Cir. 1997)

Trial counsel's failure to introduce lab reports of scientific tests on semen found in complainant's underpants, which suggested that semen could <u>not</u> have come exclusively from petitioner, constituted ineffective assistance of counsel. **See also** *Dorsey v. Irvin, 56 F.3d 425 (2nd Cir. 1995)*

Toney v. Gammon, 79 F.3d 693 (8th Cir. 1996)

Trial counsel's failure to obtain defendant's requested blood test in order to exonerate himself from the semen of the assailant blood-type could constitute ineffective assistance and required an evidentiary hearing to resolve the ineffectiveness claim.

Washington v. Murray, 952 F.2d 1472 (4th Cir. 1991)

Trial counsel's failure to develop and present to jury the results of exculpatory laboratory tests on semen stains found on blanket recovered from bed where rape occurred, which showed that the bodily fluids did not come from defendant, entitled defendant to evidentiary hearing to resolve ineffective assistance of counsel claim.

Shoot-Out Defense

Phillips v. Woodford, **267 F.3d 966, 978-81 (9th Cir. 2001)**

Trial counsel's failure to investigate "shoot out" defense, in lieu of alibi defense where counsel had information in his possession at the time of trial, which a "shoot-out" defense to first degree murder could have been fashioned amounted to ineffective assistance of counsel. The shoot-out defense might have led the jury to find that defendant did not form intent to rob until after killing, and therefore that special circumstance for imposition of death penalty that murder was "committed during the commission of robbery," did not apply, and warranted an evidentiary hearing.

Spousal Relationship

Tucker v. Renico, **317 F.Supp. 2d 766, 774-75 (E.D. Mich. 2004)**

Trial counsel was constitutionally ineffective by failing to introduce evidence at trial for criminal sexual conduct and breaking and entering charges, proving that petitioner and victim had a long term spousal relationship, and victim held herself out as petitioner's wife, where said evidence would have been useful for impeachment of the victim testimony.

Tattoo Evidence

Beltran v. Cockrell, **294 F.3d 730, 734-35 (5th Cir. 2002)**

Counsel was constitutionally ineffective for failing to investigate whether codefendant, Rubin Plata, had a tattoo on his upper left arm, and introduce evidence that witnesses had tentatively identified Rubin Plata because of this tattoo. The victim was murdered with a derringer. Rubin Plata had committed an aggravated assault with a derringer four hours before the murder. The fact that Beltran's codefendant had such a tattoo, and had been tentatively identified by witnesses would have cast doubt in the jury's mind, and established counsel's omission were prejudicial.

Time of Death

Helton v. Singletary, **85 F.Supp.2d 1323 (S.D. Fla. 1999)**

Counsel's failure to pursue time of death as a defense strategy constituted ineffective assistance of counsel.

Withdraw From Conspiracy Defense

United States v. United States Gypsum Co., **438 U.S. 442, 57 L.Ed.2d 854, 98 S.Ct. 2864 (1978)**

In order to establish a withdrawal defense to a conspiracy charge, the defendant is only required to establish affirmative acts inconsistent with the object of the conspiracy and to communicate in a manner reasonably calculated to reach co-conspirators are generally regarded as sufficient to establish withdrawal or abandonment.

Trial Ineffectiveness

U.S. v.Johnson, 995 F. Supp. 1259 (D. Kan. 1998)

Trial counsel's failure to pursue defense of lack of intent and withdrawal from conspiracy to distribute phenyl-2-propanone required an evidentiary hearing to resolve ineffective assistance claim.

U.S. v. Martin, 965 F.2d 839 (10th Cir. 1992)

Trial counsel who represented defendant and co-defendant constituted a conflict of interest where counsel refused to present defendant's withdrawal defense from conspiracy due to conflict of interest.

Other Defense/Evidence Claims

Groseclose v. Bell, 130 F.3d 1161 (6th Cir. 1997)

Trial counsel's failure to have any defense theory compounded with other errors constituted ineffective assistance.

Sager v. Maass, 907 F.Supp. 1412 (D. Or. 1995)

Trial counsel's introduction of the entire victim impact statement into evidence as a handwriting sample and as impeachment evidence constituted ineffective assistance of counsel. This blunder alone factually tainted the trial.

Demarest v. Price, 905 F.Supp. 1432 (D.Col. 1995)

Counsel presented an impossible defense theory under existing case law constituted ineffective assistance of counsel.

Scarpa v. Dubois, 38 F.3d 1 (1st Cir. 1994)

Trial counsel pursued a conduit defense in drug case where, under state law, persons who knowingly served as agents or intermediaries in narcotics transaction were punishable as principals constitutes ineffective assistance of counsel.

Vick v. Lockhart, 952 F.2d 999 (8th Cir. 1991)

Trial counsel's failure to present evidence that defendant's water had been turned off to his home at time of the alleged rape where the victim claimed defendant forced her to take bath, constituted ineffective assistance of counsel and required evidentiary hearing.

U.S. v. Cronic, 839 F.2d 1401 (10th Cir. 1988)

Trial counsel's failure to use evidence of security to cover overdrafts and object to improper testimony amounted to ineffective assistance.

FAILED TO OBJECT TO . . .

Kastigar Objection

United States v. Hylton, 294 F.3d 130, 134-36 (D.C. Cir. 2002)

Counsel was constitutionally ineffective for failure to make a *Kastigar* objection to codefendant Wright's testimony. Hylton's "debriefing agreement" with the government prohibited Wright's testimony against Hylton. During Hylton's debriefing he gave the government a range of general information relating how he imported drugs from Jamaica, and specific information concerning his relationship with his co-conspirator, Adrian Wright. Hylton claimed that the government used his debriefing statements to coerce or induce Wright to testify. Counsel's failure to raise the **Kastigar** objection with respect to Wright was simply inexcusable.

Prejudicial Evidence

Sager v. Maass, 907 F.Supp. 1412 (D. Or. 1995)
Trial counsel's failure to object to irrelevant and unduly prejudicial statements which implied that petitioner was a habitual criminal, allowed the prosecution to introduce evidence of defendant's "unsavory character merely to show that he is a bad person and, thus, more likely to have committed the crime" constitutes ineffective assistance of counsel. The Court found that jurors are not likely to remain impartial after hearing evidence which "permits them to believe that acquitting the defendant may mean releasing an exceedingly dangerous" person (quoting *U.S. v. Bland, 908 F.2d 471, 473 (9th Cir. 1990)*).

Clark v. Duckworth, 906 F.2d 1174 (7th Cir. 1990)
Trial counsel's failure to move for a mistrial over Isaac's prejudicial testimony constituted ineffective assistance of counsel and deprived defendant of a fair trial.

Vela v. Estelle, 708 F.2d 954 (5th Cir. 1983)
Defense counsel's failure to object to prejudicial testimony which was used to inflame minds of jury, constitutes ineffective assistance.

United States v. Rusmisel, 716 F.2d 301 (5th Cir. 1983)
Trial counsel's failure to object to inflammatory remarks made by prosecution during closing arguments amounted to ineffective assistance of counsel.

Nero v. Blackburn, 597 F.2d 991 (5th Cir. 1979)
Trial counsel's failure to move for a mistrial based on prosecutorial misconduct for presenting prejudicial remarks to the jury concerning defendant's prior convictions, which evidence was not admissible under Louisiana law, constitutes ineffective assistance of counsel. See also *Lyons v. McCotter, 770 F.2d 529 (5th Cir. 1985).*

Marzullo v. State of MD., 561 F.2d 540 (1977)
Trial counsel's failure to move to exclude the jury during a discussion to dismiss one count of a rape charge, or to request a limiting jury instruction to disregard the prejudicial remarks of the first rape count amounted to ineffective assistance of counsel.

Evidence of Defendant's Tattoos

Boliek v. Delo, 912 F.Supp. 1199 (W.D. Mo. 1995)
Trial counsel's failure to object to the introduction of evidence of defendant's tattoos constituted ineffective assistance.

Juvenile Record

Williams v. Arn, 654 F.Supp. 226 (N.D. Ohio 1986)
Trial counsel's introduction of defendant's prior juvenile criminal record amounted to deficient performance.

Inadmissible Evidence

Parle v. Runnels, 505 F.3d 922, 932 (9th Cir. 2007)
The cumulative effect of two errors, the wrongful admission of Dr. Acenas' testimony, and the erroneous exclusion of portions of Dr. Jackman's rendered Parle's defense "far less persuasive" depriving him of a fair trial and due process warranting habeas relief. The California Court of Appeals decision to the contrary was objectively unreasonable.

Olesen v. Class, 962 F. Supp. 1556 (D.S.D. 1997)
Defense counsel's failure to object to expert testimony that defendant's daughter would not fabricate story of abuse constitutes deficient performance, but no prejudice shown.

U.S. v. Tatum, 943 F.2d 370 (4th Cir. 1991)
Trial counsel's failure to object to admissions of inadmissible evidence due to a conflict of interest demonstrates actual lapses in defense and can constitute ineffective assistance of counsel.

Lombard v. Lynaugh, 868 F.2d 1475 (5th Cir. 1989)
Trial counsel's failure to object to the admission of extraneous armed robbery offense constitutes ineffective assistance of counsel.

Morrison v. Kimmelman, 650 F.Supp. 801 (D.N.J. 1986)
Trial counsel's failure to object to the admission of bed sheets illegally seized evidence from defendant's residence constituted ineffective assistance. **See also** *U.S. Ex. Rel. Henderson v. Brierly*, 300 F.Supp. 638 (E.D. Pa. 1969)

Lyons v. McCotter, 770 F.2d 529 (5th Cir. 1985)
Trial counsel's failure to object to highly inflammatory inadmissible evidence has no strategic value and failure to request a limiting instruction constitutes ineffective assistance of counsel.

United States v. Rusmisel, 716 F.2d 301 (5th Cir. 1983)
Trial counsel's failure to object to the prosecutorial questioning various witnesses about drug usage of defendant constitutes ineffective assistance of counsel.

Child Wouldn't Fabricate Story

Olesen v. Class, 164 F.3d 1096 (8th Cir. 1999)
Defense counsel's performance fell below an objective standard of reasonableness where counsel failed to object to testimony of medical expert that child would not fabricate story of sexual abuse, which usurped jury's function of evaluating credibility of child. However, prejudice was not shown due to court's jury instruction on child's credibility.

Defendant Killed A Cop

Crotts v. Smith, 73 F3d 861 (9th Cir. 1996)

Trial counsel's failure to object, to request a limiting instruction where the prosecution presented highly prejudicial untrue testimony that the defendant made statements that he had " killed a cop", deprived the defendant of due process and constituted ineffective assistance.

Admission of Coerced Statement

Lam v. Kelchner, 304 F.3d 256 (3rd Cir. 2002)

The trial court's admission of petitioner's coerced statements into evidence was not harmless error; given credible threats of violence made by undercover officers because petitioner's statement provided necessary elements of this offense.

Admission of Co-Defendant's Confession-Bruton Violation

Gray v. Maryland, 523 U.S. 185, 140 L.Ed.2d 294, 118 S.Ct. 1151 (1998)

Use of non-testifying codefendant's redacted confession at trial, with defendant's name replaced with obvious indications of alteration, held to violate rule of **_Bruton v. United States._**

Wenglikowski v. Jones, 306 F.Supp. 2d 688, 701-03 (E.D. Mich. 2004)

Trial court's failure to suppress a nontestifying accomplice's confession was "contrary to" clearly established Supreme Court precedent **_Douglas v. State of Alabama_, 380 U.S. 415, 85 S.Ct. 1074, 13 L.Ed.2d 934 (1965)**, at the time of petitioner's conviction; the accomplice was tried separately for the same crimes, which renders his confession prejudicial to petitioner. Admitting the accomplice's confession before the jury, without being subjected to cross-examination violates the Confrontation Clause of the United States Constitution.

Bulls v. Jones, 274 F.3d 329, 335 (6th Cir. 2001)

The state's introduction of **_Hill's_** statement, a non testifying codefendant, which tended to shift blame to Bulls violated the confrontation clause and had a substantial and injurious effect on the jury's determination of verdict in felony murder trial and warranted habeas relief.

Henry v. Scully, 78 F.3d 51 (2nd Cir. 1996)

Trial counsel's failure to object to admissions of co-defendant's confession as evidence against defendant constituted ineffective assistance of counsel.

Williams v. Washington, 59 F.3d 673 (7th Cir. 1995)

Trial counsel's failure to take appropriate measures to limit the use of a co-defendant's confession or to attempt to have the statement redrafted to eliminate any reference to defendant constitutes ineffective assistance.

Admission of Expert's Testimony on Bite-Mark

Ege v. Yukins, 380 F.Supp.2d 852, 880 (E.D. Mich. 2005)
Counsel's failure to object to the admission of Dr. Warnick's erroneous testimony that the bite-mark on murder victim's cheek belonged to petitioner constituted ineffective assistance of counsel.

Admission of 911 Taped Recording

Sager v. Maass, 907 F.Supp. 1412 (D. Or. 1995)
Trial counsel's failure to object to the admission of the taped 911 telephone call and move to delete inflammatory reference to petitioner constituted ineffective assistance of counsel.

Atomic Absorption Test

Chatom v. White, 858 F.2d 1479 (11th Cir. 1988)
Trial counsel's failure to object to introduction of atomic absorption test results constituted ineffective assistance of counsel because under the conditions which test's results occurred were questionable, and defendant's guilt beyond a reasonable doubt was a close call.

Hypnotically Induced Testimony

Pruett v. Norris, 959 F. Supp 1066 (E. Ark. 1997)
Hypnotically induced testimony by bank teller who was a witness to robbery and murder violated defendant's right under confrontation clause.

Prosecutor's Failure to Produce Witness

Hicks v. Straub, 239 F.Supp. 2d 697, 711-13 (E.D. Mich. 2003)
Counsel was constitutionally ineffective by failing to object to the prosecutor's failure to produce Mr. Brand as a witness, where the prosecutor claimed, during opening statements to the jury, that petitioner confessed to committing the crime to Mr. Brand, which violated petitioner's right to confrontation.

Taped Conversation

Eslaminia v. White, 136 F.3d 1234 (9th Cir. 1998)
The court held that jury's consideration of taped interview between police and defendant's brother that was not admitted into evidence had substantial and injurious effect on the verdict warranting habeas corpus relief.

Government of Virgin Islands v. Nicholas, 759 F.2d 1073 (3rd Cir. 1985)
Trial counsel's failure to object to testimony concerning incriminating statements, presumably to have been made by defendant in taped conversation with government informant required an evidentiary hearing to resolve the claim of ineffective assistance of counsel. See also *Whelchel v. Wood*, 996 F. Supp. 1019 (E.D. Wash. 1997).

United States v. Baynes, 687 F.2d 659 (3rd Cir. 1982)
> Trial counsel's failure to investigate possibilities of distinguishing exemplar of defendant's voice from voice on intercepted tape recording, where intercepted tape recording was the only evidence against defendant amounted to ineffective assistance of counsel.

Pinnell v. Cauthorn, 540 F.2d 938 (8th Cir. 1976)
> Trial counsel's failure to move to suppress tape recordings that discussed defendant's prior conviction and object to the admission of the tapes into evidence amounted to ineffective assistance of counsel.

Specific Objections Requested by Defendant

Government of Virgin Islands v. Forte, 865 F.2d 59 (3rd Cir. 1989)
> Trial counsel's failure to make a specific objection that was specifically requested by the defendant amounted to ineffective assistance of counsel.

Defendant's Post Arrest Silence/Statments

Girts v. Yani, 501 F.3d 743, 757 (6th Cir. 2007)
> Trial counsel provided constitutionally ineffective assistance for failing to object to the prosecutor's improper and prejudicial statements concerning Girts' failure to testify and exercising his Fifth Amendment right to remain silent.

Combs v. Coyle, 205 F.3d 269 (6th Cir. 2000)
> Failure to object to the prosecution's use of defendant's statement at the scene of the crime, where defendant told police officer to talk to his lawyer violated the defendant's Fifth Amendment Right against self- incrimination and amounted to ineffective assistance of counsel.

Freeman v. Class, 95 F.3d 639 (8th Cir. 1996)
> Trial counsel's failure to object or move for a mistrial based on prosecutor's improper comments regarding defendant's exercise of right to remain silent constitutes ineffective assistance of counsel.

Gravley v. Mills, 87 F3d 779 (6th Cir. 1996)
> Trial counsel's failure to object to prosecution's improper comments concerning defendant's post arrest silence where jury could infer that defendant's failure to assert his story earlier was evidence of guilty constitutes ineffective assistance of counsel.

Noland v. Dixon, 808 F.Supp. 485 (W.D.N.C. 1992)
> Counsel's failure to object to the introduction of evidence concerning petitioner's exercise of his right to remain silent required an evidentiary hearing to resolve ineffectiveness of counsel claim.

Martire v. Wainwright, 811 F.2d 1430 (11th Cir. 1987)
> Appellant counsel's failure to raise issue of improper admission of evidence concerning comments of defendant's post-arrest silence was prejudicial in light of state court rule of automatic reversal.

Exclusion of Absent Witness's Grand Jury Testimony

Phan v. Greiner, 165 F.Supp.2d 385, 401 (E.D.N.Y. 2001)
> The State court's exclusion of absent witness's grand jury testimony deprived petitioner of his right to present a defense and required granting habeas corpus relief.

Exclusion of Prior Sexual Relations

Smelcher v. Attorney General of Alabama, 947 F.2d 1472 (11th Cir. 1991)
> Trial counsel was ineffective in failing to object to the state court's exclusion of evidence of prior sexual relations between defendant and the rape victim and warranted an evidentiary hearing.

Hearsay Evidence

Wallace v. Price, 265 F.Supp. 2d 543, 552-553 (W.D. Pa. 2003)
> The trial court erred refusing to admit the testimony of the codefendant's girlfriend, under the hearsay exception rule for prior inconsistent statement. The codefendant's testimony was instrumental in the state securing a conviction against the defendant. The codefendant made a statement to his girlfriend, that he shot the victim. The jury should have been afforded an opportunity to hear the codefendant's statements to his girlfriend to scrutinize the codefendant's testimony. The trial court's exclusion of the codefendant's girlfriend testimony deprived the defendant of a fair trial and warranted habeas relief.

Gray v. Klauser, 282 F.3d 633, 647-48 (9th Cir. 2002)
> The trial court used two different analytical frameworks in considering the admissibility of the state's and defendants proffered hearsay statements, which resulted in admission of statements favoring state and exclusion of statements offered by the defendant. This type of action denied the defendant his fundamental right to present a defense and to present witnesses.

Gochicoa v. Johnson, 53 F.Supp. 2d 943 (W.D. Tex. 1999)
> Counsel's failure to object to hearsay statements made by an informant, which implicated defendant in the crime, constituted ineffective assistance of counsel.

Mason v. Hanks, 97 F.3d 887 (7th Cir. 1996)
> Appellate counsel's failure to raise issue of inadmissible hearsay of informant's out-of-court statements that defendant was dealing heroin where the issue was preserved for review constitutes ineffective assistance of counsel.

Henry v. Scully, 78 F.3d 51 (2nd Cir. 1996)
> Trial counsel's failure to object to hearsay testimony explaining reasons why defendant did not possess drugs constituted ineffective assistance of counsel.

Mason v. Scully, 16 F.3d 38 (2nd Cir. 1994)
> Trial counsel's failure to object to the state's introduction of hearsay statements of non-testifying co-defendants constituted ineffective assistance of counsel where there was no physical evidence that implicated the defendant. There existed a reasonable probability

that the outcome of the trial would have been different, absent counsel's unprofessional errors and omissions.

Bolander v. State of Iowa, 978 F.2d 1079 (8th Cir. 1992)
Trial counsel's failure to object to introduction of hearsay evidence, which was principal evidence on premeditation element, constitutes ineffective assistance. **See also *Harris v. Housewright, 697 F.2d 202 (8th Cir. 1982); Hollines v. Estelle, 569 F.Supp. 146 (W.D. Tex. 1983); Gaines v. Thieret, 846 F.2d 402 (7th Cir. 1988)***

Prejudicial Remarks Made by Prosecutor

Hodge v. Hurley, 426 F.3d 368, 387 (6th Cir. 2005)
Counsel was constitutionally ineffective for failing to object to prosecutorial misconduct calculated to cast Hodge in a negative light and bolster Fenn's credibility, that likely affected the jury's verdict.

Dubria v. Smith, 197 F.3d 390 (9th Cir. 1999)
Trial counsel's failure to object to the prosecutor's inflammatory statements that the defendant was a "Piece of garbage" and "The biggest liar you've ever encountered" constituted ineffective assistance of counsel.

Lombard v. Lynaugh, 868 F.2d 1475 (5th Cir. 1989)
Trial counsel's failure to object to the trial court and the prosecutor's comments by reading to the jury the indictment that showed Lombard's prior convictions, which revealed Lombard was a habitual offender constitutes ineffective assistance of counsel. Likewise, appellate counsel's failure to raise trial counsel's ineffectiveness amounted to ineffective assistance.

U.S. v. Wolf, 787 F.2d 1094 (7th Cir. 1986)
Trial counsel's failure to object to improper and inflammatory remarks by the prosecution used to show defendant's bad character constitutes ineffective assistance of counsel. **See also *United States v. Rusmisel, 716 F.2d 301 (5th Cir. 1983); Seehan v. State of Iowa, 37 F.3d 389 (8th Cir. 1994)***

Lyons v. McCotter, 770 F.2d 529 (5th Cir. 1985)
Defense counsel's failure to object to the prosecutor's allusion in closing argument to Lyons' propensity to commit aggravated robbery in light of his prior conviction for a similar crime, and his failure to seek a limiting jury instruction constituted ineffective assistance of counsel. **See also *Weygandt v. Ducharme, 774 F.2d 1491 (9th Cir. 1985)***

Marzullo v. State of MD., 561 F.2d 540 (1977)
Trial counsel's failure to object and move for a new jury panel, when the prosecutor dismissed one of the two rape charges, after the alleged victim could not identify the defendant, constituted ineffective assistance of counsel.

Prejudicial Remarks Made by Court

Porcaro v. United States, 784 F.2d 38 (1st Cir. 1986)
Trial counsel's failure to object to improper comments and prejudicial remarks made by trial court may constitute ineffective assistance of counsel.

Advocate-Witness Rule

U. S. v. Sayakhom, 186 F.3d 928 (9th Cir. 1999)
The "advocate-witness rule" prohibits an attorney from appearing as both a witness and an advocate in the same litigation.

Prosecutor Misconduct for Acting as Witness

Walker v. Davis, 840 F.2d 834 (11th Cir. 1988)
The Court held that: (1) Prosecutor's misconduct in acting as both witness and prosecutor in murder proceeding was so egregious and prejudicial to fair trial as to undermine confidence in its outcome; and (2) evidentiary hearing was required to determine whether habeas corpus petitioner had cause for procedural default in failing to object at trial to district attorney's misconduct in acting as both witness and prosecutor. Remanded.

Prosector Threatening Witness

Earp v. Ornoski, 431 F.3d 1158, 1170-1171 (9th Cir. 2005)
Prosecutorial misconduct claim required an evidentiary hearing because of the prosecutor threatening and verbally abusing witness Taylor, fed him an untrue story, forced him to recant the impeaching statement by Morgan on tape, and punished Taylor for assisting Earp by having Taylor removed from his job as a trustee and transferred to a less desirable jail.

Hemstreet v. Greiner, 367 F.3d 135, 140-41 (2nd Cir. 2004)
Counsel was constitutionally ineffective for failing to pursue issue of state's intimidation of a crucial defense witness; to secure testimony of defense witness through subpoena because witness' testimony would have offered significant exculpatory information that could have led the jury to acquit petitioner.

U.S. v. Aguilar, 90 F.Supp.2d 1152 (D. Col. 2000)
Prosecutor's statements to defense witness' that government might void witnesses plea agreement and reinstate previously dismissed charges unless he invoked his Fifth Amendment privilege against self-incrimination, deprived defendant of his right to due process and compulsory process.

Prosecutor Vouching for Witness

Kindler v. Horn, 291 F.Supp.2d 323, 361-364 (E.D. Pa. 2003)
Prosecutor's comments during closing arguments of penalty phase that it was the position of District Attorney's Office to seek death penalty against petitioner, but not against codefendant constituted improper vouching that required reversal.

Prosecution's Use of Two Conflicting Theories

Stumpf v. Mitchell, 367 F.3d 594, 611 (6th Cir. 2004)
Prosecution's use of two conflicting theories concerning shooter's identity to convict petitioner and accomplice of same aggravated murder violates due process.

Multiplicitous Indictment

U.S. v. Weathers, 186 F.3d 948 (D.C. Cir. 1999)
> Counsel's failure to object an indictment that was improperly multiplicitous warranted an evidentiary hearing to resolve claim of ineffective assistance of counsel.

Videotaped Testimony of Incarcerated Witness

Brumley v. Wingard, 269 F.3d 629 (6th Cir. 2001)
> Videotaped deposition testimony of incarcerated witness where witness indicated petitioner handed revolver to shooter and told shooter to "waste" victim, and testified about the shooting itself, violated the Sixth Amendment Confrontation Clause and warranted habeas relief.

Due Process Violation

Thomas v. Calderon, 120 F.3d 1045 (9th Cir. 1997)
> The State's prosecutor pursuit of fundamentally inconsistent theories in separate trials of defendants charged with same murder violated due process and required reversal.

Incriminating Statements

Government of Virgin Islands v. Nicholas, 759 F.2d 1073 (3rd Cir. 1985)
> Trial counsel's failure to object to testimony concerning incriminating statements, presumably to have been made by defendant in taped conversation with government informant, may constitute ineffective assistance of counsel and required an evidentiary hearing to resolve the claim.

Henry v. Scully, 78 F.3d 51 (2nd Cir. 1996)
> Trial counsel's failure to object to admissions of co-defendant's confession as evidence against defendant constituted ineffective assistance of counsel.

Improper Predicate Offense

Summit v. Blackburn, 795 F.2d 1237 (5th Cir. 1986)
> Trial counsel's failure to object to lack of corroborating evidence of attempted armed robbery that formed the basis of aggravating felony needed for first-degree murder conviction constituted ineffective assistance.

Court Directing Verdict Against Defendant

Hardin v. Davis, 878 F.2d 1341 (11th Cir. 1989)
> Trial counsel's failure to object when district judge directed verdict against defendant constituted ineffective assistance of counsel per se, without a showing of prejudice.

Directed Jury to Continue Deliberation After Reaching a
Verdict on a Lesser Included Charge

Colin v. v. Lampert, 233 F.Supp. 2d 1293, 1302-03 (D. Or. 2002)
> Counsel's failure to object to the trial court's directing the jury to continue deliberations on charge of first degree kidnapping, after the jury had rendered their guilty verdict on the lesser included offense, and to object to trial court's receipt of the subsequent guilty verdict on the charge offense constituted ineffective assistance.

Other Objectionable Problems

Groseclose v. Bell, 130 F.3d 1161 (6th Cir. 1997)
> Trial counsel's failure to conduct any meaningful adversarial challenge, as shown by his failure to cross-examine more than half of the prosecution's witness or object to any evidence, constituted ineffective assistance.

U.S. v. Hansel, 70 F.3d 6 (2nd Cir. 1995)
> Trial counsel's failure to object to specific counts of the indictment which were barred by statute of limitations constitutes ineffective assistance of counsel.

U.S. v. Myers, 892 F.2d 642 (7th Cir. 1990)
> Trial counsel's failure to object to suggestive photo lineup, after fourteen months, may constitute ineffective assistance of counsel.

Rice v. Marshall, 816 F.2d 1126 (6th Cir. 1987)
> Trial counsel's failure to object at second trial to the introduction of the handgun into evidence constitutes ineffective assistance of counsel.

Miller v. Wainwright, 798 F.2d 426 (11th Cir. 1986)
> Trial counsel's failure to object to court's failure to define sexual battery as the underlying felony in the felony murder charge may constitute ineffective assistance.

Summit v. Blackburn, 795 F.2d 1237 (5th Cir. 1986)
> Trial counsel's failure to object to lack of corroborating evidence of attempted armed robbery that formed the basis of aggravating felony needed for first-degree murder conviction constituted ineffective assistance.

Counsel "Opened Door" For Prejudicial Testimony

Berryman v. Morton, 100 F.3d 1089 (3rd Cir. 1996)
> Counsel was ineffective for "opening door" to admission of testimony concerning co-defendant robbing a bank and homicide investigation.

FAILED TO MOVE FOR A MISTRIAL

Freeman v. Class, 95 F.3d 639 (8th Cir. 1996)
> Trial counsel's failure to object or move for a mistrial based on prosecutor's improper comments regarding defendants exercise of right to remain silent constitutes ineffective assistance of counsel.

Clark v. Duckworth, 906 F.2d 1174 (7th Cir. 1990)
> Trial counsel's failure to move for a mistrial over Isaac's prejudicial testimony deprived defendant of a fair trial and constituted ineffective assistance of counsel.

Crowe v. Sowders, 864 F.2d 430 (6th Cir. 1988)
> Trial counsel's failure to object or move for a mistrial, or file a motion for a new trial after the judge erroneously instructed jury based on parole "consequences", which was not a matter for the jury, constituted ineffective assistance of counsel.

Harris v. Housewright, 697 F.2d 202 (8th Cir. 1982)
> Trial counsel failure to object to hearsay evidence, move for a mistrial and failure to object to improper prejudicial comments by the prosecutor amounted to ineffective assistance of counsel.

Nero v. Blackburn, 597 F.2d 991 (5th Cir. 1979)
> Trial counsel's failure to move for a mistrial based on prosecutorial misconduct for presenting prejudicial remarks to the jury concerning defendant's prior convictions, which evidence was not admissible under Louisiana law, constitutes ineffective assistance of counsel.

Cross v. United States, 392 F.2d 360 (8th Cir. 1968)
> Trial counsel failed to subpoena any witnesses, failed to prepare for trial because the defendant did not pay him all his money, and claimed his own ineffectiveness in a motion for mistrial warranted an evidentiary hearing.

FAILED TO PRESERVE ERROR

Kimmelman v. Morrison, 477 U.S. 365, 91 L.Ed.2d 305, 106 S.Ct. 2574 (1986)
> The Supreme Court explained that an attorney who chooses to default a Fourth Amendment claim, he also loses the opportunity to obtain direct review under the harmless error standard of *Chapman v. California*, 386 U.S. 18, 17 L.Ed.2d 705, 87 S.Ct. 824 (1967), which requires the State to prove that the defendant was not prejudiced by the error. By defaulting, counsel shifts the burden to the defendant to prove that there exists a reasonable probability that, absent his attorney's incompetence, he would not have been convicted. *Id.* 477 U.S. 383 footnote 7.

U.S. v. Matos, 905 F.2d 30 (2nd Cir. 1990)
> Trial counsel's failure to file suppression motion and preserve issue for review on appeal may constitute ineffective assistance of counsel and requires a remand.

Government of Virgin Islands v. Forte, 865 F.2d 59 (3rd Cir. 1989)
> Trial counsel's ineffectiveness for failing to preserve error denied defendant just result on appeal. **See also** *Lyons v. McCotter*, 770 F.2d 529 (5th Cir. 1985); *Hollines v. Estelle*, 569 F.Supp. 146 (W.D. Tex. 1983)

Hawkins v. Lynaugh, 862 F.2d 482 (5th Cir. 1988)
> Trial counsel's failure to preserve the *Franklin-Penny* arguments for appeal constitutes ineffective assistance. **See also** *Vela v. Estelle*, 708 F.2d 954 (5th Cir. 1983)

Pecuniary Gain Evidence

Starr v. Lockhart, 23 F.3d 1280 (8th Cir. 1994)

Trial counsel's failure to object to either "pecuniary gain" or "heinous atrocious or cruel" aggravating circumstances jury instructions during penalty phase, amounted to ineffective assistance of counsel.

Snell v. Lockhart, 791 F.Supp. 1363 (E.D. Ark. 1992)

Trial counsel's failure to object to "pecuniary gain" during penalty phase of capital murder trial, amounted to ineffective assistance.

Prejudicial Ex Parte Information Provided to Court

Osborn v. Shillinger, 861 F.2d 612 (10th Cir. 1988)

Defense counsel's performance was not only ineffective, but counsel abandoned the required duty of loyalty to his client; counsel did not simply make poor strategic or tactical choices; he acted with reckless disregard for his client's best interest and, apparently, with the intention to weaken his client's case.

Due Process Requirements

Scott v. Anderson, 58 F.Supp.2d 767 (N.D. Ohio 1998)

The trial court's incorrect jury instruction during sentencing phase of capital trial, that jurors had to unanimously recommend life rendered the imposition of death sentence unconstitutionally unfair violating Scott's Fourteenth Amendment Right to be free from deprivation of life without due process of law.

Porter v. Singletary, 49 F.3d 1483 (11th Cir. 1995)

Sentencing judge's lack of impartiality satisfies prejudice prong for hearing.

U.S. v. Pugliese, 805 F.2d 1117,1123 (2d Cir. 1986)

The Fifth Amendment Due Process Clause requires defendant not be sentenced on basis of "materially untrue" assumptions or "misinformation."

Closing Arguments in Penalty Phase/Reasons For Sparing Defendant's Life

Marshall v. Hendricks, 313 F.Supp.2d 423, 455-456 (D. N.J. 2004)

Counsel was constitutionally ineffective during penalty phase for failure to investigate, present witnesses who were available to asked jury to spare defendant's life, and to testify concerning the impact that the defendant's execution would have on family, where defendant was charged with killing his wife.

Callahan v. Haley, 313 F.Spp.2d 1252, 1265 (N.D. Ala. 2004)

Counsel was constitutionally ineffective for failure to investigate, present mitigating evidence from defendant's mother, who would have testified about petitioner's father being abusive, alcoholic man who was a Golden Glove boxer, and had chased petitioner with a knife and physically abused him as a child. This would have explained petitioner's dysfunctional upbringing and paranoid personally disorder and his cognitive defects and presented reasons for sparing defendant's life to the jury which recommended his death.

Smith v. Stewart, 140 F.3d 1263 (9th Cir. 1998)

Trial counsel's failure to present mitigating evidence of defendant's sociopathic personality, thereby showing a mitigating factor to avoid death penalty, constitutes ineffective assistance of counsel.

Abdur Rahman v. Bell, 999 F. Supp. 1073 (M.D. Tenn. 1998)

Defense counsel's failure to investigate defendant's background and mental history constituted ineffective assistance of counsel where there was reasonable probability that at least one juror would have voted for life imprisonment as opposed to death sentence.

Dobbs v. Turpin, 142 F.3d 1383 (11th Cir. 1998)

Defense counsel's closing arguments, which likely minimized the jury's responsibility for determining the appropriateness of the death penalty, failed to focus on defendant's case in specific and failed to request mercy from the jury to spare defendant's life constitutes ineffective assistance of counsel.

Hall v. Washington, 106 F.3d 742 (7th Cir. 1997)

Trial counsel's failure to present any reasons during closing arguments, other than blatant disregard of state law for sparing defendant's life, constituted ineffective assistance of counsel. **See also _Mathis v. Zant_, 704 F.Supp. 1062 (N.D.Ga. 1989)**

Harris By and Through Ramseyer v. Wood, 64 F.3d 1432 (9th Cir. 1995)

Trial counsel's argument during guilt phase that defendant was a liar and thief in first-degree murder trial constituted ineffective assistance.

Wade v. Calderon, 29 F.3d 1312 (9th Cir. 1994)

Defense counsel's closing argument to the jury that executing the defendant would free him of his mental illness amounted to a breakdown in the adversarial perches and constituted ineffective assistance of counsel.

Waters v. Zant, 979 F.2d 1473 (11th Cir. 1992)

Defense counsel's presentation of closing arguments during penalty phase was ineffective assistance of counsel, where counsel requested jury to allow defendant to be studied as specimen by those interested in mental illnesses, instead of pleading for mercy.

Noland v. Dixon, 808 F.Supp. 485 (W.D.N.C. 1992)

Counsel's failure to prepare to present arguments for second-degree murder charge amounted to ineffective assistance of counsel.

Kwan Fai Mak v. Blodgett, 754 F.Supp. 1490 (W.D. Wash. 1991)

Trial counsel's failure to present mitigating evidence, at penalty phase of capital murder prosecution, was prejudicial and constituted ineffective assistance of counsel, in light of the fact that co-defendant convicted of 13 murders did not receive the death penalty, and the prosecutor's closing argument focused on counsel's failure to present any positive human qualities in the defendant. **See also _Douglas v. Wainwright_, 714 F.2d 1532 (11th Cir. 1983)**

State And Federal Sentences To Be Served Concurrently

U.S. v. Smith, *101 F.Supp.2d 332 (W.D. Pa. 2000)*
Defense counsel's failure to move to continue federal sentencing hearing until pending state charges had been prosecuted to completion and sentences imposed so that court would be able to run the federal sentence concurrent to state sentence or failing to request that court to make a non- binding recommendation to the Bureau of Prisons to run the federal sentence concurrent to any state sentence on the pending state charges required an evidentiary hearing to resolve the ineffective assistance of counsel claim.

Lesser Included Offense

U.S. v. McDonald, *981 F.Supp. 942 (D.Md. 1997)*
Counsel's failure to object to defendant being sentenced to bank robbery which was lesser included offense of armed robbery required the sentence to be vacated on the lesser included offense and constituted ineffective assistance.

Victims Good Character Evidence

Vela v. Estelle, *708 F.2d 954 (5th Cir. 1983)*
Defense counsel, in murder prosecution, allowed the jury to hear evidence of victim's "good character" at sentencing, which was not material, resulting in actual and substantial disadvantage to defendant and constitutes ineffective assistance.

PRIOR CONVICTION RELATED INEFFECTIVENESS

Burgett v. Texas, *389 U.S. 109, 19 L.Ed.2d, 319, 88 S.Ct. 258 (1967)*
During the course of Burgett's trial, while the jury was present, the state offered into evidence a certified copy of one of the Tennessee convictions. The conviction read, in part, "Came the Assistant Attorney General for the State and the Defendant in proper person and without counsel." Burgett's counsel objected to the introduction of the record on the ground that the judgment, on its face, showed that Burgett was not represented by counsel, in violation of the Fourteenth Amendment. The state court admitted the Tennessee prior conviction into evidence but instructed the jury not to consider the prior offenses for any purpose whatsoever in arriving at the verdict.

Burgett filed a motion for new trial, which was denied. The Court of Appeals for the State of Texas affirmed the conviction. *(397 S.W.2d 79)*. The United States Supreme Court granted certiorari and reversed finding that the records of the Tennessee prior conviction raised a presumption that Burgett, in the Tennessee prosecution, had been denied his right to counsel under the Sixth Amendment that was made applicable to the states by the Fourteenth Amendment, and therefore, that Tennessee conviction was void. The Supreme Court also found that the admission into evidence in the Texas case of the second record of Tennessee conviction, in effect, resulted in Burgett's suffering a new deprivation of his Sixth Amendment right, which was inherently prejudicial, requiring reversal of the Texas conviction, even though the enhanced punishment had not been imposed and even though the Texas trial court had instructed the jury not to consider the prior offense for any purpose.

**United States v. Russell**, *221 F.3d 615, 621 (4th Cir. 2000)*
> Counsel was constitutionally ineffective by failing to investigate or confirm the status of two of Russell's three prior convictions used to impeach Russell's credibility, after Russe11 informed counsel that convictions had been "overturned" and were invalid, counsel could have verified that convictions had been vacated because Russell's credibility was paramount to the jury's deliberation.

**Strachan v. Army Clemency and Parole BD.**, *151 F.3d 1308 (10th Cir. 1998)*
> District court's findings that inmate's state court conviction was counseled was clearly erroneous where court relied on petitioner's plea agreement which contained a location for counsel's signature, but there was no signature of counsel and petitioner was entitled to hearing to determine the validity of conviction.

**Abdur Rahman v. Bell**, *999 F. Supp. 1073 (M.D. Tenn. 1998)*
> Defense counsel's failure to investigate defendant's prior murder conviction where evidence existed to mitigate prior murder conviction constituted ineffective assistance of counsel.

**Berryman v. Morton**, *100 F.3d 1089 (3rd Cir. 1996)*
> Counsel was ineffective for "opening door" to admission of testimony concerning co-defendant robbing a bank and homicide investigation.

**Lombard v. Lynaugh**, *868 F.2d 1475 (5th Cir. 1989)*
> Trial counsel's failure to object to the admission of extraneous armed robbery offense constitutes ineffective assistance of counsel. **See also** _**Pinnell v. Cauthorn**_, *540 F.2d 938 (8th Cir. 1976)*

**Blackburn v. Foltz**, *828 F.2d 1177 (6th Cir. 1987)*
> Trial counsel's failure to move to suppress three prior armed robbery convictions constituted ineffective assistance.

**Lyons v. McCotter**, *770 F.2d 529 (5th Cir. 1985)*
> Defense counsel's failure to object at the proper time to the introduction of Lyon's prior conviction, or to seek to limit the use by requesting a limiting jury instruction of such evidence constituted constitutionally deficient assistance of counsel.

**Williams v. Arn**, *654 F.Supp. 226 (N.D. Ohio 1986)*
> Trial counsel's introduction of defendant's prior juvenile criminal record amounted to deficient performance.

**Douglas v. Wainwright**, *714 F.2d 1532 (11th Cir. 1983)*
> Trial and appellate counsel's failure to raise fact that defendant's prior conviction used was invalid constitutes ineffective assistance of counsel.

**United States v. Bosch**, *584 F.2d 1113 (1st Cir. 1978)*
> Trial counsel's failure to move to redact a statement attached to motion concerning defendant's prior convictions before submitting the document to the jury was ineffective assistance of counsel.

FAILED TO CHALLENGE COMPETENCY OF WITNESS

Medina v. Diguglielmo, 461 F.3d 417, 429-433 (4th Cir. 2006)
> Trial counsel's performance was deficient for failing to object to the state's 12 year old witness's competency under Pennsylvania law, but there was no prejudiced shown because of overwhelming evidence of guilt.

LAWYER SKIPS MULTIPLE DAYS OF TRIAL

United States v. Patterson, 215 F.3d 776, 786 (7th Cir. 2000)
> Defendant whose lawyer skipped multiple days of trial where client had not agreed to substitute representation constitutes a denial of counsel.

FAILED TO CONSULT WITH DEFENDANT

Mitchell v. Mason, 257 F.3d 554, 566 (6th Cir. 2001)
> Defense counsel's failure to consult with client prior to trial violates the defendant's Sixth Amendment right to counsel during a critical stage of the proceedings and prejudiced is presumed.

Crandell v. Bunnell, 144 F.3d 1213 (9th Cir. 1998)
> Defense counsel's failure to confer with defendant, to seek discovery, to investigate crime charged or to interview witnesses, or to develop a working relationship with defendant in capital case amounted to incompetent representation and required appointment substitute of counsel. **See also *Noland v. Dixon*, 808 F.Supp. 485 (W.D.N.C. 1992)**; *Hollines v. Estelle*, 569 F.Supp. 146 (W.D. Tex. 1983)

White v. Godinez, 143 F.3d 1049 (7th Cir. 1998)
> Counsel's failure to consult with petitioner resulted in counsel's poor understanding of case and constitutes ineffective assistance of counsel.

Harris By and Through Ramseyer v. Wood, 64 F.3d 1432 (9th Cir. 1995)
> Trial counsel's failure to consult adequately with defendant amounted to ineffectiveness of counsel.

Douglas v. Wainwright, 739 F.2d 531 (11th Cir. 1984)
> Trial counsel's failure to consult with defendant and inform him of option of taking stand and testifying in his own behalf at sentencing amounted to ineffective assistance of counsel and required an evidentiary hearing.

United States v. Tucker, 716 F.2d 576 (9th Cir. 1983)
> Trial counsel's failure to consult with defendant during trial due to the complexity of the case and defendant's knowledge of the documentary evidence and witnesses amounted to ineffective assistance. **See also *Jones v. Jones*, 988 F. Supp. 1000 (E.D.La. 1997)**

JURY MISCONDUCT RELATED INEFFECTIVENESS

Cannon v. Mullin, 383 F.3d 1152, 1177 (10th Cir. 2004)
Counsel's failure to inform the Court of improper jury contact warranted an evidentiary hearing.

Fields v. Woodford, 281 F.3d 963, 974 (9th Cir. 2002)
Juror in rape, murder and robbery trial, concealed material facts and gave misleading answer relating to kidnap, robbery, and rape of his wife and the fact that the jurors wife had discussions with juror during the trial concerning facts of the case, and wife suspected that her accoster may have been the defendant required an evidentiary hearing to determine jury bias.

Davidson v. U.S., 951 F. Supp. 555 (W.D. Pa. 1996)
Trial counsel who was aware of juror misconduct and failed to advise trial court that juror had started its deliberation prior to the close of evidence constitutes ineffective assistance of counsel.

Government of Virgin Islands v. Weatherwax, 20 F.3d 572 (3rd Cir. 1994)
Trial counsel's failure to seek voir dire of jurors who were exposed to newspaper article, which distorted defendant's trial testimony, constitutes ineffective assistance of counsel and required an evidentiary hearing.

Robison v. Maynard, 829 F.2d 1501 (10th Cir. 1987)
Appellant's counsel's failure to raise issue of prosecutorial misconduct in state appeal required an evidentiary hearing where Oklahoma court granted other defendants relief from same kind of conduct by same prosecutor.

Attempting to Bribe a Verdict

Remmer v. United States, 347 U.S. 227, 228, 74 S.Ct. 450, 98 L.Ed.654 (1954)
The Court ordered an evidentiary hearing where an unnamed person had allegedly told juror that the juror could "profit by bringing in a verdict favorable to the petitioner." Without notifying the defense, the state trial court sent in an FBI Agent to investigate the juror during the trial before the verdict. **_Remmer_, 347 U.S. at 228, 74 S.Ct. 450.** The petitioner was subsequently convicted. Id. The Supreme Court criticized the trial court's unilateral handling of this issue and ordered an inquiry "with all interested parties permitted to participate." **Id. at 230, 74 S.Ct. 450.**

Biased Jurors

Williams v. Taylor, 529 U.S. 420, 440-41, 120 S.Ct. 1479, 1492-93, 146 L.Ed.2d 435 (2000)
Evidentiary hearing required to determine juror bias because of her failure to disclose during voir dire that she had formerly been married to a prosecution witness, and she had been represented in her divorce by one of the prosecutors, and to determine whether the prosecutor committed misconduct by failing to disclose his knowledge of the juror's possible bias.

Trial Ineffectiveness

Smith v. Phillips, 455 U.S. 209, 215, 102 S.Ct. 940, 71 L.Ed.2d 78 (1982)
> The remedy for allegations of juror partiality is a hearing at which the defendant has the opportunity to prove actual basis.

Miller v. Webb, 385 F.3d 666, 677 (6th Cir. 2004)
> Counsel's failure to object to empaneling an actual biased jury was presumptively prejudicial constituting ineffective assistance.

Fields v. Woodford, 281 F.3d 963, 975 (9th Cir. 2002)
> Evidentiary hearing required to determine juror bias where juror in rape, murder and robbery trial failed to disclose that his wife had been raped during a robbery.

Fields v. Woodford, 309 F.3d 1095, 1105-1106 (9th Cir. 2002)
> Evidentiary hearing was required to determine whether juror intentionally concealed fact that his wife had been raped during robbery-rape trial, which hid juror's bias against the defendant.

Dyer v. Calderon, 151 F.3d 970 (9th Cir. 1998)
> A biased juror's presence cannot be harmless error; it requires a new trial without a showing of prejudice because it amounts to a structural defect under *Arizona v. Fulminante, 499 U.S. 279, 307-10, 111 S.Ct. 1246, 113 L.Ed. 2d 302 (1991),* which is not subject to harmless error analysis.

U.S. v. Lawhorne, 29 F.Supp. 2d 292 (E.D. Va. 1998)
> Juror and prosecutor communications during trial and juror's conduct evinced an actual bias in favor of prosecution violated defendant's rights to a fair trial under the Sixth Amendment and constitutes plain error requiring reversal of the conviction.

Juror Improperly Influenced

Fullwood v. Lee, 290 F.3d 665 (4th Cir. 2002)
> Allegations that juror was improperly influenced by her husband in voting for death sentence required an evidentiary hearing, where petitioner was entitled to exploration whether the jury considered prejudicial, and outside information that petitioner had previously received death sentence from another jury.

WITNESS RELATED INEFFECTIVENESS

Witnesses in General

Ramonez v. Berghuis, 490 F.3d 482, 489 (6th Cir. 2007)
> Counsel provided constitutionally ineffective assistance for failing to investigate and to call three witnesses to the crime, which counsel recognized could provide beneficial testimony to Ramonez, which would effectively defeat the essential elements of the State's breaking and entering of the home invasion crime.

Adams v. Bertrand, 453 F.3d 428, 436-438 (7th Cir. 2006)
> Counsel was ineffective by failing to investigate, locate and call Demain as a witness because counsel knew before trial that Demain could have swung the case in his

client's favor. Demain could have explained what occurred prior to the sexual encounter, the women invitations of the men to visit their rooms, and he witnessed S.E.S. downstairs with three men after the time of the sexual encounter.

Tenny v. Dretke, 416 F.3d 404, 408-409 (5th Cir. 2005)
Counsel was constitutionally ineffective for failing to investigate, to call two monks and a nun as witnesses, and to elicit critical evidence from witnesses called that Mulvey was the aggressor which would have supported Tenny's self-defense theory.

Avila v. Galaza, 297 F.3d 911, 921-924 (9th Cir. 2002)
Counsel's failure to investigate and present evidence from about eight (8) different witnesses that petitioner's brother, Ernesto, was the shooter, not the petitioner constituted ineffective assistance of counsel.

Gardner v. Barnett, 175 F.3d 580 (7th Cir. 1999)
The district court's failure to grant petitioner's continuance at trial to obtain unavailable witnesses was a violation of due process.

Berryman v. Morton, 100 F.3d 1089 (3rd Cir. 1996)
Failure to investigate and call defense witnesses constituted ineffective assistance of counsel. See also *White v. Godinez, 143 F.3d 1049 (7th Cir. 1998)*

Siripongs v. Calderon, 35 F.3d 1308 (9th Cir. 1994)
Trial counsel's failure to interview witnesses and follow up leads indicating multiple involvement in the crime stated a valid claim of ineffectiveness of counsel and required an evidentiary hearing.

Gills v. U.S., 586 A.2d 726 (D.C. App. 1991)
Trial counsel's failure to call security guards as witnesses, who would have testified that defendant was in their custody at the time of the shooting, was sufficient allegation to constitute ineffective assistance of counsel claim and required a remand for an evidentiary hearing.

Martinez-Macias v. Collins, 810 F.Supp. 782 (W.D. Tex. 1991)
Trial counsel's failure to call defense investigator, who had previously obtained a different story from witness who was testifying, constituted ineffective assistance of counsel.

Beasley v. United States, 491 F.2d 687 (6th Cir. 1974)
Trial counsel called an FBI agent as an expert witness over petitioner's protest. The FBI agent's testimony supported petitioner's guilt and criticized petitioner's character. The government was allowed to introduce damaging evidence through the FBI agent's testimony. In this pre-*Strickland* case, the district court found that calling this witness amounted to incompetency on counsel's behalf.

Alibi Witnesses

Raygoza v. Hulick, 474 F.3d 958, 963-966 (7th Cir. 2007)
Counsel provided constitutionally ineffective assistance for failure to investigate ten alibi witnesses whose testimony would have placed Raygoza at his mother's birthday party on the night of the shooting.

Trial Ineffectiveness

Stewart v. Wolfenbarger, 468 F.3d 338, 357-360 (6th Cir. 2006)
Counsel was constitutionally ineffective for failure to give proper alibi notice and disclosing the alibi location under Michigan law, failed to investigate the alibi witnesses, which resulted in the trial court limiting alibi testimony. The additional alibi testimony would have corroborated petitioner's alibi defense and cast doubt of the prosecution's key witness's testimony.

Matthews v. Abramajtys, 319 F.3d 780, 789-790 (6th Cir. 2003)
Counsel's failure to present two alibi witnesses, who would have testified that petitioner was with them shortly before the time of the murder, and to highlight the discrepancies in prosecution's case based on petitioner's and suspects height, constituted ineffective assistance of counsel.

Alcala v. Woodford, 334 F.3d 862, 868-871 (9th Cir. 2003)
Counsel's failure to adequately present alibi defense and call material witness who would have placed petitioner at Knott's Berry Farm on June 20, 1979, between 3:00 and 3:30 p.m., constituted ineffective assistance of counsel. There exists more than a reasonable probability that the result of the proceedings would have been different, had the jury heard that petitioner could not have been in Huntington Beach at that time when the crime was committed.

Luna v. Cambra, 306 F.3d 954, 961-963 (9th Cir. 2003)
Counsel's failure to investigate and call defendant's mother and sister as alibi witnesses' to corroborate defendant's testimony that he was at home sleeping the night of the crime, constitutes ineffective assistance of counsel.

Kane v. Kyler, 201 F.Supp. 2d 392, 398-399 (E.D. Pa. 2001)
Appellant counsel was constitutionally ineffective for failing to appeal the district court's denial of defendant's motion for continuance for purposes of obtaining alibi testimony from defendant's nonambulatory father.

Washington v. Smith, 219 F.3d 620, 634 (7th Cir. 2000)
Counsel's failure to investigate, subpoena, and call alibi witnesses amounted to ineffective assistance of counsel.

Matthews v. Abramajtys, 92 F.Supp.2d 615 (E.D. Mich. 2000)
Trial counsel's failure to call favorable witness and present alibi witness or defense theory constituted ineffective assistance of counsel.

Brown v. Myers, 137 F.3d 1154 (9th Cir. 1998)
Trial counsel's failure to investigate alibi defense or to present any alibi witnesses to corroborate petitioner's testimony undermined confidence in outcome of trial and constituted ineffective assistance of counsel. **See also *Thames v. Dugger, 848 F.2d 149 (11th Cir. 1988); Beasley v. United States, 491 F.2d 687 (6th Cir. 1974); U.S. Ex. Rel. Patterson v. Neal, 678 F.Supp. 749 (N.D. Ill. 1988); U.S. v. Mills, 760 F.2d 1116 (11th Cir. 1985); Wade v. Armontrout, 798 F.2d 304 (8th Cir. 1986); Tosh v. Lockhart, 879 F.2d 412 (8th Cir. 1989)***

Grooms v. Solem, *923 F.2d 88 (8th Cir. 1991)*
> Trial counsel's failure to investigate or attempt to locate potential alibi witnesses, or to argue on the record for admission of alibi witnesses' testimony constituted ineffective assistance of counsel.

Lawrence v. Armontrout, *900 F.2d 127 (8th Cir. 1990)*
> Failure of counsel to contact and investigate all potential alibi witnesses when defendant provided counsel with their names, which would have supported counsel's defense of misidentification constituted ineffectiveness of counsel.

U.S. v. Dawson, *857 F.2d 923 (3rd Cir. 1988)*
> Trial counsel's failure to interview and call alibi witness, who put the defendant in another town at the time of the crime, constituted performance below an objective standard of reasonableness. There existed a reasonable probability that the results of the trial would have been different, absent trial counsel's unprofessional errors and omissions.

Montgomery v. Petersen, *846 F.2d 407 (7th Cir. 1988)*
> Trial counsel's failure to investigate and interview the only disinterested alibi witness, a store clerk whom Petitioner purchased a bicycle from on the same day of robbery, constituted ineffective assistance of counsel.

Nealy v. Cabana, *764 F.2d 1173 (5th Cir 1985)*
> Trial counsel's failure to contact potential alibi witnesses constitutes ineffective assistance of counsel. **See also *Martinez-Macias v. Collins*, *810 F.Supp. 782 (W.D. Tex. 1991)***

Corroborating Witness

Mitchell v. Ayers, *309 F.Supp.2d. 1146, 1153 (N.D. Cal. 2004)*
> Counsel was constitutionally ineffective for failing to investigate corroborating witnesses to burglary because of the defendant's claim that he did not enter victim's home to commit a felony, but rather to escape from people who were threatening his life; corroborating witnesses testimony would have created a reasonable probability that the jury would have reached a verdict more favorable to the defendant.

Riley v. Payne, *352 F.3d 1313, 1319-1320 (9th Cir. 2003)*
> Counsel's failure to interview petitioner's associate who was with petitioner during initial confrontation with victim constituted ineffective assistance of counsel. The assault trial boiled down to a swearing match between petitioner and victim. The victim testified that petitioner approached them with his gun drawn to rob them. The petitioner testified that the victim threatened him. The associates' testimony would have corroborated petitioner's testimony, and under Washington's law, petitioner was not entitled to self-defense jury instruction if he was the first aggressor. Therefore, absent counsel's omissions, there is a reasonable probability that had the jury heard the testimony of petitioner's associate and been given the self-defense jury instruction, the results of the trial would have been different.

Trial Ineffectiveness

Berry v. Gramley, 74 F.Supp.2d 808 (N.D. Ill. 1999)
　　Counsel's failure to visit the crime scene or employ an investigator to locate and interview witnesses to corroborate defendant's testimony amounted to ineffective assistance of counsel.

Hart v. Gomez, 174 F.3d 1067 (9th Cir. 1999)
　　Defense counsel's failure to investigate and present evidence corroborating witness' testimony that she accompanied defendant and his children to their ranch during time the alleged molesting occurred constituted ineffective assistance where evidence could have precluded conviction.

Fuller v. Attorney General of State of Alabama, 36 F.Supp. 2d 1323 (N.D. Ala. 1999)
　　Defense counsel's failure to interview or call corroborating witness who would have supported petitioner's version of the events to all counts constitutes ineffective assistance of counsel. See also ***Chambers v. Armontrout, 907 F.2d 825 (8th Cir. 1990).***

Eyewitnesses

Harrison v. Quarterman, 496 F.3d 419, 425-429 (5th Cir. 2007)
　　Trial counsel's failure to investigate and call eyewitnesses concerning Harrison, West and the victim engaging in consensual three-way sexual acts on date of the alleged sexual assault required a remand to resolve the ineffective assistance of counsel claim.

United States v. Holder, 410 F.3d 651, 655-56 (10th Cir. 2005)
　　Trial counsel's failure to call the second of the only two witnesses, to the shooting required an evidentiary hearing to determine whether counsel's actions were strategy or ineffective.

Davis v. Lambert, 388 F.3d 1052, 1062 (7th Cir. 2004)
　　Trial counsel's failure to investigate or interview potential eye-witnesses and impeachment witnesses that Davis wanted to call as witnesses to bolster his self - defense claim required a federal evidentiary hearing to resolve the ineffectiveness of counsel claim.

Anderson v. Johnson, 338 F.3d 382, 392-394 (5th Cir. 2003)
　　Counsel's failure to interview or call Arthur Gary one of two eyewitnesses to the crime whose testimony would have shown that Ronald Anderson was nowhere around the scene of the shooting, and that his testimony would have contradicted the victim and her daughter's testimony constituting ineffective assistance of counsel.

United States Ex Rel. Hampton v. Leibach, 347 F.3d 219, 249-251 (7th Cir. 2003)
　　Counsel's failure to investigate or call eyewitnesses whose names had been given to him, to make any effort on his own to locate occurrence witnesses; where there was at least one witness who would have testified that petitioner did not participate in the attacks amounted to ineffective assistance of counsel.

Dixon v. Snyder, 266 F.3d 693, 702-03 (7th Cir. 2001)
　　Trial counsel's failure to cross-examine sole eyewitness due to counsel's ignorance of Illinois statute, section **115.10.1**, permitting state to admit eyewitness' statement

identifying defendant as murderer as substantive evidence, after eyewitness recanted statement at trial, and his statement could have been excluded if eyewitness invoked the Fifth Amendment on cross-examination amounted to ineffective assistance of counsel. Counsel's error was prejudicial to petitioner, eyewitness' identification was the only direct evidence against petitioner.

Matthews v. Abramajtys, 92 F.Supp.2d 615 (E.D. Mich. 2000)
Trial counsel was ineffective in failing to call witness who would have testified that the defendant was not one of the three men he saw running from the murder scene.

Lord v. Wood, 184 F.3d 1083 (9h Cir. 1999)
Counsel's failure to interview or call three witnesses who claimed to have seen the victim alive after petitioner was suppose to have killed her constituted ineffective assistance of counsel.

Workman v. Tate, 957 F.2d 1339 (6th Cir. 1992)
Trial counsel's failure to call or contact two witnesses that were with defendant during events that led to defendant's arrest for felonious assault and having weapon while under a disability, where witnesses' testimony would have contradicted testimony of police officers that arrested defendant, and constituted ineffective assistance of counsel.

Byrd v. U.S., 614 A.2d 25 (D.C. App. 1992)
Trial counsel's failure to call three eyewitnesses that were on the scene at the time the narcotic drop was allegedly made, and the eyewitnesses' testimony would have contradicted the investigator's testimony constituted ineffective assistance of counsel. Counsel's failure to call eyewitnesses forced defendant to testify and opened door for introduction of prior convictions which were used to impeach defendant's testimony.

Harris v. Reed, 894 F.2d 871 (7th Cir. 1990)
Trial counsel's failure to call eye witnesses who saw another man run from scene of shooting constituted ineffective assistance of counsel.

Chambers v. Armontrout, 885 F.2d 1318 (8th Cir. 1989)
Trial counsel's failure to interview and call eyewitness which supported Petitioner's self-defense claim constituted ineffective assistance of counsel.

Sullivan v. Fairman, 819 F.2d 1382 (7th Cir. 1987)
Trial counsel was ineffective for failure to locate and call five witnesses who had no apparent reason to help defendant, after witnesses made statements to police that were exculpatory or inconsistent with prosecution witnesses' statements and there were significant reasons to conclude that their testimony would have been believed because they were eye-witnesses and their testimony was consistent in essential respects.

Exculpatory Witness

Berry v. Gramely, 74 F.Supp.2d 808 (N.D. Ill. 1999)
Failure to call known exculpatory witness amounted ineffective assistance of counsel.

Identification Witnesses

Berryman v. Morton, 100 F.3d 1089 (3rd Cir. 1996)
Counsel's failure to use victim's inconsistent identification testimony from an accomplice's previous trial constituted ineffective assistance.

Toney v. Gammon, 79 F.3d 693 (8th Cir. 1996)
Counsel's failure to pursue issue of mistaken identity could constitute ineffective assistance of counsel and required evidentiary hearing to resolve claim. **See also** *Eldridge v. Atkins, 665 F.2d 228 (8th Cir. 1981); Lawrence v. Armontrout, 900 F.2d 127 (8th Cir. 1990)*

Thomas v. Lockhart, 738 F.2d 304 (8th Cir. 1984)
Counsel's failure to interview police officers involved in taking defendant's statement and who participated in his pre-trial identification constitutes ineffective assistance of counsel.

Moore v. United States, 432 F.2d 730 (3rd Cir. 1970)
Trial counsel's failure to prepare for trial and locate witnesses, who could not identify the defendant as the robber from a line-up warranted an evidentiary hearing to resolve the ineffectiveness of counsel claim.

Character Witnesses

Smith v. Dretke, 417 F.3d 438, 442-444 (5th Cir. 2005)
Counsel was constitutionally ineffective for failing to call witnesses to testify about the victim's character for violence and aggressive behavior to support the defendant's self-defense theory.

Hampton v. Leibach, 290 F.Supp.2d 905, 923-925 (N.D. Ill. 2001)
Counsel was constitutionally ineffective because of his failure to investigate, interview and present exculpatory occurrence and character witnesses, where the jury would have reached a different verdict had they heard the testimony from the witnesses.

Cave v. Singletary, 971 F.2d 1513 (11th Cir. 1992)
Trial counsel's failure to call character witnesses who were prepared to testify at sentencing required an evidentiary hearing to develop the facts.

Dillion v. Duckworth, 751 F.2d 895 (7th Cir. 1985)
In this case, the attorney admitted his own incompetence and filed two affidavits to his ineffectiveness. The attorney offered no character witnesses, either at trial or at the subsequent death penalty hearing. The Court found that it would be standard practice for an attorney defending an eighteen-year-old with no criminal record to present character witnesses and evidence, and that the non-existence of the attorney's efforts to avoid the death penalty once Dillion's guilt was established, is incomprehensible and was extremely prejudicial to Dillion. In sum, the attorney's errors prejudiced Dillion's trial sufficiently to warrant a retrial. *Id. at 901.*

**Kemp v. Leggett**, 635 F.2d 453 (5th Cir. 1981)

Trial counsel's failure to prepare for trial, to interview a single witness, to call several character witnesses who were present in the courtroom, to prepare a defense and to proffer a written charge on voluntary manslaughter charge constituted ineffective assistance.

Medical Witness

**Barnes v. Elo**, 231 F.3d 1025, 1029 (6th Cir. 2000)

Counsel's failure to investigate or call medical witnesses to establish the fact that petitioner could not run in the manner that the sexual complainant stated that her assailant ran. Therefore, a remand for an evidentiary hearing was required to resolve ineffectiveness of counsel claim.

EXPERT WITNESSES

**Kumho Tire Co. v. Carmichael**, 526 U.S. 227 , 143 L.Ed.2d 238, 119 S.Ct. 1215 (1999)

Federal trial judge's gatekeeping obligation under Federal Rules of Evidence – to insure that expert witness' testimony rests on reliable foundation and is relevant to the fact at hand – held to apply to all expert testimony, not only scientific.

**General Electric Co. v. Joiner**, 522 U.S. 136 , 139 L.Ed.2d 508, 118 S.Ct. 512 (1997)

Abuse of discretion standard is proper standard governing district court's decision to **admit** or **exclude** expert scientific testimony.

Arson Expert

**Richey v. Bradshaw**, 498 F.3d 344, 362 (6th Cir. 2007)

Defense counsel was constitutionally ineffective for failing to consult with his retained expert in a timely manner and to investigate state's arson conclusion. Counsel knew that there were gaps in the State's evidence having to do with the lack of accelerant on Richey's clothing and boots, and the greenhouse owner's failure to say that any accelerant were missing, which warranted investigating the State's arson conclusion. Had counsel investigated he would have learned that there were two experts Armstrong and Custer who would have testified on Richey's behalf, if they had been contacted. Their testimony would have attached the State's gas chromatography analysis as out of prevailing scientific standards, disputed the gasoline or paint thinner theory, and shown that the burn patterns were consistent with a naturally occurring fire and would have then concluded that the fire was probably started by a cigarette smoldering in the cushion of the couch. There is a reasonable probability that this evidence would have created a different verdict.

**Dugas v. Coplan**, 428 F.3d 317, 328-331 (1st Cir. 2005)

Counsel was constitutionally ineffective for failing to consult an arson expert as part of his investigation, and to develop a "not arson" defense.

Ballistic Expert

**Harris By and Through Ramseyer v. Wood**, 64 F.3d 1432 (9th Cir. 1995)

Counsel's failure to object to evidence of ballistic test constituted ineffective assistance of counsel.

Expert On Battered Woman Syndrome

Paine v. Massie, 339 F.3d 1194, 1201-1204 (l0th Cir. 2003)
>Counsel failure to offer expert testimony based on battered woman syndrome (BWS) to support self-defense claim, for murder of abusive husband constituted ineffective assistance of counsel, where self-defense claim required expert witness' testimony that petitioner suffered from battered woman syndrome.

Expert Chemist

United States v. Bounds, 943 F.2d 541 (1991)
>For the first time on appeal, Bounds provides an impressive scientific explanation of precursor chemicals, theoretical yields, and the dramatic differences between phenylacetone and phenylacetic acid. He claims that the calculations of the government's expert witness were erroneous, that the government's expert witness was not qualified in forensic chemistry, and that the government failed to prove that the chemicals found could have been used to produce amphetamine. Evidence not produced at sentencing will not be considered on appeal. Bounds' only alternative at this stage is to show, if he can, that his attorney's failure to produce evidence, to challenge witnesses, and to assert a failure of proof constituted ineffective assistance of counsel.

Expert on Diabetes

Collier v. Turpin, 155 F.3d 1277 (11th Cir. 1998)
>Counsel's failure to retain or seek expert opinion on effects of defendant's **diabetes** which resulted in defendant being unable to control his behavior and was mitigating evidence for sentencing purposes constitutes ineffective assistance of counsel.

Expert on Drug Use

Miller v. Wainwright, 798 F.2d 426 (11th Cir. 1986)
>Trial counsel's failure to secure expert on drug use, who would have cast serious doubt on the state's witnesses' credibility, who had mental as well as drug-related problems, may constitute ineffective assistance of counsel.

DNA-Expert

Leonard v. Michigan, 287 F.Supp.2d 765, 791 (W.D. Mich. 2003)
>Counsel was constitutionally ineffective by failing to investigate the state's DNA testing, consult an expert in DNA, and because of his inability to challenge the DNA evidence.

Leonard v. Michigan, 256 F.Supp. 2d 723, 730-731 (W.D. Mich. 2003)
>Counsel was constitutionally ineffective because he failed to obtain an expert witness on DNA evidence, prepare for the suppression hearing testimony and to conduct a vigorous cross-examination of expert, and stipulated to the admission of expert witnesses suppression hearing testimony at trial.

Miller v. Anderson, 255 F.3d 455, 459 (7th Cir. 2001)

Defense counsel's failure to consult with a hair, DNA, treadmark and footprint experts, and to present evidence from these experts that Miller was not at the scene of the crime, which would have undermined state's only direct evidence placing Miller at crime scene amounted to ineffective assistance of counsel.

Phoenix v. Matesanz, 189 F.3d 20 (1st Cir. 1999)

Counsel's failure to call expert witness to rebut blood and fingerprint evidence which was basically the only state evidence linking the defendant to crime required a remand for reconsideration, where the district court failed to obtain the trial transcripts necessary to review defendant's claims.

Holsomback v. White, 133 F.3d 1382 (11th Cir. 1998)

Trial counsel's failure to conduct any pretrial investigation into the lack of medical evidence of sexual abuse in sodomy prosecution, where treating physician who performed rectal examination shortly after last alleged incident revealed that victims claims of abuse and were medically impossible constituted ineffective assistance of counsel.

Jones v. Wood, 114 F.3d 1002 (9th Cir. 1997)

Petitioner demonstrated "good cause" for conducting discovery to obtain notes for trial counsel implicating another suspect and to conduct test on blood samples from both him and his wife's as well as hair found in murdered wife's hands, where test might establish prejudice on his ineffectiveness of counsel claims.

Toney v. Gammon, 79 F.3d 693 (8th Cir. 1996)

Habeas petitioner was entitled through discovery to access to state's evidence to conduct DNA and other scientific testing; court's denial of discovery is an abuse of discretion if discovery is indispensable to a fair rounded development of material facts.

Fingerprint Expert

Phoenix v. Matesanz, 189 F.3d 20 (1st Cir. 1999)

Counsel's failure to call expert witness to rebut blood and fingerprint evidence which was basically the only state evidence linking the defendant to crime, required a remand for reconsideration, because the district court failed to obtain the trial transcripts necessary to review defendant's claims.

Schell v. Witek, 181 F.3d 1094 (9th Cir. 1999)

Counsel's failure to consult with a fingerprint expert where the only evidence connecting petitioner to the alleged crime was a single fingerprint warranted an evidentiary hearing to resolve claim of ineffectiveness of counsel. **See also *Beasley v. United States, 491 F.2d 687 (6th Cir. 1974)***

Forensic Expert

Steidl v. Walls, 267 F.Supp. 2d 919, 936 (C.D. Ill. 2003)

Counsel was constitutionally ineffective by failing to investigate and present forensic evidence that Rienbolt's knife was not the murder weapon because it was incompatible with the wounds, which would have had a devastating impact on Rienbolt's credibility.

Trial Ineffectiveness

Thomas v. Calderon, 120 F.3d 1045 (9th Cir. 1997)
Defense counsel's failure to investigate and present evidence rebutting the State's forensic evidence of rape constituted ineffective assistance.

Jones v. Wood, 114 F.3d 1002 (9th Cir. 1997)
Trial counsel's failure to test blood on petitioner's clothing or hairs found on his wife's hands and body constitutes ineffective assistance of counsel and required an evidentiary hearing.

Siripongs v. Calderon, 35 F.3d 1308 (9th Cir. 1994)
Trial counsel failure to conduct any forensic testing of the physical evidence constitutes ineffective assistance and required an evidentiary hearing.

Maddox v. Lord, 818 F.2d 1058 (2nd Cir. 1987)
Defense counsel's failure to investigate state's forensic evidence fell below an objective standard of reasonableness.

Miller v. Wainwright, 798 F.2d 426 (11th Cir. 1986)
Counsel's failure to obtain a forensic pathology expert to rebut the state's expert testimony that the alleged victim was alive when burned, may constitute ineffective assistance of counsel.

Handwriting Expert

U.S. v. Tarricone, 996 F.2d 1414 (2nd Cir. 1993)
Trial counsel's failure to consult with handwriting expert required evidentiary hearing.

Medical Expert

Bell v. Miller, 500 F.3d 149, 155-157 (2nd Cir. 2007)
Trial counsel's failure to consult with a medical expert concerning the reliability of victim's identification of Bell as shooter because the victim gave a different description at the scene of the crime, and the victim was shot in the thigh, lost half his blood, and was heavily medicated and in a coma for eleven days constituted ineffective assistance of counsel.

Investigate Expert's Opinion

Combs v. Coyle, 205 F.3d 269 (6th Cir. 2000)
Defense counsel's failure to investigate expert's opinion prior to presenting expert testimony concerning defendant's intoxication defense amounted to ineffective assistance of counsel.

Smith v. Stewart, 189 F.3d 1004 (9th Cir. 1999)
Counsel's failure to investigate and inform defense expert witnesses about essential information going to the heart of capital defendant's case for mitigation amounted to ineffective assistance of counsel.

Wallace v. Stewart, 184 F.3d 1112 (9th Cir. 1999)

Counsel's failure to present mental health evidence to defense expert which would have showed defendant's dysfunctional family history in penalty phase in capital murder sentencing constituted ineffective assistance of counsel.

Caro v. Calderon, 165 F.3d 1223 (9th Cir. 1999)

Defense counsel's failure to investigate defendant's organic brain damage or other mental impairments and failure to seek expert opinion on defendant's extraordinary exposure to neurotoxicants, neurological impairments and personal background required an evidentiary hearing to resolve claim of ineffectiveness of counsel. **See also** *Deutscher v. Whitley, 884 F.2d 1152 (9th Cir. 1989)*

Bean v. Calderon, 163 F.3d 1073 (9th Cir. 1998)

Counsel's failure to investigate, present mitigating evidence, and prepare experts for their testimony during penalty phase of trial constituted ineffective assistance.

Rogers v. Israel, 746 F.2d 1288 (7th Cir. 1984)

Trial counsel's failure to investigate expert's opinions constituted ineffective assistance where expert opinion could have resulted in different degree of verdict. **See also** *Stephens v. Kemp, 846 F.2d 642 (11th Cir. 1988)*

Expert on Ineffectiveness of Counsel Standards

Ainsworth v. Calderon, 138 F.3d 787 (9th Cir. 1998)

The court held that "admission of expert testimony on question of ineffective assistance of counsel was not abuse of discretion . . ."

Noland v. Dixon, 808 F. Supp. 485 (W.D.N.C. 1992)

The Court found that Noland was entitled to an evidentiary hearing to allow expert testimony from Jame Ferguson to testify based on the objective standards of reasonableness under which attorneys trying capital murder cases operated at the time of petitioner's trial.

Expert on Neurological Evaluation

Williamson v. Reynolds, 904 F.Supp. 1529 (E.D. Okl. 1995)

Trial counsel's failure to raise issue that defendant was mentally incompetent to stand trial and move for a continuance to have neurological evaluation may constitute ineffective assistance.

Expert Pathologist

Weddell v. Weber, 290 F.Supp.2d 1011, 1022-1023 (D.S.D, 2003)

Counsel was constitutionally ineffective for failing to retain an expert pathologist to rebut state's expert testimony about causation of victim's death.

Trial Ineffectiveness

Expert Psychiatrist

Barkell v. Crouse, 468 F.3d 684, 692-693 (l0th Cir. 2006)
Counsel failure to investigate victim's school records and counseling records, which indicated that victim had tendency to lie and failed to consult with child expert psychiatrist required an evidentiary hearing to resolve claim of ineffectiveness of counsel.

Jennings v. Woodford, 290 F.3d 1006, 1016-20 (9th Cir. 2002)
Trial counsel's failure to investigate psychiatric evidence and possible medical defense in capital murder trial deprived Jennings of an opportunity to present a defense, which would have negated the mental state necessary for a first degree murder conviction and required a new trial.

Miller v. Anderson, 255 F.3d 455, 458-59 (7th Cir. 2001)
Defense counsel was ineffective for calling a psychologist to testify that Miller was incapable of the kind of violence that had been perpetrated against the victim. Counsel knew that Miller had been previously convicted of kidnapping, rape, and sodomy. Miller was on parole for kidnapping at the time of the crime. The state brought out these facts during its cross-examination of the defense psychologist and it bolstered the jury's confidence in Miller's guilt. There was no "tactic" decision and counsel's performance was deficient.

U.S. Ex Rel. Foster v. Gilmore, 35 F.Supp. 2d 626 (N.D.111. 1998)
Defense counsel's failure to consult with an expert psychiatrist prior to or during capital murder trial constitutes ineffective assistance of counsel. **See also** *Anderson v. Butler, 858 F.2d 16 (1st Cir. 1988)*

Bloom v. Calderon, 132 F.2d 1267 (9th Cir. 1997)
Trial counsel's failure to prepare psychiatric expert or provide expert with readily available material and present expert as witness, which would have changed outcome of the trial, constituted ineffective assistance of counsel.

Halton v. Hesson, 803 F.Supp. 1272 (M.D. Tenn. 1992)
Trial counsel's failure to call physician who had performed psychiatric evaluation of defendant prior to the alleged rape and sexual battery crime amounted to ineffective assistance of counsel.

Bouchillon v. Collins, 907 F.2d 589 (5th Cir. 1990)
Defense counsel's failure to ask for a psychiatric evaluation of petitioner constituted ineffective assistance. The standard of proof in this case was based on the preponderance of evidence.

Loyd v. Smith, 899 F.2d 1416 (5th Cir. 1990)
Trial counsel's failure to retain independent psychiatrist in order to present evidence during sentencing phase constitutes ineffective assistance of counsel. **See also** *Noland v. Dixon, 808 F.Supp. 485 (W.D.N.C. 1992); United States v. Fessel, 531 F.2d 1275 (5th Cir. 1976); Loyd v. Whitley, 977 F.2d 149 (5th Cir. 1992); Wood v. Zahradnick, 611 F.2d 1383 (4th Cir. 1980)*

112

<h2 style="text-align:center">Expert Treating Physician</h2>

Miller v. Dretke, 420 F.3d 356, 362 (5th Cir. 2005)
> Counsel was constitutionally ineffective for failing to contact Miller's treating physicians, and to call them as expert witnesses concerning Miller's medical and psychological problems during the punishment phase.

<h2 style="text-align:center">Expert on Social History</h2>

Harris By and Through Ramseyer v. Wood, 64 F.3d 1432 (9th Cir. 1995)
> Trial counsel's failure to obtain an expert to prepare a social history amounted to ineffectiveness of counsel.

<h2 style="text-align:center">Voice/Tape Expert</h2>

United States v. Baynes, 687 F.2d 659 (3rd Cir. 1982)
> Trial counsel's failure to investigate possibilities of distinguishing exemplar of defendant's voice from voice on intercepted tape recording, where intercepted tape recording was the only evidence against defendant amounted to ineffective assistance of counsel.

<h2 style="text-align:center">Surprise Witnesses</h2>

Hudson v. Lockhart, 679 F.Supp. 891 (E.D. Ark. 1986)
> Trial counsel's failure to move for a severance and to object to the State's surprise witness, or move for a continuance to prepare for the surprise witness' testimony amounted to ineffective assistance of counsel.

IMPEACHMENT RELATED INEFFECTIVENESS

Alberni v. McDaniel, 458 F.3d 860, 873 (9th Cir. 2006)
> Alberni was entitled to evidentiary hearing to determine whether his trial counsel's performance was adversely affected by a conflict of interest because of successive representation of the state's rebuttal witness Mr. Flamrn. Counsel failed to impeach Mr. Flamm during cross-examination with his prior conviction, probation status, and on multiple points of his testimony.

Reynoso v. Giurbino, 462 F.3d 1099, 1110-1116 (9th Cir. 2006)
> Trial counsel's failure to investigate the reward issue and to use the reward as impeachment evidence for cross-examination of the two state's eyewitnesses about their motivation (collecting the reward) for testifying amounted to deficient performance. Reynoso was prejudice because "[i]f the jury had known the other two prosecution witnesses were eligible to receive the award, this would have cast the prosecution's case in an entirely different light," and such information "would have cast considerable doubt on the credibility of the two identification witnesses by suggesting they were promised a reward for identifying Reynoso."

Davis v. Lambert, 388 F.3d 1052, 1062 (7th Cir. 2004)
> Trial counsel's failure to investigate or interview potential eye-witnesses and impeachment witnesses that Davis wanted to call as witnesses to bolster his self -

defense claim required a federal evidentiary hearing to resolve the ineffectiveness of counsel claim.

Harris v. Senkowski, 298 F.Supp.2d 320, 327 (E.D.N.Y. 2004)
Counsel was constitutionally ineffective because of counsel's failure to confront robbery victim with her prior inconsistent statement describing the robbery victim as being eight inches shorter and 100 pounds lighter.

Thomas v. Kuhlman, 255 F.Supp. 2d 99, 109-111 (E.D.N.Y. 2003)
Counsel's failure to investigate crime scene, to read the police reports released by the State as _**Rosario**_ material, which would have impeached Artis's testimony that she observed the defendant on the fire escape of the victim's building constituted ineffective assistance of counsel.

Steidl v. Walls, 267 F.Supp. 2d 919, 934-935 (C.D. Ill. 2003)
Counsel was constitutionally ineffective by failing to investigate or call the supervisor of the government's eyewitness, who would have testified that this eyewitness was at work during the time frame she claimed to have witnessed the acts leading up to the murders, which would have impeached the government's eyewitness.

Cargle v. Mullins, 317 F.3d 1196, 1213-1214 (10th Cir. 2003)
Counsel failure to investigate, to call Dewonna Cargle and Angel Harris as witnesses, to impeach two state key witnesses testimony based upon undisclosed bias, and state inducement for their testimony constituted ineffective assistance of counsel.

Harris v. Artuz, 288 F.Supp. 2d 247, 259-260 (E.D. N.Y. 2003)
Counsel was constitutionally ineffective by failing to impeach witness with medical evidence that he was stabbed, not shot, so as to suggest that witness and his friends might have colluded to frame petitioner for homicide which they actually committed.

Gonzalez-Soberal v. United States, 244 F.3d 273, 279 (1st Cir. 2001)
Counsel's failure to impeach Negron with his letter, which suggested he had not been completely truthful during his cooperation, and Maya with a psycho diagnostic report, which would have undermined Maya's testimony and identification of Gonzalez, and required an evidentiary hearing to determine whether Gonzalez was prejudiced by counsel'serrors.

Tucker v. Prelesnik, 181 F.3d 747 (6th Cir. 1999)
Defense counsel's failure to move for a continuance, to obtain medical records of assault victim which would have impeached his ability to remember, failed to obtain and use evidence of earlier contradictory statements by victim, which would have cast serious doubt about the victims credibility, constitutes ineffective assistance of counsel.

U.S. v. Kliti, 156 F.3d 150 (2nd Cir. 1998)
Defense counsel who was a witness to potentially exculpatory statements made by a witness created a conflict of interest where counsel's testimony about exculpatory statements would have been valuable impeachment evidence attacking witnesses credibility. **See also _United States v. Iorizzo, 786 F.2d 52 (2nd Cir. 1986)_**

**Thomas v. Calderon**, 120 F.3d 1045 (9th Cir. 1997)
> Defense counsel's failure to seek-discovery regarding informant where two police agencies for whom he informed considered informant unreliable and his family considered him a pathological liar, amounted to ineffective assistance where evidence could have been used to impeach informants testimony. **See also _Lindh v. Murphy,_ 124 F.3d 899 (7th Cir. 1997)**

**Berryman v. Morton**, 100 F.3d 1089 (3rd Cir. 1996)
> Counsel's failure to use victim's inconsistent identification testimony from an accomplice's previous trial constituted ineffective assistance.

**Hadley v. Groose**, 97 F.3d 1131 (8th Cir. 1996)
> Trial counsel's failure to use police report to impeach police officer's testimony relating because footprints who counsel knew officer's testimony was contradicted by body of police report constituted ineffective assistance of counsel.

**Williamson v. Reynolds**, 904 F.Supp. 1529 (E.D. Okl. 1995)
> Trial counsel's failure to properly cross-examine prosecution's witness about witness' participation in other case where witness claimed to hear jailhouse confession was ineffective assistance.

**Driscoll v. Delo**, 71 F.3d 701 (8th Cir. 1995)
> Trial counsel's failure to properly utilize witness' prior inconsistent statements for impeachment purposes constitutes ineffective assistance. **See also _U.S. Ex.Rel. McCall v. O'Grady_, 714 F.Supp. 374 (N.D. Ill. 1989); _United States v. Tucker_, 716 F.2d 576 (9th Cir. 1983); _Hyman v. Aiken_, 824 F.2d 1405 (4th Cir. 1987); _Eldridge v. Atkins_, 665 F.2d 228 (8th Cir. 1981)**

**Williams v. Washington**, 59 F.3d 673 (7th Cir. 1995)
> Trial counsel has a duty to investigate leads affecting the credibility of witnesses, which would serve to bolster his client's credibility and undercut the state's witnesses' testimony. **See also _Miller v. Wainwright_, 798 F.2d 426 (11th Cir. 1986); _Harris v. Housewright_, 697 F.2d 202 (8th Cir. 1982); _Byrd v. U.S._, 614 A.2d 25 (D.C. App. 1992)**

**Workman v. Tate**, 957 F.2d 1339 (6th Cir. 1992)
> Trial counsel's failure to call or contact two witnesses that were with defendant during events that led to defendant's arrest for felonious assault and having weapon, while under a disability, where witnesses' testimony would have contradicted testimony of police officers that arrested defendant constituted ineffective assistance of counsel.

**Martinez-Macias v. Collins**, 810 F.Supp. 782 (W.D. Tex. 1991)
> Trial counsel's failure to call defense investigator who had previously obtained a different story from witness who was testifying constituted ineffective assistance of counsel.

**Moffett v. Kolb**, 930 F.2d 1156 (7th Cir. 1991)
> Trial counsel's failure to introduce prior inconsistent statements of state's witness who twice told detective that petitioner's brother, not petitioner, had fired the gun at victim constituted ineffective assistance of counsel. **See also _Nixon v. Newsome_, 888 F.2d 112 (11th Cir. 1989); _U.S. Ex. Rel. McCall v. O'Grady_, 908 F.2d 170 (7th Cir. 1990)**

Smith v. Wainwright, 799 F.2d 1442 (11th Cir. 1986)

Trial counsel's failure to make jury aware during trial that Smith's named accomplice (Johnson) had confessed to the crime and gave a detailed statement constituted ineffective assistance of counsel. "The district court found and (the 11th Circuit) affirmed that, at his trial, Smith was deprived of evidence, which was critical to the determination of his guilt or innocence." The conviction rested upon the testimony of Johnson. His credibility was the central issue in the case. Available evidence would have had great weight in the assertion that Johnson's testimony was not true. That evidence was not used and the jury had no knowledge of it. There is a reasonable probability that, had their original statements been used at trial, the result would have been different. **See also** *Smith v. Wainwright, 741 F.2d 1248 (11th Cir. 1984)*

CROSS-EXAMINATION INEFFECTIVENESS

Higgins v. Renico, 470 F.3d 624, 632-636 (6th Cir. 2006)

Trial counsel provided constitutionally ineffective assistance for failing to cross-examine the sole eyewitness and possible perpetrator of the shooting giving rise to the prosecution. The eyewitness gave inconsistent accounts of the shooting, had gunpowder residue on his hands, and without the witnesses testimony the state's case was weak.

Stanley v. Bartley, 465 F.3d 810, 813-814 (7th Cir. 2006)

Trial counsel provided constitutionally ineffective assistance for failing to interview any witnesses or prospective witnesses and to effectively cross-examination Stanley's sister, a state witness. A prospective witness, Robert Brock, made a statement to the police that a few hours before the murder, that James Dean (the state's principal witness) and Sammie Wilborn (the murder victim) had an argument over cocaine that resulted in pushing and shoving. According to Brock's testimony during a federal habeas hearing, Wilborn struck Dean with a wine bottle and Dean punched Wilborn in the head and knocked him down and that when the fight was over Dean told Wilborn, "I'll catch your ass later on." The state did not call Robert Brock as a witness at trial. Defense counsel failed to call Brock as a witness, and failed to question Stanley's sister about the date of Stanley's alleged confession and the date she'd seen Stanley with the gun.

Fisher v. Gibson, 282 F.3d 1283, 1298 (10th Cir. 2002)

Trial counsel's hostility toward his client and eliciting damaging testimony from his client constitutes a breach of counsel's duty to act as an advocate for his client constituting ineffective assistance of counsel.

Dixon v. Snyder, 266 F.3d 693, 702-03 (7th Cir. 2001)

Trial counsel's failure to cross-examine sole eyewitness due to counsel's ignorance of Illinois statute, section **115.10.1**, permitting state to admit eyewitness' statement identifying defendant as murderer as substantive evidence, after eyewitness recanted statement at trial, and his statement could have been excluded if eyewitness invoked the Fifth Amendment on cross-examination amounted to ineffective assistance of counsel. Counsel's error was prejudicial to petitioner, eyewitness' identification was the only direct evidence against petitioner.

Kibbe v. Dubois, 120 F.Supp. 2d 114 (D. Mass. 2000)
The prosecutor's cross-examination and closing arguing violated defendant's Fourteenth Amendment right to due process under *Doyle v. Ohio*, **426 U.s. 610, 96 S.Ct. 2240, 49 L.Ed.2d 91 (1976)** and the *Doyle* violation was not harmless error.

Matthews v. Abramajtys, 92 F.Supp.2d 615 (E.D. Mich. 2000)
Trial counsel's failure to cross-examine witness about his description of man seen fleeing from murder scene amounted to ineffective assistance of counsel.

Moore v. Johnson, 194 F.3d 587 (5th Cir. 1999)
Trial counsel elicited damaging evidence against Moore during cross-examination of the arresting officer Autrey's testimony, which established the elements of the offense and defeated Moore's alibi's defense, amounted to ineffective assistance.

Steinkuehier v. Meschner, 176 F.3d 441 (8th Cir. 1999)
Trial counsel's failure to cross-examine sheriff about pressuring jail supervisor to "forget" petitioner's condition after shooting and sheriff's purported practice of "forgetting" facts favoring defendants constituted ineffective assistance of counsel.

U.S. v. Johnson, 995 F. Supp. 1259 (D. Kan. 1998)
Trial counsel's failure to properly examine or cross-examine witnesses required an evidentiary hearing to resolve ineffective assistance of counsel claim. **See also** *Jones v. Jones, 988 F. Supp. 1000 (E.D.La. 1997)*; *Whelchel v. Wood, 996 F. Supp. 1019 (E.D. Wash. 1997)*; *Wilson v. Mintzes, 761 F.2d 275 (6th Cir. 1985)*; *U.S. v. Wolf, 787 F.2d 1094 (7th Cir. 1986)*; *Miller v. Wainwright, 798 F.2d 426 (11th Cir. 1986)*; *Pilchak v. Camper, 741 F.Supp. 782 (W.D. Mo. 1990)*; *United States v. Tucker, 716 F.2d 576 (9th Cir. 1983)*; *United States v. Hammonds, 425 F.2d 597 (D.C. Cir. 1970)*; *Hollines v. Estelle, 569 F.Supp. 146 (W.D. Tex. 1983)*; *Jemison v. Foltz, 672 F.Supp. 1002 (E.D. Mich. 1987)*; *Pinnell v. Cauthorn, 540 F.2d 938 (8th Cir. 1976)*; *Williamson v. Reynolds, 904 F.Supp. 1529 (E.D. Okl. 1995)*

Johnson v. Norris, 999 F. Supp. 1256 (E.D. Ark. 1998)
Defense counsel's failure to investigate circumstances of case and by conducting inadequate cross-examination of key witness whose testimony had several discrepancies regarding chain of custody of the cocaine, allegedly sold by defendant, and the key witness had medical problems, which included loss of memory amounted to ineffective assistance.

Sparman v. Edwards, 26 F. Supp. 2d 450 (E.D.N.Y. 1997)
Trial counsel's failure to discover exculpatory medical evidence and failing to cross-examine victims about inconsistencies in their statements to police and their trial testimony constituted ineffective assistance of counsel.

Hogan v. McBride, 79 F.3d 578 (7th Cir. 1996)
Defendant was entitled to evidentiary hearing on ineffective assistance of counsel claim based on counsel's handling of a confrontation issue during trial.

Holmes v. Bartlett, 810 F.Supp. 550 (S.D. N.Y. 1993)
The court found that Mr. Holmes was entitled to review on merits of his claim that trial court improperly restricted his counsel's ability to cross-examine detective.

Trial Ineffectiveness

U.S. v. Tatum, 943 F.2d 370 (4th Cir. 1991)
Trial counsel's failure to pursue cross-examination of government witness whose testimony is material can show adverse effect on counsel's performance because of conflict of interest and establish ineffective assistance of counsel.

Clark v. Duckworth, 906 F.2d 1174 (7th Cir. 1990)
Trial counsel's failure to cross-examine or move for a mistrial when witness refused to testify because he received threats constituted grounds for relief under habeas corpus.

Lyons v. McCotter, 770 F.2d 529 (5th Cir. 1985)
Trial counsel's failure to object, exclude, or limit cross-examination testimony that indicated defendant had prior convictions for aggravated robbery amounted to ineffective assistance.

Mills v. Scully, 653 F.Supp. 885 (S.D. N.Y. 1987)
Trial counsel's failure to elicit testimony during cross-examination of state's witness that she had testified before grand jury that she had not seen defendant shoot victim, which was different from her trial testimony, amounted to ineffective assistance of counsel.

Baumann v. United States, 692 F.2d 565 (9th Cir. 1982)
Trial counsel failed to interview prosecution witnesses and prevented the defendant from doing so, and failed to effectively cross-examine two witnesses that provided the evidence of defendant's involvement in the crime. Defendant was entitled to an evidentiary hearing to resolve his ineffective assistance of counsel claim.

Thomas v. Wyrick, 535 F.2d 407 (8th Cir. 1976)
Trial counsel's failure to interview any witnesses, which was apparently against his policy amounted to a breach of his essential duty owed to his client. Prejudice turns on when evidence is uncovered which could have been admitted that would have afforded the jury sufficient weight in assessing defendant's guilt or innocence. The record established in this case that had counsel conducted a reasonable investigation and interviewed witnesses, that counsel would have uncovered evidence which would have been useful during cross-examination and in its case in chief and granted the issuance of the writ. The Eighth Circuit reversed and remanded for a new trial.

Voyles v. Watkins, 489 F.Supp. 901 (1980)
Trial counsel's failure to elicit testimony during cross-examination from co-defendant that he expected favorable consideration from the state if the trial resulted in conviction of defendant constituted ineffective assistance of counsel.

Coaching of a Witness

Crutchfield v. Wainwright, 803 F.2d 1103 (11th Cir. 1986)
Coaching a witness has to come the meaning of improperly directing a witness' testimony in such a way as to have it conform with, conflict with, or supplement the testimony of other witnesses.

Hypnotically Induced Testimony

Pruett v. Norris, 959 F. Supp 1066 (E. Ark. 1997)
> Hypnotically induced testimony by bank teller, who was a witness to robbery and murder, violated defendant's right under confrontation clause because at time of the hypnotic session, hypnotist, six (6) FBI agents plus, FBI visual information specialist were present when the witness's inaccurate recollection was reinforced during hypnosis.

Introduction of Preliminary Hearing Testimony

Cook v. McKune, 323 F.3d 825, 836-37 (10th Cir. 2003)
> The admission of preliminary hearing testimony of absent witness during trial violated defendant's confrontation rights in murder trial. The state failed to diligently secure the witness for trial and this witness was the only individual who identified the defendant as the killer.

Seating Arrangement Prejudicial

Walker v. Butterworth, 599 F.3d 1074 (1st Cir. 1999)
> Seating arrangements prejudicial.

TESTIFYING RELATED INEFFECTIVENESS

Girts v. Yani, 501 F.3d 743, 757 (6th Cir. 2007)
> Trial counsel provided constitutionally ineffective assistance for failing to object to the prosecutor's improper and prejudicial statements concerning Girts' failure to testify and exercising his Fifth Amendment right to remain silent.

Owens v. United States, 483 F.3d 48, 57 (1st Cir. 2007)
> Trial counsel's failure to advise Owens of his right to testify warranted an evidentiary hearing to resolve ineffective assistance of counsel claim.

Cannon v. Mullin, 383 F.3d 1152, 1172 (10th Cir. 2004)
> Trial counsel's refusal to allow defendant to testify in his own behalf required an evidentiary hearing to resolve ineffectiveness of counsel claim.

Ward v. Sternes, 334 F.3d 696, 704-705 (7th Cir. 2003)
> Mental ill defendant did not knowingly and intelligently waive his fundamental right to testify during trial by stating that "I guess, I don't know," thus requiring the writ to be granted.

United States v. Rodriquez, 153 F.Supp.2d 590 (E.D. Pa 2001)
> Counsel's failure to allow defendant to testify during trial required an evidentiary hearing to resolve claim of ineffective assistance.

Rock v. Arkansas, 483 U. S. 44, 49052, 107 S.Ct. 2704, 97 L.Ed.2d 37 (1987)
> A criminal defendant has the right to testify in his own defense and that right is personal to the defendant and may not be waived by his attorney.

Trial Ineffectiveness

Ferguson v. Georgia, *365 U.S. 570, 5 Led 2d 783, 81 S. Ct. 756 (1961)*
   Due process guarantees the defendant an opportunity for his counsel to question him in open court.

U.S. v. Martiner, *181 F.3d 627 (5th Cir. 1999)*
   The Fifth Circuit vacated the district court's summary dismissal of Martinez's *§2255* motion to vacate. Martinez alleged he was denied effective assistance of counsel where he advised counsel that he wanted to testify on his own behalf, but counsel failed to call him to testify, thus, depriving him of an opportunity to present his side of the story to the jury. The Fifth Circuit mindful both of the judiciary's obligations to provide the accused with an adequate mechanism to fairly address his claims and of our heavy indulgence of pleadings by pro se prisoners, Martinez's vague and conclusory assertion alone did not warrant a hearing. At the same time, in keeping with the strictures of *§2255*, stated that we do not think summary dismissal was appropriate. Thereafter, the Court remanded the case to afford Martinez an opportunity to state with greater specificity his complaints regarding ineffective assistance of counsel and his right to testify. The Court noted that if Martinez fails to present more than his present conclusory allegation; summary dismissal of his petition would be appropriate. **See also *Gallego v. U.S.*, *174 F.3d 1196 (11th Cir. 1999)***

White v. Godinez, *143 F.3d 1049 (7th Cir. 1998)*
   Defense counsel's failure to pursue defense that defendant's brother hired hit men to kill victim and to call defendant and his girlfriend as witnesses to support defense constituted ineffective assistance of counsel. **See also *U.S. v. Scott*, *909 F.2d 488 (11th Cir. 1990)***

U.S. v. McKinnon, *995 F. Supp. 1404 (M.D. Fla. 1998)*
   Trial counsel instructed defendant not to testify on her own behalf based on inappropriate conflict concerns for the well-being of the co-defendants which required an evidentiary hearing to resolve ineffective assistance of counsel and conflict of interest claim.

U.S. v. Johnson, *995 F.Supp. 1259 (D. Kan. 1998)*
   Trial counsel's refusal to allow defendant to testify, despite defendant's request to testify, required an evidentiary hearing to resolve ineffective assistance claim. **See also *U.S. v. DiSalvo*, *726 F.Supp. 596 (E.D. Pa. 1989); U.S. v. Lore*, *26 F.Supp. 2d 729 (D. N.J. 1998)***

Harris By and Through Ramseyer v. Wood, *64 F.3d 1432 (9th Cir. 1995)*
   Counsel calling defendant as witness to allow jury to hear defendant's statement to police from defendant instead of police constituted ineffective assistance because counsel failed to attempt to enhance defendant's credibility. **See also *Jones v. Jones*, *988 F. Supp. 1000 (E.D.La. 1997)***

Jordan v. Hargett, *34 F.3d 310 (5th Cir. 1994)*
   Trial counsel's refusal to call defendant to witness stand stated a sufficient claim of ineffective assistance of counsel and, required an evidentiary hearing.

Wogan v. United States, *846 F.Supp. 135 (D.Me. 1994)*
   Defense counsel's advice to Wogan not to testify at sentencing was erroneous. Wogan's testimony would have reasonably established that Wogan was not responsible for 750

grams of heroin and would have established a lower base offense. Defense counsel's advice amounted to ineffective assistance of counsel.

Nichols v. Butler, 953 F.2d 1550 (11th Cir. 1992) (en banc)
Trial counsel's refusal to allow defendant to testify denied the jury an opportunity to observe defendant's demeanor and to judge his credibility first hand against that of the prosecution's witness and constitutes ineffective assistance and entitled defendant to a new trial. **See also** *U.S. v. Butts, 630 F.Supp. 1145 (D. Me. 1986)*

U.S. v. Long, 857 F.2d 436 (8th Cir. 1988)
Trial counsel notifying courts that defendant would commit perjury if he testifies may constitute ineffective assistance of counsel.

Blackburn v. Foltz, 828 F.2d 1177 (6th Cir. 1987)
Counsel's erroneous legal advice concerning possible use of prior convictions if defendant testified compounded with other errors amounted to ineffective assistance of counsel.

Douglas v. Wainwright, 739 F.2d 531 (11th Cir. 1984)
Trial counsel's failure to consult with defendant and inform him of option of testifying in his own behalf compounded with other errors at sentencing, amounted to ineffective assistance of counsel and required an evidentiary hearing.

United States v. Campbell, 616 F.2d 1151 (9th Cir. 1980)
Trial counsel advising the jury that defendant is testifying against counsel's advice may constitute ineffective assistance of counsel.

Whiteside v. Scurr, 744 F.2d 1323 (8th Cir. 1984)
Trial counsel's actions threatening to withdraw and tell judge and testify against Petitioner, if Petitioner testified constituted ineffective assistance of counsel. **See also** *Nichols v. Butler, 917 F.2d 518 (11th Cir. 1990); Whiteside v. Scurr, 750 F.2d 713 (8th Cir. 1984); Pilchak v. Camper, 741 F.Supp. 782 (W.D. Mo. 1990)*

Fifth Amendment Privileges Against Self-Incrimination

Ohio v. Reiner, 532 U.S. 17, 149 L.Ed.2d 158, 121 S.Ct. 1252 (2001)
A witness who had denied all culpability in manslaughter trial had valid privilege against self-incrimination under the Fifth Amendment, where witness had reasonable cause to apprehend danger from her answers, if questioned at the involuntary manslaughter trial.

Dixon v. Snyder, 266 F.3d 693, 702-703 (7th Cir. 2001)
Counsel was constitutionally ineffective by failing to research the law, cross-examine the sole eyewitness whose statement was introduced at trial identifying defendant as murdered as substantive evidence, after eyewitness recanted statement at trial, eyewitnesses statement could have been excluded if eyewitness invoked Fifth Amendment on cross-examination. Therefore, prejudice occurred since eyewitness' identification was the only direct evidence against defendant.

Perjured Testimony

U.S. v. Agurs, 427 U.S. 97, 103, 96 S. Ct. 2392, 49 LEd.2d 342 (1976)
The Supreme Court has "Consistently held that a conviction obtained by the knowing use of perjured testimony is fundamentally unfair, and must be set aside if there is any reasonable likelihood that the false testimony could have affected the judgment of the jury". This rule seems to also apply whether the prosecution knew of the perjury or merely "should have known" of the perjury. Id. **See also _U.S. v. McLaughlin, 89 F.Supp.2d 617 (E.D. Pa. 2000)_**

Mooney v. Holohan, 294 U.S. 103, 108 (1935)
Due process violated when prosecutor learned during trial that witness committed perjury but failed to inform defense counsel.

Hayes v. Brown, 399 F.3d 972, 978-980 (9th Cir. 2005)
The state violated Hayes Fourteenth Amendment right to process by knowingly presenting false testimony from prosecution witness, A.J. James, who denied that the state agreed to dismiss the felony charge in exchange for his testimony.

Phillips v. Woodford, 267 F.3d 966, 984-86 (9th Cir. 2001)
Key prosecution witness's allegedly false testimony that she had not been offered a deal in exchange for her testimony required an evidentiary hearing.

CLOSURE OF COURTROOM

Bell v. Jarvis, 198 F.3d 432 (4th Cir. 1999)
Appellate counsel's failure to raise issue that district court violated defendant's right to a public trial when Court closed court room during young victims testimony of a sex crime constituted ineffective assistance of counsel.

Brown v. Andrews, 180 F.3d 403 (2nd Cir. 1999)
The Court of appeals held that "record was insufficient to justify closure of criminal trial during testimony of undercover officer, consistent with right to public trial, on ground either of officer's continued effectiveness, or of concerns for officers safety." **Reversed and writ granted.** See also **_English v. Artuz, 164 F.3d 105 (2nd Cir. 1998)_**.

Mason v. Schriver, 14 F. Supp. 2d 323 (S.D.N.Y. 1997)
Judge's conclusory statement is plainly insufficient under **_Press-Enterpise Company v. Superior Court of California, 478 U.S. 1, 13-14, 106 S.Ct. 2735, 2743, 92 L.Ed.2d 1 (1986),_** and its progeny as it fails far short of the "explicit" and "specific" recorded findings necessary to support **closure of the courtroom during undercover officer"** testimony **and the Sixth Amendment to justify closure without** application of the four prong analysis of the Supreme Court in **_Wallace v. Georgia, 467 U.S. 39, 46, 104 S.Ct. 2210, 2215, 81 L.Ed.2d 31 (1984);_ also see, e.g., _In re Oliver, 333 U.S. 257, 266-72, 68 S.Ct. 499, 504-07, 92 L.Ed. 682 (1948)._** The Supreme Court in **_Wallace_** established a four-part test to determine when a criminal trial may be closed to the public: [1] "the party seeking to close the hearing must advance an overriding interest that is likely to be prejudiced, [2] the closure must be

no broader than necessary to protect that interest, [3] the trial court must consider reasonable alternatives to closing the proceeding, and [4] [the trial court] must make findings adequate to support the closure."

CLOSED-CIRCUIT TELEVISION TESTIMONY

U.S. v. Weekley, 130 F.3d 747 (6th Cir. 1997)
The district court before invoking alternative procedures for live, in-court testimony of child, by testimony on closed-circuit television, court must make factual finding that child would be traumatized by defendant's presence.

CORROBORATING EVIDENCE

Berry v. Gramley, 74 F.Supp.2d 808 (N.D. Ill. 1999)
Counsel's failure to visit the crime scene or employ an investigator to locate and interview witnesses to corroborate defendant's testimony amounted to ineffective assistance of counsel.

Capps v. Sullivan, 921 F.2d 260 (10th Cir. 1990)
Trial counsel's failure to interview or subpoena the witness, who would have substantially corroborated Capps' testimony material to entrapment defense, constituted ineffective assistance of counsel.

Summit v. Blackburn, 795 F.2d 1237 (5th Cir. 1986)
Trial counsel's failure to object to lack of corroborating evidence of attempted armed robbery that formed the basis of aggravating felony needed for first-degree murder conviction constituted ineffective assistance.

COUNSEL PROMOTED DEFENDANT TO LIE

Johnson v. Baldwin, 114 F.3d 835 (9th Cir. 1997)
Trial counsel promoted defendant to lie and deny being present at the alleged rape scene, which constitutes deficient performance. Defendant testified and denied his presence at scene, which enabled jury to conclude that he was lying, because he committed the rape and established prejudice under Strickland.

FAILED TO INVOKE THE SEQUESTRATION
OF WITNESS RULE

Spicer v. Warden of Roxbury Correctional Institute, 31 F.Supp. 2d 509 (D.-Md. 1998)
Defense counsel's failure to object to the prosecutions violation of the sequestration rule during the suppression hearing after the State specifically indicated that the "identification witness" would-not be called as witness and witness remained in courtroom while other witnesses testified. The State called identification witness to testify without objections for counsel constituting ineffective assistance of counsel.

Hollines v. Estelle, 569 F.Supp. 146 (W.D. Tex. 1983)
Trial counsel's failure to invoke the sequestration of witness's rule compounded with other errors amounted to ineffective assistance of counsel.

Lufkins v. Solem, 716 F.2d 532 (8th Cir. 1983)
> Trial counsel's failure to move to sequester the witnesses amounted to ineffective assistance of counsel.

FAILED TO CORRECT FALSE OR MISLEADING TESTIMONY

Mills v. Scully, 653 F.Supp. 885 (S.D. N.Y. 1987)
> Defense counsel's failure to move to correct testimony, which he knew was false or misleading, constitutes ineffective assistance of counsel.

FAILED TO INTRODUCE VIDEO/CONFESSION OF ANOTHER INDIVIDUAL

Chambers v. Missisippi, 410 U.S. 284, 93 S.Ct. 1038, 35 L.Ed.2d 297 (1973)
> Due process precluded a mechanistic application of hearsay rule to prevent a criminal defendant from introducing into evidence exculpatory third-party confessions when surrounding circumstances provide "considerable assurance of their reliability." **Id. at 300-03, 93 S.Ct. 1038**.

Wynne v. Renico, 279 F.Supp. 2d 866, 882 (E.D. Mich. 2003)
> Defendant's constitutional right to present a defense was violated by state court's refusal to allow jury to consider relevant and highly probative evidence of guilt of a third person who also happened to be the prosecution's key witness.

Luna v. Cambra, 306 F.3d 954, 961-963 (9th Cir. 2003)
> Counsel's failure to investigate and call defendant's mother and sister as alibi witnesses' to corroborate defendant's testimony that he was at home sleeping the night of the crime, constitutes ineffective assistance of counsel.

Cheung v. Maddock, 32 F.Supp. 2d 1150 (N.D. Cal. 1998)
> Defense counsel's failure to investigate defense that companion, not petitioner, was shooter and failed to present companion's tape recorded statement for admission into evidence constituted ineffective assistance of counsel.

Williamson v. Ward, 110 F.3d 1509 (10th Cir. 1997)
> Trial counsel's failure to investigate and present to the jury that another man had made a video tape confession to the murder that Williamson was charged with deprived Williamson of a fair trial and constitutes ineffective assistance of counsel. See also *Whelchel v. Wood, 996 F. Supp. 1019 (E.D. Wash. 1997)*; *Williamson v. Reynolds, 904 F.Supp. 1529 (E.D. Okl. 1995)*

Sanders v. Ratelle, 21 F.3d 1446 (9th Cir. 1994)
> Failure to investigate that another suspect purported confessed to crime constituted ineffective assistance of counsel.

Smith v. Wainwright, 799 F.2d 1442 (11th Cir. 1986)
> Trial counsel's failure to make jury aware during trial that Smith's named accomplice (Johnson) had confessed to the crime and gave a detailed statement constituted ineffective assistance of counsel. "The district court found and (the 11th Circuit)

affirmed that, at his trial, Smith was deprived of evidence which was critical to the determination of his guilt or innocence." The conviction rested upon the testimony of Johnson. His credibility was the central issue in the case. Available evidence would have had great weight in the assertion that Johnson's testimony was not true, that evidence was not used, and the jury had no knowledge of it. There is a reasonable probability that, had their original statements been used at trial, the result would have been different.

COUNSEL VERBALLY ASSAULTED DEFENDANT AND USED RACIAL COMMENTS

Frazer v. U.S., 18 F.3d 778 (9th Cir. 1994)
   Trial counsel who verbally assaulted defendant and used racial comments toward defendant and threatened to compromise defendant's rights constitutes ineffective assistance and requires an evidentiary hearing.

COUNSEL ACTING AS PROSECUTION WITNESS

Government of Virgin Island v. Zepp, 748 F.2d 125 (3rd Cir. 1984)
   Trial counsel stipulated to conduct that amounted to counsel acting as a prosecution witness by stipulating that when counsel arrived at Zepp's residence that counsel did not flush any drugs down the toilets.

COUNSEL PROVOKED ERRORS

Taylor v. Starnes, 650 F.2d 38 (4th Cir. 1981)
   Trial counsel provoked error by remaining silent instead of requesting lesser included jury instruction for assault and battery and such conduct falls below the wide range of competence demanded of attorneys in criminal cases.

COUNSEL SLEEPING DURING TRIAL

Burdine v. Johnson, 262 F.3d 336, 349 (5th Cir. 2001) (en banc)
   Unconscious counsel does not analyze, object, listen or in any way exercise judgment on behalf of a client, and where counsel slept repeatedly through trial prejudice is presumed.

Burdine v. Johnson, 66 F.Supp.2d 854 (S.D. Tex. 1999)
   Trial counsel who slept through substantial portion of trial deprived the defendant of his right to his effective assistance of counsel. **See also *Tippins v. Walker*, 77 F.3d 682 (2nd Cir. 1996).**

COUNSEL SILENT THROUGHOUT TRIAL

Harding v. Davis, *878 F.2d 1341 (11th Cir. 1989)*
> Counsel was virtually silent throughout the entire trial and failed to object when judge directed verdict against defendant. There was no need for a showing of prejudice as ineffective assistance was established, per se.

COUNSEL REFUSED TO PARTICIPATE IN TRIAL

Martin v. Rose, *744 F.2d 1245 (6th Cir. 1984)*
> Trial counsel refused to participate in the trial because he erroneously believed that participation would either waive pretrial motions or render their denial harmless error constitutes ineffective assistance of counsel.

FAILED TO DEVELOP FACTS

Roberts v. Dretke, *356 F.3d 632, 640 (5th Cir. 2004)*
> Counsel's failure to develop evidence of petitioner's mental illness and suicide intentions and make adequate use of court-appointed psychiatrist stated a valid claim of ineffective assistance and warranted a certificate of appealability (COA).

Rogers v. Israel, *746 F.2d 1288 (7th Cir. 1984)*
> Trial counsel's failure to establish facts through defendant's expert witness, which were favorable and would have cast a reasonable doubt about respecting guilt on the charge of first-degree murder, constituted ineffective assistance of counsel, and entitled defendant to an evidentiary hearing. **See also *Smith v. Wainwright*, *799 F.2d 1442 (11th Cir. 1986)***

COUNSEL HAD ALZHEIMER DISEASE

Pilchak v. Camper, *741 F.Supp. 782 (W.D. Mo. 1990)*
> Just because defense counsel was suffering from Alzheimer's did not constitute ineffective assistance of counsel without a showing of prejudice. The defendant established prejudice based on numerous cumulative unprofessional errors and omissions.

COUNSEL ABSENT DURING TRIAL

Caver v. Straub, *349 F.3d 340, 349-352 (6th Cir. 2003)*
> Counsel's absences during re-instruction to the jury was a critical stage of the proceedings and constitutes ineffective assistance of counsel per se.

Olden v. United States, *224 F.3d 561, 569-70 (6th Cir. 2000)*
> Counsel's absence during trial at critical stages triggers presumption of prejudice and required a new trial, if Olden can establish that he did not voluntarily, knowingly, and intelligently waive his right to have his own counsel.

French v. Jones, *41 F.Supp. 2d 726 (E.D. Mich. 1999)*
> Defense counsel's absence from courtroom while trial court reinstructed deadlocked

jury violated the defendant's Sixth Amendment right to counsel and a fair trial and required granting of writ of habeas corpus.

***Green v. Arn*, 809 F.2d 1257 (6th Cir. 1987)**
Trial counsel absent from trial during taking of evidence constituted a denial of counsel and is prejudicial, per se, justifying granting of the writ. Under these circumstances, the harmless error inquiry cannot be applied.

COUNSEL CALLED PROSECUTOR A JERK

***Loving v. O'keefe*, 960 F. Supp. 46 (S.D.N.Y. 1997)**
Defense counsel engaged in improper behavior calling the prosecutor a "jerk", and made faces and repeated answers to witness, all in the eyes of the jury. The court found trial counsel provided vigorous representation and may have been overzealous at times because counsel obtained an acquittal on the most serious charges.

COUNSEL STIPULATED TO ELEMENTS OF DRUG OFFENSE

***United States v. McCoy*, 410 F.3d 124, 130-135 (3rd Cir. 2005)**
Trial counsel's decision to enter into the ***Jemal*** stipulation where there was no reasonable or tactical basis for counsel to stipulate away the elements of knowledge and intent on the drug charges, required an evidentiary hearing to resolve the ineffective assistance of counsel claim.

CONCEDED DEFENDANT'S GUILT

***Haynes v. Cain*, 272 F.3d 757, 761 (5th Cir. 2001)**
Counsel's strategy conceding petitioner's guilt on felonies underlying the murder charge, and claiming only issue in the case is, whether petitioner intended to commit murder was per se ineffective, because counsel failed to subject the prosecution's case to a meaningful adversarial testing process. Petitioner was constructive denied his right to counsel in violation of the Sixth and Fourteenth Amendments.

***Cave v. Singletary*, 971 F.2d 1513 (11th Cir. 1992)**
Trial counsel admitted to the jury the defendant's guilt on armed robbery because counsel misunderstood the concept of felony-murder and resulted in performance below an objective standard of reasonableness for defense counsel in criminal cases.

***U.S. v. Byfield*, 795 F.Supp. 468 (D. D.C. 1992)**
Trial counsel's opening argument placed defendant with alleged drug courier at times other than date of defendant's arrest and suggested that shoe box carried by courier had contained defendant's shoes, which provided a basis for jury's guilty verdict and amounted to ineffective assistance of counsel.

***U.S. v. Swanson*, 943 F.2d 1070 (9th Cir. 1991)**
Trial counsel conceded factual issues in dispute, and such conduct by counsel failed to hold the government to its burden of persuading the jury that Petitioner is guilty. Thus, Petitioner was deprived of effective assistance of counsel.

Young v. Zant, 677 F.2d 792 (11th Cir. 1982)
> Trial counsel conceded defendant's guilt on all three crimes in guilt phase of trial based on mistaken belief that such action was necessary to plead for mercy at sentencing, which constituted ineffective assistance.

COUNSEL INTRODUCED IRRELEVANT OR PREJUDICIAL EVIDENCE

Dubria v. Smith, 197 F.3d 390 (9th Cir. 1999)
> Trial counsel suggested that evidence not presented to jury supported murder charges constituted ineffective assistance of counsel.

Sager v. Maass, 907 F.Supp. 1412 (D. Or. 1995)
> Trial counsel's introduction of the entire victim impact statement into evidence as a handwriting sample and as impeachment evidence constituted ineffective assistance of counsel. This blunder alone factually tainted the trial. **See also *Ward v. U.S., 995 F.2d 1317 (6th Cir. 1993)***

Martinez-Macias v. Collins, 810 F.Supp. 782 (W.D. Tex. 1991)
> Trial counsel's failure to research the law and call disinterested alibi witnesses who were available regardless of risk of opening door to the presentation of extraneous criminal incident constituted ineffective assistance of counsel.

United States v. Bosch, 584 F.2d 1113 (1st Cir. 1978)
> Trial counsel introduced prejudicial evidence concerning defendant's prior convictions, which were otherwise inadmissible, constituted ineffective assistance of counsel.

FAILED TO SUBJECT PROSECUTION'S CASE TO MEANINGFUL ADVERSE TESTING PROCESS

Bell v. Cone, 535 U.S. 685, 152 L.Ed.2d 914, 122 S.Ct. 1843, 1850 (2002)
> ***Cronic*** applies when counsel entirely fails to subject the prosecution's case to a meaningful adversarial testing process. The ***Bell*** Court clarified that an attorney's failure must be complete, noting the difference between the situations addressed by ***Strickland*** and ***Cronic*** is "not of degree but of kind." ***Bell*, 122 S.Ct. at 1581**. The Court identified three situations implicating the right to counsel, where the Court would presume petitioner has been prejudiced. ***Bell*, 122 S.Ct. at 1850**. First, where petitioner is denied counsel at a critical stage of the criminal proceeding. Second, where petitioner is represented by counsel at trial, but counsel "entirely fails to subject the prosecution's case to a meaningful adversarial testing." Third, prejudice is presumed when the circumstances surrounding a trial prevent petitioner's attorney from rendering effective assistance of counsel. **Id.**

U.S. v. Theodore, 345 F. Supp. 2d 123, 130 (D. Mass. 2004)
> Counsel was constitutionally ineffective because he failed to subject the prosecution's case to a meaningful adversarial testing process by failing to prepare for trial, had no focused defense strategy, failed to call any witnesses, and failed to oppose the government's motion to squash his one properly executed subpoena.

U.S. v. Cronic, 466 U.S. 648, 80 L.Ed.2d 657, 104 S.Ct. 2039 (1984)
> Trial counsel's failure to subject the prosecution's case to a meaningful adversary testing process may constitute a denial of due process and establish a per se violation of defendant's right to effective assistance of counsel. See also ***Rickman v. Bell, 131 F.3d 1150 (6th Cir. 1997)***; ***Groseclose v. Bell, 130 F.3d 1161 (6th Cir. 1997)***.

Patrasso v. Nelson, 121 F.3d 297 (7th Cir. 1997)
> Defense counsel at sentencing made no effort to contradict prosecution's case, or to present mitigating factors, thus, leaving defendant without a defense at sentencing or an opportunity to argue for a sentence less than statutory maximum, which he received. The Seventh Circuit found under these circumstance counsel failed to subject the prosecution's case to a meaningful adversarial testing and applied the Cronic, standard, where prejudice was presumed.

U.S. v. Glover, 97 F.3d 1345 (10th Cir. 1996)
> Counsel's failure to hold the government to the burden of proof, that D-methamphetamine rather than L-methamphetamine was involved in the offense constituted performance that undermined the proper functioning of the adversarial process, which cannot be relied on has having produced a just result, and constitutes ineffective assistance of counsel.

U.S. v. Byfield, 795 F.Supp. 468 (D. D.C. 1992)
> Trial counsel's opening arguments placed defendant with alleged drug courier at times other than date of defendant's arrest and suggested that shoe box carried by courier had contained defendant's shoes, which provided a basis for jury's guilty verdict, and amounted to ineffective assistance of counsel.

U.S. v. Swanson, 943 F.2d 1070 (9th Cir. 1991)
> Trial counsel abandoned Petitioner's only defense, which was inherently prejudicial because counsel conceded only factual issue in dispute in closing arguments constituting ineffective assistance of counsel. See also ***Cave v. Singletary, 971 F.2d 1513 (11th Cir. 1992);Daniel v. Thigpen, 742 F.Su pp. 1535 (M.D. Ala. 1990)***

Harding v. Davis, 878 F.2d 1341 (11th Cir. 1989)
> Counsel was virtually silent throughout the entire trial and failed to object when judge directed verdict against defendant. There was no need for a showing of prejudice as ineffective assistance was established, per se.

Osborn v. Shillinger, 861 F.2d 612 (10th Cir. 1988)
> Defense counsel's performance was not only ineffective, but counsel abandoned the required duty of loyalty to his client; counsel did not simply make poor strategic or tactical choices; he acted with reckless disregard for his client's best interest, and apparently with the intention to weaken his client's case.

U.S. Ex. Rel. Potts v. Chrans, 700 F.Supp. 1505 (N.D. Ill. 1988)
> Trial counsel's failure to offer evidence or make closing arguments on defendant's behalf amounted to failure to hold government to burden of proof and deprived defendant of the right to effective assistance of counsel.

**Young v. Zant**, 677 F.2d 792 (11th Cir. 1982)
> Trial counsel conceded defendant's guilt on all three crimes in guilt phase of trial based on mistaken belief that such action was necessary in order to plead for mercy, and such action constituted ineffective assistance.

FAILED TO RAISE INSUFFICIENCY OF EVIDENCE

**Fiore v. White**, 531 U.S. 225, 148 L.Ed.2d 629, 121 S.Ct. 712 (2001)
> Fiore was convicted absent proof of an essential element of the offense (operating hazardous waste facility without a permit), the Supreme Court found that lack of evidence supporting the criminal offense violates due process and reversed the conviction.

**Richey v. Mitchell**, 395 F.3d 660, 681-82 (6th Cir. 2005)
> Trial and appellate counsel was ineffective for failing to challenge the sufficiency of evidence, the State failed to prove one of the elements, that is, Richey's specific intent to kill the victim.

**Plaskowski v. Casperson**, 126 F.Supp. 1149 (E.D. Wis. 2001)
> The Court held that there was insufficient evidence to support defendant's conviction and the Wisconsin appellate court's decision holding to the contrary was an unreasonable application of the constitutional standard set forth by the Supreme Court in _**Jackson v.Virginia**_, 443 U.S. 307, 319, 99 S.Ct. 2781, 61 L.Ed.2d 560 (1979).

**Carpenter v. Mohr**, 163 F.3d 938 (6th Cir. 1998)
> Appellate counsel's failure to challenge sufficiency of evidence supporting conditional guilty plea constituted ineffective assistance of counsel.

**Buggs v. U.S.**, 153 F.3d 439 (7th Cir. 1998)
> Insufficiency of evidence raises a constitutional issue cognizable on collateral review.

**Quatararo v. Hanslmaier**, 28 F. Supp. 2d 749 (E.D.N.Y. 1998)
> Where the evidence was insufficient to support conviction for second-degree murder habeas corpus relief was granted.

**Whaley v Thompson**, 22 F. Supp. 2d 1146 (D. Or. 1998)
> Where the evidence was insufficient to sustain aggravated kidnapping conviction under Oregon law habeas corpus relief was warranted pursuant to _28 U.S.C. §2254._

**Holsclaw v. Smith**, 822 F.2d 1041 (11th Cir. 1987)
> Trial counsel's failure to raise issue of insufficient evidence at the end of trial or move for dismissal based on insufficient evidence constituted ineffective assistance of counsel.

FORFEITURE PHASE OF TRIAL

**United States v. Arbolaez**, 450 F.3d 1283, 1294-1295 (11th Cir. 2006)
> Failure to allow counsel to present evidence and argument during forfeiture phase of trial was not harmless error beyond a reasonable doubt and warranted reversal.

CLOSING ARGUMENTS RELATED INEFFECTIVENESS

Herring v. New York, 422 U.S. 853, 45 LEd.2d 593, 95 S.Ct. 2550 (1975)
Defense counsel in a criminal case has a right to present closing arguments to the jury which is a basic element of the adversary factfinding process.

Spisak v. Mitchell, 465 F.3d 684, 704 (6th Cir, 2006)
Counsel provided constitutionally ineffective assistance during closing arguments to the jury where he stressed his own hostility towards Spisak because of the brutality and the aggravating factors of the crimes.

Humphries v. Ozmint, 366 F.3d 266, 275-78 (4th Cir. 2004)
Counsel's failure to object to prosecutor's closing argument that compared the life of murdered victim to that of petitioner constituted ineffective assistance of counsel.

Gentry v. Roe, 320 F.3d 891, 902-903 (9th Cir. 2003)
Counsel was ineffective because his closing arguments detailed a host of things that hurt petitioner's defense; failed to discuss important factors of the case to the jury; there was not overwhelming evidence of petitioner's guilt, and the jury deliberated over six hours before returning a guilty verdict.

Gentry v. Roe, 300 F.3d 1007, 1013-15 (9th Cir. 2002)
Trial counsel failed to address the only aspects of the trial that mattered during closing arguments, focused on things that did not matter, and mentioned a host of details that hurt his client's position, such as, his client was a "bad person, lousy drug addict, stinking thief, and jail bird," which amounted to ineffective assistance of counsel.

Fisher v. Gibson, 282 F.3d 1283, 1305 (10th Cir. 2002)
Trial counsel failed to present a closing argument to the jury. A closing argument may have overcome the impact of counsel's hostility towards his client while he was on the stand or advance a theory of defense constitutes ineffective assistance of counsel.

Hunter v. Moore, 304 F.3d 1066, 1069-1072 (11th Cir. 2002)
Defendant was deprived of his right to effective assistance of counsel; the trial court issued its verdict in a bench trial without affording defense counsel an opportunity to present closing arguments, constituting a denial of counsel at a critical stage of the proceeding. Thus, reversal was warranted without a showing of prejudice under **_Cronic_**.

Washington v. Hofbauer, 228 F.3d 689, 704-05 (9th Cir. 2000)
Counsel's failure to object to the prosecutor using Washington's "bad character" evidence as a basis to argue his guilt during closing arguments constitutes ineffecttive assistance of counsel.

Werts v. Vaughn, 228 F.3d 178, 206 (3rd Cir. 2000)
Counsel's failure to object to the prosecutor's comment that petitioner would be a marked man during closing argument was deficient performance, but no prejudiced was shown.

Burns v. Gammon, 260 F.3d 892, 897-98 (8th Cir. 2001)
> Counsel was constitutionally ineffective for failing to object to the prosecutor's closing arguments that defendant forced victim to relive the attack by exercising his constitutional right to trial by jury or request a cautionary instruction.

Agard v. Portuondo, 159 F.3d 98 (2nd Cir. 1998)
> The Court found that "prosecutor's closing argument comments suggesting that defendant" credibility was less than that of prosecution witnesses, solely because he attended entire trial, while witnesses were present only during their own testimony, was not harmless error and warranted habeas corpus relief." **Id.**

U.S. v. Maddox, 156 F.3d 1280 (D.C. Cir. 1998)
> Prosecutor's closing arguments which referred to and suggested that uncalled witnesses would have supported government's case was reversible error.

Tejeda v. Dubois, 142 F.3d 18 (1st Cir. 1998)
> Trial counsel's failure to present a coherent argument to the judge and jury based on defense of police fabrication rendered defendant's trial fundamentally unfair, unreliable, and constituted ineffective assistance of counsel.

Waters v. Zant, 979 F.2d 1473 (11th Cir. 1992)
> Trial counsel's failure to argue that defendant was only guilty of manslaughter was ineffective assistance of counsel.

U.S. v. Swanson, 943 F.2d 1070 (9th Cir. 1991)
> Trial counsel abandoned Petitioner's only defense, which was inherently prejudicial, where counsel conceded only factual issue in dispute in closing arguments and deprived Petitioner of effective assistance of counsel, and due process. Thus, no showing of prejudice was necessary. **See also** *Jones v. Jones*, **988 F.Supp. 1000 (E.D.La.1997)**; *Demarest v. Price*, **905 F.Supp. 1432 (D.Col. 1995)**; *Weygandt v. Ducharme*, **774 F.2d 1491 (9th Cir. 1985)**; *United States v. Hammonds*, **425 F.2d 597 (D.C. Cir. 1970)**; *Jemison v. Foltz*, **672 F.Supp. 1002 (E.D. Mich. 1987)**;

Lyons v. McCotter, 770 F.2d 529 (5th Cir. 1985)
> Defense counsel's failure to object to the prosecutor's allusion in closing argument to Lyons' propensity to commit aggravated robbery in light of his prior conviction for a similar crime, and his failure to seek a limiting jury instruction constituted ineffective assistance of counsel.

United States v. Rusmisel, 716 F.2d 301 (5th Cir. 1983)
> Trial counsel's failure to object to prosecutor's closing arguments where prosecutor attempted to prove guilt by association was ineffective assistance of counsel.

JURY INSTRUCTIONS RELATED INEFFECTIVENESS

Accomplice Instructions

Lankford v. Arave, 468 F.3d 578, 584-591 (9th Cir. 2006)
> Counsel was constitutionally ineffective for requesting a jury instruction eliminating Idaho's requirement that an accomplice's testimony must corroborated by other

evidence in order to convict, which relieved the prosecution of its burden of proof in capital murder case.

Everett v. Beard, 290 F.3d 506,510-19 (3rd Cir. 2002)
Trial counsel's failure to object to accomplices jury instruction, which permitted jury to convict defendant of first degree murder, if his accomplices intended to cause the victims death, violates due process and constitutes ineffectiveness of counsel.

Freeman v. Class, 95 F.3d 639 (8th Cir. 1996)
Trial counsel's failure to request a special cautionary instruction on the credibility of accomplice testimony pursuant to South Dakota Pattern Jury Instructions 1-14-8, which provides that a conviction cannot be had upon the testimony of an accomplice unless it is corroborated by other evidence which tends to connect the defendant with the commission of offense. S.D. Codified Laws Ann. §23A-22-8(1994), constitutes ineffective assistance of counsel.

Com. v. Chmiel, 639 A.2d 9 (Pa. 1994)
Trial counsel's failure to request an accomplice jury instruction constituted ineffective assistance.

Voyles v. Watkins, 489 F.Supp. 901 (1980)
Trial counsel's failure to request an accomplice jury instruction for the key prosecution's witness' testimony to be scrutinized with caution and suspicion, amounted to ineffective assistance of counsel and constituted "cause" for failure to raise the issue. **See also** *Harris v. Housewright, 697 F.2d 202 (8th Cir. 1982)*

Ambiguous Instruction

Boyde v. California, 494 U.S. 370, 379-80, 110 S.Ct. 1190, 108 L .Ed. 2d 316 (1990)
The Supreme Court established that, with respect to ambiguous jury instructions, "[i]n some instances . . . we have held that when a case is submitted to the jury on alternative theories, the unconstitutionality of any of the theories requires that the conviction be set aside." **Id. at 379-80, 110 S.Ct. 1190**. **See also** *Martinez v. Garcia, 379 F.3d 1034, 1041 (9th Cir. 2004)*.

Payton v. Woodford, 346 F.3d 1204, 1211-13 (9th Cir. 2003)
California model instruction requiring death penalty jury to take into account "any other circumstances which extenuates the gravity of the crime even though it is not a legal excuse for the crime," was unconstitutionally ambiguous as applied to post-crime evidence; the instructional error was not harmless and required the death sentence to be set aside.

Aggravating Circumstances Instructions

Joseph v. Coyle, 469 F.3d 441, 460-465 (6th Cir. 2006)
Trial counsel was constitutionally ineffective for failing to object to the indictment and charge to the jury that incorrectly charged Joseph with the capital specification for being the principal offender in commission of kidnapping when the statute required the defendant to be the principal offender in the commission of the aggravated murder. A little research would have revealed that being the principal

offender in the commission of the aggravated murder means that the defendant must have "actually killed" the victim.

Starr v. Lockhart, 23 F.3d 1280, 1285-86 (8th Cir. 1994)
Trial counsel's failure to object to either "pecuniary gain" or "heinous atrocious or cruel" aggravating circumstances jury instructions during penalty phase amounted to ineffective assistance of counsel.

Buyer-Seller Instructions

Schmidt v. U.S., 987 F.2d 536, 537 (8th Cir. 1993)
Counsel's failure to request a jury instruction that explained buyer-seller relationship of cocaine transaction not ineffective assistance when jury instructions adequately covered the substance of defendant's buyer-seller defense theory.

Cautionary Instruction

Burns v. Gammon, 260 F.3d 892, 897-98 (8th Cir. 2001)
Counsel was constitutionally ineffective for failing to object to the prosecutor's closing arguments that defendant forced victim to relive the attack by exercising his constitutional right to trial by jury or request a cautionary instruction.

Coercive Instruction

Jenkins v. United States, 380 U.S. 445, 13 L.Ed. 957, 85 S.Ct. 1059 (1965)
A jury instruction directing the jury that it had to reach a verdict was coercive and constitutes reversible error.

U.S. v. Eastern Medical Billing, Inc., 230 F.3d 600, 614 (3rd Cir. 2000)
A coercive supplemental instruction, given after two days of deliberation because the jury was hung on some of the charges was not harmless error and required reversal.

Defective or Improper Instructions

Smith v. Wainwright, 741 F.2d 1248 (11th Cir. 1984)
Appellate counsel's failure to challenge defective jury instruction constituted ineffective assistance of counsel. See also *Luchenburg v. Smith, 79 F.3d 388 (4th Cir. 1996)*

Diminished Capacity Instruction

Pirtle v. Morgan, 313 F.3d 1160, 1172 (9th Cir. 2002)
Counsel's failure to request a diminished capacity jury instruction during penalty phase of capital murder trial constituted ineffective assistance.

Excessive Force Theory Instruction

U.S. v. Span, 75 F.3d 1383 (9th Cir. 1996)
Defense counsel's failure to request an excessive force theory jury instruction was ineffective assistance.

Erroneous Instructions

Baker v. Horn, 383 F.Supp.2d 720, 778-780 (E.D. Pa. 2005)
> Counsel's failure to object to the trial court's erroneous jury instruction permitting jury to convict of first degree murder as an accomplice without a finding that petitioner possessed the specific intent to kill amounted to ineffective assistance of counsel.

Luchenburg v. Smith, 79 F.3d 388 (4th Cir. 1996)
> Trial counsel's failure to request a jury instruction that correctly stated the law and defined a predicate crime of violence to the jury, so it could not convict defendant unless it first found him guilty of the predicate crime of violence and that common-law assault was not a predicate offense constitutes ineffective assistance of counsel.

Gray v. Lynn, 6 F.3d 265 (5th Cir. 1993)
> Trial counsel's failure to object to erroneous jury instruction, which expanded the elements of attempted first degree murder charge constitutes ineffective assistance of counsel.

Kubat v. Thieret, 867 F.2d 351 (7th Cir. 1989)
> Defense counsel's failure to object to court's erroneous jury instruction during death penalty phase constituted ineffective assistance of counsel. See also **_Goodwin v. Balkcom, 684 F.2d 794 (11th Cir. 1982)._**

Crowe v. Sowders, 864 F.2d 430 (6th Cir. 1988)
> Trial counsel's failure to object or move for a mistrial, file a motion for a new trial, after the judge erroneously instructed jury based on parole "consequences", which was not a matter for the jury, constituted ineffective assistance of counsel.

United States v. Bosch, 584 F.2d 1113 (1st Cir. 1978)
> Trial counsel's failure to object to the trial court's erroneous reply to the jury note which referred to the information that contained Bosch's prior convictions amounted to ineffective assistance of counsel.

Entrapment Instruction

Jones v. Jones, 988 F. Supp. 1000 (E.D.La. 1997)
> Counsel's failure to present the only viable defense of entrapment amounted to ineffective assistance.

Capps v. Sullivan, 921 F.2d 260 (10th Cir. 1990)
> Trial counsel's failure to request an entrapment jury instruction, after defendant Capps took the stand at trial and admitted all of the elements of the crime and there was evidence to support an entrapment defense constituted ineffective assistance of counsel.

Good Faith Defense Instruction

U.S. v. Cronic, 839 F.2d 1401 (10th Cir. 1988)
> Trial counsel's failure to request a good faith defense jury charge amounted to ineffective assistance.

Omission of Essential Elements

Lombard v. Lynaugh, 868 F.2d 1475 (5th Cir. 1989)
> Trial counsel's failure to contest the omission of an essential element from the jury charge constitutes ineffective assistance of counsel.

Failed to Request Any Instructions

United States v. Hammonds, 425 F.2d 597 (D.C. Cir. 1970)
> Trial counsel's failure to request any jury instructions compounded with other errors amounted to ineffective assistance of counsel.

Intent Instructions

U.S. v. Wolf, 787 F.2d 1094 (7th Cir. 1986)
> Trial counsel's failure to object to the jury instruction on intent or offer a dominant purpose jury instruction constituted ineffective assistance of counsel. **See also** *Steinkuehier v. Meschner, 176 F.3d 441 (8th Cir. 1999)*

Rummel v. Estelle, 498 F.Supp. 793 (W.D. Tex 1980)
> Trial counsel's failure to investigate the facts of the offense and pursue defense of lack of intent to write the hot check constituted ineffective assistance of counsel.

Intoxication Defense

Jackson v. Calderon, 211 F.3d 1148 (9th Cir. 2000)
> Defense counsel's failure to investigate and compile social history and develope mitigating factors based on the defendant's intoxication from (PCP) phencydicline which could have established a 90% medical certainly that defendant was unable to think consciously when he committed crime amounted to ineffective assistance of counsel.

Harich v. Wainwright, 813 F.2d 1082 (11th Cir. 1987)
> Trial counsel's failure to request a jury instruction based on Harich's intoxication defense may constitute ineffective assistance of counsel.

Instruction Constructively Amended Indictment

Lucas v. O'Dea, 179 F.3d 412 (6th Cir. 1999)
> Trial counsel's failure to object to a jury instruction which constructively amended the indictment creating a fatal variance and rendered murder defense meaningless constituted ineffective assistance of counsel.

Gray v. Lynn, 6 F.3d 265 (5th Cir. 1993)
> Trial counsel's failure to object to erroneous jury instruction, which expanded the elements of attempted first degree murder charge, constitutes ineffective assistance of counsel.

Thomas v. Harrelson, 942 F.2d 1530 (11th Cir. 1991)

> Trial counsel's failure to object or raise issue to constructive amendment of indictment constituted ineffective assistance.

Instruction Relieved Prosecution of Burden of Proof

Medley v. Runnels, 506 F.3d 857, 863-868 (9th Cir. 2007)

> The trial court's jury instructions relieved the prosecution of its burden of proof that a flare gun was designed to be used as a weapon as defined by statute and violated due process warranting habeas relief.

Instruction Shifted Burden of Proof

Cox v. Donnelly, 432 F.3d 388, 390 (2nd Cir. 2005)

> Counsel was constitutionally ineffective for failing to object to erroneous jury instruction that impermissibly shifted the burden of proof to defendant because of counsel's misunderstanding of the law.

Cox v. Donnelly, 387 F.3d 193, 198 (2nd Cir. 2004)

> Counsel was constitutionally ineffective for failing to object to an unconstitutional instruction that shifted the burden of proof onto defendant, which could not be deemed strategic and prejudiced the outcome of Cox's trial.

Cox v. Donnelly, 267 F.Supp. 2d 418, 424 (E.D.N.Y. 2003)

> Counsel's failure to object to the jury instruction on "intent to kill" that improperly shifted the burden of proof from the prosecution to petitioner constitutes ineffective assistance of counsel.

Law Enforcement Agents Dual Role as Fact and Expert Witness Cautionary Instruction

United States v. Lopez-Medina, 461 F.3d 724, 743-749 (6th Cir. 2006)

> The trial court's failure to give a cautionary jury instruction about law enforcement agents' dual roles in testifying both as fact and expert witness, along with the introduction of irrelevant criminal histories of Medina's acquaintances was prejudicial and plain error warranting reversal.

Lesser Included Instruction

Turrentine v. Mullin, 390 F.3d 1181, 1191-93 (10th Cir. 2004)

> Erroneous second-degree murder instruction that deprived defendant of his right to have jury instructed on lesser included offense warranted habeas relief where defendant presented substantial evidence of his own diminished capacity at the time of the murders.

Daniel v. Thigpen, 742 F.Supp. 1535 (M.D. Ala. 1990)

> Trial counsel's failure to object to jury instruction or request an instruction for a lesser included offense constituted ineffective assistance of counsel and established "cause" for procedural default.

Trial Ineffectiveness

Summit v. Blackburn, 795 F.2d 1237 (5th Cir. 1986)
> Trial counsel's failure to move for a post-verdict judgment of acquittal or a modification of the verdict for a conviction on a lesser included charge constitutes ineffective assistance of counsel.

Young v. Zant, 677 F.2d 792 (11th Cir. 1982)
> Trial counsel's failure to request the court to give a voluntary manslaughter charge to the jury constitutes ineffective assistance.

Taylor v. Starnes, 650 F.2d 38 (4th Cir. 1981)
> Failure to request a lesser included misdemeanor offense jury instruction based on assault and battery, where the evidence supported said instruction constitutes ineffective assistance of counsel.

Limiting Instruction

White v. McAninch, 235 F.3d 988, 997 (6th Cir. 2000)
> Trial counsel in prosecution for oral sex with child victim elicited extensive testimony from several witnesses concerning uncharged acts of sexual intercourse and failed to request a limiting instruction on the use of uncharged acts of sexual intercourse evidence, which constituted ineffective assistance of counsel because the victim's testimony about oral sex acts were largely uncorroborated.

Crotts v. Smith, 73 F3d 861 (9th Cir. 1996)
> Trial counsel's failure to object, to request a limiting instruction where the prosecution presented highly prejudicial untrue testimony that the defendant made statements that he had " killed a cop", constituted ineffective assistance.

Williams v. Washington, 59 F.3d 673 (7th Cir. 1995)
> Trial counsel's failure to take appropriate measures to limit the use of a co-defendant's confession or to attempt to have the statement redrafted to eliminate any reference to defendant constitutes ineffective assistance.

U.S. v. Myers, 892 F.2d 642 (7th Cir. 1990)
> Trial counsel's failure to seek a limiting instruction as to co-defendant Nelson's out-of-court statement that would tell the jury to consider the statement only in relation to Neal's guilt or innocence constituted ineffective assistance.

Lyons v. McCotter, 770 F.2d 529 (5th Cir. 1985)
> Defense counsel's failure to object at the proper time to the introduction of Lyon's prior conviction, or to seek to limit the use by requesting a limiting jury instruction of such evidence constituted ineffective assistance of counsel.

Marzullo v. State of MD., 561 F.2d 540 (1977)
> Trial counsel's failure to request a specific jury instruction to disregard the prejudicial remarks, which the jury heard, about the first rape charge that had been dismissed at the prosecutor's request constituted ineffective assistance of counsel.

Materiality Element Instruction

United States v. Alferahin, 433 F.3d 1148, 1162 (9th Cir. 2006)

Counsel was constitutionally ineffective for failing to request jury instructions on materiality element of the offense for charge of knowingly procuring naturalization contrary to law.

Missing Witness Instruction

Henry v. Scully, 78 F.3d 51 (2nd Cir. 1996)

Trial counsel's failure to request a missing witness jury instruction with respect to confidential informant who did not testify at trial constituted ineffective assistance of counsel.

Mitigating Evidence Instructions

Noland v. Dixon, 808 F. Supp. 485 (W.D.N.C. 1992)

The Court found that Noland was entitled to a new sentencing because of a jury instruction defect allowed the jury to discredit mitigating factors in order to come to an unanimous decision. Noland was entitled to evidentiary hearing to resolve his ineffective assistance of counsel claims.

Hawkins v. Lynaugh, 862 F.2d 482 (5th Cir. 1988)

Trial counsel's failure to request a jury instruction for the jury to be able to consider mitigating evidence based on the defendant's history of mental illness and his difficult childhood constitutes ineffective assistance of counsel.

Woodard v. Sargent, 806 F.2d 153 (8th Cir. 1986)

Defense counsel's failure to request a jury instruction based on mitigating circumstances and lack of prior criminal activity constitutes ineffective assistance.

Multiple Conspiracy Instruction

U.S. v. Chandler, 950 F.Supp. 1545 (N.D. Ala. 1996)

Trial counsel's failure to request a multiple conspiracy jury instruction **may** constitute ineffective assistance, if the evidence supports multiple conspiracies. This case did not support the theory of multiple conspiracy defenses, and the Court held counsel to be effective.

Prior Inconsistent Statement Instruction

Phylle v. Leapley, 66 F.3d 154 (8th Cir. 1995)

Trial counsel's failure to request a jury instruction that a witness's credibility may be attacked by the use of prior inconsistent statements was <u>explained</u> away by counsel at an evidentiary hearing, and held <u>not</u> to be ineffective assistance.

Presumed to be Innocent Instruction

U.S. Ex. Rel. Castleberry v. Sielaff, 446 F.Supp. 451 (N.D. Ill. 1978)

Trial counsel's failure to request a jury instruction that the defendant is presumed innocent and the burden of proof beyond a reasonable doubt is on the State to prove, constituted ineffective assistance of counsel.

Reasonable Doubt Instruction

In re Winship, 397 U.S. 358, 364, 90 S.Ct. 1068, 25 L.Ed.2d 368 (1970)

The Due Process Clause protects the accused against conviction except upon proof beyond a reasonable doubt of every fact necessary to constitute the crime with which he is charged.

Franics v. Franklin, 471 U.S. 307, 309, 105 S.Ct. 1965, 85 L.Ed.2d 344 (1985)

Due process requires the government to prove every element of a criminal offense beyond a reasonable doubt.

Bloomer v. U.S., 162 F.3d 187 (2nd Cir. 1998)

Defense counsel's failure to object to and raise issue that the jury instruction on reasonable doubt is constitutionally deficient constituted ineffective assistance of counsel. **See also** *McKee v. U.S., 167 F.3d 103 (2nd Cir. 1999); Brown v. U.S., 167 F.3d 109 (2nd Cir. 1999)*

Simpson v. Matesanz, 29 F.Supp. 2d 11 (D. Mass. 1998)

The reasonable doubt jury instruction violated the defendant's Sixth Amendment right to a fair trial where the instruction stated that jury must be sure of defendant's guilt to a "moral certainty" of same degree juror's used to make "decisions of importance" in their own lives, and stated that juror's should give defendant benefit of the doubt if they had any "serious unanswered questions" about his guilt. The defective reasonable doubt jury instruction was held to be a "structural defect" which defies analysis by "harmless-error" and required granting federal habeas relief.

Self-Defense Instruction

U.S. v. Sanchez-Lima, 161 F.3d 545 (9th Cir. 1998)

District court's failure to give jury instruction that clearly indicated that government had burden of disproving self-defense was reversible error.

Sanders v. U.S., 8 F. Supp. 2d 674 (N.D. Ohio 1998)

Petitioner collaterally attacked his state prior conviction used to enhance his current federal sentence under the **Armed Career Criminal Act** pursuant to *28 U.S.C.§2255* motion to vacate even through state prior conviction had expired decades ago. The Court held that the Armed Career Criminal Act sentence enhancement could not be applied where said prior conviction was the result of ineffectiveness of counsel where counsel failed to object to an inadequate jury instructions on self-defense state assault case.

U.S. v. Span, 75 F.3d 1383 (9th Cir. 1996)
>Trial counsel's failure to pursue an affirmative of self-defense and request a jury instruction on self-defense in this assault of a federal officer case constituted ineffective assistance of counsel.

Supplemental Instruction

Fillippon v. Albion Vein Slate Co., 250 U.S. 76, 63 L.Ed. 853, 39 S.Ct. 435 (1919)
>The Supreme Court observed "that the orderly conduct of trial by jury essential to the proper protection of the right to be heard, entitles the parties who attend for the purposes to be present in person, or by counsel, at all proceeding from the time the jury is impaneled until it is discharged after rendering the verdict." **Id., at 81, 63 L.Ed 893, 39 S.Ct. 435**. In applying that principle, the Court found that the trial judge had "erred in giving a supplementary instruction to the jury in the absence of the parties and without affording them an opportunity either to be present or to make timely objections to the instructions. **See also *Shields v. United States*, 273 U.S. 583, 71 L.Ed. 787, 47 S.Ct. 478 (1927)**.

French v. Jones, 332 F.3d 430, 438 (6th Cir. 2003)
>The trial court erred delivering a supplemental instruction to the deadlocked jury without affording defense counsel an opportunity to respond to the juries note or the supplemental instruction. This type of action by the court violated petitioner's right to be present and his right to counsel at critical stages of the proceedings in violation of *Cronic*.

Arguments Cannot Cure Defective Instruction

Carter v. Kentucky, 450 U.S. 288, 67 L.Ed.2d 241, 101 S.Ct. 1112 (1981)
>Defense counsel's arguments to the jury cannot substitute for an instruction by the court to the jury.

Goodwin v. Balkcom, 684 F.2d 794 (11th Cir. 1982)
>Trial counsel's arguments can never substitute for a jury instruction given by the trial court and argument cannot cure defective jury instructions.

Insufficient CCE Instruction

Rutledge v. U.S., 22 F. Supp. 2d 871, 877 (C.D. Ill. 1998)
>The Court **VACATED** the **Continuing Criminal Enterprise count (CCE)**. When the Court instructed the jury on the elements required to convict on Count V. It did not instruct the jury that the drug trafficking crime must be a felony. The Court instructed the jury "that the firearm was used or carried during and in relation to a **drug trafficking crime for which he may be prosecuted in a court of the United States."** The Court then found this instruction was insufficient, because it simply does not inform the jury that the predicate offense needs to be a felony. Some drug trafficking crimes are not felonies. **See** *21 U.S.C. §844,* making possession for small amount of controlled substances punishable by imprisonment of one year or less. **It was for the above reasons, the CCE conviction was improper and is accordingly VACATED.**

Voluntary Manslaughter Instruction

Kemp v. Leggett, 635 F.2d 453 (5th Cir. 1981)
> Trial counsel's failure to prepare for trial, to interview a single witness, to call several character witnesses who were present in the courtroom, failed to prepare a defense and failed to proffer a written charge on voluntary manslaughter charge constituted ineffective assistance.

U.S. Ex Rel. Barnard v. Lane, 819 F.2d 798 (7th Cir. 1987)
> Defense counsel's deliberate withholding a manslaughter instruction constituted ineffective assistance of counsel because the jury was reluctant about returning verdict on murder count.

Trustworthiness of Statement Instruction

Arrowood v. Clusen, 732 F.2d 1364 (7th Cir. 1984)
> Trial counsel's failure to request a limiting instruction based on trustworthiness of statement made by defendant and failure to abstract critical testimony for defendant concerning the alleged statements constituted ineffective assistance of counsel.

Other Instruction Problems

Waye v. Morris, 469 U.S. 908, 83 LEd.2d 218, 105 S.CT.282 (1984)
> Trial counsel's failure to object to a constitutionally defective jury instruction may constitute ineffective assistance of counsel. (Dissenting opinion.) Certiorari granted on other grounds.

Patterson v. Dahm, 769 F.Supp. 1103 (D. Neb. 1991)
> Trial counsel offering instruction for conspiracy to commit murder as a lesser-included offense of first-degree murder constitutes ineffective assistance.

Miller v. Wainwright, 798 F.2d 426 (11th Cir. 1986)
> Trial counsel's failure to object to court's failure to define sexual battery as the underlying felony in the felony murder charge may constitute ineffective assistance.

Poll of Jury Problems

Sincox v. United States, 571 F.2d 876 (5th Cir. 1978)
> Counsel's failure to object during poll of jury because a juror indicated that he had a reasonable doubt concerning petitioner's guilt showed that the verdict was not a unanimous and constitutes ineffective assistance of counsel.

JURY NOTE

U.S. v. Clark, 409 F.3d 1039, 1044 (8th Cir. 2005)
> Defendant had no right to be present during two meetings between judge and trial counsel in which jury notes were read and discussed or during in chambers conference and brief hearing regarding note from individual juror.

United States v. Bosch, 584 F.2d 1113 (1st Cir. 1978)
> Trial counsel's failure to object to the trial court's erroneous reply to the jury note, which referred to the information that contained Bosch's prior convictions, amounted to ineffective assistance of counsel.

Juror Excused from Deliberations

U.S. v. Davis, 177 F.3d 552 (6th Cir. 1999)
> The district court's handling of juror's request to be excused from deliberations and not questioning all jurors about effect upon them of prejudicial and extraneous information violated the defendant's Sixth Amendment right to a fair trial and required remand for an evidentiary hearing.

Ex Parte Meeting with Deliberating Jury

United States v. United States Gypsum. Co., 438 U.S. 422, 57 L.Ed.2d 854, 98 S.Ct. 2864 (1978)
> Any ex parte meeting or communication between the trial judge and jury foreman of a deliberating jury is pregnant with possibilities for error.

United States v. Cowan, 819 F.2d 89 (5th Cir. 1987)
> District judge's improper ex parte meeting with deliberating jury's impermissibly influenced jury to return guilty verdict and required reversal.

Extrinsic Information During Deliberation

U.S. v. Santana, 175 F.3d 57 (1st Cir. 1999)
> The district court abused its discretion after the close of the evidence and while the jury was in deliberations, by allowing the jury to return to the courtroom and observe defendant's ears, which were covered by headphones throughout trial, that allowed the jury to consider extrinsic information not admitted into evidence and was not harmless error requiring reversal.

U.S. v. Martinez, 151 F. 3d 384 (5th Cir. 1998)
> Where a colorable showing of extrinsic influence on the jury appears, a court must investigate the asserted impropriety.

Dyer v. Calderon, 151 F.3d 970 (9th Cir. 1998)
> Where a court is faced with a colorable claim of juror bias it must conduct an investigation of the pertinent facts and circumstances.

Special Verdict Form

United States v. Barnes, 158 F.3d 662, 672 (2nd Cir. 1998)
> The burden of requesting a special verdict falls on the government.

Reinstructed Deadlock Jury

French v. Jones, 332 F.3d 430, 438 (6th Cir. 2003)
The trial court erred delivering a supplemental instruction to the deadlocked jury without affording defense counsel an opportunity to respond to the juries note or the supplemental instruction. This type of action by the court violated petitioner's right to be present and his right to counsel at critical stages of the proceedings in violation of *Cronic*.

Caver v. Straub, 349 F.3d 340, 349-352 (6th Cir. 2003)
Counsel's absences during re-instruction to the jury was a critical stage of the proceedings and constitutes ineffective assistance of counsel per se.

French v. Jones, 41 F.Supp. 2d 726 (E.D. Mich. 1999)
Defense counsel's absence from courtroom when trial court reinstructed deadlocked jury violated the defendant's Sixth Amendment right to counsel and a fair trial, thus it required granting of writ of habeas corpus.

Read Back Testimony to Jury

La Crosse v. Kernan, 211 F.3d 468, 474 (9th Cir. 2000)
La Crosse's due process constitutional right to be present during read back of testimony to jury was violated. La Cross was entitled to an evidentiary hearing to determine whether the read back outside the presence of La Crosse and his counsel, had a "substantial and injurious effect or influence" in the determination of the jury verdict.

General Verdict Form

Griffin v. United States, 502 U.S. 46, 58-59, 112 S.Ct. 466, 116 L.Ed.2d 371 (1991)
A general verdict cannot be sustained if any of the possible bases for conviction were legally erroneous. **See also** *Zant v. Stephens,* **462 U.S. 862, 881, 103 S.Ct. 2733, 2745, 77 L.Ed.2d 235 (1983)** (if the jury was instructed that it could rely on any of two or more independent grounds, and one of those grounds is legally insufficient, because the verdict may have rested exclusively on the insufficient ground, reversal is required).

Ballard v. U.S., 400 F.3d 404, 408-09 (6th Cir. 2005)
Appellate counsel was constitutionally ineffective for failing to raise Ballard's *Apprendi* and *Dale* claims where the indictment charged two drugs in one count and where the jury **never** determined which drug it used to convict Ballard because the trial court used a general verdict form, and then imposed sentence based on cocaine which carries a greater sentence than marijuana.

United States v. Conley, 349 F.3d 837, 840-842 (5th Cir. 2003)
Counsel failed to object to the imposition of the **120** month sentence for conspiracy to commit money laundering, where the indictment charged two separate statutes and the Court used a general verdict form making it impossible to tell which statute the jury convicted petitioner by the verdict, and **18 U.S.C. §371** charged in the

indictment carried a five year maximum penalty, and constituted ineffective assistance of counsel.

Wicks v. Lockhart, 569 F. Supp. 549, 567 (E.D. Ark. 1983)

Counsel's failure to object to the verdict form where single count charged two separate crimes and the Court used a general verdict form was so egregious as to deprive petitioner of his Sixth Amendment right to effective assistance of counsel. The separate counts are fundamental and the petitioner was substantially and actually prejudiced by counsel's failure to object to the courts use of a general verdict form.

Unanimous Verdict

Richardson v. United States, 119 S. Ct. 1707, 143 L.Ed.2d 985 (1999)

The Supreme Court found that the jury must reach a **unanimously verdict** on the three specific predicate violations constituting the "continuing series" of the Continuing Criminal Enterprise charge.

Johnson v. Louisiana, 406 U.S. 356, 92 S.Ct. 1620, 32 L.Ed.2d 152 (1972)

The Supreme Court held that the Sixth Amendment requires a unanimous verdict in federal criminal trials despite the fact that the Sixth Amendment, which is applicable to the states through the Fourteenth Amendment under ***Duncan v. Louisiana*, 391 U.S. 145, 88 S.Ct. 1444, 20 L.Ed.2d 491 (1968)**, does not impose a similar requirement on state criminal proceedings.

U.S. Ex Rel. Madej v. Schomig, 223 F.Supp. 2d 968, 973-74 (N.D. Ill. 2002)

Counsel was constitutionally ineffective by failing to advise petitioner of jury unanimity requirement to impose death sentence.

U.S. v. Holley, 942 F.2d 916, 929 (5th Cir. 1991)

The district court's failure to give specific unanimity instruction was reversible error and required a new trial.

United States v. Gipson, 553 F.2d 453, 457-58 (5th Cir. 1977)

The unanimity rule requires jurors to be in substantial agreement as to just what the defendant did. Thus, requiring the vote of twelve (12) jurors to convict a defendant does little to insure that his Sixth Amendment right to a unanimous verdict is protected unless this prerequisite of jury consensus as to the defendant's course of actions is also required.

Hibdon v. United States, 204 F.2d 834 (6th Cir. 1953)

A federal criminal defendant has a constitutionally based right to a unanimous jury verdict. This right may not be waived.

Scott v. Anderson, 58 F.Supp.2d 767 (N.D. Ohio 1998)

The trial court's incorrect jury instruction during sentencing phase of capital trial and that jurors had to unanimously recommend life rendered the imposition of death sentence unconstitutionally unfair violating Scott's Fourteenth Amendment Right to be free from deprivation of life without due process of law.

JONES/APPRENDI/BOOKER

The Supreme Court *Jones* Decision

Jones v. United States, 119 S. Ct. 1215, 1228 (1999)

The Supreme Court construed the federal carjacking statute, 18 USC. §2119, "As establishing three separate offenses by the specification of distinction [Penalty] elements, each of which must be charged by indictment, proven beyond a reasonable doubt, and submitted to a jury for its verdict." The Court highlighted that under the Due Process Clause of the Fifth Amendment and the notice and jury trial guarantees of the Sixth Amendment, any fact (Other than prior conviction) that increases the maximum penalty for a crime must be charged in an indictment, submitted to a jury, and proven beyond reasonable doubt.

The Supreme Court *Apprendi* Decision

Apprendi v. New Jersey, 147 LEd.2d 435 (2000)

At issue was a conviction and lengthy sentence under state statue allowing the sentencing judge to impose a sentence greater than statutory maximum based upon the court's finding that the crime was motivated by racial bias. The Supreme Court reversed, concluding that, under the Fifth and Sixth Amendments as made applicable to the States by the Due Process Clause of the Fourteenth Amendment, "Other than the fact of a prior conviction, any fact that increases the penalty for a crime beyond the prescribed statutory maximum must be submitted to a jury, and proved beyond reasonable doubt." Id.

Julian v. Bartley, 495 F.3d 487, 495-496 (7th Cir. 2007)

Counsel provided constitutionally ineffective assistance for misinterpreting *Apprendi v. New Jersey* maximum sentence, and incorrectly advised Julian of the maximum penalty, if he proceeded to trial in light of *Apprendi* and warranted a new trial.

Nichols v. United States, 501 F. 3d 542, 547-548 (6th Cir. 2007)

Trial counsel provided constitutional ineffective assistance for failing to preserve claim that use of mandatory Sentencing Guidelines to increase Nichols' sentence violated his Sixth Amendment right to jury trial in light of *Apprendi*.

United States v. Sheppard, 219 F.3d 766 (8th Cir. 2000)

Drug quantity must be treated as an element of the offense under 21 USC. §841 and the jury must determine the type of drug involved in the crime under *Apprendi*.

U.S. v. Nordby, 225 F.3d 1053 (9th Cir. 2000)

The Court found that *Apprendi* required any fact that increases the prescribed statutory maximum penalty must be submitted to the jury and proven beyond a reasonable doubt. The district court's failure to submit issue of amount of marijuana to jury was plain error requiring a remand for resentencing to statutory maximum of five years based on the facts as found by jury beyond a reasonable doubt.

The Supreme Court _Booker_ Decision

United States v. Booker, 125 S.Ct. 738, 160 L.Ed.2d 621 (2005)
The Supreme Court applied the rule of _**Apprendi**_ to the guidelines so that "[a]ny fact (other than a prior conviction) which is necessary to support a sentence exceeding the maximum [mandatory guideline range] authorized by the facts established by a plea of guilty or a jury verdict must be admitted by the defendant or proved to a jury beyond a reasonable doubt." **125 S.Ct. at 756.** The Court then held that two provisions of the statute creating the federal guidelines system must be excised to make it compatible with the Sixth Amendment. **18 U.S.C. §3553(b)(l)** which made the guidelines mandatory and **§3742(e)** which made their application subject to de novo review. _**Booker**_, **125 S.Ct. at 764.** The constitutional remedy chosen by the Court was to make the guidelines advisory and their application subject to review for reasonableness. **See id.** Nevertheless, federal courts still "must consult [the] Guidelines and take them into account when sentencing." **id. 125 S.Ct. at 767.** Sentencing courts should also consider the sentencing factors created by Congress in **18 U.S.C. §3553(a). See id. 125 S.Ct. at 765.** Sentencing remains a court function under _**Booker**_. **125 S.ct. at 760.** Judicial fact finding is permitted as long as it is understood that the guidelines are not mandatory. **id. 125 S.Ct. at 767.** Reasonableness may be demonstrated by a court's consideration of the guidelines, relevant conduct, and statutory sentencing factors. _**Booker**_, **125 S.ct. at 764-765. See also _U.S. v. Mooney_, 401 F.3d 940, 949 (8th Cir. 2005).**

United States v. Holland, 380 F.Supp.2d 1264, 1273-75 (N.D. Ala. 2005)
Trial and appellate counsel was constitutionally ineffective where they failed to test the constitutionality of restitution award procedure because court imposed a penal sanction of restitution that was never charged in the indictment, nor proved beyond a reasonable doubt by the government as required by _**Booker**_.

U.S. v. Dunmire, 403 F.3d 722, 724-27 (10th Cir. 2005)
The evidence was insufficient to support a finding that _**Dunmire**_ conspired and agreed to distribute more than five grams of crack cocaine in light of _**Booker**_, and the court vacated the conspiracy conviction.

McReynolds v. U.S., 397 F. 3d 479,480-81 (7th Cir. 2005)
The Supreme Court's decision in _**Booker**_ announced a new procedural rule that does not apply retroactively on initial 2255 motions under _**Teague v Lane**_, **489 U.S. 288, 311, 109 S. Ct. 1060, 103 L. Ed. 2d 334 (1989)**, to cases on collateral review. **See also _U.S. v Helmos Food Produts Inc._, 407 F. 3d 848, 849 (7th Cir. 2005)**; relief under writ of error coram nobis is not warranted because _**Booker**_ does not apply retroactively to criminal cases that became final before its release on January 12, 2005.

U.S. v. Williams, 408 F. 3d 1073, 1078 (8th Cir. 2005)
The district court's factual findings that defendant used a firearm in connection with another offense to enhance defendant's base offense which was not admitted by defendant nor proved to a jury beyond a reasonable doubt were in violation of the Sixth Amendment in light of _**Booker**_ and required resentencing.

United States v. Vazquez-Rivera, 407 F.3d 476, 488-90 (1st Cir. 2005)
> The district court's factual findings as to the drug quantity, defendant's role in the offense, and possession of a firearm, which were not reflected in the jury verdict or admitted by the defendant, but were used to enhance punishment, were in violation of defendant's Sixth Amendment rights in light of ***Booker*** and required resentencing.

THE SUPREME COURT BLAKELY DECISION

Blakely v. Washington, 542 U.S. 296, 159 L.Ed.2d 403, 124 S.Ct. 2531 (2004)
> The Supreme Court dealt with a determinative sentencing scheme similar to the Federal Sentencing Guideline. Blakely pleaded guilty to kidnaping his estranged wife. A class B felony punishable by a term of not more than 10 years. Other provisions of Washington law, comparable to the Federal Sentencing Guidelines, mandate a standard sentence of 49-to-53 months, unless the judge found aggravating facts justifying an exceptional sentence. Although the prosecutor recommended a sentence in the standard range, the judge found that Blakely had acted with "deliberate cruelty" and sentenced him to 90 months. Id. at 300, 159 L.Ed.2d 403, 124 S.Ct. 2531. The Supreme Court held that the district court sentence exceeding the general statutory maximum violated he Sixth Amendment because the facts supporting the findings of deliberate cruelty had been neither admitted to by Blakely, nor found by a jury. The Supreme Court, reversed and remanded for further proceedings.

FAILED TO MOVE FOR JUDGMENT OF ACQUITTAL

U.S. v. Jimenez Recio, 258 F.3d 1069 (9th Cir. 2001)
> Trial counsel's failure to move for judgment of acquittal on drug possession charge under **U.S. v. Cruz, 127 F.3d 791, 795 (9th Cir. 1997)**, which held that a defendant could not be charged with conspiracy to distribute illegal drugs when the defendant was brought into the drug scheme only after law enforcement authorities had already intervened, and defendant's involvement was prompted by the intervention, and constituted ineffective assistance of counsel. The conspiracy convictions were **REVERSED,** and dismissed with prejudice because of insufficient evidence.

THE RIGHT TO COUNSEL

Gideon v. Wainwright, 372 U.S. 335, 9 L.Ed.2d 799, 83 S.Ct. 792, 93 A.L. R.2d 733 (1963)

The trial court refused Mr. Gideon appointment of counsel under Florida law, due to the fact that Gideon wasn't charged with a capital offense. Gideon informed the trial court that the United States Supreme Court said that he was entitled to be represented by counsel. The trial court refused Gideon's request. Gideon was forced to trial and had to conduct his own defense and did about as well as could be expected for a layman. He made an opening statement to the jury, cross-examined the State's witnesses, presented witnesses in his own defense, declined to testify himself, and made a short argument "emphasizing his innocence to the charge contained in the information filed in this case." The jury returned a verdict of guilty and Gideon was sentenced to serve five years in the state prison.

Gideon filed a petition for habeas corpus in the Florida Supreme Court attacking his conviction and sentence on the ground that the trial court's refusal to appoint counsel for him denied him rights "guaranteed by the Constitution and the Bill of Rights." The state Supreme Court denied the petition without an opinion. Gideon filed a pro se petition for writ of certiorari to the United States Supreme Court. The United States Supreme Court granted certiorari and held that the Sixth Amendment's provision, that in all criminal prosecutions, the accused shall enjoy the right to have the assistance of counsel for his defense was made obligatory upon the states by the Fourteenth Amendment and reversed Gideon's conviction.

McNeil v. Wisconsin, 501 U.S. 171, 115 L.Ed.2d 158, III S.Ct. 2204 (1991)

The Sixth Amendment right [to counsel] . . .is offense specific. It cannot be invoked once for all future prosecutions, for it does not attach until a prosecution is commenced, that is, at or after the initiation of adversary judicial criminal proceedings-whether by way of formal charge, preliminary hearing, indictment, or arraignment.

Texas v. Cobb, 532 U.S. 162, 149 L.Ed.2d 321, 121 S.Ct. 1335 (2001)

Defendant's Sixth Amendment right to counsel held to apply to the "offense specific" and not necessary to extend to crimes "factually related" to charged offense.

Argersinger v. Hamlin 407 U.S. 25, 32 L.Ed.2d 530, 92 S.Ct. 2006 (1972)

Argersinger, an indigent defendant, was tried and convicted of a charge of carrying a concealed weapon, an offense punishable by imprisonment up to 6 months and a $1,000 fine. Argersinger had no counsel and had to proceed to trial without counsel. The trial was by a state judge. Argersinger was convicted and sentenced to 90 days in jail, and brought a habeas corpus to the Florida Supreme Court, alleging that he was being deprived of his right to counsel, he was an indigent layman and unable to raise and present to the trial court a good and sufficient defense to the charges. The Florida Supreme Court denied relief, relying on ***Duncan v. Louisiana, 391 U.S. 145, 159, 20 L.Ed.2d 491, 501, 88 S.Ct. 1444 (1969)*** concluding that the right to counsel extends only to trials "for non-petty offenses punishable by more than six-months imprisonment."

The United States Supreme Court granted certiorari and reversed finding that absent a knowing and intelligent waiver, no person may be imprisoned for any offense, regardless of whether it is classified as petty, misdemeanor, or felony, unless he or she was represented by counsel at trial.

Powell v. Alabama, 287 U.S. 45, 77 L.Ed. 158, 53 S.Ct. 55, 84 ALR 527 (1932)
"The right to be heard would be, in many cases, of little avail if it did not comprehend the right to counsel ... [A defendant] is unfamiliar with the rules of evidence ... He lacks both skill and knowledge to adequately prepare his defense, even though he [may] have a perfect one. He requires the guiding hand of counsel at every step of the proceeding against him."

Police Custodial Interrogation

Miranda v. Arizona, 384 U.S. 436, 16 Led.2d 694, 86 S.Ct. 1602 (1966)
The accused must be advised that he/she has a right to counsel before a custodial police interrogation.

Manning v. Bowersox, 310 F.3d 571, 576 (8th Cir. 2002)
The government violated petitioner's Sixth Amendment right to counsel, after petitioner had been charged with a crime by using informants to elicit incriminating information from petitioner, and warranted habeas relief.

Misdemeanor Case

Berry v. Cincinnati, 414 U.S 29, 38 L.Ed.2d 187, 94 S.Ct. 193 (1973)
Berry was convicted of a misdemeanor without counsel and was free on bail pending action on his claim that his conviction should be invalidated by application of the Supreme Court's decision in *Argersinger v. Hamlin , 407 U.S. 25, 32 L.Ed. 530, 92 S.Ct. 2006 (1972)*. The Supreme Court agreed and reversed Berry's conviction.

Revocation of Probation or a Deferred Sentencing

Mempa v. Rhay, 389 U.S. 128. 19 L.Ed.2d 336, 88 S.Ct. 254 (1967)
This case stands for the proposition that the federal constitution requires an indigent defendant to have appointed counsel at every stage of a criminal proceeding including revocation of probation or a deferred sentencing.

Discretionary Review By Court of Appeals

Blankenship v. Johnson, 118 F.3d 312 (5th Cir. 1997)
Defendant had right to counsel during discretionary review by Court of Appeals under due process and equal protection clauses, when state sought such review after appellate court reversed defendant's conviction.

Child Neglect Proceedings

Garramone v. Romo, 94 F.3d 1446 (10th Cir. 1996)
Mother had right to counsel in neglect of child proceedings.

Motion For New Trial

Robinson v. Norris, 60 F.3d 457 (8th Cir. 1995)
Defendant is entitled to counsel for motion for new trial proceeding, a critical stage of the proceedings, which constitutional right to counsel attaches.

§2255 Evidentiary Hearing

U.S. v. Vasquez, 7 F.3d 81 (5th Cir. 1993)
Trial court's failure to appoint indigent petitioner, counsel for evidentiary hearing on §2255 motion to vacate sentence required reversal. **See also _Richardson v. Miller, 721 F.Supp. 1087 (W.D. Mo. 1989); United States v. Barnes, 662 F.2d 777 (D.C. Cir. 1980)_**

Pretrial Lineup Identification

Frisco v. Blackburn, 782 F.2d 1353 (5th Cir. 1986)
Defendant has right to counsel for pretrial lineup identification by robbery victim.

Grand Jury Proceedings

Young v. Duckworth, 733 F.2d 482 (7th Cir. 1984)
Defendant's constitutional right to counsel attached at initial hearing where there was sufficient evidence to present case to grand jury.

Civil Contempt

United States v. Anderson, 553 F.2d 1154 (8th Cir. 1977)
The Sixth Amendment of the United States Constitution requires the Court to appoint counsel for indigent defendants that face incarceration pursuant to a finding of civil contempt.

Counsel of Defendant's Choice

United States v. Gonzalez-Lopez, 548 U.S. 140, 126 S.Ct. 2557, 2564, 165 L.Ed.2d 409 (2006)
The "erroneous deprivation of the right to counsel choice" is a structural error requiring reversal of subsequent conviction. **Id. at 2564.**

Crooker v. California, 357 U.S. 433, 2 Led 2d 1448, 78 S.Ct. 1287 (1958)
An accused has a right to secure counsel of his own choice.

Reynolds v. Cochran, 365 U.S. 525, 5 LEd.2d 754, 81 S. Ct. 723 (1961)
The Supreme Court held that "the trial court's refusal to grant the accused's motion for a continuance, in order that he might have the assistance in the proceeding of counsel whom he had retained, deprived the accused of due process in the constitutional sense."

U.S. v. Childress, 58 F.3d 693 (D.C. Cir. 1995)
The Court remanded to determine whether defendant was denied counsel of his choice in murder trial.

Deportation Proceedings

Almendarez-Torres v. United States, **523 U.S. 224, 140 L.Ed.2d 350, 118 S.Ct. 1219 (1998)**
Provision of *8 USCS §1326 (b) (2)* authorizing increased sentence for deported alien's illegal return if deportation was subsequent to aggravated felony conviction held to be penalty provision, so that aggravated felony need not be charged in indictment.

Mustata v. U.S. Dept. of Justice, **179 F.3d 1017 (6th Cir. 1999)**
The Sixth Amendment right to effective assistance of counsel does not extend to civil deportation proceedings.

Extradition Proceedings

DeSilva v. DiLeonardi, **181 F.3d 865 (7th Cir. 1999)**
The defendant has no Sixth Amendment right to effective assistance of counsel in an **extradition proceeding.**

SELF-REPRESENTATION

Farrett v. California, **422 U.S. 806, 45 L.Ed.2d 562, 95 S.Ct. 2525 (1975)**
Sixth Amendment right to represent oneself in a criminal proceeding.

United States v. Davis, **285 F.3d 378 (5th Cir. 2002)**
The Fifth Circuit held that the district court's decision to appoint independent counsel for a pro se defendant at penalty phase of capital murder trial, to present mitigating evidence of kind that defendant had specifically declined to present, violated defendant's Sixth Amendment right to self-representation.

Vega v. Johnson, **149 F. 3d 354 (5th Cir. 1998)**
Defendant has a Sixth Amendment right to file a pro se Appellant's brief on direct appeal.

Moore v. Calderon, **108 F.3d 261 (9th Cir. 1997)**
Moore requested to represent himself two weeks before trial. The trial court refused to allow Moore to represent himself, which abridged Moore's right to self-representation under the Sixth Amendment. The Ninth Circuit affirmed the grant of Moore's new trial.

Larrabee v. Bartlett, **970 F. Supp. 102 (N.D.N.Y. 1997)**
The trial court denial of defendant's motion to proceed with pro se representation made a week before trial constituted a denial of the defendant's Sixth Amendment to self-representation.

U.S. v. Moskouits, **86 F.3d 1303 (3rd Cir. 1996)**
The district court's failure to inform defendant that punishment might be increased at retrial rendered defendant's waiver of counsel and chooses to proceed with self-representation invalid requiring resentence to the original sentence.

U.S. v. Baker, 84 F.3d 1263 (10th Cir. 1996)
>The district court's refusal to allow defendant to represent himself without findings that defendant was incompetent to represent him constituted reversible error and required new trial.

Myers v. Johnson, 76 F.3d 1330 (5th Cir. 1996)
>The district court's denial of defendant's right to file pro se briefs on direct appeal was not subject to harmless error, remedy was to afford defendant an opportunity to present out-of-time pro se appellate brief to State Court of Appeals.

Moore v. Calderon, 56 F.3d 39 (9th Cir. 1995)
>Defendant's right to represent himself was violated and he was entitled to release pending appeal where state failed to make sufficiently strong showing that it was likely to succeed on the merits.

U.S. v. Treff, 924 F.2d 977 (10th Cir. 1991)
>A criminal defendant has a statutory and constitutional right to represent himself.

Hybrid Representation

McKaskle v. Wiggins, 465 U.S. 168, 169, 104 S.Ct. 944, 79 L.Ed.2d 122 (1984)
>There is no constitutional right to hybrid representation. **See also *Neal v. Texas*, 870 F.2d 312, 315-16 (5th Cir. 1989) (same); *Myers V. Johnson*, 76 F.3d 1330, 1335 (5th Cir. 1996).**

IMMIGRATION APPEAL PROCEEDINGS

Saba v.I.N.S., 52 F.Supp. 2d 1117 (N.D. Cal. 1999)
>Counsel's failure to advise aliens to apply for adjustment of status to that of legal permanent United States residence within a reasonable time after their mother's naturalization constituted ineffective assistance of counsel.

FADIGA v. Attorney General U.S., 488 F.3d 142, 157 (3rd Cir. 2007)
>Counsel provided constitutionally ineffective assistance during immigration proceeding for failing to present evidence, and to advise the client that he could produce witnesses or affidavits or declarations to prove his relationship to Guinean government officials.

United States v. Scott, 394 F.3d 111, 117-120 (2nd Cir. 2005)
>Counsel was constitutionally ineffective for failing to apply for waiver of deportation pursuant to **8 U.S.C. §212(c)**, after the Immigration Judge directed counsel to do so because he believed *Scott* qualified for such relief.

Jie Lin v. Ashcroft, 377 F. 3d 1014, 1024-27 (9th Cir. 2004)
>Counsel's failure to collect material testimony, documentary evidence, to present legal and factual arguments for asylum claim constituted ineffective assistance of counsel and required reopening asylum hearing.

__Mandarino v. Ashcroft__, 290 F.Supp.2d 253, 261-263 (D. Conn. 2002)
Counsel was constitutionally ineffective during sentence for failing to move for a downward departure and inform the sentencing court of relevant immigration law, i.e., the relevant sentence ceiling of five years for seeking a waiver from deportation pursuant to **8 U.S.C. §212(c)**.

Notice of Appeal

__Siong v. I.N.S.__, 376 F. 3d 1030, 1037 (9th Cir. 2004)
Alien counsel's failure to file timely requested notice of appeal of denial of asylum constituted ineffective assistance of counsel and required reopening of removal proceeding.

INEFFECTIVENESS vs. STRATEGY DECISIONS

Florida v. Nixon, 543 U.S. 175, 160 L.Ed.2d 565, 125 S.Ct. 551 (2004)

Counsel's strategy in capital murder trial, with overwhelming evidence of guilt, was to concede guilt and concentrate on sparing the defendant's life, held not to be ineffective assistance.

Alvord v. Wainwright, 469 U.S. 956, 83 LEd.2d 291, 105 S.Ct. 355 (1984)

Counsel's failure to investigate defendant's only plausible line of defense and defers to his client's wishes on defense strategy when it was clear that client lacked his knowledge or ability to understand the law and facts constituted ineffective assistance. Certiorari was denied in this case, but Justice Marshall and Brennan wrote dissenting opinions.

Darden v. Wainwright, 477 U.S.168, 91 LEd.2d 144, 106 S.Ct. 2464 (1986)

Trial counsel's strategy decision not to attempt to portray petitioner as a nonviolent man, which would have opened door for state to rebut with evidence of petitioner's prior conviction, did <u>not</u> constitute ineffective assistance.

Smith v. Murray, 477 U.S. 527, 91 L.Ed.2d 434, 106 S.Ct. 2661 (1986)

Defense counsel's calculated tactical decision not to raise self-incrimination claim on direct appeal held not to show "cause" for procedural default rule.

Hall v. Washington, 106 F.3d 742 (7th Cir. 1997)

Trial counsel's failure to present mitigation witnesses during capital sentencing of defendant because of counsel's failure to investigate has no strategic value and constitutes ineffective assistance.

Berryman v. Morton, 100 F.3d 1089 at 1096 (3rd Cir. 1996)

For counsel to rest on "strategy" necessitates the existence of one. This case lacked strategy. Instead, it was a "useless charade." *(citing __United States v. Cronic__, 466 U.S. 648, n.19, 104 S.Ct. 2039, n.19, 80 L.Ed.2d 657 (1984))*.

Berryman v. Morton, 100 F.3d 1089 at 1096 (3rd Cir. 1996)

The question of whether counsel's strategy was reasonable goes directly to the performance prong of __Strickland__ test, thus requiring the application of legal principles, and **de novo review**.

Freeman v. Class, 95 F.3d 639 (8th Cir. 1996)

There is no reasonable trial strategy for counsel's failure to request the cautionary accomplice testimony instruction and corroboration instruction.

De Luca v. Lord, 77 F.3d 578 (3rd Cir. 1996)

Trial counsel's ineffective assistance of counsel claim will stand, even if a well-intentioned lawyer earnestly pursues a strategy that is objectively unreasonable under professional norm and results in prejudiced to defendant.

Odle v. Calderon, 919 F.Supp. 1367 (N.D. Cal. 1996)

Defense counsel's tactical choices based on proper understanding of law and facts are virtually unchallengeable.

Ineffectiveness vs. Strategy Decisions

Jackson v. Herring, 42 F.3d 1350 (11th Cir. 1995)
Defense counsel's failure to investigate his options and make a reasonable choice between them forecloses any "strategic decision " that might exists.

Jones v. Scotts, 59 F.3d 143 (10th Cir. 1995)
A criminal defendant can overcome trial counsel's strategy and prevail on an ineffective assistance of counsel claim when he proves trial counsel's strategy would not be considered sound.

Weekly v. Jones, 56 F.3d 889 (8th Cir. 1995)
Failure to investigate insanity defense has no strategy value.

Bryant v. Scott, 28 F.3d 1411 (5th Cir. 1994)
Failure to investigate potential alibi witnesses was not a "strategic choice" that precludes claims of ineffective assistance.

Loyd v. Whitley, 977 F.2d 149 (5th Cir. 1992)
Failure of counsel to pursue an independent psychological analysis of defendant was not a strategic choice made after investigation. It was not a strategic choice made, in light of the limited investigation conducted since there was no limitations for funds.

Nelson v. Hargett, 989 F.2d 847 (5th Cir. 1993)
Trial counsel's failure to pursue speedy trial claim may constitute ineffective assistance of counsel and has no strategic value.

Johnson v. Armontrout, 961 F.2d 748 (8th Cir. 1992)
There exists no strategic move for defense counsel's failure to remove biased jurors from panel where jurors had heard prejudicial and damaging testimony in prior trial.

Osborn v. Shillinger, 861 F.2d 612 (10th Cir. 1988)
Defense counsel's performance was not only ineffective, but counsel abandoned the required duty of loyalty to his client; counsel did not simply make poor strategic or tactical choices; he acted with reckless disregard for his client's best interest and apparently with the intention to weaken his client's case.

U.S. v. Gray, 878 F.2d 702 (3rd Cir. 1989)
The *Gray* Court found where the deficiencies in counsel's performance are severe and cannot be characterized as a strategic judgment in the first prong of *Strickland* is met.

Wilson v. Butler, 813 F.2d 664 (5th Cir. 1987)
Trial counsel's failure to pursue mental impairment as a mitigating factor at sentencing may constitute ineffective assistance of counsel and an evidentiary hearing was warranted to determine whether counsel's action was a strategic decision.

Armstrong v. Dugger, 833 F.2d 1430 (11th Cir. 1987)
Trial counsel was ineffective at sentencing where he failed to investigate or present mitigating evidence due to inexperience and counsel's conduct was not a tactical or strategic decision.

Hyman v. Aiken, 824 F.2d 1405 (4th Cir. 1987)
Trial counsel's lack of preparation and research cannot be considered the result of deliberate, informed trial strategy.

Lyons v. McCotter, 770 F.2d 529 (5th Cir. 1985)
Trial counsel's failure to object to highly inflammatory inadmissible evidence has no strategic value and failure to request a limiting instruction constitutes ineffective assistance of counsel.

Martin v. Rose, 744 F.2d 1245 (6th Cir. 1984)
Trial counsel's tactics can constitute ineffective assistance of counsel if they fall outside the wide range of professionally competent assistance or the prevailing professional norms.

Crisp v. Duckworth, 743 F.2d 580, 584 (7th Cir. 1984)
Trial counsel cannot stand behind the shield of trial strategy after failing to interview readily available witness whose testimony would have been noncumulative and potentially aided the defense.

House v. Balkcom, 725 F.2d 608 (11th Cir. 1984)
Trial counsels failure to develop strategy of consequence, and being absent from crucial portions of trial, amounted to having no representation at all, and constitutes ineffective assistance of counsel.

BREAKDOWN IN COMMUNICATIONS BETWEEN DEFENDANT AND COUNSEL

U.S. v. Cronic, 466 U.S. 648, 80 L.Ed.2d 657, 104 S.Ct. 2039 (1984)
Trial counsel's failure to subject the prosecution's case to a meaningful adversary testing process may constitute a denial of due process and establish a per se violation of defendant's right to effective assistance of counsel.

U.S. v. D'Amore, 56 F.3d 1202 (9th Cir. 1995)
Defendant is entitled to substitute counsel when there is evidence of a breakdown of communication between defendant and counsel, even in a probation revocation hearing.

Wilson v. Mintzes, 761 F.2d 275 (6th Cir. 1985)
The court should allow substitution of counsel where there is a conflict of interest or a complete breakdown in communication between the defendant and counsel.

CONFLICT OF INTEREST

United States Supreme Court

Mickens v. Taylor, 535 U.S. 162, 152 L.Ed.2d 291, 122 S.Ct. 1237 (2002)
>In order to establish a Sixth Amendment violation based on a potential conflict of interest, a defendant is required to show that the conflict of interest adversely affected counsel's performance, even if the trial court failed to inquire into potential conflict about which the trial judge knew or reasonably should have known.

Burden v. Zant, 498 U.S. 433, 112 LEd.2d 962, 111 S.Ct. 862 (1991)
>Defendant's pretrial counsel who reached informal understanding with prosecutor that second suspect in murders who counsel also represented, would not be prosecuted in exchange for his testimony against defendant, sufficiently stated a conflict of interest. Also see, *Burden v. Zant, 24 F.3d 1298 (11th Cir. 1994).*

Wheat v. United States, 486 U.S. 153, 100 L.Ed.2d 140, 108 S.Ct. 1692 (1988)
>The *Wheat* court explained "the dilemma facing a trial court confronted with a potential conflict of interest. Trial courts confronted with multiple representations face the prospect of being "whipsawed" by assertions of error no matter which way they rule." *Id. at 161, 108 S.Ct. at 1698.* Where multiple representations are allowed, advocacy of counsel is impaired and the defendant may assert a claim for ineffective assistance of counsel regardless of whether the defendant waived his or her right to conflict-free representation. *Id at 161-62, 108 S.Ct. at 1698-99.* If multiple representation is prohibited, the defendant may raise a Sixth Amendment violation. *Id at 161, 108 S.Ct. at 1698.* The independent interest of the trial court "in ensuring that criminal trials are conducted within the ethical standards of the profession and that legal proceeding appear fair to all who observe them," *Id at 160, 108 S.Ct. at 1698*, the "institutional interest in the rendition of just verdicts in criminal cases," *Id.*, as well as the "interest of a criminal defendant," *Id.*, require flexibility in the trial court to decline a proffer of waiver if it justifiably finds an actual or potential conflict. *Id. at 162-63, 108 S.Ct. at 1698-99.*

Burger v. Kemp, 483 U.S. 776, 97 L.Ed.2d 638, 107 S.Ct. 3114 (1987)
>Appointment of law partners to represent co-defendants in joint trial is <u>not</u> a per se effective assistance of counsel. No conflict of interest was shown in this case.

Holloway v. Arkansas, 435 U.S. 475, 489-490, 55 L.Ed.2d 426, 98 S.Ct. 1173 (1978)
>In defining what constitutes a "conflict of interest", the Supreme Court stated that "an actual, relevant conflict of interests [exists] if, during the course of representation, the defendants' interests do diverge with respect to a material, factual or legal issue, or to a course of action." *Cuyler, 446 U.S. at 356 n.3, 100 S.Ct. at 1722 n.3.* The *Holloway* Court further explained that whenever a trial court improperly requires joint representation over timely objections by defendant, requires reversal automatic.

Flanagan v. United States, 465 U.S. 259, 79 L.Ed.2d 288, 104 S.Ct. 1051 (1984)
>Disqualification of criminal defense counsel for potential conflict of interest is not immediately appealable.

Wood v. Georgia, 450 U.S. 261, 67 L.Ed.2d 220, 101 S.Ct. 1097 (1981)
Conflict of interest issue, where a third party retained counsel, required an evidentiary hearing.

Cuyler v. Sullivan, 446 U.S. 335, 100 S.Ct. 1708, 64 L.Ed.2d 333 (1980)
In order to find a Sixth Amendment violation based on a conflict of interest, the reviewing court must find: (1) that counsel actively represented conflicting interests; and (2) that an actual conflict of interest adversely affected the attorney's performance. *Id. at 348, 100 S.Ct. at 1718.* Under *Cuyler*, the court must presume prejudice if the conflict of interest adversely affected the attorney's performance. *Id.* Although *Cuyler* involved a conflict of interest between clients, the presumption of prejudice extends to a "conflict between a client and his lawyer's personal interest. *See, Mannhalt v. Reed, 847 F.2d 576, 580 (9th Cir.), cert. denied, 488 U.S. 908, 109 S.Ct. 260, 102 L.Ed.2d 249 (1988).*

District of Columbia

U.S. v. Taylor, 139 F.3d 924 (D.C. Cir. 1998)
Trial counsel's failure to advise defendant of advice of counsel defense because of a conflict of interest required evidentiary hearing.

U.S. v. Harris, 846 F.Supp. 121 (D.D.C. 1994)
Counsel had an intimate relationship with a police officer that testified in defendant's case creating a conflict of interest.

United States v. Hurt, 543 F.2d 162 (D.C. Cir. 1976)
Competition between the client's interests and counsel's own interests and corrupts the relationship and creates a conflict of interest.

First Circuit

United States v. Segarra-Rivera, 473 F.3d 381, 383 (1st Cir. 2007)
Evidentiary hearing warranted to determine whether counsel was burdened with a conflict of interest because the defendant accused counsel of failing to file his requested motion to withdraw guilty plea based on counsel concealing exculpatory evidence, manipulated defendant into signing plea agreement to avoid trial for which counsel failed to prepare, used improper means to obtain defendant's signature on plea.

U.S. v. Rodriguez-Rodriguez, 929 F.2d 747 (1st Cir. 1991)
Trial counsel's failure to inform defendant of plea offer as a result of a conflict of interest stated a Sixth Amendment claim warranting an evidentiary hearing.

U.S. v. Diozzi, 807 F.2d 10 (1st Cir. 1986)
Government's motion to disqualification of defendant's attorney violated the defendant's Sixth Amendment right to effective assistance of counsel.

Conflict of Interest

Second Circuit

Eisemann v. Herbert, 274 F.Supp. 2d 283, 301-304 (E.D.N.Y. 2003)

Counsel's dual representation of petitioner and his father, who were both charged on the same day for sexual molesting petitioner's seven year old daughter labored under a conflict of interest. Counsel committed numerous violations of the rules of professional responsibility and the law because he billed the Eisemann family large sums of money, fabricated affidavits to excuse his conduct, threatened to put petitioner in jail if he did not vouch for the fabricated affidavits, failed to consider reasonable alternative defense strategies on petitioner's behalf, and advised petitioner to flee while the jury was deliberating which resulted in counsel's disbarment. This conflict violated petitioner's right to effective assistance of counsel and warrants habeas relief.

United States v. Massino, 303 F.Supp.2d 258, 262-264 (E.D. N.Y. 2003)

Counsel in a racketeering and murder conspiracy trial had an unwaivable conflict of interest where counsel had previously represented a potential government witnesses and learned confidential information protected by the attorney-client privilege from the potential witness, which warranted disqualifying counsel.

United States v. Davis, 239 F.3d 283, 287 (2nd Cir. 2001)

A conflict of interest exists where defendant made specific factual allegations that counsel threatened not to investigate, file pretrial motions if defendant did not accept guilty plea offer, and counsel remained silent at withdrawal of plea hearing with respect to defendant's allegation of coercion.

Armienti v. United States, 234 F.3d 820, 824-25 (2nd Cir. 2000)

Counsel who was being criminally investigated by the same U.S. Attorney's Office that was prosecuting petitioner created a possible conflict of interest. Adverse performance was shown through counsel's failure to conduct a pretrial investigation and vigorously cross-examination government witnesses, and required an evidentiary hearing to resolve the claim.

Guzman v. Sabourin, 124 F.Supp. 2d 828 (S.D.N.Y. 2000)

Conflict of interest arose between petitioner and counsel, during motion to withdraw guilty plea, when counsel testified against petitioner disputing petitioner's factual allegations concerning counsel coercing the guilty plea.

U.S. v. Kliti, 156 F.3d 150 (2nd Cir. 1998)

District court's failure to conduct a ***Curcio*** **hearing** upon learning that defense counsel was witness to statement by witness that tended to exculpate defendant was prejudicial error violating defendant's Sixth Amendment right.

U.S. v. Gotti, 9 F. Supp. 2d 320 (S.D.N.Y. 1998)

Defense counsel who previously represented a codefendant who turned government witness combined with allegation that counsel's involvement in the conduct underlying the indictment warranted disqualification due to conflict of interest.

U.S. v. Jiang, 140 F.3d 124 (2nd Cir. 1998)

Defense counsel's legal partner who represented defendant's co-conspirator in related forfeiture proceedings, may present a potential conflict of interest and the court remanded case for determination whether actual conflict existed and if it had effects on defendant.

__U.S. v. Cruz__, 982 F.Supp. 946 (S.D.N.Y. 1997)
Disqualification of attorney was required where a serious potential conflict of interest existed where attorney's former client's wife was expected to testify as a confidential informant for government.

__U.S. v. Martel__, 958 F. Supp. 211 (D.N.J. 1997)
The court held that: (1)"payment of attorney fees by principal of owner of van driven by defendants created insurmountable conflict of interest precluding attorney's from representing either defendant, and (2) record did not support finding that either defendant made knowing, intelligent and voluntary waive of right to conflict-free representation."

__U.S. v. Malpiedi__, 62 F.3d 465 (2nd Cir. 1995)
Trial counsel had previously represented and accompanied records custodian to the grand jury session where she allegedly provided false testimony. The defendant's counsel failed to vigorously cross-examine record custodian due to his duty owed to custodian. Counsel represented conflict of interests and prejudice was presumed.

__CIAK v. U.S.__, 59 F.3d 296 (2nd Cir. 1995)
Trial counsel had previously represented an important government witness and counsel presented a theory to impeach the governments witness with statements that the government's witness made to counsel while being represented by him. Counsel's actions amounted to counsel being an unsworn witness in the proceedings. The defendant asserted that a conflict of interest existed and that counsel abandoned plausible defense because that specific approach would have been inherently in conflict with the position counsel had taken representing the potential witness. The Court of Appeals reversed and remanded for an evidentiary hearing.

__Lopez v. Scully__, 58 F.3d 38 (2nd Cir. 1995)
Lopez in a pro se motion to withdraw his guilty plea asserted that counsel had coerced him into pleading guilty. At that point, counsel had a conflict of interest; to argue in favor of his client's motion would require admitting serious ethical violations and possibly subject him to liability for malpractice; on the other hand, "Any contention by counsel that defendant's allegations were not true would... contradict his client." The court remanded for resentencing with appointment of new counsel.

__U.S. v. Levy__, 25 F.3d 146 (2nd Cir. 1994)
Counsel represented Levy and his accomplice, and assisted the accomplice in his flight from prosecution to a different country, which stated sufficient grounds for a conflict of interest.

__U.S. v. Levy__, 25 F.3d 146 (2nd Cir. 1994)
Counsel's prosecution on unrelated criminal charges by the same prosecuting attorney's office, which prosecuted the defendant stated a valid claim for a conflict of interest.

Conflict of Interest

Hinkler v. Keane, 7 F.3d 304 (2d Cir. 1993)
Defense counsel was burdened with a conflict of interest based on a contingency fee agreement which counsel would receive an additional $25,000 if defendant was acquitted.

U.S. v. Fulton, 5 F.3d 605 (2d Cir. 1993)
The government's witness during trial testified that the defendant's trial counsel had engaged in heroin trafficking which related to charge defendant was on trial, created a per se conflict of interest.

Mathis v. Hood, 937 F.2d 790 (2nd Cir. 1991)
A conflict of interest between defendant and his appellate counsel, where defendant had filed disciplinary proceedings against appellate counsel, because of appellate counsel's delay in filing appeal, warranted new appeal.

U.S. v. Gotti, 771 F.Supp. 552 (E.D. N.Y. 1991)
Counsel who may be called as a witness by the prosecution establishes a conflict of interest.

United States v. Iorizzo, 786 F.2d 52 (2d Cir. 1986)
Trial counsel was burdened with a conflict of interest where counsel had represented prosecution's witness and, the prior testimony of the prosecution's witness could not be used to attack witness' credibility and defendant was denied opportunity to properly cross-examine prosecution's witness because of conflict of interest.

Lace v. United States, 736 F.2d 48 (2nd Cir. 1984)
Petitioner alleged that trial counsel's brother was potential prosecution witness and this allegation stated a sufficient claim of conflict of interest requiring an evidentiary hearing.

Third Circuit

Cates v. Superintendent Indiana Youth, 752 F.Supp. 854 (S.D. Ind. 1990)
Joint representation of defendant and co-defendant constituted a conflict of interest and violated defendant's Sixth Amendment right to effective assistance of counsel. Counsel negotiated a plea agreement on defendant's co-defendant's behalf, which required co-defendant to testify against defendant.

Government of Virgin Island v. Zepp, 748 F.2d 125 (3rd Cir. 1984)
Trial counsel was burdened with a conflict of interest where counsel faced potential criminal liability on same charges and such conflict affected counsel's cross-examination of witnesses.

Fourth Circuit

United States v. Nicholson, 475 F.3d 241, 245 (4th Cir. 2007)
Nicholson was denied his right to effective representation because of a conflict of interest that occurred during the sentencing stage. Counsel simultaneously represented Nicholson and the individual who threatened to kill Nicholson. Counsel's performance was adversely affected because he could not file a motion for

a downward departure from the Sentencing Guidelines based on Nicholson's self-defense theory because counsel would have to accuse his other client of criminal acts to prove Nicholson's self-defense theory.

Rubin v. Gee, 292 F.3d 396, 403 (4th Cir. 2002)
Rubin's pretrial attorneys instructed her to flee the crime scene and check into a hospital under an assumed name. These pretrial attorneys recommended that she hire a specific trial attorney and they would remain on the defense team. The prosecutor during trial relied on the fact that Rubin fled the crime scene and lied about her name when she checked into the hospital. The only way for Rubin to refute the state's allegations was to call her pretrial attorneys. However, Rubin's pretrial attorneys interest in concealing their role in the events following the homicide that would have exposed them to potential criminal charges conflicted with Rubin's interest and prevented them from testifying. Rubin was denied effective assistance of counsel because her pretrial attorneys who remained on her defense team had a conflict of interest and habeas relief was warranted.

U.S. v. Scott, 980 F. Supp. 165 (E.D. Va. 1997)
Counsel who was retained for defendant in drug conspiracy case by other members of the conspiracy and had taken up representation of a second individual involved in the conspiracy, which created an actual and potential conflict and court concluded that no counsel could not represent anybody in the case.

U.S. v. Thomas, 977 F. Supp. 771 (N.D.W. Va. 1997)
Attorney's representation of defendant's brother in pending criminal action for conspiracy to distribute "crack" cocaine, created an actual conflict which precluded attorney from representing defendant on charges against both defendant and his brother, who were part of one big conspiracy.

U.S. v. Magini, 973 F.2d 261 (4th Cir. 1992)
The Court of Appeals held that evidentiary hearing was required to determine whether counsel's alleged actual conflict of interest had adverse effect on petitioner's defense. *Id.* **Reversed and Remanded**. Magini claimed her Sixth Amendment right to counsel was violated because her counsel was operating under a private, pecuniary conflict of interest while representing her. Magini alleged that the adverse effect of counsel's private, pecuniary interest is that counsel persuaded her to plead guilty, rather than proceed to trial. Magini also claimed that counsel did not negotiate a forfeiture provision in the North Carolina plea agreement because such a provision would have deprived him of his fee. Magini's thesis is that counsel might have negotiated forfeiture in exchange for a lighter prison term. *Id. at 263*.

U.S. v. Swartz, 975 F.2d 1042 (4th Cir. 1992)
Trial counsel and co-counsel created a conflict of interest requiring defendant's conviction to be vacated and set aside where defendant's attorney and co-counsel advanced legal arguments that benefited co-defendant to defendant's detriment.

U.S. v. Tatum, 943 F.2d 370 (4th Cir. 1991)
Trial counsel's representation of defendant can be tainted if counsel relies on previous counsel as source of information where previous counsel had a conflict of interest. This ineffectiveness claim was resolved on direct appeal.

U.S. v. Tatum, *943 F.2d 370 (4th Cir. 1991)*
Trial counsel's failure to pursue cross-examination of government witness whose testimony is material can show adverse effect on counsel's performance because of conflict of interest and establishes ineffective assistance of counsel.

U.S. v. Tatum, *943 F.2d 370 (4th Cir. 1991)*
Trial counsel's failure to object to admissions of inadmissible evidence due to a conflict of interest demonstrates actual lapses in defense and can constitute ineffective assistance of counsel.

U.S. v. Tatum, *943 F.2d 370 (4th Cir. 1991)*
Trial counsel who had to account to two masters, when the two masters have separate defenses, constitutes a conflict of interest, especially where counsel's representation of one master adversely affects the other master.

Hoffman v. Leeke, *903 F.2d 280 (4th Cir. 1990)*
Joint representation of defendant and co-defendant by counsel in murder case, prosecution created actual conflict of interest, especially where counsel advised co-defendant to enter guilty plea which implicated defendant.

Fifth Circuit

United States v Culverhouse, *507 F.3d 888, 893-894 (5th Cir. 2007)*
Counsel assisted his prior client in debriefing against petitioner, prior to inducing petitioner to plead guilty, and the prior clients' statements made during debriefing were used to determine petitioner's relevant conduct, warranted an evidentiary hearing to resolve the claim of conflict of interest.

U.S. v. Infante, *404 F.3d 376, 390 (5th Cir. 2005)*
Trial counsel Anthony Foster labored under a conflict of interest where he pled two prior clients guilty (Gallegos-Natera and Rivera-Hernandez) who testified against Infante during trial. Counsel indicated in the **Fed. R. of Crim. Proc., Rule 44** conflict of interest hearing, that if Gallegos-Natera and Rivera-Hernandez testified against Infante that he would pull their files and run over to the government's attorney's office and ask for a **Rule 35** motion to reduce their sentence. The *Infante* Court remanded for the district court's determination of whether the conflict adversely affected counsel's performance.

Perillo v. Johnson, *205 F.3d 775 (5th Cir. 2000)*
Defense counsel who previously represented robbery defendant who testified against defense counsel's second client in murder trial created a conflict of interest.

Blankenship v. Johnson, *118 F.3d 312 (5th Cir. 1997)*
Counsel was burdened with a conflict of interest, where counsel had been elected as county attorney, and failed to take any action in defendant's behalf during state-requested discretionary review by state criminal court of last resort after intermediate appellate court reversed defendant's conviction.

Beets v. Scott, *65 F.3d 1258 (5th Cir. 1995)*
The Fifth Circuit in *Beets* held that the *Strickland* test, rather than the *Cuyler* test, offers superior framework for addressing conflict of interest outside the multiple or

serial client context. However, *footnote 17*, pointed out that "a powerful argument can be made that a lawyer who is a potential co-defendant with his client is burdened by a 'multiple representation' conflict that ought to be analyzed under *Cuyler*."

U.S. v. Santiago, 993 F.2d 504, 507 (5th Cir. 1993)
The Court held that (4) Defendant was entitled to evidentiary hearing on claim that trial counsel had conflict of interest. Santiago argued that his trial counsel, without his knowledge, also represented the Albrechts at all relevant times. Santiago stated that he learned of the conflict for the first time in June 1992, which was after the district court had dismissed his §2255 motion. This allegation raised serious concerns given the apparent plethora of evidence connecting the Albrechts with the drugs and the fact that they were never prosecuted for this offense. The Fifth Circuit found that this claim of conflict of interest could be raised on appeal for the first time, because the failure to consider it would result in a manifest injustice. This case was remanded for an evidentiary hearing to resolve the conflict of interest.

U.S. v. Greig, 967 F.2d 1018 (5th Cir. 1992)
When counsel places himself in a position of simultaneously having to defend himself as well as his client for their potentially criminal activity, a conflict of interest exists. Counsel by having an unethical meeting with co-defendant, opened himself up for an indictment for obstruction of justice and disciplinary matters. The court's failure to conduct a *Garcia* hearing was reversible error.

Nealy v. Cabana, 782 F.2d 1362 (5th Cir. 1986)
Trial counsel was burdened with a conflict of interest where he represented Nealy and his brother who was tried separately for the same crime. Trial counsel was placed in an awkward situation whether to call Nealy's brother as a witness, because he felt it may harm his brother's case. The district court granted the petition for habeas corpus. The state appealed and the Fifth Circuit affirmed.

United States v. Garcia, 517 F.2d 272 (5th Cir. 1975)
Waiver of conflict must be on the record by clear and unequivocal language.

Sixth Circuit

Whiting v. Burt, 266 F.Supp. 2d 640, 644 (E.D. Mich. 2003)
Appellate counsel labored under a conflict of interest because he was petitioner's trial counsel and refused to raise claim of ineffectiveness of counsel against himself on direct appeal. The appropriate remedy was to grant a new appeal.

Harris v. Carter, 337 F.3d 758, 762-764 (6th Cir. 2003)
Counsel's joint representation of defendant and codefendant created a conflict of interest where the codefendant was testifying against defendant under the grant of immunity. Counsel advised the trial court of the actual conflict, the court failed to inquire into the conflict as mandated by *Holloway*, and habeas relief was granted.

Conflict of Interest

Tyler v. U.S., 78 F.Supp.2d 626 (E.D. Mich. 1999)
Counsel being absent from pre- arranged plea negotiations, due to the fact that counsel felt that Petitioner would be more willing to provide information about counsel's other client, created a conflict of interest.

Jamison v. Collins, 100 F.Supp.2d 521 (S.D. Ohio 1998)
Where trial counsel was one of petitioner's two appellate attorneys, a conflict existed preventing counsel from raising trial counsel's ineffectiveness on direct appeal and established "cause" for procedural default. Also see **_Jamison v. Collins, 100 F.Supp.2d 647 (S.D. Ohio 2000)._**

Groseclose v. Bell, 130 F.3d 1161 (6th Cir. 1997)
Trial counsel abdicated defendant's case to counsel for co-defendant, whose defense was completely antagonistic to that of defendant, and prejudice resulting from such actions was substantial and constituted ineffective assistance of counsel.

U.S. v. Boling, 869 F.2d 965 (6th Cir. 1989)
Trial counsel was former associate of co-defendant and failed to call several witnesses whose testimony would have bolstered defendant Boling's argument that she was just an employee of the co-defendant and was not aware of co-defendant's activities, amounted to a conflict of interest and deprived Boling of effective assistance of counsel.

Thomas v. Foltz, 818 F.2d 476 (6th Cir. 1987)
The Court held that: "Habeas corpus petitioner was denied effective assistance of counsel due to his counsel's actual conflict of interest arising out of representation of petitioner and co-defendants in murder prosecution."

Wilson v. Mintzes, 761 F.2d 275 (6th Cir. 1985)
Trial counsel's failure to cross-examine a state's key witness due to a conflict of interest, constitutes ineffective assistance of counsel.

Seventh Circuit

Hall v. United States, 371 F.3d 969, 973-75 (7th Cir. 2004)
Counsel for defendant was burdened by conflict of interest because he represented the informant who provided FBI Agents with information about co-conspirator's drug distribution activities at federal prison and required an evidentiary hearing to resolve claim of ineffective assistance.

U.S. v. Morris, 259 F.3d 894, 899 (7th Cir. 2001)
Morris established that an actual conflict of interest existed, the district court did not inquire into the conflict. Morris alleged that he should be able to withdraw his guilty plea on the basis that his attorney falsely led him to believe that the plea would not waive his ability to appeal the admissible of evidence issue in a motion. The district court conducted a hearing on the motion. Morris was forced against his wishes to choose between allowing his (conflict) attorney to speak for him, or arguing the motion pro se. Morris' allegations warranted a remand for an evidentiary hearing to resolve the ineffectiveness of counsel claim.

U.S. v. Messino, 181 F.3d 826 (7th Cir. 1999)
>Excluding a government witness' testimony due to conflict of interest created by fact that defendant's defense counsel had previously represented witness constituted an abuse of discretion.

Stoia v. U.S., 109 F.3d 392 (7th Cir. 1997)
>Defense counsel who had entered a plea agreement, requiring counsel to cooperate with the federal government as a confidential informant and to refrain from representing individuals charged with crimes under investigation by federal authorities created a conflict of interest, but caused no adverse effect on defense. The Court denied the ineffectiveness of counsel claim.

Griffin v. McVicar, 84 F.3d 830 (7th Cir. 1996)
>Defense counsel's joint representation of Griffin and codefendant established a conflict of interest where counsel failed to assert defense that Griffin was an innocent bystander and shift the blame onto codefendant.

Griffin v. McVicar, 84 F.3d 880 (7th Cir. 1996)
>Counsel was burdened with actual conflict in joint representation where counsel knew information suggesting alterative, albeit unpromising, defense asserting defendant was innocent bystander and shifting blame on codefendant. However, counsel presented hopeless joint alibi defense and arguments that were favorable to codefendant and detrimental to defendant.

U.S. v. Shorter, 54 F.3d 1248 (7th Cir. 1995)
>Defendant's accusing attorney of forcing him to plead guilty and attorney claiming that the defendant's statements were false constitutes a conflict of interest.

Castillo v. U.S., 34 F.3d 443 (7th Cir. 1994)
>Counsel advising defendant not to testify because his testimony would hurt codefendant whom was represented by same lawyer in joint prosecution showed that lawyer's conflict adversely affected his representation of defendant.

Stoia v. U.S., 22 F.3d 766 (7th Cir. 1994)
>Defense counsel, who had signed a consent degree with the government under which counsel had agreed to work with the government undercover to uncover drug crimes, was burdened with a conflict of interest where he was retained by Stoia to help prepare and participate in Stoia defense. Stoia had two other defense counsels who handled the trial but were instructed by counsel who was burdened with conflict of interest. The Seventh Circuit remanded for an evidentiary hearing.

Rosenwald v. U.S., 898 F.2d 585 (7th Cir. 1990)
>Rosenwald's §2255 motion alleged ineffective assistance of counsel due to attorney simultaneous representation, on unrelated civil matter, of government's key witness, and if established, constitutes "cause" under the Frady Rule.

U.S. v. Ziegenhagen, 890 F.2d 937 (7th Cir. 1989)
>A conflict of interest is established where defense counsel previously appeared against defendant at state sentencing hearing 20 years earlier, and any subsequent representation of same defendant in defense capacity was not proper.

Conflict of Interest

U.S. Ex Rel Duncan v. O'Leary, 806 F.2d 1307 (7th Cir. 1986)

Defense counsel was the prosecutor's campaign manager and at an evidentiary hearing, the court found that there was collusion between the prosecutor and defense counsel, which created a conflict of interest that adversely affected counsel's performance.

Dently v. Lane, 695 F.2d 113 (7th Cir. 1981)

Dently claimed he was denied effective assistance of counsel because of a conflict of interest, where he "fired" his public defender and the court reappointed another public defender. The case was vacated and remanded for an evidentiary hearing.

U.S. v. Ellison, 798 F.2d 1102 (7th Cir. 1986)

Ellison filed a motion to withdraw his guilty plea in the context of a letterform. Ellison claimed his guilty pleas were the result of psychological pressures of solitary confinement, the exclusion from family and friends, and the erroneous advice of his court-appointed attorney "that an immediate guilty plea would place [him] in better and more humane living conditions and renew [my] contact with family and friends" (emphasis added). The court conducted an evidentiary hearing on defendant's motion. Counsel testified against Ellison at the hearing. The court denied the motion to withdraw guilty plea. The Seventh Circuit reversed and remanded, holding that there was no doubt that a conflict of interest existed, where counsel testified against Ellison, but without counsel Ellison was deprived of his right to cross-examine counsel, in violation of the Sixth Amendment.

Eighth Circuit

Koste v. Dormire, 260 F.3d 872,879-881 (8th Cir. 2001)

Koste advised the trial court that his attorney had a conflict of interest because she represented him in another case, where she provided constitutionally ineffective assistance of counsel, and that claim was the subject of a pending post-conviction relief motion. The trial court failed to adequate inquiry into the potential conflict which was "contrary to" clearly established federal law by the Supreme Court in *Holloway v. Arkansas*, **435 u.s. 475, 98 S .Ct. 1173, 55 L.Ed.2d 426 (1978)**, and required reversal.

Atley v. Ault, 191 F.3d 865 (8th Cir. 1999)

Where the district court fails to discharge its duty to inquire into a known conflict of interest under the *Holloway* standard said error is not subject to the harmless error analysis but rather is constitutional defect that entitles petitioner relief in habeas proceeding.

Burns v. Gammon, 173 F.3d 1089 (8th Cir. 1999)

Trial counsel and appellate counsel who came from same office as trial counsel created a conflict of interest where appellate counsel failed to raise trial counsel's ineffective assistance of counsel claims on direct appeal which could have been reviewed based on the record on appeal and constituted "cause" for procedural default.

Dawn v. Lockhart, 31 F.3d 718 (8th Cir. 1994)

Trial counsel was burden with a conflict of interest where he represented defendant and a co-defendant, and codefendant pleads guilty and implicated defendant in the offense charged. Counsel failed to bring to the jury's attention that codefendant made prior inconsistent statements, which established adverse performance. **See also _Dawan v. Lockhart_, 980 F.2d 470 (8th Cir. 1992)**

Jamison v. Lockhart, 975 F.2d 1377 (8th Cir. 1992)

Defendant's trial counsel, who was also City Attorney, created a conflict of interest and constitutes "cause" for procedural default.

Simmons v. Lockhart, 915 F.2d 372 (8th Cir. 1990)

Post-conviction counsel's failure to raise in petition that trial counsel was burdened with a conflict of interest, where prosecution's witness was trial counsel's former client, lifting procedural bar to habeas corpus claim.

Williams v. Lockhart, 849 F.2d 1134 (8th Cir. 1988)

Petitioner's allegation that counsel was burdened with a conflict of interest, where counsel allegedly represented the victim, would be addressed on remand even though petitioner failed to properly object to the Magistrate's report, which did not specifically address the conflict of interest claim.

Edgemon v. Lockhart, 768 F.2d 252 (8th Cir. 1985)

Trial counsel representing Edgemon also represented the Sheriff, who helped investigate the case and was a key prosecution witness, constituted a conflict of interest and required an evidentiary hearing.

U.S. v. Averbach, 745 F.2d 1157 (8th Cir. 1984)

The Court held that representation of both father and son by same counsel resulted in conflict of interest that denied father effective assistance of counsel.

United States v. Unger, 665 F.2d 251 (8th Cir. 1981)

Trial counsel's joint representation of defendant and co-defendant, where there was no valid waiver of conflict of interest, and counsel failed to make efforts to distant defendant from aggravating circumstances, failed to exonerate defendant at expense of co-defendant, constitutes a conflict of interest and required an evidentiary hearing.

Ninth Circuit

Plumlee v. Del Papa, 465 F.3d 901, 921-923 (9th Cir. 2006)

Plumlee asserted that his lawyer had betrayed him where members of the Public Defender's Office were leaking information about his case to another suspect and to the District Attorney. The lack of trust on both sides were so severe that Plumlee's attorney not only corroborated Plumlee's claim that the relationship had broken down, but even made his own motion to be relieved. The district court denied the motion. Plumlee then chose self-representation because of the irreconcilable conflict with his attorney. An erroneous denial of a motion to substitute counsel that prompts a defendant to choose self-representations warrants reversal despite the defendant's "choice" to represent himself.

Alberni v. McDaniel, 458 F.3d 860, 873 (9th Cir. 2006)

Alberni was entitled to evidentiary hearing to determine whether his trial counsel's performance was adversely affected by a conflict of interest because of successive representation of the state's rebuttal witness Mr. Flamrn. Counsel failed to impeach

Conflict of Interest

Mr. Flamm during cross-examination with his prior conviction, probation status, and on multiple points of his testimony.

Daniel v. Woodford, 428 F.3d 1181, 1197 (9th Cir. 2005)

Daniels was constructively denied his right to counsel because of a conflict of interest resulting in a failure to communicate between Daniels and the public defender's office.

Campbell v. Rice, 302 F.3d 892, 898 (9th Cir. 2002)

The trial court violated defendant's due process right to be present when it excluded the defendant from a private in-chambers hearing in which defense counsel, prosecutor and judge discussed the conflict of interest because defense counsel was being prosecuted for a felony by the same district attorney's office that was prosecuting Campbell.

Campbell v. Rice, 265 F.3d 878, 884 (9th Cir. 2001)

Trial counsel who was being prosecuted by the same district attorney's office on unrelated criminal charges as defendant created a conflict of interest, and the court's failure to inquiry into the potential conflict of interest required reversal.

U.S v. Moore, 159 F.3d 1154 (9th Cir. 1998)

Moore claimed that his trial counsel Cozens' had loyalties to LeMaux, a co-defendant, which were in conflict with Cozens' duty towards Moore, since Moore desired to pursue a withdrawal defense which would have undermined LeMauz's defense that the conspiracy never existed. Moore also alleged that Cozens failed to investigate and present Moore's withdrawal defense, failed to communicate a written plea offer, failed to file a motion to serve and, as such, constituted ineffective assistance of counsel. The Ninth Circuit did not reach the merits of Moore's ineffective assistance of counsel claims, but held an irreconcilable conflict of interest existed and **reversed and remanded the case for a new trial.**

U.S. v. DelMoro, 87 F.3d 1078 (9th Cir. 1996)

The district court created a conflict of interest by forcing counsel to prove his own ineffectiveness which violated defendant's Sixth Amendment to effective counsel.

Sanders v. Ratelle, 21 F.3d 1446 (9th Cir. 1994)

Defense counsel represented defendant burdened with a conflict of interest where he also represented defendant's brother who had confessed to the crime, and counsel advised defendant's brother to take the Fifth Amendment if called to the stand in defendant's trial.

U.S. v. Miskinis, 966 F.2d 1263 (9th Cir. 1992)

Defendant has a right to present an "advice of counsel defense" and continued representation of defendant by counsel who gave said advice can constitute ineffective assistance of counsel when defense of "advice of counsel" is not presented and requires an evidentiary hearing to resolve the claim.

Fitzpatrick v. McCormick, 869 F.2d 1247 (9th Cir. 1989)

Trial counsel actively represented defendant with a conflict of interest where evidence showed counsel's successive representation of petitioner at second trial, after counsel represented petitioner's co-defendant in petitioner's first trial, constituted a violation of the petitioner's right to effective assistance of counsel.

Mannhalt v. Reed, *847 F.2d 576 (9th Cir. 1988)*

A conflict of interest exists when a government witness testifies that he sold the stolen goods to the defendant's attorney and attorney's failure to withdraw and to testify to rebut the witness' allegation affected the attorney's cross-examination denying defendant the right to effective assistance of counsel.

Mannhalt v. Reed, *847 F.2d 576 (9th Cir. 1988)*

Failure to explore possible plea bargain due to a conflict of interest deprives defendant of the right to effective assistance of counsel.

Tenth Circuit

Hammon v. Ward, *466 F.3d 919, 929-930 (10th Cir. 2006)*

Glenn and Demarcus Hammon were represented by the same counsel with the intention of proceeding to trial with a planned trial strategy. However, trial counsel negotiated a plea bargain with the State for Demarcus Hammon, which the State agreed to recommend to five year deferred sentence, if Demarcus agreed to inculpate Glenn. Trial counsel never informed Glenn that Demarcus had pleaded guilty, and Glenn declined a fifteen (15) year plea offer. Glenn did not know that Demarcus plead guilty until after the trial started when counsel informed Glenn that Demarcus Hammon had already plead guilty and would not be able to testify for Glenn because Demarcus' plea agreement required him to inculpate Glenn. Trial counsel's performance was adversely affected by an actual conflict of interest because trial counsel could not simultaneously negotiate the most favorable deal for Demarcus Hammon—a five (5) year deferred sentence--without disqualifying Demarcus Hammon from providing exculpatory testimony for Glenn Hammon. Demarcus' plea agreement basically sabotaged Glenn's viable defense strategy. An evidentiary hearing was warranted to resolve the factual disputes related to the conflict of interest claim.

U.S. v. Martin, *39 F.Supp. 2d 1333 (D. Utah 1999)*

Conflict of interest prevented former Assistant United States Attorney from representing the defendant because he had personally participated in the investigation of the defendant.

U.S. v. Gallegos, *108 F.3d 1272 (10th Cir 1997)*

The Tenth Circuit found the district court committed reversible error where the "court failed to resolve conflict of interest which arose when co-defendant called witness who had previously been represented by defendant's attorney and possessed information that was exculpatory to defendant by inculpatory of witness."

Edens v. Hannigan, *87 F.3d 1109 (10th Cir. 1996)*

Counsel was burden with actual conflict of interest in joint representation case, where counsel failed to make opening arguments in defendant's behalf, failed to put on evidence in defendant's behalf and did not permit defendant to testify where counsel knew defendant's only defense was in conflict with co-defendant's defense and where conflict between two defenses were consistently resolved in favor of codefendant's defense.

Conflict of Interest

Edens v. Hannigan, 87 F3d 1109 (10th Cir. 1996)
    Counsel's failure to pursue favorable plea negotiations on defendant's behalf, which was motivated by a conflict of interest, established ineffective assistance of counsel.

Selsor v. Kaiser, 81 F.3d 1492 (10th Cir. 1996)
    Joint representation was called to the trial court's attention due to a possible conflict of interest and the two defendants moved for a severance in trial. The Court failed to appoint separate counsel, prejudice was presumed.

U.S. v. Cook, 45 F.3d 388 (10th Cir. 1995)
    Trial court created a conflict of interest, which denied defendant effective assistance of counsel, where district court ordered counsel to advise government witness of consequences for her failure to comply with the provisions of her plea agreement to testify against defendant and required reversal of conviction.

Selsor v. Kaiser, 22 F.3d 1029 (10th Cir. 1994)
    The district court applied the incorrect legal standard applying Culver where the defendant objected to joint representation. The Court remanded for reconsideration under the Holloway standard.

U.S. v. Martin, 965 F.2d 839 (10th Cir. 1992)
    Trial counsel who represented defendant and co-defendant constituted a conflict of interest where counsel refused to present defendant's withdrawal defense from conspiracy due to conflict of interest.

Church v. Sullivan, 942 F.2d 1501 (10th Cir. 1991)
    Trial counsel was burdened with a conflict of interest where counsel was required to present defense theory, which inculpated his former client and was intertwined with petitioner's case. These allegations stated a significant claim warranting an evidentiary hearing.

Moore v. U.S., 950 F.2d 656 (10th Cir. 1991)
    A defendant has a right to conflict-free representation during guilty plea negotiations which includes investigations.

Eleventh Circuit

Reynolds v. Chapman, 253 F.3d 1337, 1347 (11th Cir. 2001)
    Counsel who represented Reynolds in rape, kidnapping, and aggravated sodomy case was appointed to represent a co-defendant as well as Reynolds in post-trial proceedings. Counsel labored under a conflict of interest, which adversely effected his performance. Counsel for Reynolds could have advanced the following arguments but didn't: (1) the jury unfairly failed to distinguished him from Curtis, when the evidence against Curtis, but not Reynolds, was overwhelming, and (2) Reynolds was unfairly prejudiced by the perjurious testimony of Curtis and Curtis's mother. Counsel declined to advance these arguments on Reynolds behalf because of the effect those arguments would have on Curtis. This type of circumstances satisfies the "actual conflict" prong of the *Cuyler* test.

Trejo v. U.S., *66 F.Supp.2d 1274 (S.D. Fla. 1999)*
> Defense counsel who refused to represent his client who decided to cooperate with the government and left co-defendant's counsel's to handle his client cooperation agreement with the government created a conflict of interest, which tainted all three defendant's convictions.

U.S. v. McKinnon, *995 F. Supp. 1404 (M.D. Fla. 1998)*
> Trial counsel instructed defendant not to testify on her own behalf based on inappropriate conflict concerns for the well-being of the co-defendants, these claims, required an evidentiary hearing to resolve ineffective assistance of counsel and conflict of interest claim.

Freud v. Butterworth, *117 F3d 1543 (11th Cir. 1997)*
> Trial counsel who cross-examines former client/witness inherently encounters divided loyalty, where prior representation likely provided counsel's law firm with information that could be used to impeach former client/witness, which establishes an actual conflict of interest.

Burden v. Zant, *498 U.S. 433, 112 LEd.2d 962, 111 S.Ct. 862 (1991)*
> Defendant's pretrial counsel who reached informal understanding with prosecutor that second suspect in murders whom counsel also represented, would not be prosecuted in exchange for his testimony against defendant, sufficiently stated a conflict of interest. Also see, *Burden v. Zant, 24 F.3d 1298 (11th Cir. 1994).*

Hamilton v. Ford, *969 F.2d 1006 (11th Cir. 1992)*
> A timely notice or objections to joint representation requires the trial court to inquire into the conflict and failure of the court to do so requires automatic reversal.

Buenoano v. Singletary, *963 F.2d 1433 (11th Cir. 1992)*
> Ms. Buenoano stated a sufficient claim that her trial counsel was burdened with a conflict of interest arising out of book and movie contract that was entered into by counsel, his wife and petitioner. There was a wealth of significant evidence which was available and which should have been presented but wasn't. Buenoano claimed this lack of efforts resulted because of the book and movie contract and that her attorney failed to investigate, discover and present mitigating evidence concerning her background and mental health.

U.S. v. Urbana, *770 F.Supp. 1552 (S.D. Fla. 1991)*
> Trial counsel being implicated in criminal activity creates a conflict of interest and required disqualification of counsel.

McConico v. State of Ala., *919 F.2d 1543 (11th Cir. 1990)*
> James McConico argued that an actual conflict existed where counsel simultaneously represented him in his criminal trial and Brenda McConico in her insurance claim. James McConico contended that counsel faced divided loyalties when he cross-examined his client Brenda McConico at James' trial especially as the matters were so closely related. The insurance policy contained an exclusion clause that denied payment if the policyholder died from "participation in, or as a result of having committing of an assault or felony." At trial, counsel argued that James' shot in self-defense and that Morton was the aggressor in the incident that resulted in his death. In order for counsel to preserve the insurance proceeds payable upon Morton's death to counsel's second

client, Brenda McConico, and to avoid the exclusion clause of the policy. However, counsel was required to take the position in the insurance claim that Morton was not the aggressor in the incident. This position negated James' claim of self-defense. A vigorous defense of James' based on self-defense that could have resulted in acquittal would necessarily have made Morton the aggressor in the shooting incident. Counsel by placing himself between two adverse parties and actively representing both, constituted a conflict of interest.

Porter v. Wainwright, 805 F.2d 930 (11th Cir. 1986)

Trial counsel representing the defendant, after he had previously represented a prosecution's key witness, stated a sufficient claim of conflict of interest and warranted an evidentiary hearing.

Ruffin v. Kemp, 767 F.2d 748 (11th Cir. 1985)

The Court held that: "(1) Attorney who had been appointed to represent co-defendants and who attempted to work out plea bargain for one which would call for that one to testify against the other labored under actual conflict of interest, and (2) that conflict precluded attorney from seeking to plea bargain on behalf of prisoner, and thus adversely affected representation of prisoner." Reversed and Remanded.

INEFFECTIVENESS CAUSED BY COURT OR THE GOVERNMENT

DENIAL OF MOTION FOR PRO HAV VICE

Fuller v. Diesslin, 868 F.2d 604 (3rd Cir. 1989)
The Court held that: "(1) State trial court's wooden approach and its failure to make record-supported findings balancing right to counsel with demands of administration of justice resulted in arbitrary denial of defendant's motion for counsel pro hac vice, and such arbitrary denial constituted per se constitutional error justifying issuance of writ."

U.S. v. Costanzo, 740 F.2d 251 (3rd Cir. 1984)
Just because attorney had been suspended in New York and Wisconsin State Courts, but he was a member and in good standing in the Federal District of the Eastern District of New York and the Second Circuit, did not provide trial court with reasons not to allow attorney's admission for pro hav vice in federal district court in New Jersey.

COURT REFUSED TO APPOINT COUNSEL

Mempa v. Rhay, 389 U.S. 128. 19 L.Ed.2d 336, 88 S.Ct. 254 (1967)
The Supreme Court held that as a matter of federal constitutional law, a lawyer must be afforded at the proceeding described above, whether they are labeled a revocation of probation or a deferred sentencing.

Green v. United States, 262 F.3d 715, 718 (8th Cir. 2001)
The district court's denial of counsel to indigent petitioner during an evidentiary hearing to resolve claims presented in **28 U.S.C. §2255** motion, is not subject to harmless error analysis, but required automatic reversal.

Roney v. U.S., 205 F.3d 1061 (8th Cir. 2000)
District court's failure to appoint Mr. Roney counsel for an evidentiary on his 28 U.S.C. §2255 motion to vacate as mandated by Rule 8(c) governing §2255 proceeding was not harmless. The district court's ruling is Reversed and Remanded for a new evidentiary hearing.

O'Rourke v. Endell, 153 F,3d 560 (8th Cir. 1998)
The State Court deprived Petitioner of due process of law where it failed to appoint counsel to argue during competency hearing that Petitioner lacked capacity to waive his appeal in a post-conviction proceedings, plus the state court's findings that petitioner was competent was not entitled to presumption of correctness.

U.S. v. Vasquez, 7 F.3d 81 (5th Cir. 1993)
Trial court's failure to appoint indigent petitioner at evidentiary hearing on '2255 motion to vacate sentence required reversal.

175

Ineffectiveness Caused
By Court Or The Government

Smith v. Lockhart, *923 F.2d 1314 (8th Cir. 1991)*
The trial court violated defendant's Sixth Amendment rights by refusing to appoint new counsel, when defendant presented sufficient cause for substitution of counsel to assist defendant at omnibus hearing.

U.S. v. Wadsworth, *830 F.2d 1500 (9th Cir. 1987)*
The trial court's denial of the defendant's right to counsel is per se reversal.

United States v. Anderson, *553 F.2d 1154 (8th Cir. 1977)*
The Court of Appeals held that: "Trial court's failure to determine whether alleged contemnor who was faced with prospect of imprisonment was indigent required remand for a finding on such issue; if alleged contemnor were found to be indigent, judgment of contempt would be vacated and district court would be ordered to appoint counsel and re-adjudicate civil contempt charge." Remanded.

COURT FAILED TO APPOINT AN INTERPRETER

Gonzalez v. Phillips, *147 F.Supp. 2d 791, 804 (E.D. Mich. 2001)*
A federal habeas corpus evidentiary hearing was required, to determine whether the trial court's failure to provide petitioner an interpreter violated his rights of confrontation, effective assistance of counsel, right to be present, right to participation in his defense, and a fair trial.

COURT REFUSED TO GRANT CONTINUANCE

Reynolds v. Cochran, *365 U.S. 525, 5 LEd.2d 754, 81 SCt. 723 (1961)*
The Supreme Court held that "the trial court's refusal to grant the accused's motion for a continuance, in order that he might have the assistance in the proceeding of counsel whom he had retained, deprived the accused of due process in the constitutional sense."

Gardner v. Barnett, *175 F.3d 580 (7th Cir. 1999)*
The district court's failure to grant petitioner's continuance at trial to obtain unavailable witnesses was a violation of due process.

U.S. v Garrett, *149 F.3d 1019 (9th Cir. 1998)*
District court's failure to grant a motion for a 30-day continuance where defendant's newly retained counsel could adequately prepare for trial was an abuse of discretion and required **REVERSAL of GARRETT'S conviction and a REMAND for new trial. See also *McKenna v. Ellis*, 280 F.2d 592 (5th Cir. 1960); *Hintz v. Beto*, 379 F.2d 937 (5th Cir. 1967); *United States ex. rel. Spencer v. Warden, Pontiac Corr. Ctr.*, 545 F.2d 21 (7th Cir. 1976)**

U.S. v. Verderame, *51 F.3d 249 (11th Cir. 1995)*
The trial court's failure to grant a continuance deprived the defendant of an opportunity to confer, to consult and prepare a defense with counsel. The Court of Appeals reversed the conviction and remanded for a new trial.

Wade v. Armontrout, 798 F.2d 304 (8th Cir. 1986)
> The trial court's denial of defendant's motion for continuance attributed to the defendant receiving ineffective assistance of counsel, because counsel was not prepared for trial, and required an evidentiary hearing to resolve the claim.

COURT PROVOKED COUNSEL'S ERRORS

Wilson v. Mintzes, 761 F.2d 275 (6th Cir. 1985)
> Where trial counsel provoked into acts inconsistent with his duties of loyalty to his client, by the trial court, such interference effects the fairness of the trial and prejudice is presumed. The *Strickland* standards have no applicability.

JUDGE THREATENS COUNSEL

U.S. v. Cruz, 977 F.2d 732 (2nd Cir. 1992)
> Trial judge's threat to impose maximum sentence if defendant went to trial without "good defense" required remand for resentencing in front of different judge.

Walberg v. Israel, 766 F.2d 1071 (7th Cir. 1985)
> The trial judge's threats to trial counsel that if he pushed too hard during trial that he would be jeopardizing future appointments by the court, reduced defendant's likelihood to receive a vigorous defense, regardless of the fact there was overwhelming evidence.

PREVENTING DEFENDANT FROM CONSULTING WITH COUNSEL

Geders v. United States, 425 U.S. 80, 47 L.Ed.2d 592, 96 S.Ct. 1330 (1976)
> The Supreme Court held that "a trial court's order directing a defendant not to consult his attorney during an overnight recess, called while the defendant was on the witness stand, violated his Sixth Amendment right to counsel." **See also** *Milton v. Morris, 767 F.2d 1443 (9th Cir. 1985)*; *Sanders v. Lane, 861 F.2d 1033 (7th Cir. 1988)*

Perry v. Leeke, 488 U.S. 272, 102 L.Ed.2d 624, 109 S.Ct. 594 (1989)
> The Supreme Court held that: (1) a trial court's order directing an accused not to consult his attorney during a brief recess, called while the accused is on the witness stand, does not violate the accused's Sixth Amendment right to counsel; and (2) a showing of prejudice is not an essential component of a violation of the *Geders* rule.

Norde v. Keane, 294 F.3d 401, 414-15 (2nd Cir. 2002)
> The trial court denied defense counsel's request for adjournment to consult with her client upon his removal from the courtroom for disruptive behavior during voir dire in burglary prosecution, and then required counsel to communicate with client through a court officer, rather than his counsel, as to whether he wanted to return to the courtroom, which was an impermissible denial of defendant's right to counsel.

Moore v. Purkett, 275 F.3d 685 (8th Cir. 2001)
> The trial court violated petitioner's Sixth Amendment right to counsel by prohibiting petitioner from talking quietly with his attorney in the courtroom during trial.

U.S. v. Santos, 201 F.3d 953 (7th Cir. 2000)
> The district court erred instructing defendant's lawyer not to discuss his client's testimony with his client during an overnight recess.

SURREPTITIOUS QUESTIONING DEFENDANT BY GOVERNMENT

U.S. v. Geittmann, 733 F.2d 1419 (10th Cir. 1984)
> Geittmann had been arrested, indicted and released on bond for a marijuana conspiracy charge. A co-defendant, Patrick Callihan, agreed to cooperate with the government. Callihan made tape-recorded conversations between himself and Geittmann. The Court found that Geittmann's statement during post-indictment period to Callihan violated Geittmann's Sixth Amendment right to counsel and suppressed the tape conversations.

FAILED TO RELEASE *Brady* MATERIAL

Parkus v. Delo, 33 F.3d 933 (8th Cir. 1994)
> The State falsely informed defendant's lawyer that defendant's mental health records had been destroyed, and, as such constitute "cause" for procedural default. An evidentiary hearing was required to resolve this claim.

Tate v. Wood, 963 F.2d 20 (2d Cir. 1992)
> Tate was entitled to evidentiary hearing on **Brady** claim concerning failure to disclose evidence that victim was initial aggressor. The test of materiality in the context of a guilty plea is whether there is a reasonable probability that, but for the failure to produce such information, the defendant would not have entered the plea but instead would have insisted on going to trial. The inquiry is an objective one that is resolved largely on the basis of the persuasiveness of the withheld evidence. *See, Miller v. Angliker, 848 F.2d 1312, 1322 (2nd Cir.), cert. denied, 488 U.S. 890, 109 S.Ct. 224, 102 L.Ed.2d 214 (1988))*.

PUNISHMENT MIGHT BE INCREASED

U.S. v. Moskouits, 86 F.3d 1303 (3rd Cir. 1996)
> The district court's failure to inform defendant that punishment might be increased at retrial rendered defendant's waiver of counsel and chooses to proceed with self-representation invalid requiring resentence to the original sentence.

INTRUSION BY GOVERNMENT

U.S. v. Amlani, 111 F.3d 705 (9th Cir. 1997)
The prosecutor repeatedly disparaged Amlani's original chosen trial attorney in front of Amlani. The government told Amlani and his wife that his attorney did not care about him and was not competent, and could not prevent a conviction. Amlani claimed the disparagement violated his Sixth Amendment because it caused him to change attorney to a less competent counsel. The Court of Appeals remanded for an evidentiary hearing, and new trial if Amlani's allegations were established as true.

Shillinger v. Haworth, 70 F.3d 1132 (10th Cir. 1995)
The state's use of a deputy sheriff's presence during Petitioner's trial preparation conference with defense counsel amounted to prosecutorial intrusion into attorney-client relationship and constituted a per se violation of Petitioner's Sixth Amendment rights.

U.S. v. Kelly, 790 F.2d 130 (D.C. Cir. 1986)
Kelly contended that his Sixth Amendment rights were violated when Davenport, a government agent, invaded his defense strategy sessions and stole relevant and important documents. District court's failure to develop any evidentiary record or to make any findings constituted abuse of discretion.

INTERFERENCE WITH DEFENSE WITNESS'

U.S. v Vavages, 151 F.3d 1185 (9th Cir. 1998)
Governmental interference with a defense witness' choice of whether to testify constitutes a violation of due process and requires a reversal and a remand for new trial.

ORDERS COUNSEL TO PROVE INEFFECTIVENESS

U.S. v. DelMoro, 87 F.3d 1078 (9th Cir. 1996)
The district court created a conflict of interest by forcing counsel to prove his own ineffectiveness which violated defendant's Sixth Amendment to effective counsel.

STATE LOST DEFENDANT'S POST CONVICTION MOTIONS

Footman v. Singletary, 978 F.2d 1207 (11th Cir. 1992)
The state was precluded from claiming that petitioner had not raised claims of ineffectiveness of counsel, where state lost copy of defendant's motion for post-conviction relief.

ATTORNEY'S FEES EXEMPT FROM FORFEITURE

U.S. v. Monsanto, 852 F.2d 1400 (2nd Cir. 1988)
Defendant was entitled to assets for attorney fees in criminal case and fees were exempted from subsequent forfeiture.

FAILED TO WARN DEFENDANT OF RISK OF SELF-REPRESENTATION

United States v. Virgil, 444 F.3d 447, 454-457 (5th Cir. 2006)
Failure to give *Faretta* warning at sentencing to ensure that defendant's waiver of his right to counsel was knowing and intelligent warranted reversal.

U.S. v. Akins, 276 F.3d 1141, 1149 (9th Cir. 2002)
The government was prohibited from using defendant's prior state misdemeanor conviction for domestic assault charge, to support federal conviction for possession of a firearm following conviction for a misdemeanor domestic violence crime because the waiver of right to counsel did not include a *Faretta* warning, explaining the dangers and disadvantage of proceeding pro se without counsel. Therefore, the state conviction was obtained in violation of Akins' Sixth Amendment right to counsel.

U.S. v. Davis, 269 F.3d 514 (5th Cir. 2001)
The district court did not give an adequate **Farretta warning** of the perils of self-representation and thus defendant did not make a knowing and intelligent waiver of his Sixth Amendment right to counsel.

Shafer v. Bowersox, 168 F.Supp.2d 1055, 1066-1094 (E.D. Mo. 2001)
The state court, during change of plea hearing, failed to advise *Shafer* of the dangers and disadvantages of self-representation as required by the U.S. Supreme Court precedent in *Faretta v. California*, rendering his guilty plea, waiver of counsel and mitigation not knowingly and voluntary entered, requiring the conviction to be vacated to afford *Shafer* the opportunity to plead anew.

Hall v. Moore, 253 F.3d 624, 628 (11th Cir. 2001)
Hall failed to clearly and unequivocally assert his right to self-representation. The court failed to conduct a hearing to ensure that Hall was fully aware of the dangers and disadvantages of proceeding without counsel, therefore there is a presumption of prejudice established.

U.S. v. Proctor, 166 F.3d 396 (1st Cir. 1999)
Where the court of appeals could not tell whether defendant Proctor's self-representation at trial resulted from a valid waiver of his Sixth Amendment right to counsel, the Court **VACATED** his conviction and **REMANDED** for a new trial.

Henderson v. Franks, 155 F.3d 159 (3rd Cir. 1998)
Trial court's failure to make certain that defendant knowingly, voluntarily and intelligently waived his right to counsel required reversal.

U.S. v. Sandles, **23 F.3d 1121 (7th Cir. 1994)**
> Trial court's failure to properly warn defendant of risk and disadvantages of self-representation did not constitute a valid waiver of the right to counsel.

Sanchez v. Mondragon, **858 F.2d 1462 (10th Cir. 1988)**
> The Court held that: "(1) Standard used to review defendant's decision to represent himself at trial was same in collateral proceeding as it was on direct review; (2) defendant's decision to represent himself was not knowing and intelligent; and (3) violation of Sixth Amendment Rights in connection with defendant's decision to represent himself was not harmless." Reversed and Remanded.

U.S. v. Wadsworth, **830 F.2d 1500 (9th Cir. 1987)**
> A criminal defendant, who chooses to represent himself, must make a knowing and intelligent waiver on the record.

FAILED TO INQUIRE INTO REASONS WHY DEFENDANT REQUESTED SUBSTITUTE COUNSEL

Plumlee v. Del Papa, **465 F.3d 901, 921-923 (9th Cir. 2006)**
> Plumlee asserted that his lawyer had betrayed him where members of the Public Defender's Office were leaking information about his case to another suspect and to the District Attorney. The lack of trust on both sides were so severe that Plumlee's attorney not only corroborated Plumlee's claim that the relationship had broken down, but even made his own motion to be relieved. The district court denied the motion. Plumlee then chose self-representation because of the irreconcilable conflict with his attorney. An erroneous denial of a motion to substitute counsel that prompts a defendant to choose self-representations warrants reversal despite the defendant's "choice" to represent himself.

Bland v. California Dept. of Corrections, **20 F.3d 1469 (9th Cir. 1994)**
> The trial court's failure to inquire into the reasons why defendant sought to substitute counsel violated defendant's Sixth Amendment right to counsel and harmless error doctrine did not apply. The prosecution's failure to dispute factual allegation in habeas petition and traverse amounted to admitting the allegations were true.

EX PARTE CONVERSATIONS

Yohn v. Love, **76 F.3d 508 (3rd Cir. 1996)**
> The Court found that Mr. Yohn's Sixth Amendment right to counsel was violated where the prosecutor had an ex parte conversation with a Supreme Court Justice who advised trial judge to admit certain evidence into defendant's trial. Thus, violating defendant's due process rights.

STATE ATTRIBUTED TO COUNSEL'S FAILURE
TO PERFECT APPEAL

Harris v. Kuhlman, 601 F.Supp. 987 (E.D. New York 1985)
> Counsel's failure to perfect appeal, which was attributed to state, constituted ineffective assistance of counsel.

COURT REFUSED TO ALLOW DEFENDANT TO BE PRESENT
AT AN INCAMERA HEARING

U.S. v. Bohn, 890 F.2d 1079 (9th Cir. 1989)
> A defendant has a right to be present with counsel at an in-camera hearing to determine the validity of his Fifth Amendment claim. The court's refusal to allow defendant to be accompanied by counsel denied defendant his right to counsel.

REFUSED REQUEST FOR EXPERT MENTAL HEALTH
WITNESS

Starr v. Lockhart, 23 F.3d 1280 (8th Cir. 1994)
> The trial court's failure to grant petitioner's request for appointment of expert mental health witness violated due process.

ADVISED DEFENDANT HE WOULD HAVE TO PROCEED
PRO SE IF HE TESTIFIED

U.S. v. Scott, 909 F.2d 488 (11th Cir. 1990)
> The Court held that: District court's advising defendant that he could be precluded from testifying, without confirmation that defendant intended to commit perjury, or could proceed pro se impermissibly forced defendant to choose between his constitutional right to counsel and his constitutional right to testify. Vacated and Remanded.

FAILED TO ASK DEFENDANT IF SHE READ PSR

U.S. v. Sustaita, 1 F.3d 950 (9th Cir. 1993)
> A criminal defendant is entitled to read and review a presentence report prior to the imposition of sentence in the Federal Court system. Just because defense counsel stated to the court "we" twice discussed the PSR did not satisfy the requirements of *Federal Rules of Civil Procedure, Rule 32*.

DEFENSE ORDERED TO RELEASE EXPERTS OPINION

U.S. v. Beckford, 962 F. Supp. 748 (E.D. Va. 1997)

A requirement that the defense provides the government any and all material supplied to defense by the defense expert, which forms the basis of expert's opinion on defendant's mental illness, would violate defendant's right to effective assistance of counsel.

OTHER CLAIMS

Brooks v. Tennessee, 406 U.S. 605, 32 LEd.2d 358, 92 S.Ct. 1891 (1972)

The Supreme Court found that Brooks, was deprived of his constitutional rights when the trial court excluded him from the stand for failing to testify first.

Lewis v. Lane, 832 F.2d 1446 (7th Cir. 1987)

The Court held that: (1) Petitioner's procedural default with respect to contesting validity of prior felony convictions was caused by States' concealment of evidence of their invalidity; (2) defense counsel's stipulation to existence of convictions, ultimately determined to be nonexistent, constituted ineffective assistance of counsel, prejudicial to petitioner and entitled him to new sentencing hearing.

MISCELLANEOUS INEFFECTIVENESS

COUNSEL ADMITS HIS OWN INCOMPETENCE

U.S. v. Galloway, 56 F.3d 1259 (10th Cir. 1995)
Counsel can raise his own ineffectiveness at trial on appeal.

Dillion v. Duckworth, 751 F.2d 895 (7th Cir. 1985)
In this case, the attorney admitted his own incompetence and filed two affidavits to his ineffectiveness. The attorney offered no character witnesses, either at trial or at the subsequent death penalty hearing. The Court found that it would be standard practice for an attorney defending an eighteen-year-old with no criminal record to present character witnesses and evidence. The non-existence of the attorney's efforts to avoid the death penalty once Dillion's guilt was established was incomprehensible and extremely prejudicial to Dillion. In sum, the attorney's errors prejudiced Dillion's trial sufficiently to warrant a retrial. *Id. at 901.*

COUNSEL NOT REQUIRED TO RAISE HIS OWN INEFFECTIVENESS

Nichols v. U.S., 75 F.3d 1137 (7th Cir. 1996)
Trial counsel is not required to raise his own ineffectiveness on appeal, or at any other time.

Page v. U.S., 884 F.2d 300 (7th Cir. 1989)
Appellate counsel is not required to raise his own ineffectiveness on appeal in order to preserve claim for *28 U.S.C. §2255* motion.

COUNSEL USE OF DRUGS DURING TRIAL

Payne v. U.S., 697 A.2d 1229 (D.C.App. 1997)
Counsel's alleged drug use during trial did not constitute ineffective assistance.

COURT OF APPEALS REMANDS TO AFFORD DEFENDANT AN OPPORTUNITY TO AMEND HIS INEFFECTIVE ASSISTANCE OF COUNSEL CLAIMS

Ellerby v. U.S., 187 F.3d 257 (2nd Cir. 1999)
The Court of Appeals remanded the district court's denial of *Ellerby's* §2255 motion to afford *Ellerby* an opportunity to amend his ineffective assistance of counsel claims with instructions to hold an evidentiary hearing on counsel's failure to subpoena alibi witness.

U.S. v. Martiner, 181 F.3d 627 (5th Cir. 1999)

The Fifth Circuit vacated the district court's summary dismissal of Martinez's *§2255* motion to vacate. Martinez alleged he was denied effective assistance of counsel where he advised counsel that he wanted to testify on his own behalf, but counsel failed to call him to testify, thus, he was deprived of an opportunity to present his side of the story to the jury. The Fifth Circuit mindful both of the judiciary's obligations to provide the accused with an adequate mechanism to fairly address his claims and of our heavy indulgence of pleadings by pro se prisoners, Martinez's vague and conclusory assertion alone did not warrant a hearing. At the same time, in keeping with the strictures of *§2255*, stated that we do not think summary dismissal was appropriate. Thereafter, the Court remanded the case to afford Martinez an opportunity to state with greater specificity his complaints regarding ineffective assistance of counsel and his right to testify. The Court noted that, if Martinez fails to present more than his present conclusory allegation, summary dismissal of his petition would be appropriate.

Dorsey v. Irvin, 56 F.3d 425 (2nd Cir. 1995)

The Court of Appeals remanded to allow Dorsey an opportunity to amend his ineffective assistance of counsel claims based on failure to investigate or use available scientific evidence of the semen on the underwear, which apparently was inconclusive to Dorsey's blood type, or prosecutorial misconduct for failure to comply with the Brady rule.

Jones v. Lockhart, 851 F.2d 1115 (8th Cir. 1988)

The Court of Appeals affirmed the district court's dismissal of petitioner's pro se petition without prejudice to afford the petitioner an opportunity to file a new petition in the district court where, petitioner raised a new substantial factual issue that he did not received actual notice of the nature of the charge against him and a claim of ineffective assistance of counsel in relation to defendant being illegally sentenced as an habitual offender.

Petty v. McCotter, 779 F.2d 299 (5th Cir. 1986)

The Court held, in pertinent part, that petitioner was entitled to opportunity to amend his pleadings in district court to raise contention that he was denied effective assistance of counsel due to his trial attorney's failure to investigate possible insanity defense.

COUNSEL'S OWN PHYSICAL AND MENTAL PROBLEMS

United States v. Theodore, 354 F.3d 1, 7 (1st Cir. 2003)

Counsel misrepresented to court his past trial experience and history of alcohol abuse; failed to review or even glance at thousands of pages of evidence disclosed by the government, failed to appear at hearing on motion to quash subpoena and required an evidentiary hearing to resolve claim of ineffective assistance.

Bellamy v. Cogdell, 952 F.2d 626 (2nd Cir. 1991)

Trial counsel who admitted to physical and mental incapacity two weeks before trial without defendant knowing of counsel's incapacity, constituted ineffective assistance of counsel per se. But see *974 F.2d 302 (2nd Cir. 1992)* which vacated this opinion of the panel in *952 F.2d 626.*

COUNSEL PERJURED HIMSELF AT HEARING

Lahay v. Armontrout, 923 F.2d 578 (8th Cir. 1991)
The Eighth Circuit remanded this case for an evidentiary hearing to determine whether trial counsel perjured himself in the original evidentiary hearing on an ineffective assistance of counsel claim filed against counsel.

COUNSEL SUSPENDED IN SOME COURTS, BUT IN GOOD STANDING IN OTHER COURTS

Mitchell v. Mason, 325 F.3d 732, 741-744 (6th Cir. 2003)
Counsel who spent approximately six minutes spanning over three separate meetings with petitioner prior to trial and was suspended from practice a month before trial resulted in a complete denial of counsel. The state court's application of **Strickland** standard was an unreasonable application of clearly established Supreme Court law in **Cronic**.

Cole v. U.S., 162 F.3d 957 (7th Cir. 1998)
Just because counsel had not been admitted to practice in the federal district court did not render a per se claim of ineffective assistance of counsel.

U.S. v. Maria-Martinez, 143 F.3d 914 (5th Cir. 1998)
Just because defendant's attorney had been barred from practicing before the Fifth Circuit Court of Appeals did not compel a per se finding that counsel was ineffective.

Kieser v. People of State of New York, 56 F.3d 16 (2nd Cir. 1995)
The Court of Appeals held that fact that trial counsel was not licensed to practice in New York at time of arraignment and trial, because he had been temporarily suspended from practice in New Jersey for nonpayment of State bar dues failed to make motion in New York to be admitted pro hav vice, did not amount to per se violation of Sixth Amendment.

U.S. v. Costanzo, 740 F.2d 251 (3rd Cir. 1984)
Just because attorney had been suspended in New York and Wisconsin State Courts, but he was a member and in good standing in the Federal District of the Eastern District of New York and the Second Circuit, did not provide trial court with reasons not to allow attorney's admission for pro hav vice in federal district court in New Jersey.

COUNSEL ALLOWED DEFENDANT TO MAKE INCRIMINATING STATEMENTS

Harris By and Through Ramseyer v. Wood, 64 F.3d 1432 (9th Cir. 1995)
Trial counsel's performance fell below an objective standard of reasonableness where counsel allowed defendant to make incriminating statements to the prosecutor, where the prosecutor refused to promise a reduction in charges or an offer of immunity.

ATTORNEY-CLIENT PRIVILEGE

Swidler & Berlin v. United States, 524 U.S. 399 , 141 L.Ed.2d 379, 118 S.Ct. 2081 (1998)
> Attorney-client privilege protect initial interview notes that were (1) written by White House official's attorney shortly before official's death, and (2) subpoenaed by Independent counsel in criminal investigation after official's death.

COUNSEL'S FRAUDULENT DEALING WITH THE FEDERAL JUDICIARY

United States v. Levy, 377 F.3d 259, 265 (2nd Cir. 2004)
> An ineffective assistance of counsel claim based on counsel's criminal indictment for fraudulent conduct, dealing with the federal judiciary, the government, submitting fraudulent application for appointment of counsel under Criminal Justice Act, making false statements to a United States District Court, and to the criminal investigator required a remand for additional fact finding.

FRAUDULENTLY OBTAINED ADMISSION TO BAR

U.S. v. Novak, 903 F.2d 883 (2nd Cir. 1990)
> Novak was represented by an individual, who fraudulently obtained admission to bar, and the Court found that representation by the individual was per se insufficient to satisfy the Sixth Amendment.

COUNSEL REFUSED TO PRESENT PERJURY TESTIMONY

Nix v. Whiteside, 475 U.S. 157, 89 L.Ed.2d 123, 106 S.Ct. 988 (1986)
> Attorney's refusal to assist defendant in presenting perjury at trial not ineffective assistance of counsel.

FAILED TO PRESENT CONSTITUTIONAL ISSUE IN HABEAS PETITION

Griffin v. Delo, 961 F.2d 793 (8th Cir. 1992)
> Failure to properly present constitutional issues by habeas counsel can constitute ineffective assistance of counsel. But see **1996 Antiterrorist Act**.

ATTORNEY DISCLOSED CONFIDENTIAL COMMUNICATION

Whiteside v. Scurr, 750 F.2d 713 (8th Cir. 1984)
> Trial counsel threatened to withdraw as counsel, tell the judge that defendant was going to testify falsely, and agree to testify against defendant, deprived the defendant of his right to present a defense, due process of law and effective assistance of counsel.

ALL OR NOTHING APPROACH

U.S. Ex Rel. Barnard v. Lane, 819 F.2d 798 (7th Cir. 1987)
> Trial counsel's action that all or nothing approached by withholding manslaughter and justification jury instruction, in light of the fact the jury was hesitant about returning a guilty verdict, constituted ineffective assistance of counsel.

FAILED TO FILE NOTICE OF APPEAL, BUT FILED AN UNTIMELY AMENDED MOTION TO VACATE

Clay v. Director Juvenile Div., Dept. of Corr., 749 F.2d 427 (7th Cir. 1984)
> Counsel's failure to file notice of appeal in a timely manner, but instead filed an amended motion to vacate, which was subsequently denied as untimely on grounds of res judicata, amounted to ineffective assistance of counsel.

COURT-APPOINTED COUNSEL ACCEPTED MONEY FROM DEFENDANT'S FAMILY

Harris v. Housewright, 697 F.2d 202 (8th Cir. 1982)
> Trial counsel accepted money from defendant's family for payment when he was court-appointed attorney, and the failed to properly handle change of venue issue, which amounted to ineffective assistance of counsel.

OTHER CLAIMS

U.S. v. Myers, 892 F.2d 642 (7th Cir. 1990)
> Trial counsel's failure to cooperate or provide replacement counsel with pertinent information, may constitute ineffectiveness.

Hardin v. Davis, 878 F.2d 1341 (11th Cir. 1989)
> Defendant's refusal to cooperate with court-appointed counsel did not amount to waiver of counsel.

Jemison v. Foltz, 672 F.Supp. 1002 (E.D. Mich. 1987)
> Trial counsel waived a jury trial and allowed defendant to be tried before a judge that was fully aware of defendant's long criminal history, along with numerous other errors, constituted ineffective assistance of counsel.

DENIAL OF COUNSEL

Williams v. Taylor, 529 U.S. 362, 375, 20, S.Ct. 1495, 146 L.Ed.2d 389 (2000)
The deprivation of the right to effective assistance of counsel is a structural error, which harmless error review does not apply.

Geders v. United States, 425 U.S. 80, 47 L.Ed.2d 592, 96 S.Ct. 1330 (1976)
The Supreme Court held that "a trial court's order directing a defendant not to consult his attorney during an overnight recess, called while the defendant was on the witness stand, violated his Sixth Amendment right to counsel."

Perry v. Leeke, 488 U.S. 272, 102 L.Ed.2d 624, 109 S.Ct. 594 (1989)
The Supreme Court held that: (1) a trial court's order directing an accused not to consult his attorney during a brief recess, called while the accused is on the witness stand, does not violate the accused's Sixth Amendment right to counsel; and (2) a showing of prejudice is not an essential component of a violation of the **_Geders_** rule.

Penson v. Ohio, 488 U.S. 75, 102 L.Ed.2d 300, 109 S.Ct. 346 (1988)
The Supreme Court found that the lower court of appeals erred allowing counsel to withdraw as appellate counsel after it determined that there were several arguable claims of error and, that such a complete denial of counsel on appeal can never be harmless error and prejudice is automatically presumed.

Robinson v. Ignacio, 360 F.3d 1044, 1059-61 (9th Cir. 2004)
Trial court's denial of Robinson's timely request for appointment of counsel at sentencing on the notion that Robinson had waived his right to counsel violated his Sixth Amendment right to counsel.

Mitchell v. Mason, 325 F.3d 732, 741-744 (6th Cir. 2003)
Counsel who spent approximately six minutes spanning over three separate meetings with petitioner prior to trial and was suspended from practice a month before trial resulted in a complete denial of counsel. The state court's application of **_Strickland_** standard was an unreasonable application of clearly established Supreme Court law in **_Cronic_**.

Hunter v. Moore, 304 F.3d 1066, 1069-1072 (11th Cir. 2002)
Defendant was deprived of his right to effective assistance of counsel; the trial court issued its verdict in a bench trial without affording defense counsel an opportunity to present closing arguments, constituting a denial of counsel at a critical stage of the proceeding. Thus, reversal was warranted without a showing of prejudice under **_Cronic_**.

Mitchell v. Mason, 257 F.3d 554, 566-74 (6th Cir. 2001)
Defense counsel's failure to consult, or visit with Mitchell, prior to trial and spent approximately six minutes with Mitchell prior to jury selection, spanning over three separate meetings in court bullpen, counsel was suspended from practice for one month immediately prior to trial and Mitchell sought new counsel for six months, amounted to a complete denial of counsel.

Probation Revocation Proceedings
Ineffective Assistance Of Counsel

Childress v. Johnson, 103 F.3d 1221 (5th Cir. 1997)
> Appointment of counsel in an earlier state court proceeding to stand with the defendant in Court, execute a jury waiver and plea was not counsel at all, as required by the Sixth Amendment. The earlier conviction could not be used to enhance defendant's sentence in a subsequent proceeding.

Tucker v. Day, 969 F.2d 155 (5th Cir. 1992)
> Counsel's failure to provide the defendant with any assistance at the resentencing hearing amounted to a constructive denial of the right to counsel which warranted relief.

U.S. v. Mateo, 950 F.2d 44 (1st Cir. 1991)
> Defendant was entitled to resentencing where counsel sought to withdraw as counsel and failed to act as an advocate for defendant at sentencing.

U.S. Ex. Rel. Gibson v. McGinnis, 773 F.Supp. 126 (C.D. Ill. 1991)
> Gibson's Sixth Amendment right to counsel was violated when a jailhouse informant was placed in his cell and said claim required an evidentiary hearing to determine whether the error was harmless.

Lofton v. Whitley, 905 F.2d 885 (5th Cir. 1990)
> When a defendant is constructively denied his right to counsel on appeal by counsel's actions, then prejudice is presumed. See also *Lombard v. Lynaugh, 868 F.2d 1475 (5th Cir. 1989).*

U.S. v. Allen, 895 F.2d 1577 (10th Cir. 1990)
> The trial court's failure to conduct an inquiry as to defendant's waiver of his right to counsel, rendered defendant's purported waiver was invalid and the harmless error analysis did not apply.

Fuller v. Diesslin, 868 F.2d 604 (3rd Cir. 1989)
> The Court held that: "(1) State trial court's wooden approach and its failure to make record-supported findings balancing right to counsel with demands of administration of justice resulted in arbitrary denial of defendant's motion for counsel pro hac vice, and such arbitrary denial constituted per se constitutional error justifying issuance of writ."

U.S. v. Golden, 854 F.2d 31 (3rd Cir. 1988)
> Trial counsel's failure to file a motion for reduction of sentence within time limits, after denial of certiorari, at the defendant's request constituted a denial of counsel and deprived defendant of opportunity to have sentencing judge to exercise discretion over the reduction of sentence.

Green v. Arn, 809 F.2d 1257 (6th Cir. 1987)
> Trial counsel absent from trial during taking of evidence constituted a denial of counsel and is prejudicial per se justifying granting of the writ. Under these circumstances, the harmless error inquiry cannot be applied.

U.S. v. Diozzi, 807 F.2d 10 (1st Cir. 1986)
> Government's motion to disqualification of defendant's attorney violated the defendant's Sixth Amendment right to effective assistance of counsel.

Siverson v. O'Leary, 764 F.2d 1208 (7th Cir. 1985)

Counsel's absence from courtroom amounts to a denial of the right to counsel and is per se prejudicial.

Martin v. Rose, 744 F.2d 1245 (6th Cir. 1984)

Trial counsel's actions in his refusal to participate in the trial because he erroneously believed that participation would either waive pretrial motions or render their denial harmless error, constitutes ineffective assistance of counsel.

U.S. v. Geittmann, 733 F.2d 1419 (10th Cir. 1984)

Geittmann had been arrested, indicted and released on bond for a marijuana conspiracy charge. A co-defendant, Patrick Callihan, agreed to cooperate with the government. Callihan made tape-recorded conversations between himself and Geittmann. The Court found that Geittmann's statement during post-indictment period to Callihan violated Geittmann's Sixth Amendment right to counsel and suppressed the tape conversations.

U.S. Ex. Rel. Potts v. Chrans, 700 F.Supp. 1505 (N.D. Ill. 1988)

Trial counsel's failure, in murder prosecution during bench trial, to offer evidence, to make closing arguments on defendant's behalf, which amounted to failure to hold government to burden of proof, and deprived defendant of the right to effective assistance of counsel.

PROBATION REVOCATION PROCEEDINGS INEFFECTIVE ASSISTANCE OF COUNSEL

PROBATION REVOCATION PROCEEDINGS

Mempa v. Rhay, 389 U.S. 128. 19 L.Ed.2d 336, 88 S.Ct. 254 (1967)

This case stands for the proposition that the federal constitution requires an indigent defendant to have appointed counsel at every stage of a criminal proceeding including revocation of probation or a deferred sentencing.

U.S. v. Dodson, 25 F.3d 385 (6th Cir. 1994)

Defendant was entitled to counsel at revocation of probation hearing where case was complex and counsel was needed to ensure procedural due process safeguards to call witnesses and present case in mitigation.

U.S. v. Yanzey, 827 F.2d 83 (7th Cir. 1987)

Yanzey asserted that his counsel ignored his request to call witnesses. Also, Yanzey argued that there is no indication in the record that his attorney interviewed potential witnesses prior to the revocation of probation. The Court concluded that Yanzey established sufficient issue of ineffective assistance of counsel, if he had a right to counsel at a revocation hearing.

EVIDENTIARY HEARING

Federal Habeas Evidentiary Hearing For 28 U.S.C.S. §2254 Petition's under the 1996 AEDPA

Federal habeas petitioner requesting an evidentiary hearing on a §2254 petition must be evaluated under 28 U.S.C. §2254 (e)(2), which provides, in pertinent part :

If the applicant has failed to develop the factual basis of a claim in State court proceedings, the court shall not hold an evidentiary hearing on the claim unless the applicant shows that-
(A)   the claim relies on-
    (i)   a new rule of constitutional law, made retroactive to cases on collateral review by the Supreme Court, that was previously unavailable; or
    (ii)   a factual predicate that could not have been previously discovered through the exercise of due diligence...

See, *McDonald v. Johnson, 139 F.3d 1056 (5th Cir. 1998),* where the Court found "because McDonald does not allege that his ineffective assistance claim relies on a new rule of constitutional law or a hidden factual predicate, he cannot secure an evidentiary hearing if he failed to develop a factual basis for his claim in state court proceedings." Id. The Third and Seventh Circuits' have understood the phrase "failed to develop" in §2254 (e) (2) as requiring some sort of omission by the petitioner; in other words, he cannot be deemed to have failed to develop a factual basis for his claim if the basis was left undeveloped through no fault of his own. See, *Love v. Morton, 112 F.3d 131, 136 (3rd Cir. 1997),* where the court held that the petitioner could not be said to have failed to develop the factual record when the trial judges abrupt declaration of a mistrial prevented him from doing so. The court concluded that "factors other than the defendant's action prevented a factual record from being developed,"; therefore the petitioner was entitled to an evidentiary hearing. Id. In *Burris v. Parke, 116 F.3d 256, 258, 259 (7th Cir.),* cert. denied *522 U.S. 990 118 S.Ct. 462, 139 L.Ed. 2d 395 (1997),* the court explained: "'Failure' implies' omission-a decision not to introduce evidence when there was an opportunity, or a decision not to seek an opportunity." It then concluded that "the word 'fail' cannot bear a strictliability reading under which a federal court would disregard the reason for the shortcoming of the record." Id.

United States Supreme Court

Williams v. Taylor, 529 U.S. 420, 44041, 120 S.Ct. 1479, 1492-93, 146 L.Ed.2d 435 (2000)
Evidentiary hearing required to determine juror bias because of her failure to disclose during voir dire that she had formerly been married to a prosecution witness, and she had been represented in her divorce by one of the prosecutors; and to determine whether the prosecutor committed misconduct by failing to disclose his knowledge of the juror's possible bias.

Michael Williams v. Taylor, 529 U.S. 420, 120 S.Ct. 1479, 146 L.Ed.2d 435 (2000)
The Supreme Court confirmed that *28 U.S.G. §2254(e)(2)* did not bar evidentiary hearing when the failure to develop the record did not result from the prisoner's neglect or lack of due diligence.

**Smith v. Phillips**, 455 U.S. 209, 215, 102 S.Ct. 940, 71 L.Ed.2d 78 (1982)
The remedy for allegations of juror partiality is a hearing at which the defendant has the opportunity to prove actual basis.

**Remmer v. United States**, 347 U.S. 227, 228, 74 S.Ct. 450, 98 L.Ed.654 (1954)
The Court ordered an evidentiary hearing where an unnamed person had allegedly told juror that the juror could "profit by bringing in a verdict favorable to the petitioner." Without notifying the defense, the state trial court sent in an FBI Agent to investigate the juror during the trial before the verdict. _Remmer_, **347 U.S. at 228, 74 S.Ct. 450.** The petitioner was subsequently convicted. Id. The Supreme Court criticized the trial court's unilateral handling of this issue and ordered an inquiry "with all interested parties permitted to participate. **Id. at 230, 74 S.Ct. 450.**

-----------------------------*---------------------------

DISTRICT OF COLUMBIA

**United States v. Rashad**, 331 F.3d 908, 911-912 (D.C. Cir. 2003)
Counsel advised petitioner to reject the government's favorable plea offer. Counsel assured petitioner that the government's evidence could not support a conviction, and that he only faced 10 to 15 years if convicted at trial. An evidentiary hearing was required to determine whether counsel was ineffective, and if petitioner understood his sentencing exposure before rejecting the plea offer.

**U.S. v. Weaver**, 281 F.3d 228, 234 (D.C. Cir. 2002)
The general practice of the D.C. Circuit is to remand to the district court for an evidentiary hearing when ineffectiveness of counsel claims are first raised on direct appeal, unless it is clear from the record that counsel was or was not ineffective.

**U.S. v. Klat**, 156 F.3d 1258 (D.C. Cir. 1998)
District court's failure to appoint a pro se defendant counsel for a competency hearing when the Court had found "reasonable cause" to believe that defendant was mentally incompetent to stand trial required a remand for an evidentiary hearing to determine whether the competency hearing would have had a different outcome.

**Gills v. U.S.**, 586 A.2d 726 (D.C. App. 1991)
Trial counsel's failure to call security guards as witnesses who would have testified that defendant was in their custody at the time of the shooting, was sufficient allegation to constitute ineffective assistance of counsel claim and required a remand for an evidentiary hearing.

**U.S. v. Kelly**, 790 F.2d 130 (D.C. Cir. 1986)
Kelly contended that his Sixth Amendment rights were violated when Davenport, a government agent, invaded his defense strategy sessions and stole relevant and important documents. District court's failure to develop any evidentiary record or to make any findings constituted abuse of discretion.

**United States v. Barnes**, 662 F.2d 777 (D.C. Cir. 1980)
Trial court violated defendant's Sixth Amendment right to counsel where it conducted an evidentiary hearing on defendant's petition to vacate sentence in absence of defendant's chosen counsel.

United States v. DeCoster, 487 F.2d 1197 (D.C. Cir. 1973)
   Trial counsel's lack of pretrial preparations and failure to conduct investigation required a remand for a supplemental hearing on ineffective assistance of counsel claims.

FIRST CIRCUIT

United States v. Segarra-Rivera, 473 F.3d 381, 383 (1st Cir. 2007)
   Evidentiary hearing warranted to determine whether counsel was burdened with a conflict of interest because the defendant accused counsel of failing to file his requested motion to withdraw guilty plea based on counsel concealing exculpatory evidence, manipulated defendant into signing plea agreement to avoid trial for which counsel failed to prepare, used improper means to obtain defendant's signature on plea.

Gonzalez-Soberal v. United States, 244 F.3d 273, 279 (1st Cir. 2001)
   Counsel's failure to impeach Negron with his letter, which suggested he had not been completely truthful during his cooperation, and Maya with a psycho diagnostic report, which would have undermined Maya's testimony and identification of Gonzalez, and required an evidentiary hearing to determine whether Gonzalez was prejudiced by counsel's errors.

U.S. v. De Alba Pagan, 33 F.3d 125 (1st Cir. 1994)
   Counsel's failure to advise defendant that the court could use relevant conduct to determine sentence may constitute ineffective assistance of counsel and require a remand for an evidentiary hearing.

Hernandez-Hernandez v. U.S., 904 F.2d 758 (1st Cir. 1990)
   Counsel informed petitioner that he would receive a ten-year sentence if he pleaded guilty in front of five (5) witnesses who submitted affidavits stating that they heard the attorney say that he had spoken with the government's attorney and that petitioner would receive a ten (10) year sentence if he pleaded guilty. The petitioner pleaded guilty and received a 99-year sentence based on counsel's erroneous advice. The Court was to conduct an evidentiary hearing to resolve this claim.

Porcaro v. United States, 784 F.2d 38 (1st Cir. 1986)
   Trial counsel's failure to call witness to show that defendant was not a high-pressure salesman and made cash refunds when required in mail fraud sales case, may constitute ineffective assistance and required an evidentiary hearing to resolve ineffectiveness of counsel claim. See also *U.S. v. Giardino, 797 F.2d 30 (1st Cir. 1986).*

SECOND CIRCUIT

Armienti v. United States, 234 F.3d 820, 824-25 (2nd Cir. 2000)
   Counsel who was being criminally investigated by the same U.S. Attorney's Office that was prosecuting petitioner created a possible conflict of interest. Adverse performance was shown through counsel's failure to conduct a pretrial investigation and vigorously cross-examination government witnesses, and required an evidentiary hearing to resolve the claim.

Ellerby v. U.S., 187 F.3d 257 (2nd Cir. 1999)
> The Court of Appeals remanded the district court's denial of **Ellerby's** §2255 motion to afford **Ellerby** an opportunity to amend his ineffective assistance of counsel claims with instructions to hold an evidentiary hearing on counsel's failure to subpoena alibi witness.

Sparman v. Edwards, 154 F.3d 51, 52 (2nd Cir. 1998)
> Defense counsel charged with an ineffectiveness of counsel claim should be afforded an opportunity to be heard and present evidence either by live testimony or in the form of affidavit.

CIAK v. U.S., 59 F.3d 296 (2nd Cir. 1995)
> Trial counsel had previously represented an important government witness and counsel presented a theory to impeach the governments witness with statements that the government's witness made to counsel while being represented by him. Counsel's actions amounted to counsel being an unsworn witness in the proceedings. The defendant asserted that a conflict of interest existed and that counsel abandoned plausible defense because that specific approach would have been inherently in conflict with the position counsel had taken representing the potential witness. The Court of Appeals reversed and remanded for an evidentiary hearing.

U.S. v. Tarricone, 996 F.2d 1414 (2d Cir. 1993)
> Trial counsel's failure to consult with handwriting expert may constitute ineffective assistance of counsel and required evidentiary hearing.

Holmes v. Bartlett, 810 F.Supp. 550 (S.D. N.Y. 1993)
> The court found that Mr. Holmes was entitled to review on merits of his claim that trial court improperly restricted his counsel's ability to cross-examine detective.

Tate v. Wood, 963 F.2d 20 (2d Cir. 1992)
> Tate was entitled to evidentiary hearing on **Brady** claim concerning failure to disclose evidence that victim was initial aggressor. The test of materiality in the context of a guilty plea is whether there is a reasonable probability that, but for the failure to produce such information, the defendant would not have entered the plea but instead would have insisted on going to trial. The inquiry is an objective one that is resolved largely on the basis of the persuasiveness of the withheld evidence. *See, **Miller v. Angliker**, 848 F.2d 1312, 1322 (2nd Cir.), cert. denied, 488 U.S. 890, 109 S.Ct. 224, 102 L.Ed.2d 214 (1988).*

U.S. v. Matos, 905 F.2d 30 (2nd Cir. 1990)
> Trial counsel's failure to file suppression motion and preserve issue for review on appeal may constitute ineffective assistance of counsel and requires a remand. See also **Nell v. James, 811 F.2d 100 (2nd Cir. 1987).**

Maddox v. Lord, 818 F.2d 1058 (2nd Cir. 1987)
> Defense counsel's failure to present affirmative defense of extreme emotional disturbance in state murder case constitutes ineffective assistance of counsel and required an evidentiary hearing.

Allah v. LeFevere, 623 F.Supp. 987 (D.C. N.Y. 1985)

Trial counsel's failure to make motion for suppression of evidence of stolen property required an evidentiary hearing to resolve ineffective assistance of counsel claim, where stolen property constituted the only evidence linking defendant to robbery.

Lace v. United States, 736 F.2d 48 (2nd Cir. 1984)

Petitioner alleged that trial counsel's brother was potential prosecution witness and this allegation stated a sufficient claim of conflict of interest requiring an evidentiary hearing.

THIRD CIRCUIT

U. S v. Baird, 218 F.3d 221, 232 (3rd Cir. 2000)

Defense counsel's failure to challenge the presentence report or sentence under U.S.S.G. §1B1.8 prohibiting the prosecutors assurance that defendant's statements will in no way be used against them warranted an evidentiary hearing to resolve the ineffectiveness of counsel claim.

Government of Virgin Islands v. Weatherwax, 20 F.3d 572 (3rd Cir. 1994)

Trial counsel's failure to seek voir dire of jurors who were exposed to newspaper article, which distorted defendant's trial testimony, constitutes ineffective assistance of counsel and required an evidentiary hearing.

Hull v. Freeman, 932 F.2d 159 (3rd Cir. 1991)

An evidentiary hearing was required to determine whether defendant was prejudiced because of counsel's failure to contest defendant's competence.

U.S. v. Gray, 878 F.2d 702 (3rd Cir. 1989)

Trial counsel's failure to conduct pretrial investigation by failing to go to the scene of the crime and locate potential witnesses amounted to ineffective assistance of counsel and required a evidentiary hearing.

Government of Virgin Islands v. Forte, 865 F.2d 59 (3rd Cir. 1989)

Trial counsel's failure to object to prosecutor's peremptory challenges to excuse white prospective jurors in prosecution of white man for rape of black female constituted ineffective assistance of counsel and required an evidentiary hearing.

U.S. v. Dawson, 857 F.2d 923 (3rd Cir. 1988)

Defendant was entitled to evidentiary hearing to resolve ineffective assistance of counsel claim. Trial counsel's failure to call or interview witnesses whose testimony would have shown that the voice on the taped conversation used as evidence was not the voice of defendant.

Government of Virgin Islands v. Nicholas, 759 F.2d 1073 (3rd Cir. 1985)

Trial counsel's failure to object to testimony concerning incriminating statements, presumably to have been made by defendant in taped conversation with government informant, may constitute ineffective assistance of counsel and required an evidentiary hearing to resolve the claim.

U.S. v. Baynes, 687 F.2d 659 (3rd Cir. 1982)

Trial counsel's alleged strategy decision not to refer to voice exemplar of defendant, which was the sole evidence against defendant, consisting of an electronically intercepted telephone conversation fails, and the Court found counsel ineffective. Trial counsel could have made a strategic decision <u>only</u> after he carefully compared the two recordings and investigated the voice exemplar evidence, which he did not do, an evidentiary hearing was required.

United States ex.rel. Caruso v. Zelinsky, 689 F.2d 435 (3rd Cir. 1982)

Counsel's ineffectiveness in failing to inform defendant of state's plea offer constitutes "cause" for procedural default and requires an evidentiary hearing.

Moore v. United States, 432 F.2d 730 (3rd Cir. 1970)

Trial counsel's failure to properly consult with defendant and prepare for an identification defense constituted ineffective assistance of counsel and required an evidentiary hearing to resolve the claim.

FOURTH CIRCUIT

Fullwood v. Lee, 290 F.3d 665 (4th Cir. 2002)

Allegations that juror was improperly influenced by her husband in voting for death sentence required an evidentiary hearing, where petitioner was entitled to exploration whether the jury considered prejudicial, and outside information that petitioner had previously received death sentence from another jury.

U.S. v. Magini, 973 F.2d 261 (4th Cir. 1992)

Trial counsel who was influenced by private pecuniary concerning and made private agreement with U.S. Attorney to exclude defendant's jewelry from forfeiture proceeding to collect attorney's fee; failed to prepare for trial, and advised defendant to plead guilty constituted a conflict of interest and required an evidentiary hearing.

Noland v. Dixon, 808 F. Supp. 485 (W.D.N.C. 1992)

The Court found that Noland was entitled to an evidentiary hearing to allow expert testimony from Jame Ferguson to testify based on the objective standards of reasonableness under which attorneys trying capital murder cases operated at the time of petitioner's trial.

Washington v. Murray, 952 F.2d 1472 (4th Cir. 1991)

Trial counsel's failure to develop and present to jury the results of exculpatory laboratory tests on semen stains found on blanket recovered from bed where rape occurred, which showed that the bodily fluids did not come from defendant, entitled defendant to evidentiary hearing to resolve ineffective assistance of counsel claim.

Becton v. Barnett, 920 F.2d 1190 (4th Cir. 1990)

Counsel's failure to investigate defendant's competence and failure to appeal, stated a 'colorable' claim of ineffective assistance of counsel and required evidentiary hearing to resolve the ineffective assistance claims.

FIFTH CIRCUIT

United States v. Herrera, 412 F.3d 577, 581-82 (5th Cir. 2005)
Evidentiary hearing required to determine whether counsel misadvised Herrera about sentencing exposure because the attorney misunderstood the actual sentencing exposure under the Guidelines which caused Herrera to reject a 48 month plea offer and ended up with a 78 month sentence.

U.S. v. Santiago, 993 F.2d 504, 507 (5th Cir. 1993)
The Court held that (4) Defendant was entitled to evidentiary hearing on claim that trial counsel had conflict of interest. Santiago argued that his trial counsel, without his knowledge, also represented the Albrechts at all relevant times. Santiago stated that he learned of the conflict for the first time in June 1992, which was after the district court had dismissed his §2255 motion. This allegation raised serious concerns given the apparent plethora of evidence connecting the Albrechts with the drugs and the fact that they were never prosecuted for this offense. The Fifth Circuit found that this claim of conflict of interest could be raised on appeal for the first time, because the failure to consider it would result in a manifest injustice. This case was remanded for an evidentiary hearing to resolve the conflict of interest.

U.S. v. Borders, 992 F.2d 563 (5th Cir. 1993)
Trial counsel who induced defendant to plead guilty to a plea agreement, which was ambiguous, amounted to ineffective assistance of counsel and required an evidentiary hearing.

Nelson v. Hargett, 989 F.2d 847 (5th Cir. 1993)
Trial counsel's failure to pursue defendant's request for speedy trial may constitute ineffective assistance and requires an evidentiary hearing to determine whether defendant was prejudiced by counsel's unprofessional errors and omissions.

Loyd v. Smith, 899 F.2d 1416 (5th Cir. 1990)
Trial counsel's failure to present mitigating evidence of defendant's mental disease or defects constituted ineffective assistance of counsel and required evidentiary hearing.

Wilson v. Butler, 813 F.2d 664 (5th Cir. 1987)
Trial counsel's failure to pursue mental impairment as a mitigating factor at sentencing may constitute ineffective assistance of counsel; thus, an evidentiary hearing was warranted to determine whether counsel's action was a strategic decision.

Kirkpatrick v. Blackburn, 777 F.2d 272 (5th Cir. 1985)
Trial counsel's failure to move to suppress evidence obtained during illegal search of petitioner's residence may constitute ineffective assistance and requires an evidentiary hearing to develop the record on claim.

Mack v. Smith, 659 F.2d 23 (5th Cir. 1981)
Appellate counsel hiding the fact that defendant's appeal had been dismissed for more than a year and assuring defendant that counsel was still waiting for a copy of the trial transcripts, was sufficient allegation for an evidentiary hearing.

Clark v. Blackburn, 619 F.2d 431 (5th Cir. 1980)

Trial counsel's failure to file any pre-trial motions on defensive issues, failed to seek pre-trial discovery, failed to obtain a transcript of testimony before the grand jury, warranted an evidentiary hearing to resolve the ineffectiveness of counsel claim.

Friedman v. United States, 588 F.2d 1010 (5th Cir. 1979)

Trial counsel's failure to subpoena certain witnesses at government's expense on behalf of his indigent client, required an evidentiary hearing to resolve the ineffectiveness of counsel claim.

United States v. Sanderson, 595 F.2d 1021 (5th Cir. 1979)

Trial counsel's misrepresented material facts, withhheld information, and exerted pressure on defendant to induce a guilty plea, which constitutes ineffective assistance and requires an evidentiary hearing to resolve claim.

Greer v. Beto, 379 F.2d 923 (5th Cir. 1967)

Defense counsel's failure to present testimony on sanity issue at trial after defendant had been found sane, compounded with the introduction of a jury verdict in the sanity trial, defendant stated a valid claim of ineffectiveness of counsel and warranted an evidentiary hearing.

SIXTH CIRCUIT

Griffin v. United States, 330 F.3d 733, 739 (6th Cir. 2003)

Counsel's failure to communicate government's five (5) year plea offer, and to advise petitioner that his codefendant's were planning on testifying against him required an evidentiary hearing to determine whether petitioner was prejudiced by counsel's omissions.

Greer v. Mitchell, 264 F.3d 663 (6th Cir. 2001)

Appellate counsel's failure to raise trial counsel's ineffectiveness on direct appeal for failure to investigate and present mitigating evidence during penalty phase required an evidentiary hearing.

Barnes v. Elo, 231 F.3d 1025, 1029 (6th Cir. 2000)

Counsel's failure to investigate or call medical witnesses to establish the fact that petitioner could not run in the manner that the sexual complainant stated that her assailant ran. Therefore, a remand for an evidentiary hearing was required to resolve ineffectiveness of counsel claim.

Arredondo v. U.S., 178 F.3d 778 (6th Cir. 1999)

Defense counsel's failure to object to drug quantity through relevant conduct of other codefendant's involved in the conspiracy required an evidentiary hearing to resolve ineffective assistance of counsel claim where defendant could have received eight-year difference in sentence.

Arredondo v. U.S., 178 F.3d 778 (6th Cir. 1999)

Defense counsel's failure to communicate to petitioner a plea agreement offer made by the government required an evidentiary hearing to resolve claim of ineffective assistance of counsel.

Mapes v. Coyle, 171 F.3d 408 (6th Cir. 1999)
Evidentiary hearing required to determine whether appellate counsel's failure to raise on direct appeal trial counsel's failure to investigate mitigating evidence in reference to a prior murder conviction supporting petitioner's death specification. Also, the trial court's errors in precluding jury from considering mitigating evidence during penalty phase constitutes ineffective assistance of counsel.

Sparks v. Sowders, 852 F.2d 882 (6th Cir. 1988)
Defendant's allegation that counsel misadvised him that if he did not plead guilty that he could get life without parole, would not have pleaded guilty without such incorrect advice, so, an evidentiary hearing is warranted.

Blackburn v. Foltz, 828 F.2d 1177 (6th Cir. 1987)
Counsel's erroneous legal advice concerning possible use of prior convictions if defendant testified, failure to obtain transcripts of earlier trial to impeach key eyewitness, and failure to investigate potential alibi defense constituted ineffective assistance of counsel.

Pitts v. United States, 763 F.2d 197 (6th Cir. 1985)
Trial counsel's misrepresentation of the maximum penalty on counts of indictment, which defendant pled guilty constituted ineffective assistance of counsel and warranted an evidentiary hearing.

SEVENTH CIRCUIT

Davis v. Lambert, 388 F.3d 1052, 1062 (7th Cir. 2004)
Trial counsel's failure to investigate or interview potential eye-witnesses and impeachment witnesses that Davis wanted to call as witnesses to bolster his self - defense claim required a federal evidentiary hearing to resolve the ineffectiveness of counsel claim.

Bruce v. U.S., 256 F.3d 592, 599 (7th Cir. 2001)
Defense counsel's failure to investigate and call two alibi witnesses, Thompson and Barton, where their testimony would have proved that **Bruce** was with them in Michigan during the time the armed bank robberies took place in Indiana, warranted an evidentiary hearing to resolve the ineffectiveness of counsel claim.

Paters v. U.S., 159 F.3d 1043 (7th Cir. 1998)
Counsel was ineffective in plea negotiation process and warranted an evidentiary hearing to determine whether petitioner would have accepted the Government's plea offer, which would have resulted in petitioner receiving a less harsh sentence.

Dumer v. Berge, 975 F. Supp. 1165 (E.D. Wis. 1997)
The court held in pertinent part that : "Trial Court violated federal law, as established by United States Supreme Court, by not holding evidentiary hearing on defendant's claim that refusal of his appellate counsel to take appeal was ineffective assistance." Conditional writ granted.

Hogan v. McBride, 79 F.3d 578 (7th Cir. 1996)
Defendant was entitled to evidentiary hearing on ineffective assistance of counsel claim based on counsel's handling of a confrontation issue during trial.

Daniels v. U.S., _54 F.3d 290 (7th Cir. 1995)_

Defense counsel induced guilty plea based on defendant's inability to pay counsel's fee, which created a conflict of interest, and required an evidentiary hearing to resolve the issue of ineffective assistance of counsel.

Nichols v. U.S., _75 F.3d 1137 (7th Cir. 1996)_

An evidentiary hearing was required to resolve ineffective assistance of counsel claim based on failure to object to drug quantity under the Sentencing Guidelines.

Stoia v. U.S., _22 F.3d 766 (7th Cir. 1994)_

Defense counsel. who had signed a consent degree with the government wherein counsel agreed to work with the government undercover to uncover drug crimes, was burdened with a conflict of interest where he was retained by Stoia to help prepare and participate in Stoia defense. Stoia had two other defense counsel's who handled the trial, but they were instructed by counsel who was burdened with conflict of interest. The Seventh Circuit remanded for an evidentiary hearing.

Soto v. U.S., _37 F.3d 252, 254-56 (7th Cir. 1994) (per curiam)_

Trial counsel's failure to discourage Soto from pleading guilty due to counsel's failure to perceive that the government's theory that Soto engaged in a single long-term conspiracy was a mistake, which exposed Soto to the application of the Guidelines and a mandatory minimum sentence, required an evidentiary hearing to determine the dates of the actual conspiracy that Soto was involved and resolve ineffective assistance of counsel claim.

Lee v. U.S., _939 F.2d 503 (7th Cir. 1991)_

The Court held that: "Defendant was prejudiced by trial counsel's failure at sentencing hearing to present evidence regarding defendant's legitimate income during period of his criminal activity and remand was warranted for determination of whether default brought counsel beneath constitution minimum for effective representation". _Id._

U.S. Ex. Rel. Gibson v. McGinnis, _773 F.Supp. 126 (D.C. Ill. 1991)_

Gibson's Sixth Amendment right to counsel was violated when a jailhouse informant was placed in his cell; said claim required an evidentiary hearing to determine whether the error was harmless.

Rosenwald v. U.S., _898 F.2d 585 (7th Cir. 1990)_

An evidentiary hearing is required to resolve claim that attorney represented conflicting interests, where same attorney represented government's key witness in an unrelated civil matter.

U.S. v. Ziegenhagen, _890 F.2d 937 (7th Cir. 1989)_

An evidentiary hearing is required to resolve conflict of interest issue when the conflict is called to the court's attention.

U.S. v. Myers, _892 F.2d 642 (7th Cir. 1990)_

Trial counsel's failure to submit a limiting jury instruction and read and review documents released by government during discovery required an evidentiary hearing.

Nevarez-Diaz v. U.S., *870 F.2d 417 (7th Cir. 1989)*
> Trial counsel's ineffectiveness constituted "cause" and the Court's failure, along with the prosecutor's failure to adequately inform defendant that mere presence at time crimes were committed did not constitute the elements of the offense amounted to a fundamental miscarriage of justice and required evidentiary hearing.

U.S. Ex Rel Duncan v. O'Leary, *806 F.2d 1307 (7th Cir. 1986)*
> Defense counsel was the prosecutor's campaign manager and, at an evidentiary hearing, the court found that there was collusion between the prosecutor and defense counsel, which created a conflict of interest that adversely affected counsel's performance.

U.S. Ex. Rel. Patterson v. Neal, *678 F.Supp. 749 (N.D. Ill. 1988)*
> Trial counsel's failure to call alibi witness and present an alibi defense. Defendant stated a sufficient claim of ineffective assistance of counsel and required an evidentiary hearing to resolve the claim.

Dently v. Lane, *695 F.2d 113 (7th Cir. 1981)*
> Dently claimed he was denied effective assistance of counsel because of a conflict of interest where he "fired" his public defender, and the court reappointed another public defender. The case was vacated and remanded for an evidentiary hearing.

EIGHTH CIRCUIT

Koskela v. United States, *235 F.3d 1148, 1150 (8th Cir. 2001)*
> Counsel's failure to present alibi defense or call alibi witnesses required an evidentiary hearing to resolve claim of ineffectiveness of counsel.

Kingsberry v. United States, *202 F.3d 1030, 1032 (8th Cir.), cert. denied, 531 U.S. 829, 121 S.Ct. 81, 148 L.Ed.2d 43 (2000)*
> An evidentiary hearing on a **28 U.S.C. §2255** motion must be granted unless the motion, files, and records of the case, establish conclusively that the petitioner is not entitled to relief.

Wanatee v. Auly , *39 F.Supp. 2d 1164 (N.D. Iowa 1999)*
> Defense counsel's failure to advise petitioner of applicable law on the aiding and abetting liability, or joint conduct liability during plea negotiations for second degree murder warranted an evidentiary hearing to resolve claim of ineffectiveness of counsel.

Toney v. Gammon, *79 F.3d 693 (8th Cir. 1996)*
> Trial counsel's failed to obtain defendant's requested blood test in order to exonerate himself from the semen of the assailant blood-type could constitute ineffective assistance and required an evidentiary hearing to resolve the ineffectiveness claim.

Nearly v. U.S., *998 F.2d 563 (8th Cir. 1993)*
> Trial counsel objected to enhancement of defendant's sentence for "obstruction of justice" under the Guidelines but failed to raise the issue on appeal which constituted performance below an objective standard of reasonableness and required an evidentiary hearing to resolve ineffective assistance of counsel claim.

Rogers v. U.S., 990 F.2d 1008 (8th Cir. 1993)
> Appellate counsel's failure to raise, on direct appeal, district court's failure to advise defendant that, if the district court refused to accept prosecutor's sentence recommendation, defendant had no right to withdraw guilty plea, stated a sufficient claim of ineffective assistance of counsel and warranted an evidentiary hearing.

Houston v. Lockhart, 982 F.2d 1246 (8th Cir. 1993)
> Trial counsel's failure to have the parties' stipulation that polygraph evidence could be admitted into evidence constitutes ineffective assistance of counsel. This claim required an evidentiary hearing.

Weekley v. Jones, 927 F.2d 382 (8th Cir. 1991)
> Defense counsel's failure to raise jury issue that violated fair cross-section requirement and recommending change of plea of 'not guilty' to plea of not guilty by insanity, required additional facts and conclusion of law, which required an evidentiary hearing to resolve the ineffective assistance of counsel claim.

Lahay v. Armontrout, 923 F.2d 578 (8th Cir. 1991)
> The Eighth Circuit remanded this case for an evidentiary hearing to determine whether trial counsel perjured himself in the original evidentiary hearing on an ineffective assistance of counsel claim filed against counsel.

Blalock v. Lockhart, 898 F.2d 1367 (8th Cir. 1990)
> Defense counsel's failure to inform defendant of the accomplice corroboration rule, constitutes ineffective assistance, combined with the trial court's failure to properly advise defendant of his rights to confront witnesses, remain silent, and the nature of the charges rendered the guilty plea not knowing or voluntarily entered, which required an evidentiary hearing.

Estes v. U.S., 883 F.2d 645 (8th Cir. 1989)
> Defendant was entitled to evidentiary hearing to determine whether counsel's failure to file appeal at defendant's request was ineffective assistance of counsel.

U.S. v. Long, 857 F.2d 436 (8th Cir. 1988)
> An evidentiary hearing was necessary to resolve ineffective assistance of counsel claim to determine whether counsel had a firm factual belief that defendant would commit perjury if he testified.

Williams v. Lockhart, 849 F.2d 1134 (8th Cir. 1988)
> Counsel's failure to perfect appeal required evidentiary hearing on claim of ineffective assistance of counsel where dispute existed between petitioner and his attorney as to whether petitioner requested counsel to file an appeal.

Wade v. Armontrout, 798 F.2d 304 (8th Cir. 1986)
> Trial counsel's failure to conduct a pretrial investigation and to interview alibi witnesses, warranted an evidentiary hearing to resolve the ineffective assistance of counsel claim.

Edgemon v. Lockhart, 768 F.2d 252 (8th Cir. 1985)
> The Court held that: "(2) Habeas petitioner was entitled to evidentiary hearing on allegation that trial attorney had a conflict of interest, and that trial counsel failed to make juror incompetence challenge before jury was empaneled."

Beavers v. Lockhart, 755 F.2d 657 (8th Cir. 1985)
      Appellate counsel was ineffective and required an evidentiary hearing where counsel failed to raise the issue of the trial court's imposition of consecutive sentence.

United States v. Unger, 665 F.2d 251 (8th Cir. 1981)
      Trial counsel's joint representation of defendant and co-defendant, where there was no valid waiver of conflict of interest, and counsel failed to make efforts to distant defendant from aggravating circumstances failed to exonerate defendant at expense of co-defendant, constitutes a conflict of interest and required an evidentiary hearing.

Cross v. United States, 392 F.2d 360 (8th Cir. 1968)
      Trial counsel failed to subpoena any witnesses, failed to prepare for trial because the defendant did not pay him all his money, and in a motion for mistrial, claimed his own ineffectiveness. The Eighth Circuit reversed and remanded the case for an evidentiary hearing.

NINTH CIRCUIT

Alberni v. McDaniel, 458 F.3d 860, 873 (9th Cir. 2006)
      Evidentiary hearing required to resolve claim that counsel was burdened with a conflict of interest because he failed to impeach his previous client, Mr. Flamm, with his prior conviction, probation status, and cross-examine him on multiple points of his testimony.

Boyde v. Brown, 421 F.3d 1154, 1155 (9th Cir. 2005)
      Counsel's failure to introduce evidence during the penalty phase that Boyde suffered physical abuse as a child and that his sisters were sexual abused required an evidentiary hearing to resolve ineffective assistance of counsel claim.

United States v. Leonti, 326 F.3d 1111, 1121-1122 (9th Cir. 2003)
      Counsel failed to assist defendant cooperating with government in order to obtain a sentencing reduction pursuant to **U.S.S.G. §5K1.1** for substantial assistance to the government and failed to attend debriefing meeting with defendant, required an evidentiary hearing to resolve claim of ineffectiveness of counsel.

Fields v. Woodford, 281 F.3d 963, 974 (9th Cir. 2002)
      Juror in rape, murder and robbery trial, concealed material facts and gave misleading answer relating to kidnap, robbery, and rape of his wife and the fact that the jurors wife had discussions with juror during the trial concerning facts of the case, and wife suspected that her accoster may have been the defendant required an evidentiary hearing to determine jury bias.

Turner v. Calderon, 281 F.3d 851, 891-95 (9th Cir. 2002)
      Failure to investigate and present mitigating evidence during penalty phase of capital murder and robbery trial, where mitigating evidence such as, petitioner's drug use, beatings by his mother and father using switches, extension cords, telephone wires, petitioner's mental impairment and being a slow learner constitutes ineffective assistance of counsel and required an evidentiary hearing.

Beaty v. Stewart, 303 F.3d 975, 993-994 (9th Cir. 2002)

Petitioner was entitled to an evidentiary hearing to determine whether his alleged confession to killing a thirteen year old girl was voluntary; when he signed a confidentiality agreement with jail psychiatrist before he confessed to the killing.

Fields v. Woodford, 309 F.3d 1095, 1105-1106 (9th Cir. 2002)

Evidentiary hearing was required to determine whether juror intentionally concealed fact that his wife had been raped during robbery-rape trial, which hid juror's bias against the defendant.

Summerlin v. Stewart, 267 F.3d 926, 948-53 (9th Cir. 2001)

Summerlin was entitled to evidentiary hearing on claim that trial judge's alleged use of and addiction to marijuana, deprived petitioner of due process in death penalty case.

Phillips v. Woodford, 267 F.3d 966, 978-81 (9th Cir. 2001)

Trial counsel's failure to investigate "shoot out" defense, in lieu of alibi defense where counsel had information in his possession at the time of trial, which a "shoot-out" defense to first degree murder could have been fashioned amounted to ineffective assistance of counsel. The shoot-out defense might have led the jury to find that defendant did not form intent to rob until after killing, and therefore that special circumstance for imposition of death penalty that murder was "committed during the commission of robbery," did not apply, and warranted an evidentiary hearing.

Schell v. Witek, 181 F.3d 1094 (9th Cir. 1999)

Counsel's failure to consult fingerprint expert warranted an evidentiary hearing to resolve ineffective assistance of counsel claim.

Caro v. Calderon, 165 F.3d 1223 (9th Cir. 1999)

Defense counsel's failure to investigate defendant's organic brain damage or other mental impairments and to seek expert opinion on defendant's extraordinary exposure to neurotoxicants, neurological impairments and personal background required an evidentiary hearing to resolve claim of ineffectiveness of counsel.

Turner v. Duncan, 158 F.3d 449 (9th Cir. 1998)

Trial counsel's failure to investigate and to adequately conduct a pretrial preparation was not a strategic decision and required a remand for an evidentiary hearing to determine whether a pretrial investigation would have produced a conviction of a lesser degree of homicide.

Correll v. Stewart, 137 F.3d 1404 (9th Cir. 1998)

Trial counsel's failure to present any evidence of petitioner's mental illness which may have constitute mitigating circumstances required an evidentiary hearing to resolve ineffectiveness of counsel claim.

Williams v. Calderon, 48 F.Supp. 2d 979 (C.D. Cal. 1998)

Evidentiary hearing was warranted where an issue of fact existed whether the defendant was competent to stand trial and whether counsel was ineffective in failing to present mitigating evidence.

Evidentiary Hearing

U.S. v. Gonzalez, 113 F.3d 1026 (9th Cir. 1997)

Gonzalez plead guilty. Prior to sentencing he filed a motion for appointment of new counsel claiming that he was coerced and physically intimidated by his attorney to plead guilty. Gonzalez claimed that he originally refused to plead guilty and his attorney became very agitated and threatened to "smack [Gonzalez] between the eyes" and told Gonzalez to "take the plea." The Court at sentencing asked counsel if the coercion was true, and counsel denied it. Gonzalez claimed the coercion occurred in front of the probation officer. The district court created a conflict by inviting counsel to contradict his client and to undermine his veracity, which left Gonzalez without counsel. The Court abused its discretion in failing to conduct an evidentiary hearing.

U.S. v. Duarte-Higareda, 68 F.3d 369 (9th Cir. 1995)

An indigent petitioner is entitled to appointment of counsel for an evidentiary hearing and is mandatory pursuant to *Rule 8(c), 28 U.S.C. § 2255.*

U.S. v. Blaylock, 20 F.3d 1458 (9th Cir. 1994)

Trial counsel's failure to inform defendant of government's plea offer constitutes ineffective assistance of counsel and requires an evidentiary hearing.

Frazer v. U.S., 18 F.3d 778 (9th Cir. 1994)

Trial counsel who verbally assaulted defendant, used racial comments toward defendant and threatened to compromise defendant's rights constitutes ineffective assistance and requires an evidentiary hearing.

Siripongs v. Calderon, 35 F.3d 1308 (9th Cir. 1994)

Trial counsel's failure to interview witnesses and follow up leads indicating multiple involvement in the crime stated a valid claim of ineffectiveness of counsel and required an evidentiary hearing.

Risher v. U.S., 992 F.2d 982 (9th Cir. 1993)

The Court held that: (1) Counsel's failure to warn defendant before he entered his guilty plea of risk that he might be sentenced under Sentencing Guidelines fell below level of professional competence required for effective assistance of counsel and (2) Remand was required to determine whether defendant was prejudiced. Reversed and Remanded.

Hendricks v. Vasquez, 974 F.2d 1099 (9th Cir. 1992)

Defense counsel's failure to call witnesses to support defendant's mental impairment defense during penalty phase may constitute ineffective assistance and requires an evidentiary hearing to develop the facts.

U.S. v. Miskinis, 966 F.2d 1263 (9th Cir. 1992)

Defendant has a right to present an "advice of counsel defense." The continued representation of defendant by counsel who gave said advice can constitute ineffective assistance of counsel when defense of "advice of counsel" is not presented and requires an evidentiary hearing to resolve the claim.

U.S. v. Bigman, 906 F.2d 392 (9th Cir. 1990)

Defense counsel's failure to advise defendant of the intent element of second-degree murder charge could not be resolved by attorney's affidavit and change of plea transcripts, which lead to only a certain conclusion of what might have occurred. This claim required an evidentiary hearing.

U.S. v. Burrows, 872 F.2d 915 (9th Cir. 1989)
Trial counsel's failure to investigate defendant's mental state and present evidence, at trial based on defendant's mental state constituted a significant claim of ineffective assistance of counsel and required the district court to conduct an evidentiary hearing.

U.S. v. Espinoza, 841 F.2d 326 (9th Cir. 1988)
A defendant who alleged that his guilty plea was induced by trial counsel's promise of a specific sentence was entitled to evidentiary hearing.

Iaea v. Sunn, 800 F.2d 861 (9th Cir. 1986)
Trial counsel threatened to withdraw and petitioner's brother threatened to withdraw bail if petitioner did not plead guilty. Therefore, the plea was rendered involuntary and required an evidentiary hearing to resolve the ineffective assistance of counsel claim.

Marrow v. U.S., 772 F.2d 525 (9th Cir. 1985)
Defendant's allegation that he informed trial counsel that the FBI had threatened to arrest defendant's female companion if defendant did not confess to crime, and that counsel told defendant to plead guilty and tell the judge that plea was voluntary stated a claim of ineffective assistance of counsel.

Baumann v. United States, 692 F.2d 565 (9th Cir. 1982)
Trial counsel failed to interview prosecution witnesses and prevented the defendant from doing so. He also failed to effectively cross-examine two witnesses that provided the evidence of defendant's involvement in the crime. Defendant was entitled to an evidentiary hearing to resolve his ineffective assistance of counsel claim.

TENTH CIRCUIT

United States v. Holder, 410 F.3d 651, 655-56 (10th Cir. 2005)
Trial counsel's failure to call the second of the only two witnesses, to the shooting required an evidentiary hearing to determine whether counsel's actions were strategy or ineffective.

United States v. Garrett, 402 F.3d 1262, 1267 (10th Cir. 2005)
Claim of ineffective assistance of counsel for failing to file defendant's requested notice of appeal required an evidentiary hearing to resolve factual disputes.

Mayes v. Gibson, 210 F.3d 1284 (10th Cir. 2000)
Defense counsel's failure to investigate and present mitigating evidence during penalty phase warranted an evidentiary hearing to resolve claim of ineffective assistance of counsel.

Barnett v. Hargett, 174 F.3d 1128 (10th Cir. 1999)
Petitioner is entitled to a nune pro tunc evidentiary hearing to determine whether he was incompetent at the time of trial in habeas corpus case.

Evidentiary Hearing

U.S. v. Harst, 168 F.3d 398 (10th Cir. 1999)
   Defense counsel's failure to argue that defendant was a minor or minimal participant in drug distribution case required an evidentiary hearing to resolve claim of ineffective assistance of counsel.

Stouffer v. Reynolds, 168 F.3d 1155 (10th Cir. 1999)
   Defense counsel's failed to make opening statements to the jury and failed to properly prepare exhibits for admission. Counsel cross-examination of witnesses, which had effect of reiterating state's evidence, failed to advance key defense evidence during trial and failed to present mitigating evidence during penalty phrase. Taken alone each error might not establish deficient representation, however, the cumulative effect of each error underscores a fundamental lack of formulation and direction to present a coherent defense and required an evidentiary hearing to resolve the ineffective assistance of counsel claims.

Strachan v. Army Clemency and Parole BD., 151 F.3d 1308 (10th Cir. 1998)
   District court's findings that inmate's state court conviction was counseled was clearly erroneous where court relied on petitioner's plea agreement which contained a location for counsel's signature but there was no signature of counsel, and petitioner was entitled to hearing to determine the validity of conviction.

U.S. v. Johnson, 995 F.Supp. 1259 (D. Kan. 1998)
   Trial counsel's refusal to allow defendant to testify, despite defendant's request to testify, required an evidentiary hearing to resolve ineffective assistance claim.

Medina v. Barnes, 71 F.3d 363 (10th Cir. 1995)
   Trial counsel's failure to investigate prosecution's key witness in murder case, where key witness lied about his criminal activity with victim at the time he called police, constituted "cause" for procedural default and required an evidentiary hearing, under the fundamental miscarriage of justice standard, to resolve ineffective assistance of counsel claims.

Moore v. U.S., 950 F.2d 656 (10th Cir. 1991)
   Defendant's allegation that counsel suborned perjury at plea hearing and was paid by another co-conspirator, established a conflict of interest and required an evidentiary hearing.

Church v. Sullivan, 942 F.2d 1501 (10th Cir. 1991)
   Trial counsel was burdened with a conflict of interest where counsel was required to present defense theory which inculpated his former client and was intertwined with petitioner's case. These allegations stated a significant claim warranting an evidentiary hearing.

Robison v. Maynard, 829 F.2d 1501 (10th Cir. 1987)
   Appellant's counsel's failure to raise issue of prosecutorial misconduct in state appeal required an evidentiary hearing where Oklahoma court granted other defendants relief from same kind of conduct by same prosecutor to resolve ineffective assistance of counsel claim.

ELEVENTH CIRCUIT

***Fuller v. Attorney General of State of Alabama*, 36 F. Supp. 2d 1323 (N.D. Ala. 1999)**
Witnesses uncontradicted affidavit-corroborating petitioners testimony could be used in post-evidentiary hearing in deciding petition.

***Jones v. U.S.*, 153 F.3d 1305 (11th Cir. 1998)**
Jones pleads guilty to using and carrying a firearm during and in relation to a drug trafficking offense. Jones filed a ***28 U.S.C. §2255*** motion contending that the evidence does not support the conviction and that his plea was not voluntary after the Supreme Court ruling in ***Bailey*** the district court denied the ***§2255*** motion without conducting an evidentiary hearing. Jones appealed claiming that the Supreme Court's decision in ***Bousley v. United States*, 118 S.Ct. 1604, 140 L.Ed.2d 828 (1998)**, required the case to be remanded for a hearing to determine whether Jones is actually innocent of the ***18 U.S.C. §924 (c) (1)*** charge and therefore can establish cause for procedural bar. The Eleventh Circuit **REMANDED for a hearing.**

***U.S. v. McKinnon*, 995 F. Supp. 1404 (M.D. Fla. 1998)**
Trial counsel instructed defendant not to testify on her own behalf based on inappropriate conflict concerns for the well-being of the co-defendants. These claims, required an evidentiary hearing to resolve ineffective assistance of counsel and conflict of interest claim.

***U.S. v. Chandler*, 950 F.Supp. 1545 (N.D. Ala. 1996)**
Evidentiary hearing warranted on habeas claim for government's failure to disclose results of witness' polygraph test, in violation of ***Brady***.

***Williams v. Turpin*, 87 F.3d 1204 (11th Cir. 1996)**
Counsel's failure to present mitigating evidence that petitioner had been physically and sexually abused as a child during penalty phase could constitute ineffective assistance of counsel and required evidentiary hearing to resolve claim.

***Huynh v. King*, 95 F.3d 1052 (11th Cir. 1996)**
Trial counsel's delay in filing a meritorious suppression motion in order to later obtain a more favorable federal habeas review was objectively unreasonable and required a remand for an evidentiary hearing to determine prejudice under Strickland.

***Upshaw v. Singletary*, 70 F.3d 576 (11th Cir. 1995)**
Defense counsel's failure to investigate and present defenses and mitigating circumstance regarding defendant's mental state at the time of crime constituted ineffective assistance and required evidentiary hearing.

***Glock v. Singletary*, 84 F.3d 385 (11th Cir. 1994)**
Defense counsel's failure to investigate and discovery mitigating evidence for sentencing required an evidentiary hearing to resolve ineffectiveness of counsel claim.

Evidentiary Hearing

Buenoano v. Singletary, 963 F.2d 1433 (11th Cir. 1992)
Trial counsel's failure to investigate, discover, and present mitigating evidence during Judy Buenoano's penalty phase of capital murder trial constituted ineffective assistance of counsel and required an evidentiary hearing.

Tower v. Phillips, 979 F.2d 807 (11th Cir. 1992)
A defendant is entitled to evidentiary hearing where he alleged that his attorney misrepresented the degree of the offenses in the written plea agreement, and that he would not have pled guilty had he understood the charges to which he was pleading.

Tower v. Phillips, 979 F.2d 807 (11th Cir. 1992)
An evidentiary hearing may be required to resolve attorney-client communication when record does not resolve disputed facts supporting ineffective assistance of counsel claim.

Cave v. Singletary, 971 F.2d 1513 (11th Cir. 1992)
Trial counsel's failure to call character witnesses who were prepared to testify at sentencing may constitute ineffective assistance and required an evidentiary hearing to develop the facts.

Smith v. Gearinger, 888 F.2d 1334 (11th Cir. 1989)
Trial counsel's failure to contest two prospective jurors that counsel knew were within the prohibited degree of consanguinity with victim or her mother, constituted ineffective assistance, and required an evidentiary hearing.

Holmes v. U.S., 876 F.2d 1545 (11th Cir. 1989)
Defense counsel misinformed petitioner concerning parole eligibility under plea agreement constitutes ineffective assistance of counsel, where defendant sufficiently alleged that he would not have plead guilty and would have insisted on going to trial, absent counsel's erroneous advice, required an evidentiary hearing where record did not conclusively show that petitioner was not entitled to relief.

Walker v. Davis, 840 F.2d 834 (11th Cir. 1988)
The Court held that: (1) Prosecutor's misconduct in acting as both witness and prosecutor in murder proceeding was so egregious and prejudicial to fair trial as to undermine confidence in its outcome; and (2) evidentiary hearing was required to determine whether habeas corpus petitioner had cause for procedural default in failing to object at trial to district attorney's misconduct in acting as both witness and prosecutor. Remanded.

Agan v. Dugger, 835 F.2d 1337 (11th Cir. 1987)
An evidentiary hearing was required to resolve trial counsel's ineffectiveness where record indicated that counsel neither spent much time on case and failed to request competency hearing despite defendant's conduct and mental record.

Slicker v. Wainwright, 809 F.2d 768 (11th Cir. 1987)
Trial counsel's misrepresentation that he had negotiated plea agreement which provided that defendant would not serve maximum penalty constituted ineffective assistance and required an evidentiary hearing to allow defendant an opportunity to prove he would not have plead guilty, but would have proceeded to trial, absent counsel's misrepresentation of plea.

Harich v. Wainwright, 813 F.2d 1082 (11th Cir. 1987)

Trial counsel's failure to research and understand the law based on Harich's intoxication defense may constitute ineffective assistance and required an evidentiary hearing.

Porter v. Wainwright, 805 F.2d 930 (11th Cir. 1986)

Trial counsel representing the defendant and had previously represented a prosecution's key witness, stated a sufficient claim of conflict of interest and warranted an evidentiary hearing.

McCoy v. Wainwright, 804 F.2d 1196, (11th Cir. 1986)

Failure to investigate possible insanity defense, which caused counsel not to move for a competency hearing, amounted to counsel's failure to advise defendant of affirmative insanity defense, and constitutes ineffective assistance, which requires an evidentiary hearing.

Gaddy v. Linahan, 780 F.2d 935 (11 Cir. 1986)

Failure to explain the elements of the offense of malice murder renders the guilty plea involuntary and requires an evidentiary hearing.

Downs-Morgan v. U.S., 765 F.2d 1534 (11th Cir. 1985)

The Court of Appeals held that: Petitioner was entitled to evidentiary hearing to determine if he was afforded reasonably effective assistance of counsel in deciding to plead guilty in light of petitioner's allegations that counsel advised him that guilty plea would not result in his deportation. Reversed and Remanded.

U.S. v. Mills, 760 F.2d 1116 (11th Cir. 1985)

Trial counsel had only one day to prepare. The Eleventh Circuit found, under these circumstances, counsel did not have time to prepare and Remanded the case in regards to determine whether the defendant was prejudiced by counsel's failure to locate alibi witness.

COUNSEL'S CUMULATIVE ERRORS

Taylor v. Kentucky, 436 U.S. 478, n. 15, 98 S.Ct. 1930, 56 L.Ed.2d 468 (1978)
Cumulative errors, while individually harmless, when considered together, can prejudice a defendant as much as a single reversible error and violate a defendant's right to due process of law.

Goodman v. Bertrand, 467 F.3d 1022, 1030 (7th Cir. 2006)
The cumulative effect of counsel's errors to wit: (1) opened the door for admission of Goodman's two prior convictions for armed robbery, (2) failed to subpoena the store's cashier to testify, (3) failed to request a limiting instruction regarding the threats evidence, (4) failed to properly object and preserve the record regarding the denial of Goodman's right to confront the witnesses against him, and (5) failed to object and request a mistrial based upon prosecutorial misconduct in closing argument constituted ineffective assistance of counsel.

Stouffer v. Reyon1ds, 214 F.3d 1231 (10th Cir. 2000)
Counsel's failure to make an opening statement to the jury; lay proper grounds for admission into evidence defense exhibit to impeach a key prosecution witness; eliciting incriminating testimony during cross-examination of prosecution witnesses; presented closing arguments that were ineffective for proffering any semblance of a defense theory; file an application for funds to hire experts to examine the opinions of the state's expert witnesses; call defense investigator to testify to crucial facts that 13 shots were fired into the house, rather than 5 shots as alleged by the state constituted ineffective assistance of counsel.

Lindstandt v. Keane, 239 F.3d 191, 203-06 (2nd Cir. 2001)
Counsel's cumulative errors in prosecution for sexual abuse of defendant's minor daughter amounted to ineffective assistance of counsel requiring a new trial on all counts. Counsel failed to discover and expose that daughter gave wrong date for alleged abuse; request the unnamed studies relied on by prosecution's expert witness; stated in opening argument that defendant would testify only if prosecution proved its case; failed to argue the relevance of third party testimony that defendant's wife tried to get him arrested before the alleged abuse was actually reported. There exists more than a reasonable probability that the results of the proceedings would have been different, absent counsel's unprofessional errors and omissions.

Dubria v. Smith, 197 F.3d 390 (9th Cir. 1999)
Trial counsel's cumulative errors, by failing to object to inflammatory statements made by prosecution that the defendant was a "Piece of garbage" and "The biggest liar you've ever encountered," and counsel suggesting to jury that evidence not presented supported murder charge deprived the defendant of his due process right to a fair trial.

Washington v. Smith, 48 F.Supp. 2d 1149 (E.D. Wis. 1999)
Counsel's cumulative errors and omissions by failing to investigate exculpatory information in police report, interview alibi witnesses, and subpoena alibi witnesses deprived the defendant of his due process right to a fair trial and constitutes ineffective assistance of counsel.

__Blackburn v. Foltz__, 828 F.2d 1177 (6th Cir. 1987)
> The Court held that: Defendant was denied the effective assistance of counsel based on combination of counsel's erroneous legal advice concerning possible use of prior convictions if defendant testified, failure to obtain transcripts of earlier trial to impeach key eyewitness, and failure to investigate concerning potential alibi defense. Reversed and Remanded with instructions.

__U.S. v. Tory__, 52 F.3d 207 (9th Cir. 1995)
> The Ninth Circuit found the cumulative effect of the errors deprived the defendant of a fair trial. This case was not a ineffective assistance of counsel claim; rather, the trial court's action hindered the defendant's defense.

__Thomas v. Calderon__, 120 F.3d 1045 (9th Cir. 1997)
> Counsel's cumulative errors in failing to investigate and impeach the jailhouse informants and to rebut the forensic evidence of rape cast grave doubt on his reliability of the entire proceedings, thus, constituting ineffective assistance of counsel. **See also** *__U.S. v. Kladouris__, 739 F.Supp. 1221 (N.D. Ill. 1990); __Halton v. Hesson__, 803 F.Supp. 1272 (M.D. Tenn. 1992); __United States v. Hammonds__, 425 F.2d 597 (D.C. Cir. 1970); __Hollines v. Estelle__, 569 F.Supp. 146 (W.D. Tex. 1983); __Jemison v. Foltz__, 672 F.Supp. 1002 (E.D. Mich. 1987); __Henry v. Scully__, 78 F.3d 51 (2nd Cir. 1996); __Harris By and Through Ramseyer v. Wood__, 64 F.3d 1432 (9th Cir. 1995); __Harris v. Housewright__, 697 F.2d 202 (8th Cir. 1982); __Harris v. Towers__, 405 F.Supp 497 (D. Del 1974); __Nealy v. Cabana__, 764 F.2d 1173 (5th Cir 1985)*

__Wade v. Calderon__, 29 F.3d 1312 (9th Cir. 1994)
> Defense counsel's cumulative errors and omissions during penalty phase constituted ineffective assistance of counsel.

__Demarest v. Price__, 905 F.Supp. 1432 (D.Col. 1995)
> Trial counsel's cumulative errors and omissions constituted ineffective assistance of counsel and warranted a new trial.

__Pilchak v. Camper__, 741 F.Supp. 782 (W.D. Mo. 1990)
> Just because defense counsel was suffering from Alzheimer's, did not constitute ineffective assistance of counsel without a showing of prejudice. The defendant established prejudice based on numerous cumulative unprofessional errors and omissions.

__Crisp v. Duckworth__, 743 F.2d 580 (7th Cir. 1984)
> In this case, *__Crisp__* claimed his attorney committed multiple acts and omissions which taken as a whole, amounted to ineffective assistance. The Court found that it must examine each error individually and then must also consider their cumulative effect in light of the totality of circumstances. *__Strickland__, 104 S.Ct. 15 2069; __United States v. Brown__, 739 F.2d 1136 at 1145 (7th Cir. 1984)*. On one hand, this means that an attorney's individual errors may not, looking at the trial as a whole, cast doubt on the reliability of the result and, therefore, would not merit reversal. On the other hand, even if individual acts or omissions are not so grievous as to merit a finding of incompetence or of prejudice from incompetence, their cumulative effect may be substantial enough to meet the *__Strickland test__*. *__See United States v. Merritt__, 528 F.2d 650, 651 (7th Cir. 1976) (per curiam); __United States v. Hammonds__, 425 F.2d 597, 604 (D.C. Cir. 1970)*. Looking at the alleged errors as a whole, the Court agreed that

Counsel's Cumulative Errors

Crisp overcame the presumption that his trial counsel provided reasonable professional assistance, *Strickland, 104 S.Ct. at 2065*; and had established that counsel was in fact incompetent. However, looking at the trial as a whole, the Court did not believe that Crisp's counsel's conduct so undermined the proper functioning of the adversarial process that the trial court cannot be relied on as having produced a just result. *Strickland, 104 S.Ct. at 2064*. This case was affirmed, but the language used provides a great method for attacking counsel's cumulative errors and omission.

LEGAL STANDARDS/REVIEWS FOR INEFFECTIVENESS CLAIMS

Strickland STANDARD

Strickland v. Washington, 466 U.S. 668, 104 S.Ct. 2052, 2064-74, 80 L.Ed.2d 674 (1984)
> Claims of ineffectiveness of counsel in a criminal case are evaluated under a two-prong test set forth in **_Strickland_**. To succeed on any claim of ineffective assistance of counsel claim, the defendant must show: (1) that his attorney's representation fell below an objective standard of reasonableness; and (2) due to counsel's unprofessional errors that the results of the proceedings would have been different. **_Strickland, 466 U.S. 687-688_**. Judicial scrutiny of counsel's performance must be highly deferential, and a fair assessment of attorney performance requires that every effort be made to eliminate the distorting effects of hindsight, to reconstruct the circumstances of counsel's challenged conduct, and to evaluate the conduct from counsel's perspective at the time. A court must indulge a strong presumption that counsel's conduct falls within the wide range of reasonable professional assistance. **_80 L.Ed.2d at 682_**. The Court also concluded that strategic choice made by counsel after thorough investigation of law and facts relevant to plausible options are virtually unchallengeable; strategic choices made after less than complete investigation are reasonable precisely to the extent that reasonable professional judgments support limitations on investigation.

Miller v. Wainwright, 798 F.2d 426 (11th Cir. 1986)
> The Court held that: "(1) Ineffective assistance of counsel claims had to be re-examined by district court under correct **_Strickland_** standard, where federal district court had improperly accorded presumption of correctness to State court's mixed law-fact determination of absence of ineffective assistance; (2) it was incumbent upon some court to review grand jury testimony of eye witnesses to determine whether petitioner had particularized need sufficient to overcome need for secrecy of grand jury proceedings where witnesses had testified to two different versions, both under oath."

Siverson v. O'Leary, 764 F.2d 1208 (7th Cir. 1985)
> Counsel's absence from courtroom amounts to a denial of the right to counsel and is per se prejudicial.

AMERICAN BAR ASSOCIATION STANDARDS

U.S. v. Boigerain, 155 F.3d 1183 (10th Cir. 1998)
> The American Bar Association Standards is a guide in determining reasonable professional behavior. **See _Strickland_, 466 U.S. at 668, 104 S. Ct. 2052.**

Strickland PREJUDICE PRONG STANDARD REQUIRES PROOF BY PREPONDERANCE OF EVIDENCE STANDARD

Weekly v. Jones, 56 F.3d 889 (8th Cir. 1995)
> The Court found a "defendant need not establish that the attorney's deficient performance more likely than not altered the outcome in order to establish prejudice

under Strickland and that the reasonable probability standard is not a sufficiency of evidence test." (citing)*Kyles v. Whitley, 115 S.Ct. 1555,1566,131 LEd.2d 490 (1995)*. Id. at 56 F.3d at 897.

James v. Cain, 56 F.3d 662 (5th Cir. 1995)
Proof of ineffective assistance of counsel is by the preponderance of evidence. **See also *Vela v. Estelle, 708 F.2d 954 (5th Cir. 1983)***

Lofton v. Whitley, 905 F.2d 885 (5th Cir. 1990)
When a defendant is actually denied his right to counsel on appeal, prejudice is automatically presumed. **See also *Williams v. Lockhart, 849 F.2d 1134 (8th Cir. 1988)***

Bouchillon v. Collins, 907 F.2d 589 (5th Cir. 1990)
The ***Bouchillon*** Court found the standard prejudice prong of ineffective assistance of counsel was a "reasonable probability" that he was incompetent "sufficient to undermine confidence in outcome." ***Strickland at 694, 104 S.Ct. at 2068***. This is a lower burden of proof than the preponderance standard.

Woodard v. Collins, 898 F.2d 1027 (5th Cir. 1990)
This case stands for the proposition once ineffective assistance of counsel is established, then the decision to overturn the conviction goes to the prejudiced prong of ***Strickland***. If the defendant was actually or constructively denied assistance of counsel, the prejudice prong of ***Strickland*** is not required to be shown and the conviction must be set-aside.

Blackmon v. White, 825 F.2d 1263 (8th Cir. 1987)
A defendant must establish that the result of the proceeding would have been different, after defendant demonstrates counsel's performance fell below an objective standard of reasonableness.

Wilson v. Mintzes, 761 F.2d 275 (6th Cir. 1985)
Where trial counsel was provoked into acts inconsistent with his duties of loyalty to his client by the trial court, such interference effects the fairness of the trial and prejudice is presumed. The ***Strickland*** standards have no applicability.

RULES OF LAW AND PROCEDURE

Vela v. Estelle, 708 F.2d 954 (5th Cir. 1983)
An attorney's performance is judged on the basis of the facts known to him, and the rules of law and procedure, he is held to know, as an attorney representing defendants in criminal proceedings. Unless a defendant charged with a serious offense has counsel able to invoke the procedural and substantive safeguards that distinguish our system of justice, a serious risk of injustice infects the trial itself.

MIXED QUESTION OF LAW AND FACTS

U.S. v. Signori, 844 F.2d 635 (9th Cir. 1988)
Ineffective assistance of counsel is a mixed question of law and facts, which is reviewed de novo by the Court of Appeals.

Constructive Denial of Counsel/Review

Delgado v. Lewis, 181 F.3d 1087 (9th Cir. 1999)
> The Strickland and harmless error standards are not appropriate when appellate counsel fails to raise any arguable issues in appellates brief and prejudice is presumed.

Childress v. Johnson, 103 F.3d 1221 (5th Cir. 1997)
> The standard of review to determine whether a defendant was constructively denied his right to counsel is a mixed question of law and fact, reviewed de novo.

STANDARDS FOR JUDGING GUILTY PLEA
INEFFECTIVENESS CLAIMS

Hill v. Lockhart, 474 U.S. 52, 88 L.Ed.2d 203, 106 S.Ct. 366 (1985)
> A guilty plea defendant must establish that he would not have pleaded guilty, but would have insisted on going to trial, absent counsel's unprofessional errors or omissions.

Tollet v. Henderson, 411 U.S. 258, 93 S.Ct. 1602, 36 L.Ed.2d 235 (1973)
> A criminal defendant can only attack the voluntary and intelligent character of guilty plea based on the advice he received from counsel.

Hill v. Lockhart, 877 F.2d 698 (8th Cir. 1989)
> A petitioner alleging that his guilty plea was a result of ineffective assistance of counsel must show only that there exists a reasonable probability that result of plea process would have been different absent counsel's misadvise; however, petitioner is not required to show that he probably would have been acquitted or received a shorter sentence at trial.

Wiley v. Wainwright, 793 F.2d 1190 (11th Cir. 1986)
> A guilty plea does not preclude defendant from raising a Sixth Amendment claim of ineffective assistance of counsel.

Lockhart's Incorrect Prejudiced Standard

Williams v. Taylor, 529 U.S. 362, 146 L.Ed.2d 389, 400, 120 S.Ct. 1495 (2000)
> The Supreme Court addressed the lower courts incorrect use of the prejudice standard set forth in ***Lockhart v. Fretwell***, **506 U.S. 364, 369, 122 L.Ed.2d 180, 113 S.Ct. 838 (1993)**, for determining Williams ineffective assistance of counsel claims. The Williams Court held: "Moreover, counsel's unprofessional service prejudiced Williams within ***Strickland's*** meaning. The Virginia Supreme Court's prejudice analysis was unreasonable in at least two respects: (1) It was not only 'contrary to,' but also inasmuch as it relied on the inapplicable ***Lockhart*** exception-an 'unreasonable application of,' the clear law as established [by] ***Strickland***; and (2) it failed to evaluate the totality of, and to accord appropriate weight to, the available mitigation evidence." Williams, **146 L.Ed.2d at 400**. See also ***Rose v. Lee***, **252 F.3d 679, 689 (4th Cir. 2001)**; ***Mask v. McGinnis***, **233 F.3d 132, 140 (2nd Cir. 2000)**.

STANDARDS FOR INEFFECTIVENESS CLAIMS RELATED TO SENTENCING

Glover v. United States, 531 U.S. 198, 148 L.Ed.2d 607, 611, 121 S.Ct. 696 (2001)
Defense counsel was constitutionally ineffective for failing to argue at sentencing and on direct appeal that Glover's conviction for federal labor racketeering, money laundering, and tax evasion should be grouped under **USSG §3D1.2**, which allows the grouping of counts involving substantially the same harm. As a result of counsel's ineffectiveness Glover's offense level was increased two levels, resulting in an increased sentence of between 6 and 21 months. The **_Glover_** Court held that any amount of actual jail time has Sixth Amendment significance under **_Strickland_**.

U.S. v. Acklen, 47 F.3d 739 (5th Cir. 1995)
A criminal defendant can met the prejudice prong of **_Strickland_** in non-capital sentencing cases, by showing he would have received a less harsh sentence absent counsel's unprofessional errors or omissions.

Strickland STANDARD APPLIES TO APPELLATE COUNSEL'S INEFFECTIVENESS CLAIMS

Gray v. Greer, 778 F.2d 350 (7th Cir. 1985)
The Court found the right to appellate counsel is now firmly established. **_Evitts v. Lucey_, 469 U.S. 387, 83 L.Ed.2d 821, 105 S.Ct. 830 (1985) _Strickland v. Washington_, 466 U.S. 668, 687-88, 694, 104 S.Ct. 2052, 2064-74, 80 L.Ed.2d 674 (1984)** established the standard for ineffective assistance of counsel, and though it is phrased in terms of ineffective assistance of trial counsel, it can be used as a basis for establishing a standard for effective assistance of appellate counsel. Accord **_Brown v. Foltz_, 763 F.2d 191, 195 (6th Cir. 1985) (Coutie, J., dissenting)**; **_Schwander v. Blackburn_, 750 F.2d 494, 502 (5th Cir. 1985)**; **_Mitchell v. Scully_, 746 F.2d 951, 954 (2nd Cir. 1984)**. Under **_Strickland_**, ineffective assistance of counsel will be found when "counsel's conduct so undermined the proper functioning of the adversarial process that the trial cannot be relied on as having produced a just result". **_Strickland_, 104 S.Ct. at 2064**. The **_Strickland_** standard envisions a two-prong analysis. First, counsel's performance must have been deficient, and second, the deficiency must have prejudiced the defense. **_Id._** Had appellate counsel failed to raise a significant and obvious issue, the failure could be viewed as deficient performance. If an issue which was not raised, may have resulted in a reversal of the conviction or an order for a new trial, the failure was prejudicial. **_Id._ at 352**. See also **_Gray v. Greer_, 800 F.2d 644 (7th Cir. 1986)**

SINGLE ERROR OF COUNSEL

Murray v. Carrier, 477 U.S. 478, 91 L.Ed.2d 391, 106 S.Ct. 2639 (1986)
A single error of counsel may constitute ineffective assistance of counsel.

Nero v. Blackburn, 597 F.2d 991 (5th Cir. 1979)
Trial counsel's single error, failure to move for a mistrial, constitutes ineffective assistance where that error allowed prejudicial evidence in that would not have been admissible.

INEFFECTIVENESS CLAIMS PROPERLY RAISED IN MOTION FOR NEW TRIAL OR MOTION TO VACATE

U.S. v. Cronic, 466 U.S. 648, 80 L.Ed.2d 657, 104 S.Ct. 2039 (1984)

The Supreme Court noted, in footnote 4, that the district court had jurisdiction to entertain the defendant's ineffective assistance of counsel pursuant to a motion for new trial under **_Fed. Rules of Crim. Proc. Rule 33_**.

Abbamonte v. U.S., 160 F.3d 922 (2nd Cir. 1998)

Ineffectiveness of counsel claim could be raised in a **_28 U.S.C. §2255_** motion to vacate even though defendant raised a different ineffectiveness of counsel claim on direct appeal.

U.S. v. Medina, 118 F.3d 371 (5th Cir. 1997)

New trial motion under Federal Rules of Criminal Procedure Rule 33 could not be based on "newly discovered evidence" of trial counsel's ineffectiveness.

Williams v. Turpin, 87 F.3d 1204 (11th Cir. 1996)

An ineffective assistance of counsel claim must be raised in a motion for new trial under Georgia law, or it is deemed waived. Thus, defendant has a constitutional right to effective representation in a motion for new trial.

Duarte v. U.S., 81 F.3d 75 (7th Cir. 1996)

Ineffectiveness of counsel is properly brought under motion to vacate sentence.

Riascos-Prado v. U.S., 66 F.3d 30 (2nd Cir. 1995)

Where new appellate counsel is forced to raise trial counsel's ineffectiveness on direct appeal where those claims are developed by the record and to prevent a procedural bar, the defendant is entitled to present a new claim of conflict of interest in a 28 U.S.C. §2255 motion where the record was not factually developed to resolve the claim on direct appeal. The Second Circuit vacated and remanded the district courts dismissal of this claim with instructions to the district court that in addressing this issue on remand, the district court may take into account the subject matter of the other ineffectiveness claims insofar as they may be deemed probative of the alleged conflict. Cf. **_Caballero v. Keane, 42 F.3d 738, 740-41 (2nd Cir. 1994)_** (state court's should be afforded opportunity to consider circumstances and cumulative effect of ineffectiveness claims as a whole).

U.S. v. Stockstill, 26 F.3d 492 (4th Cir. 1994)

The district court evaluated Stockstill's ineffective assistance of counsel claims under criteria of rule 33 for newly discovered evidence standard, rather than the Strickland standard, the Court of Appeals remanded for consideration under the Strickland standards.

Bond v. U.S., 1 F.3d 631 (7th Cir. 1993)

Trial counsel's failure to file motion to suppress evidence is properly raised on petition for habeas relief instead of direct appeal.

U.S. v. Busse, 814 F.2d 760 (E.D. Wis. 1993)

Trial court has jurisdiction to entertain petitioner's 2255 motion based on ineffective assistance of counsel even though direct appeal was pending.

Billy-Eko v. U.S. 8 F.3d 111 (2d Cir. 1993)

The Court held that: Ineffective assistance of counsel claims could be brought in motion to vacate without showing cause and prejudice for failure to raise them on direct appeal and the defendant was not prejudiced by his counsel's failure to appeal conviction.

U.S. v. Aquilla, 976 F.2d 1044 (7th Cir. 1992)

Ineffective assistance of counsel claims are generally best raised in motion for new trial or motion to vacate.

U.S. v. Kladouris, 739 F.Supp. 1221 (N.D. Ill. 1990)

Facts forming a basis of defendant's defense not presented at trial can constitute newly discovered evidence and form a basis for ineffective assistance of counsel claim for a new trial under *Federal Rules of Criminal Procedure Rule 33.*

COUNSEL'S PERFORMANCE IS EVALUATED DURING DISCREET PORTIONS OF TRIAL

Horton v. Zant, 941 F.2d 1449 (11th Cir. 1991)

Attorney's performance is evaluated during discreet portions of a trial without regard to attorney's performance at other points during trial.

COURT INCORRECTLY PASSED BURDEN TO DEFENDANT TO EVALUATE COUNSEL'S PERFORMANCE

Ward v. U.S., 995 F.2d 1317 (6th Cir. 1993)

The Court held that: (1) Trial court improperly reviewed counsel's performance when it passed burden to evaluate counsel's performance onto defendant and his father; and (2) defendant was deprived of effective assistance of trial counsel. Judgment vacated; petition granted; new trial ordered.

DE NOVO REVIEW REQUIREMENTS

U.S. v. Gallegos, 108 F.3d 1272 (10th Cir. 1997)

The Court of Appeals reviews district court's determination of whether actual conflict of interest existed de novo, and reviews factual findings under clearly erroneous standard.

Childress v. Johnson, 103 F.3d 1221 (5th Cir. 1997)

The standard of review to determine whether a defendant was constructively denied his right to counsel is a mixed question of law and fact that is reviewed de novo.

Wilson v. Cooke, 814 F.2d 614 (11th Cir. 1987)

District court must review transcripts or listen to tape recording to conduct a de novo review of evidentiary hearing to deny petitioner's objections to Magistrate's report and recommendations. This case was remanded because there was no transcript made of evidentiary hearing and no tape recording existed of evidentiary hearing.

AFFIDAVIT TESTIMONY TO SUPPORT CLAIM OF FAILURE TO CALL WITNESSES

Wright v. Gramley, 125 F.3d 1038 (7th Cir. 1997)

The Court held that:(1) defendant established prejudice arising from his failure to present affidavit of witness who would have affirmatively stated that defendant was not attacker in state court battery prosecution, and(2) remand was required to determine whether defendant had established cause for his failure to submit affidavit as required by state post-conviction practice. Vacated and remanded.

Fields v. U.S., 698 A.2d 485 (D.C.App. 1997)

Defendant <u>must</u> provide affidavit from witnesses showing what witnesses testimony would have been to support an ineffective assistance of counsel claim for failure to call witnesses.

U.S. v. Ashimi, 932 F.2d 643 (7th Cir. 1991)

In order to support an ineffective assistance of counsel claim for failure to call witnesses, evidence of putative witness must be presented in form of actual testimony or in an affidavit.

TRIAL FREE FROM FUNDAMENTAL UNFAIRNESS

Strickland v. Washington, 466 U.S. 668, 695-96, 80 L.Ed.2d 674, 104 S.Ct. 2052 (1984)

The ultimate focus of inquiry in challenging ineffectiveness assistance of counsel claims goes to the fundamental fairness of the proceedings being challenged and whether counsel's errors is the type that causes a breakdown in the adversarial proceeding which seriously undermines the validity of the verdict, making the adversarial process itself presumptively unreliable.

Strickland v. Washington, 466 U.S. 668, 695-96, 80 L.Ed.2d 674, 104 S.Ct. 2052 (1984)

Errors with the "pervasion effect" of "altering the evidentiary picture".

Ake v. Oklahoma, 470 U.S. 68, 84 LEd.2d 53, 105 S.Ct. 1087 (1985)

A criminal trial is fundamentally unfair if the State proceeds against an indigent defendant without making certain that he has access to the raw materials integral to the building of a effective defense.

Estelle v. Williams, 425 U.S. 501,505-06,96 S.Ct. 1691, 1693-94,48 LEd. 2d 126 (1976)

Some courtroom practices may deprive a defendant of his Sixth Amendment Right to a fair trial, which implicates the due process clause.

Nealy v. Cabana, 764 F.2d 1173 (5th Cir 1985)

The Fifth Circuit found that even if Nealy could not show by the preponderance of the evidence that counsel's errors to undermine the outcome of the trial, that counsel's errors were sufficient gravity to undermine the fundamental fairness and warranted a new trial.

***Clark v. Blackburn*, 619 F.2d 431 (5th Cir. 1980)**

A criminal defendant is guaranteed, through the due process clause, a trial free from fundamental unfairness, including any unfairness which stems from blatantly incompetent counsel.

***Beasley v. United States*, 491 F.2d 687 (6th Cir. 1974)**

When trial counsel erroneously advised defendant on clear points of law and that advice leads to the denial of a fair trial, the defendant has been denied his right to effective assistance of counsel.

TOTALITY OF COUNSEL'S ERRORS

***Arrowood v. Clusen*, 732 F.2d 1364 (7th Cir. 1984)**

Trial counsel's unprofessional errors and omissions must be considered in light of totality of the circumstances. In other words, the prejudicial effect must be considered together.

***Goodwin v. Balkcom*, 684 F.2d 794 (11th Cir. 1982)**

The totality of trial counsel's unprofessional errors and omissions constitute ineffective assistance of counsel.

Harmless Error Analysis

***Gilbert v. California*, 388 U.S. 263, 272, 87 S.Ct. 1951, 1956-1957, 18 L.Ed.2d 1178 (1967)**

Harmless error analysis required after petitioner was denied his right to counsel during post-indictment pretrial line up.

CONFLICT OF INTEREST

***Cuyler v. Sullivan*, 446 U.S. 335, 100 S.Ct. 1708, 64 L.Ed.2d 333 (1980)**

In order to find a Sixth Amendment violation based on a conflict of interest, the reviewing court must find: (1) that counsel actively represented conflicting interests; and (2) that an actual conflict of interest adversely affected the attorney's performance. *Id. at 348, 100 S.Ct. at 1718.* Under *Cuyler*, the court must presume prejudice if the conflict of interest adversely affected the attorney's performance. *Id.* Although *Cuyler* involved a conflict of interest between clients, the presumption of prejudice extends to a "conflict between a client and his lawyer's personal interest. *See*, *Mannhalt v. Reed*, 847 F.2d 576, 580 (9th Cir.), *cert. denied*, 488 U.S. 908, 109 S.Ct. 260, 102 L.Ed.2d 249 (1988).*

***Beets v. Scott*, 65 F.3d 1258 (5th Cir. 1995)**

The Fifth Circuit in *Beets* held that the *Strickland* test, rather than the *Cuyler* test, offers superior framework for addressing conflict of interest outside the multiple or serial client context. However, *footnote 17*, pointed out that "a powerful argument can be made that a lawyer who is a potential co-defendant with his client is burdened by a 'multiple representation' conflict that ought to be analyzed under *Cuyler*."

Selsor v. Kaiser, 22 F.3d 1029 (10th Cir. 1994)
> The district court applied the incorrect legal standard applying <u>Culyer</u> where the defendant objected to joint representation. The Court remanded for reconsideration under the <u>Holloway</u> standard.

U.S. v. Greig, 967 F.2d 1018 (5th Cir. 1992)
> The trial court must conduct a **_Garcia_** hearing once it has been alerted of the existence of an actual conflict of interest.

Hamilton v. Ford, 969 F.2d 1006 (11th Cir. 1992)
> A timely notice or objections to joint representation requires the trial court to inquire into the conflict and failure of the court to do so requires automatic reversal.

Rosenwald v. U.S., 898 F.2d 585 (7th Cir. 1990)
> Where attorney represents conflicting interests, prejudice is presumed for showing of ineffective assistance of counsel.

DEFENDANT MUST ALLEGE SPECIFICALLY WHAT AN INVESTIGATION BY COUNSEL MIGHT HAVE PRODUCED

Nelson v. Hargett, 989 F.2d 847 (5th Cir. 1993)
> Trial counsel's failure to investigate may constitute ineffectiveness of counsel, but defendant must allege with specificity what the investigation would have lead to and how outcome of trial would have been different.

Smith v. Wainwright, 777 F.2d 609 (11th Cir. 1985)
> A defendant must allege specific errors amounting to performance below an objective standard of reasonableness in order to support defendant's ineffective assistance claim. When a defendant demonstrates the specific unprofessional error or omission, the circumstance surrounding counsel's representation at that point give rise to the presumption of prejudice.

MISCELLANEOUS

Howell v. State Bar of Texas, 843 F.2d 205 (5th Cir. 1988)
> The Court held that: Texas disciplinary rule prohibiting lawyer from engaging in conduct that is prejudicial to administration of justice is not unconstitutionally overbroad or vague.

Green v. Arn, 809 F.2d 1257 (6th Cir. 1987)
> The Court found the **_Strickland_** test was not appropriate where the issue is a denial of counsel, as opposed to an ineffective assistance of counsel claim.

INEFFECTIVENESS CLAIMS CAN BE RESOLVED ON APPEAL

U.S. v. Director of Ill.Dept.of Corrections, 963 F. Supp. 1473 (N.D.Ill. 1997)
> Ineffective assistance of counsel claims was procedurally defaulted where argument could have been raised on direct appeal.

U.S. v. Galloway, 56 F.3d 1239 (10th Cir. 1995)
> Ineffective assistance of counsel claims raised on direct appeal do not procedurally bar ineffective assistance claims on §2255 motion if new claims are based on different grounds.

Riascos-Prado v. U.S., 66 F.3d 30 (2nd Cir. 1995)
> Ineffective assistance of counsel claim must be brought on direct appeal when defendant is represented by a new appellate counsel on direct appeal and claim is based solely on the record.

Guinan v. U.S., 6 F.3d 468 (7th Cir. 1993)
> Ineffective assistance of counsel claims may be resolved on direct appeal where defendant relies on record to support ineffectiveness claim.

WHETHER COUNSEL'S STRATEGY WAS REASONABLE

Berryman v. Morton, 100 F.3d 1089 at 1096 (3rd Cir. 1996)
> The question of whether counsel's strategy was reasonable goes directly to the performance prong of *Strickland* test, thus requiring the application of legal principles and **de novo review**.

SENTENCING INEFFECTIVENESS

JURY SELECTION FOR PENALTY PHASE

Gary v. Mississippi, 481 U.S. 648, 652 n. 3, 107 S.Ct. 2045, 95 L.Ed.2d 622 (1987)
> The erroneous exclusion of one potential juror based on her views on the death penalty was **reversible constitutional error**.

Morgan v. Illinois, 504 U.S. 719, 112 S.Ct. 2222, 119 L.Ed.2d 492 (1992)
> The Supreme Court held that "on voir dire the court must, on defendant's request, inquire into the prospective juror's views on capital punishment" because a prospective juror who would always impose the death penalty must not be empanelled, *Morgan*, **504 U.S. at 726, 112 S.Ct. 2222.** "If even one such juror is empanelled and the death sentence is imposed, the State is disentitled to execute the sentence." **Id. at 729, 112 S.Ct. 2222.**

Witherspoon v. Illinois, 391 U.S. 510, 88 S.Ct. 1770, 20 L.Ed.2d 776 (1968)
> The Supreme Court determined that it was proper to ask prospective jurors about their views concerning the death penalty during voir dire in capital cases. Such "death qualifying" questions would ensure the impartiality of jurors by allowing the state to properly exercise challenges for cause against potential jurors unwilling to return a capital sentence. **Id. 391 U.S. at 520-23, 88 S.Ct. 1770.**

United States v. Chanthadara, 230 F. 3d 1237, 1268 (10th Cir. 2000)
> The erroneous exclusion of even one potential juror mandates reversal of a death sentence.

Fuller v. Johnson, 114 F.3d 491, 500 (5th Cir. 1997)
> Where the Court finds that one juror was improperly excluded, the defendant is entitled to a new sentencing, because the right to an impartial adjudication is so basic to a fair trial that its infraction can never be treated as harmless error in a capital case.

Szuchon v. Lehman, 273 F.3d 299 (3rd Cir. 2001)
> The exclusion for cause of potential juror who stated that he did not believe in death penalty, but, was never asked whether he could be impartial required granting habeas relief.

FAILED TO INVESTIGATE, TO PRESENT EVIDENCE, OR TO CALL WITNESSES IN SUPPORT OF:

Defendant's Mental History/Mental Condition at Time of Crime/Mitigating Evidence/Expert Testimony

Williams v. Taylor, 529 U.S. 362, 146 LEd.2d 389, 120 S. Ct. 1495 (2000)
> Counsel's failure to begin to prepare for sentencing phase of trial until a week before the trial did not fulfill the obligation to conduct a thorough investigation of the defendant's background violated the standards of *Strickland*.

Sentencing Ineffectiveness

Stevens v. McBride, 489 F.3d 883, 896-897 (7th Cir. 2007)
Counsel's failure to investigate and present mitigating evidence concerning Stevens' mental health amounted to ineffective assistance of counsel. **See also** *Lambright v. Schriro*, 490 F.3d 1003, 1119-1122 (9th Cir. 2007).

Lopez v. Schriro, 491 F.3d 1029, 1040-1044 (9th Cir. 2007)
Counsel's failure to investigate and present mitigating evidence concerning Lopez' background, dysfunctional family, alcoholic parents and that he began drinking at an early age and consult with an expert witness required addressing the merits of Lopez' claim on remand.

Haliym v. Mitchell, 492 F.3d 680, 712 (6th Cir. 2007)
Counsel provided constitutionally ineffective assistance for failing to investigate Haliym's family background, abusive and violent childhood, loss of family members; mental defects and present mitigating evidence during the penalty phase.

Williams v. Anderson, 460 F.3d 789, 804-806 (6th Cir. 2006)
Counsel was constitutionally ineffective during the penalty phase of this capital murder trial for failing to present mitigating evidence concerning Williams violent upbringing where his mother was an alcoholic, neglected him and beat him upside his head with whatever she could get her hands on, and there was at least one juror that would have voted against the death sentence.

Outten v. Kearney, 464 F.3d 401, 416-420 (3rd Cir. 2006)
Counsel's failure to conduct a proper investigation into mitigating evidence was unreasonable and prejudicial in light of the Outten's abusive childhood by his father and the fact that he had been sexually abused in foster care.

Correll v. Ryan, 465 F.3d 1006, 1012-1015 (9th Cir. 2006)
Counsel's failure to investigate, call witness and present mitigating evidence during the penalty phase concerning Correll's abusive childhood, extensive drug abuse, mental illness and methamphetamine-induced psychosis at the time of the murder amounted to ineffective assistance of counsel.

Hovey v. Ayers, 458 F.3d 892, 930 (9th Cir. 2006)
Counsel was constitutionally ineffective for failing to investigate and present mitigating evidence during the penalty phase, which left the jury with the erroneous impression that petitioner had never been treated for a mental illness prior to committing the crimes, and that petitioner may have fabricated a mental illness to obtain mercy at sentencing. **See also** *Williams v. Anderson*, 460 F.3d 789, 804-06 (6th Cir. 2006); *Outten v. Kearney*, 464 F.3d 401, 420 (3rd Cirl. 2006).

Landrigan v. Schriro, 441 F.3d 638, 647 (9th Cir. 2006)
Counsel's failure to investigate and present mitigating evidence during penalty phase concerning petitioner's tortured family, history of drug abuse, and mental illness constituted ineffective assistance of counsel.

Harries v. Bell, 417 F.3d 631, 639-640 (6th Cir. 2005)
Counsel's failure to investigate mitigating evidence for penalty phase concerning Harries's traumatic childhood amounted to ineffective assistance and required resentencing.

Lewis v. Drethe, 355 F.3d 364, 367-69 (5th Cir. 2004)
Counsel was constitutionally ineffective by failing to investigate, present mitigating evidence in capital murder trial of petitioner's abusive father; call petitioner's three sisters as witnesses who would have testified that their father beat them all with extension cards, switches, sticks or anything else he could find and beat their mother in front of them, required resentencing.

McNair v. Campbell, 307 F.Supp. 2d 1277, 1316-18 (M.D. Ala. 2004)
Counsel was constitutionally ineffective for failing to obtain an expert witness to explain that McNair had a biological condition, namely, crack cocaine addiction, that he had been struggling with for several years unsuccessfully. This information would have changed the sentencing judge's understanding of the picture and might <u>not</u> have resulted in the imposition of the death penalty.

Smith v. Mullin, 379 F.3d 919, 941-942 (10th Cir. 2004)
Counsel's performance was deficient for failing to present mitigating evidence of defendant's mental retardation, brain damage, and troubled background in penalty phase. **See ABA Guidelines** for the Appointment and Performance of Defense Counsel in Death Penalty Cases 1.1, 4.1, 10.4, 10.7, 10.11. In order for the Court to grant relief, it must find that there is a reasonable probability that the jury would have concluded the balance of aggravating and mitigating circumstances did not warrant death. A reasonable probability is <u>less</u> than a <u>preponderance</u> <u>of</u> the <u>evidence</u>, but sufficient to undermine confidence in the outcome. ***Smith*, 379 F.3d at 941-942 (emphasis added)**. The Court found that counsel's errors undermine the confidence in the outcome of the proceedings because the mitigating evidence omitted from Mr. Smith's trial is exactly the type of evidence that garners the most sympathy from jurors and would have probably resulted in a life sentence. **See id**. **See also *Earp v. Stokes*, 423 F.3d 1024, 1037 (9th Cir. 2005)**.

Powell v. Collins, 332 F.3d 376, 398-401 (6th Cir. 2003)
Counsel's failure to interview or call family and friends as witnesses, and to present mitigating evidence that would have likely resulted in life sentence, as opposed to death sentence constituted ineffective assistance of counsel.

Karis v. Galderon, 283 F. 3d 1117, 1139-40 (9th Cir. 2002)
Trial counsel's failure to adequately investigate and present mitigating evidence that Karis grew up "seeing his mother regularly and violently abused by men," during penalty phase in rape case constituted ineffective assistance of counsel.

Wright v. Walls, 288 F.3d 937, 942-44 (7th Cir. 2002)
The sentencing court failed to consider the defendant's mitigating evidence concerning his troubled childhood and to evaluate the individualized circumstances of the defendant prior to imposing the death penalty.

Simmons v. Luebbers, 299 F.3d 929, 939 (8th Cir. 2002)
Defense counsel's failure to present mitigating evidence in penalty phase of capital murder case was ineffective assistance. Counsel failed to present mitigating evidence concerning Simmons childhood beatings and impoverished upbringing, where said evidence could have reasonably demonstrated that Simmons' violent reactions to rejection by women were the result of his childhood background and entitled Simmons to habeas relief.

<u>Sentencing Ineffectiveness</u>

<u>*U.S. Ex Rel. Madeja v. Schomig*</u>, *223 F.Supp. 2d 968, 974 (N.D. Ill. 2002)*

Counsel was constitutionally ineffective for failing to present mitigating evidence that petitioner suffered neurological impairments resulting from years of polysubstance abuse and physical abuse by his father as a child.

<u>*Sallahdin v. Gibson*</u>, *275 F.3d 1211, 1232 (10th Cir. 2002)*

Defense counsel's failure to investigate and present an expert psychiatrist to testify concerning Sallahdin's psychiatric effects from anabolic steroid use at the time of the crime, which altered Sallahdin's normal behavior and may have caused the jury to impose a life sentence, instead of death sentence amounted to ineffective assistance of counsel.

<u>*Sallahdin v. Gibson*</u>, *275 F.3d 1211, 1239-40 (10th Cir. 2002)*

Defense counsel was constitutionally ineffective by failing to call, Dr. Pope, as an expert witness on steroids use during the sentencing phase to explain that Sallahdin's consistent use of steroids could have transformed Sallahdin from a mild-manner law biding individual into a person capable of committing the brutal murder that he was convicted of committing. If the jury would have heard Dr. Pope's testimony there is a reasonable probability that the jury would have determined that Sallahidn did not represent a continuing threat to society and would not have sentenced Sallahdin to death.

<u>*Caro v. Woodford*</u>, *280 F.3d 1247, 1255-58 (9th Cir. 2002)*

Counsel was constitutionally ineffective for failing to investigate Caro's extraordinary history of exposure to pesticides, toxic chemicals, and seek out an expert to assess the brain damage done by those poisons, where such evidence would have provided powerful mitigating evidence during the penalty phase.

<u>*Jermyn v. Horn*</u>, *266 F.3d 257, 309-10 (3rd Cir. 2001)*

Trial counsel's failure to investigate into defendant's childhood, where defendant was severely abused by his father, and present such evidence during penalty phase of capital murder trial amounted to ineffective assistance of counsel. There was at least one juror who would have found the mitigating facts outweighed the aggravating factors and precluded the imposition of the death sentence.

<u>*Mayfield v. Woodford*</u>, *270 F.3d 915 (9th Cir. 2001)*

Trial counsel's failure to present mitigating evidence during penalty phase from testimony of experts in endocrinology and toxicology, or of friends and family members which may have caused jury not to impose death sentence amounted to ineffective assistance of counsel.

<u>*Jacobs v. Horn*</u>, *129 F.Supp.2d 391, 408-08 (M.D. Pa. 2001)*

Trial counsel was ineffective in failing to investigate, to present mitigating evidence concerning defendant's mental health and background history of abuse, in penalty phase constitutes ineffective assistance of counsel.

<u>*Wiggins v. Corcoran*</u>, *164 F.Supp.2d 538 (D. Md. 2001)*

Trial counsel's failure to present mitigating evidence concerning petitioner's mental status during penalty phase of capital sentencing constituted ineffective assistance of counsel.

Wright v. Cowan, 149 F.Supp. 2d 523, 535 (C.D. Ill. 2000)
>Trial judge's failure to consider evidence of petitioner's traumatic childhood as a mitigating factor in determining whether to impose death penalty resulted in an unconstitutional imposition of the death penalty and required death sentence to be vacated.

Lockett v. Anderson, 230 F.3d 695, 711-12 (5th Cir. 2000)
>Counsel's failure to investigate and present mitigating evidence based on defendant's mental and psychological abnormalities that seriously affected defendant's ability to control his behavior, and would have caused a reasonable juror to decide that the death penalty was not appropriate, established prejudice under *Strickland*.

Mayes v. Gibson, 210 F.3d 1284 (10th Cir. 2000)
>Defense counsel's failure to investigate and present mitigating evidence during penalty phase warranted an evidentiary hearing to resolve claim of ineffective assistance of counsel. **See also** *Bean v. Calderon*, 163 F.3d 1073 (9th Cir. 1998) ; *Christy v. Horn*, 28 F. Supp. 2d 307 (W.D. Pa. 1998) ; *U.S. Ex. Rel. Maxwell v. Gilmore* , 37 F.Supp. 2d 1078 (N.D. Ill. 1999); *Abdur Rahman v. Bell*, 999 F. Supp. 1073 (M.D. Tenn. 1998); *Correll v. Stewart*, 137 F.3d 1404 (9th Cir. 1998); *Dobbs v. Turpin*, 142 F.3d 1383 (11th Cir. 1998); *Jackson v. Herring*, 42 F.3d 1350 (11th Cir. 1995); *Baxter v. Thomas*, 45 F.3d 1501 (11th Cir. 1995); *Glock v. Singletary*, 84 F.3d 385 (11th Cir. 1994)

Carter v. Bell, 218 F.3d 581 (6th Cir. 2000)
>Defense counsel's failure to investigate and present mitigating evidence based on defendant's family, social, and psychological background during sentencing phase constitutes ineffective assistance of counsel.

Parker v. Bowersox, 188 F.3d 923 (8th Cir. 1999)
>Defense counsel's failure to call defendant's former trial attorney to testify during penalty phase that petitioner was aware prior to date of murder that victim was no longer a potential witness amounted to ineffective assistance.

Collier v. Turpin, 177 F.3d 1184 (11th Cir. 1999)
>Defense counsel's failure to present available mitigating evidence regarding defendant's background and character, including but not limited to defendant's upbringing and his mental and physical aliments, constitutes ineffective assistance where jury might not have imposed death penalty, absent counsel's errors and omissions.

Ivy v. Caspari, 173 F.3d 1136 (8th Cir. 1999)
>Defense counsel's failure to present a psychiatrist's report indicating mental illness constituted ineffective assistance of counsel.

Wallace v. Stewart, 184 F.3d 1112 (9th Cir. 1999)
>Counsel's failure to present mental health evidence to defense expert, which would have showed defendant's dysfunctional family history, in penalty phase in capital murder sentencing constituted ineffective assistance of counsel.

Antwine v. Delo, 54 F.3d 1357 (8th Cir. 1995)
>Counsel's failure to fully investigate defendant's mental condition, which would have shown defendant suffered from a "bi-polar disorder" at the time of the crime, and had

this evidence been found and presented to the jury the defendant's mental impairment, the jury might not have imposed the death sentence.

Williams v. Turpin, 87 F.3d 1204 (11th Cir. 1996)
Counsel's failure to present mitigating evidence that petitioner had been physically and sexually abused as a child during penalty phase could constitute ineffective assistance of counsel and required evidentiary hearing to resolve claim.

Austin v. Bell, 126 F.3d 843 (6th Cir. 1997)
Trial counsel's failure to investigate and present mitigating evidence at sentencing, where witnesses were available and willing to testify undermine adversarial process and, constitutes ineffective assistance.

Upshaw v. Singletary, 70 F.3d 576 (11th Cir. 1995)
Defense counsel's failure to investigate and present defenses and mitigating circumstance regarding defendant's mental state at the time of crime constituted ineffective assistance and required evidentiary hearing. **See also** *Emerson v. Gramley, 91 F.3d 898 (7th Cir. 1996)*; *Stephens v. Kemp, 846 F.2d 642 (11th Cir. 1988)*; *Tyler v. Kemp, 755 F.2d 741 (11th Cir. 1985)*; *Loyd v. Smith, 899 F.2d 1416 (5th Cir. 1990)*; *Middleton v. Dugger, 849 F.2d 491 (11th Cir. 1988)*; *Williamson v. Reynolds, 904 F.Supp. 1529 (E.D. Okl. 1995)*; *Armstrong v. Dugger, 833 F.2d 1430 (11th Cir. 1987)*; *Butler v. Summer, 783 F.Supp. 519 (D. Nev. 1991)*; *Evans v. Lewis, 855 F.2d 631 (9th Cir. 1988)*; *Mathis v. Zant, 704 F.Supp. 1062 (N.D.Ga. 1989)*; *Porter v. Wainwright, 805 F.2d 930 (11th Cir. 1986)*

Hendricks v. Vasquez, 974 F.2d 1099 (9th Cir. 1992)
Defense counsel's failure to call family members to testify about defendant's childhood during penalty phase of capital murder trial may constitute ineffective assistance and requires an evidentiary hearing to develop the facts.

Waters v. Zant, 979 F.2d 1473 (11th Cir. 1992)
Defense counsel's failure to elicit available mitigating evidence from defendant's medical expert in respect to defendant's mental illness constitutes ineffectiveness at sentencing.

Wilson v. Butler, 813 F.2d 664 (5th Cir. 1987)
Trial counsel's failure to pursue mental impairment as a mitigating factor at sentencing may constitute ineffective assistance of counsel and an evidentiary hearing was warranted to determine whether counsel's action was a strategic decision.

Ford v. Lockhart, 861 F.Supp. 1447 (E.D. Ark. 1994)
Trial counsel was ineffective in capital case where counsel failed to investigate defendant's past family history, where counsel would have learned that defendant's father had beaten defendant frequently, beat defendant's mother, and stayed drunk, which caused emotional harm to defendant and may have led jury to impose life sentence without parole instead of death sentence.

Kubat v. Thieret, 867 F.2d 351 (7th Cir. 1989)
Trial counsel's failure to introduce mitigating evidence during death penalty phase and relied solely on a plea for mercy to avoid death penalty constituted ineffective assistance of counsel and was prejudicial to defendant.

Brewer v. Aiken, 935 F.2d 850 (7th Cir. 1991)
> Counsel's failure to investigate defendant's mental and family history as well as counsel's failure to present mitigating evidence to the jury during penalty phase of capital murder trial, constituted ineffective assistance of counsel.

Kwan Fai Mak v. Blodgett, 754 F.Supp. 1490 (W.D. Wash. 1991)
> Trial counsel's failure to present mitigating evidence at penalty phase of capital murder prosecution was prejudicial and constituted ineffective assistance of counsel, in light of the fact that co-defendant convicted of 13 murders did not receive the death penalty and the prosecutor's closing argument focused on counsel's failure to present any positive human qualities in the defendant.

Johnson v. Dugger, 911 F.2d 440 (11th Cir. 1990)
> Defense counsel's failure to develop evidence relevant to defendant's psychological state of mind at the time of crime constituted ineffective assistance of counsel. **See also *U.S. v. Burrows, 872 F.2d 915 (9th Cir. 1989); Blanco v. Singletary, 943 F.2d 1477 (11th Cir. 1991); Buenoano v. Singletary, 963 F.2d 1433 (11th Cir. 1992); Cave v. Singletary, 971 F.2d 1513 (11th Cir. 1992); Boliek v. Delo, 912 F.Supp. 1199 (W.D. Mo. 1995); Bolder v. Armontrout, 713 F.Supp. 1558 (W.D. Mo. 1989);***

Deutscher v. Whitley, 884 F.2d 1152 (9th Cir. 1989)
> Counsel's failure to investigate and present mitigating evidence, through a psychiatrist who examined defendant and would have testified that defendant's history was consistent with mental disorder, characterized by episodes of uncontrollable violence, which testimony would have rebutted state's evidence, constituted ineffective assistance of counsel.

Loyd v. Whitley, 977 F.2d 149 (5th Cir. 1992)
> Trial counsel's failure to secure an independent psychological evaluation of defendant and failure to present expert testimony on defendant's mental condition at time of murder, amounted to ineffective assistance of counsel.

Hall v. Washington, 106 F.3d 742 (7th Cir. 1997)
> Trial counsel's failure to investigate defendant's mental condition where it is apparent from the crime itself and conversations with the defendant that he suffered from mental problems, which would constitute mitigating evidence for sentencing, was ineffective assistance of counsel. **See also *Martinez-Macias v. Collins, 810 F.Supp. 782 (W.D. Tex. 1991); Hendricks v. Calderon, 70 F.3d 1032 (9th Cir. 1995)***

Wood v. Zahradnick, 611 F.2d 1383 (4th Cir. 1980)
> Trial counsel's failure to present evidence that the defendant was an alcoholic and had drank too much, and failure to investigate an insanity defense, which would have explained mental state of mind at the time of crime, constituted ineffective assistance of counsel.

Sentencing Ineffectiveness

Defendant's Social History; Psychiatric Disorders; Disadvantaged Childhood; Drinking Problems; Head Injury; Mental Retardation; Socioeconomic Background; Reputation as Good Father.

Williams v. Taylor, 529 U.S. 362, 146 LEd.2d 389, 120 S. Ct. 1495 (2000)
>   Counsel's failure to introduce a comparatively voluminous amount of evidence in the accused's favor during a capital sentencing hearing constituted ineffective assistance of counsel.

Morales v. Mitchell, 507 F.3d 916, 931-936 (6th Cir. 2007)
>   Counsel provides constitutionally ineffective assistance in this aggravated murder and kidnapping case where a death sentence was imposed because counsel failed to prepare for the penalty phase. Counsel failed to investigate Morales alcoholic and dysfunctional family environment and possible mental problems which might have undermined the unanimity jury requirement in death penalty case.

Lambright v. Schriro, 485 F.3d 512, 528-532 (9th Cir. 2007)
>   Counsel provided constitutionally ineffective assistance for failing to investigate and present mitigating evidence concerning Lambright's childhood, long term drug abuse and impaired mental conditions.

Anderson v. Sirmons, 476 F.3d 1131, 1146-1148 (10th Cir. 2007)
>   Counsel provided constitutionally ineffective assistance for failing to present mitigating evidence concerning Anderson's brain damage and borderline mental illness during penalty phase.

Hovey v. Ayers, 458 F.3d 892, 930 (9th Cir. 2006)
>   Defense counsel provided constitutionally ineffective assistance for failing to prepare the defense expert psychiatrist witness, Dr. Satten, with Hovey's prior mental history, which left the jury with the erroneous impression that Hovey had never been treated for mental illness before committing his crime, and that Hovey may have fabricated a mental illness to obtain mercy at sentencing, requiring the death sentence to be set aside.

Frierson v. Woodford, 463 F.3d 982, 989 (9th Cir. 2006)
>   Counsel was constitutionally ineffective for failing to investigate for the penalty phase and present mitigating evidence concerning Frierson's extensive drug history; early childhood head trauma, mental impairment, organic brain damage; and child abuse.

Boyde v. Brown, 421 F.3d 1154, 1155 (9th Cir. 2005)
>   Counsel's failure to introduce evidence during the penalty phase that Boyde suffered physical abuse as a child and that his sisters were sexual abused required an evidentiary hearing to resolve ineffective assistance of counsel claim.

Summerlin v. Schriro, 427 F.3d 623, 642 (9th Cir. 2005)
>   Counsel's failure to investigate or interview witnesses related to Summerlin's troubled childhood history of physical and mental abuse, and to present mitigating evidence during penalty phase of capital murder trial constitutes ineffective assistance of counsel and required resentencing.

Marshall v. Cathel, *428 F.3d 452, 465 (3rd Cir. 2005)*
> Counsel's failure to investigate present mitigating evidence, to make a plea for life, and to recognize the difference between the guilt and punishment phase of capital murder trial amounted to ineffective assistance of counsel.

Daniels v. Woodford, *428 F.3d 1181, 1202 (9th Cir. 2005)*
> Counsel was ineffective for failing to investigate Daniel's mental illness, brain damage and present mitigating evidence during the penalty phase.

Stankewitz v. Woodford, *365 F.3d 706, 716-18 (9th Cir. 2004)*
> Counsel's failure to investigate, to present social background and mental health evidence during the penalty phase of capital murder trial, required a remand for an evidentiary hearing to develop the record on petitioner's claims, that he was removed from his home at the age of six because his mother had severely beat him, and spent most of the rest of his youth in state homes where he was sexually and physically abused.

Frazier v. Huffman, *343 F.3d 780, 797-799 (6th Cir. 2003)*
> Counsel's failure to investigate and present mitigating evidence based on petitioner's brain impairment, where there was at least one juror who would have voted against death penalty constituted ineffective assistance.

Cargle v. Mullin, *317 F.3d 1196, 1221 (10th Cir. 2003)*
> Counsel's failure to investigate and present mitigating evidence from petitioner's mother concerning: petitioner's premature birth, physical and learning problems, which might have prevented the imposition of the death sentence constitutes ineffective assistance of counsel.

Douglas v. Woodford, *316 F.3d 1079, 1090-1093 (9th Cir. 2002)*
> Counsel failure to investigate and present petitioner's mental health and social background from a doctor who had examined petitioner in prior case where the doctor's testimony would have revealed that petitioner had a "serious and outstanding mental illness" and explained how toxic solvents used by petitioner in his work may have exacerbated petitioner's pre-existing neurological deficit, constitutes ineffective assistance of counsel.

Brownlee v. Harley, *306 F.3d 1043, 1070 (11th Cir. 2002)*
> Counsel was constitutionally ineffective during penalty phase of capital murder trial. Counsel failed to investigate and present mitigating evidence to the jury that Brownlee was borderline mentally retarded, psychiatric disorders, a history of drug and alcohol abuse that undermines the confidence in Browlee's death sentence proceedings.

United States v. Ex Rel. Clemons v. Walls, *202 F.Supp. 2d 767, 781 (N.D. Ill. 2002)*
> Counsel was constitutionally ineffective for failing to present mitigating evidence during sentencing phase of first degree murder trial where petitioner's mother and brothers testimony at sentencing would have put case in a different light.

Turner v. Calderon, *281 F.3d 851, 892-97 (9th Cir. 2002)*
> Counsel's failure to investigate Turner's long-term drug use, abusive and difficult childhood and present evidence of such during the penalty phase required an evidentiary hearing to resolve the ineffectiveness of counsel claim.

Sentencing Ineffectiveness

Smith v. Stewart, 241 F.3d 1191 (9th Cir. 2001)
Counsel's failure to adequately investigate and present mitigating evidence concerning defendant's miserable childhood, mental disabilities and impairment at the time of the offense required an evidentiary hearing to resolve ineffectiveness of counsel claim.

Battenfield v. Gibson, 236 F.3d 1215, 1228-35 (10th Cir. 2001)
Counsel was constitutionally ineffective because counsel failed to investigate or interview any witnesses regarding the mitigating aspects of defendant's background with respect to prior conviction and personality, which could have led jury to reach a different sentence than death.

Skaggs v. Parker, 235 F.3d 261, 269 (6th Cir. 2000)
Counsel was ineffective for using an <u>incompetent</u> and <u>fraudulent</u> <u>psychologist</u> witness during mitigation. Counsel observed the same psychologist witness bizarre and eccentric testimony during guilty phase. Counsel failed to present a realistic view of Skaggs mental status that probably would have resulted in the jury imposing a life sentence, rather than death sentence.

Jackson v. Calderon, 211 F.3d 1148(9th Cir. 2000)
Defense counsel's failure to investigate and compile social history and develope mitigating factors based on the defendant's intoxication from (PCP) phencydicline which could have established a 90% medical certainly that defendant was unable to think consciously when he committed crime amounted to ineffective assistance of counsel.

Morales v. Coyle, 98 F.Supp.2d 849 (N.D. Ohio 2000)
Defense counsel's failure to present mitigating evidence during penalty phase constituted ineffective assistance of counsel.

Caro v. Calderon, 165 F.3d 1223 (9th Cir. 1999)
Defense counsel's failure to investigate defendant's organic brain damage or other mental impairments and failure to seek expert opinion on defendant's extraordinary exposure to neurotoxicants, neurological impairments, and personal background required an evidentiary hearing to resolve claim of ineffectiveness of counsel.

Valdez v. Johnson, 93 F.Supp.2d 769 (S.D. Tex. 1999)
Counsel's failure to investigate and present mitigating evidence to the jury that the defendant was mentally retarded and was a positive influence on people around him, despite his childhood of physical and emotional abuse, amounted to ineffective assistance of counsel. **See also _Thomas v. Kemp_, 796 F.2d 1322 (11th Cir. 1986)**

Glenn v. Tate, 71 F.3d 1204 (6th Cir. 1995)
Trial counsel failed to prepare case and present mitigating evidence that the defendant's family considered defendant "slow" and that defendant's clinical psychological evaluation report show a full scale IQ score of 56, placing defendant "within the mental defective range." Another evaluation showed defendant was "an ineffectual and dependent young man" who "is very anxious and insecure", that he left school virtually illiterate, that his mother beat him, and that he was hyperactive as a child. As such, counsel's deficiencies constitutes ineffective assistance of counsel.

Wade v. Calderon, 29 F3d 1312 (9th Cir. 1994)

Defense counsel's failure to argue and present evidence from defendant's sister and mother that defendant's stepfather abused him as a child constituted ineffective assistance of counsel during penalty phrase.

Cunningham v. Zant, 928 F.2d 1006 (11th Cir. 1991)

Defense counsel's failure, at penalty phase of capital murder and armed robbery prosecution, to present and argue evidence of petitioner's head injury, mental retardation, his socioeconomic background, plus petitioner's reputation as a good worker and father, constituted ineffective assistance of counsel.

Judge's Addiction to Marijuana

Summerlin v. Stewart, 267 F.3d 926, 948-53 (9th Cir. 2001)

Summerlin was entitled to evidentiary hearing on claim that trial judge's alleged use of and addiction to marijuana, deprived petitioner of due process in death penalty case.

Judge's Compensatory Bias

Bracy v. Schoming, 286 F.3d 406, 412-18 (7th Cir. 2002)

A judge in a capital murder trial who had engaged in compensatory bias during penalty phase of trial, in order to prevent suspicion that he was accepting bribes in other criminal cases, supported determination that defendant's due process rights were violated and warranted to a new penalty hearing.

Polygraph Evidence Excluded

Rupe v. Wood, 93 F.3d 1434 (9th Cir. 1996)

The trial court excluded the results of polygraph test of state's witness in penalty phase which violated defendant's due process rights to have relevant, mitigating evidence surrounding the crime to presented to the jury for deciding between penalty of life or death; were issues of relative credibility and culpability between defendant and witness, and without polygraph evidence allowed prosecutor to persuasively argue against defendant's credibility.

Plausible Defenses

Osborn v. Shillinger, 861 F.2d 612 (10th Cir. 1988)

Defense counsel's failure to adequately prepare or investigate plausible lines of defense for sentencing, constitutes ineffective assistance of counsel.

Douglas v. Wainwright, 739 F.2d 531 (11th Cir. 1984)

Trial counsel's failure to consult with defendant and inform him of option of taking stand and testifying in his own behalf compounded with other errors at sentencing amounted to ineffective assistance of counsel and required an evidentiary hearing.

Counsel's Absence During Resentencing

Hall v. Moore, 253 F.3d 624, 627 (11th Cir. 2001)

> The absence of counsel at resentencing violated *Hall's* Sixth Amendment right to counsel.

Restrictive Rules Not Applicable for Penalty Phase

Williams v. New York, 337 U.S. 241, 247, 69 S.Ct. 1079, 93 L.Ed.2d 1337 (1949)

> A judge or jury at a capital sentencing hearing should "not be denied an opportunity to obtain pertinent information by a requirement of rigid adherence to restrictive rules of evidence properly applicable to the trial."

Ex Post Facto Violation

Murtishaw v. Woodford, 255 F.3d 926 (9th Cir. 2001)

> The district court instructing the jury based on the **1978 California death penalty statute**, rather than the **1977 statute** in effect at the time of the offense, violated the ex post facto clause and warranted habeas relief from the death sentence.

Booth-El v. Nuth, 140 F.Supp.2d 495 (D.Md. 2001)

> The removal of diminished capacity as a result of intoxication as a statutory mitigating factor at defendant's 1990 re-sentencing was an unconstitutional ex post facto law and requires resentencing.

Visible Shackles & Handcuffs

Ruimveld v. Birkett, 404 F.3d 1006, 1018 (6th Cir. 2005)

> Shackling defendant in front of jury violated defendant's right to a fair trial and warranted habeas relief.

Roche v. Davis, 291 F.3d 473, 483 (7th Cir. 2002)

> Defense counsel was constitutionally ineffective because he failed to ensure that Roche's shackles were concealed from jury during the penalty phase of capital murder trial. Roche was prejudiced by counsel's omission because considerable mitigating evidence was presented during the penalty phase and the jury was unable to recommend the death penalty after eight (8) hours of deliberations.

Roche v. Anderson, 132 F.Supp. 2d 688 (N.D. Ind. 2001)

> Trial counsel was ineffective for failing to object to petitioner being shackled during the guilty and penalty phases of the trial which deprived petitioner of his due process rights to a fair trial.

Laird v. Horn, 159 F.Supp. 2d 58 (E.D. Pa. 2001)

> Petitioner's right to a fair and reliable capital sentencing was violated where he was forced to wear visible shackles and handcuffs in front of the jury.

Prosecutor's Case on Sentencing Recommendation

Thomas v. Lockhart, 738 F.2d 304 (8th Cir. 1984)
> Trial counsel's failure to investigate similarities and differences between defendant's case and case that prosecutor referred to recommending a 30-year sentence as part of plea agreement, constituted ineffective assistance of counsel.

FAILED TO INVESTIGATE OR OBJECT TO:

Aggravating Circumstance Jury Instruction

Esparza v. Mitchell, 310 F.3d 414, 420-421 (6th Cir. 2002)
> A death sentence could not be imposed because the state failed to charge aggravating circumstances in the indictment; failed to instruct the jury on aggravating circumstances, and the jury did not reach a verdict on aggravating circumstances beyond a reasonable doubt.

Banks v. Horn, 271 F.3d 527, 548-50 (3rd Cir. 2001)
> Jury instructions and verdict slip form used in capital murder trial during penalty phase which indicated jury was to have made such a finding "unanimously," could be interpreted by a reasonable jury as requiring a unanimous finding of mitigating circumstances, therefore, was unconstitutional; verdict form was confusing; and suggestive, regarding need for unanimity as to aggravating circumstances.

Thomas v. Gibson, 218 F.3d 1213 (10th Cir. 2000)
> The evidence was insufficient to satisfy heinous atrocious or cruel aggravating factors for the imposition of the death penalty under Oklahoma law and required the death sentence be reversed.

United States v. Chanthadara, 230 F.3d 1237, 1267-68 (10th Cir. 2000)
> Trial judge's smoke screen comment "might have contributed to the death sentence" due to lack of overwhelming evidence supporting statutory aggravating factor requirements and such error was not harmless.

Lockett v. Puckett, 980 F. Supp. 201 (S.D. Miss. 1997)
> The court held in pertinent part that "defendant was entitled to habeas relief on death sentence for husbands murder based on absence of factual findings to support especially heinous aggravating factor, in murder involving quick death with little or no warning to victim."

McKenna v. McDaniel, 65 F.3d 1483 (9th Cir. 1995)
> The depravity of mind aggravating circumstance instruction in capital murder case was determined unconstitutionally vague required remand for resentencing in federal habeas proceedings.

Starr v. Lockhart, 23 F.3d 1280 (8th Cir. 1994)
> Trial counsel's failure to object to either "pecuniary gain" or "heinous atrocious or cruel" aggravating circumstances jury instructions during penalty phase, amounted to ineffective assistance of counsel.

Coercive Jury Instruction

Henderson v. Collins, 101 F.Supp.2d 866 (S.D. Ohio 1999)
> The district court's supplemental jury instruction requiring jury to continue deliberations on death sentence was unconstitutionally coercive which required the death sentence to be vacated.

Eighth Amendment Claims

Mills v. Maryland, 486 U.S. 367, 108 S.Ct. 1860, 100 L.Ed.2d 384 (1988)
> The Supreme Court held that a death penalty should be vacated as violate of the Eighth Amendment if there is a substantial probability that reasonable Jurors, upon receiving the trial judge's instructions and attempting to complete the verdict form based on those instructions, may have thought that they could only consider those mitigating factors which they unanimously found to exist. **486 U.S. at 376, 108 S.Ct. 1860.**

Dickerson v. Bagley, 453 F.3d 690, 696-699 (6th Cir. 2006)
> Counsel was constitutionally ineffective for failing to investigate mitigating evidence that showed defendant's IQ score was close to retarded level and the execution of the retarded was prohibited by the Eighth Amendment.

Bigby v. Dretke, 402 F.3d 551, 571 (5th Cir. 2005)
> The special issues and supplemental instruction failed to allow the jury to consider mitigating evidence and stripped it of a vehicle for expressing its reasoned moral response to appropriateness of death penalty violated the Eighth Amendment.

Bigby v. Cockrell, 340 F.3d 259, 273-275 (5th Cir. 2003)
> The trial court's instruction which removed the jury's consideration of mitigating evidence that petitioner suffered from chronic paranoid schizophrenia violated the Eighth Amendment.

Belmontes v. Woodford, 350 F.3d 861, 895-901 (9th Cir. 2003)
> The jury instruction at sentencing was insufficient to satisfy the Eighth Amendment concerns that the jury consider and weigh all mitigating evidence presented by petitioner.

Porter v. Horn, 276 F.Supp. 2d 278, 302-05 (E.D. Pa. 2003)
> The trial court's failure to advise jury that any juror who individually found mitigating circumstances could weigh that against the aggravating circumstances found, even if there was not unanimity as to the existence of that mitigating circumstance. The penalty phase jury instructions and verdict sheet that indicated the jury had to unanimously find a mitigating circumstances before it could be given effect in the sentencing decision violated the Eighth and Fourteenth Amendments of the U.S. Constitution.

Erroneous Jury Instruction

Kubat v. Thieret, 867 F.2d 351 (7th Cir. 1989)
> Defense counsel's failure to object to court's erroneous jury instruction during death penalty phase of case, constituted ineffective assistance of counsel.

Crowe v. Sowders, 864 F.2d 430 (6th Cir. 1988)
> Trial counsel's failure to object or move for a mistrial or file a motion for a new trial, after the judge erroneously instructed jury based on parole "consequences", which was not a matter for the jury, constituted ineffective assistance of counsel.

Goodwin v. Balkcom, 684 F.2d 794 (11th Cir. 1982)
> Failure to object to a clearly erroneous jury instruction in capital case, which denied jury of opportunity to impose life sentence even though aggravating circumstances existed, constituted ineffective assistance.

Life Sentence Carried No Possibility of Parole

Shafer v. South Carolina, 532 U.S. 36, 149 L.Ed.2d 178, 121 S.Ct. 1263 (2001)
> Due Process in capital case requires whenever defendant's future dangerousness was at issue, jury be properly informed that life sentence carried no possibility of parole under South Carolina sentencing scheme.

Judge's Misleading Response About Parole Availability

Capenter v. Vaughn, 296 F.3d 138,156-59 (3rd Cir. 2002)
> Counsel's failure to object in penalty phase of capital murder trial to the trial judge's misleading response to a jury note about the availability of parole, if the defendant received a life sentence amounted to ineffective assistance of counsel.

Presentation Alone Perception of Dangerous

Comer v. Schriro, 463 F.3d 934, 963-965 (9th Cir. 2006)
> Comer's due process rights were violated by sentencing him to death while being shackled in a wheelchair and slumped to one side of the wheelchair with blood oozing from his head wounds, nearly naked, and barely conscious with only a blanket half covering him. This presentation alone certainly increased the perception of Comer's dangerousness and warranted setting aside the death sentence.

Death Sentence Barred By Double Jeopardy

Arizona v. Rumsey, 467 U.S. 203 (1984)
> A life sentence implies a defendant in a capital case was acquitted of the necessary factual findings to impose the death penalty because a sentencing proceedings is like a trial. The Court then reasoned that the imposition of the death penalty is barred by double jeopardy even if a life sentence is set- aside on appeal or results from an erroneous evidentiary ruling or legal principles.

Consecutive Sentence

Beavers v. Lockhart, 755 F.2d 657 (8th Cir. 1985)
> Appellate counsel was ineffective and required an evidentiary hearing where counsel failed to raise the issue of the trial court's imposition of consecutive sentence.

PRIOR CONVICTION RELATED INEFFECTIVENESS

Failed to Investigate Prior Conviction

Rompilla v. Beard, 545 U.S. 374, 162 L.Ed.2d 360, 125 S.Ct. 2456 (2005)
> Trial counsel was constitutionally ineffective for failing to investigate and examine the court file on Rompilla's prior conviction because the Commonwealth intended to seek the death penalty based on Rompilla's prior record, which indicated the use or threat of violence, as aggravator under state law.

United States v. Russell, 221 F.3d 615, 621 (4th Cir. 2000)
> Counsel was constitutionally ineffective by failing to investigate or confirm the status of two of Russell's three prior convictions used to impeach Russell's credibility, after Russell informed counsel that convictions had been "overturned" and were invalid, counsel could have verified that convictions had been vacated because Russell's credibility was paramount to the jury's deliberation.

Hill v. U.S., 118 F.Supp. 2d 910, 915-16 (E.D. Wis. 2000)
> Defense counsel's failure to investigate predicate offenses used for armed career criminal sentence enhancement, where predicate offenses showed through receipt of discharge certificates that previous felonies contained no firearm restrictions constituted ineffective assistance of counsel.

Collateral Challenge to State Prior Conviction

Daniels v. United States, 532 U.S. 374, 149 L.Ed.2d 590, 121 S.Ct. 1598 (2001)
> An accused is not entitled to collateral challenge his prior state convictions used to enhance his federal sentence in a **28 U.S.C. §2255** motion to vacate, set aside or correct sentence, except in a rare circumstances. The Court declined to address what the rare circumstances in which **§2255** relief would be available.

Custis v. United States, 511 U.S. 485, 128 L.Ed.2d 517, 114 S.Ct. 1732 (1994)
> A federal prisoner cannot attack the validity of his previous state convictions used to enhance his federal sentence under **28 U.S.C. §2255**, with the sole exception of the convictions obtained in violation of the right to counsel. However, a prisoner can file in state court contesting the validity of prior conviction and then commence §2255 proceedings as long as its timely.

United States v. Clark, 284 F.3d 563, 566-67 (5th Cir. 2002)
> The Fifth Circuit found that a "prisoner who has no channel of review actually available to him with respect to a prior conviction, due to no fault of his own, is excepted from the general rule" of **Daniels v. United States, 532 U.S. 374, 121 S. Ct. 1731, 149 L. Ed. 2d 590 (2001)**, and that such exception was not available to Clark,

who never attempted any attack on his state convictions until four years after his federal sentence was imposed.

Failed to Object to Maryland Prior Conviction

Somerville v. Conway, 281 F.Supp.2d 515, 522 (E.D.N.Y. 2003)
> Counsel was constitutionally ineffective by failing to object to the use of Maryland prior conviction for robbery, that should not have been used by the sentencing court in its determination, that petitioner was a second violent felony offender, which would have resulted in a lesser sentence.

Failed to Object to Commercial Burglary

Rios-Delgado v. U.S., 117 F.Supp. 2d 581 (W.D. Tex. 2000)
> Defense counsel's failure to object, in illegal reentry case, to the imposition of a 16-level enhancement based on the classification of his prior felony conviction of Commercial Burglary as an aggravated felony constituted ineffective assistance of counsel.

Validity of Conviction Used to Enhance Sentence

Strachan v. Army Clemency and Parole BD., 151 F.3d 1308 (10th Cir. 1998)
> District court's findings that inmate's state court conviction was counseled was clearly erroneous where court relied on petitioner's plea agreement which contained a location for counsel's signature, but there was no signature of counsel and petitioner was entitled to hearing to determine the validity of conviction.

Abdur Rahman v. Bell, 999 F. Supp. 1073 (M.D. Tenn. 1998)
> Defense counsel's failure to investigate defendant's prior murder conviction where evidence existed to mitigate prior murder conviction constituted ineffective assistance of counsel.

Childress v. Johnson, 103 F.3d 1221 (5th Cir. 1997)
> Appointment of counsel in an earlier state court proceeding, to stand with the defendant in Court, execute a jury waiver, and plea, was not counsel at all as required by the Sixth Amendment. The earlier conviction could not be used to enhance defendant's sentence in a subsequent proceeding.

U.S. v. Kissick, 69 F.3d 1048 (10th Cir. 1995)
> Trial counsel's failure to object or challenge the use of a prior conviction which was insufficient to fit the definition of a controlled substance offense to place defendant in the status of a career offender under the Sentencing Guidelines constitutes ineffective assistance, and prejudice was shown because defendant received a harsher sentence.

Cook v. Lynaugh, 821 F.2d 1072 (5th Cir. 1987)
> Trial counsel's failure to investigate defendant's prior convictions that were used to enhance defendant's sentence, where facts of prior would have shown that defendant's prior nolo contendere plea was unconstitutional, constitutes ineffective assistance of counsel.

**Douglas v. Wainwright**, _714 F.2d 1532 (11th Cir. 1983)_
>   Trial and appellate counsel's failure to raise fact that defendant's prior conviction used was invalid, constitutes ineffective assistance of counsel.

Nolo Contendere Prior Conviction

**Harrison v. Jones**, _880 F.2d 1279 (11th Cir. 1989)_
>   Counsel's failure to object to the admission of prior convictions at sentencing, constituted ineffective assistance of counsel. Since at least 1954, convictions based on pleas of nolo contendere have not been admissible in criminal prosecutions in Alabama for any purpose, including challenging the credibility of a witness.

Philippine Conviction

**U.S. v. Kole**, _164 F.3d 164 (3rd Cir. 1998)_
>   The Court held that the use of Philippine conviction as basis for sentence enhancement did not violate due process.

Validity of "Mexican Conviction"

**U.S. v. Moskovits**, _784 F.Supp. 183 (E.D. Pa. 1991)_
>   Trial counsel's failure to object to the validity of a Mexican conviction used to enhance defendant's sentence, constitutes ineffective assistance, where it was clear that defendant was denied counsel at critical stages of Mexican proceedings. Mexican conviction could not be used to enhance defendant's sentence.

Stipulating to Non-Existent Prior Conviction

**Lewis v. Lane**, _832 F.2d 1446 (7th Cir. 1987)_
>   The Court held that: (1) Petitioner's procedural default with respect to contesting validity of prior felony convictions was caused by States' concealment of evidence of their invalidity; (2) defense counsel's stipulation to existence of convictions, ultimately determined to be nonexistent, constituted ineffective assistance of counsel, prejudicial to petitioner and entitled him to new sentencing hearing.

Habitual Offender

**Esslinger v. Davis**, _44 F.3d 1515 (11th Cir. 1995)_
>   Defense counsel's failure to adequately investigate defendant's prior criminal history and recommended defendant to enter a blind guilty plea to a class A felony, which was subsequently enhanced under Alabama's Habitual Offender Act, constitutes ineffective assistance of counsel where there was a reasonable probability that defendant would have proceeded to trial, absent counsel's errors.

**Jones v. Lockhart**, _851 F.2d 1115 (8th Cir. 1988)_
>   The Court of Appeals affirmed the district court's dismissal of petitioner's pro se petition without prejudice to afford the petitioner an opportunity to file a new petition in the district court where petitioner raised a new substantial factual issue that he did not

receive actual notice of the nature of the charge against him and a claim of ineffective assistance of counsel in relation to defendant being illegally sentenced as an habitual offender.

Peoples v. Bowen, 791 F.2d 861 (11th Cir. 1986)
Appellate counsel's failure to advise defendant that if he appealed the twenty (20) year sentenced, that the Court of Appeals may remand for resentencing, at which time defendant would receive life under the mandatory habitual felony offender statute, constituted ineffective assistance of counsel.

Conviction Obtained in Violation of the 6th Amendment

U.S. v. Akins, 276 F.3d 1141, 1149 (9th Cir. 2002)
The government was prohibited from using defendant's prior state misdemeanor conviction for domestic assault charge, to support federal conviction for possession of a firearm following conviction for a misdemeanor domestic violence crime because the waiver of right to counsel did not include a *Faretta* warning, explaining the dangers and disadvantage of proceeding pro se without counsel. Therefore, the state conviction was obtained in violation of Akins' Sixth Amendment right to counsel.

Greene v. U.S., 880 F.2d 1299 (11th Cir. 1989)
A conviction sustained in violation of the Sixth Amendment right to counsel cannot be used to enhance sentence, but defendant was procedurally barred from contesting the validity of the prior conviction.

Juvenile Prior Convictions

Girtman v. Lockhart, 942 F.2d 468 (8th Cir. 1991)
Trial counsel's failure to object to the district court's use of a prior burglary conviction, which occurred when defendant was a juvenile, to place defendant in habitual offender category constitutes ineffective assistance of counsel.

Presentence Report Ineffectiveness Claims

U.S. v. Gordon, 172 F.3d 753 (10th Cir. 1999)
Gordon alleged that his substitute counsel was ineffective for not discussing the Presentence Report (PSR) with him, and by failing to bring to the court's attention factual inaccuracies in the PSR which were relevant to determinations of relevant conduct and acceptance of responsibility. The district court held that these claims were procedurally barred because Gordon failed to raise them on direct appeal. The Tenth Circuit **REVERSED and REMANDED** to the district court to consider the merits of these claims.

U.S. v. Davenport, 151 F.3d 1325 (11th Cir. 1998)
Presentence report must be disclosed to both defense counsel and defendant at least ten (10) days prior to sentencing as mandated by statute.

U.S. v. Sustaita, 1 F.3d 950 (9th Cir. 1993)

Sentencing judge's failure to determine whether defendant had read presentence report or discussed it with her counsel, as required by _Rules of Criminal Procedure_, was prejudicial error requiring remand for resentencing in narcotics prosecution; defense counsel made no specific objection to any fact in presentence report, and defendant could not have tried to contradict report's factual finding that conspiracy involved 5 kilograms of heroin had she been given opportunity to read or discuss it.

West v. U.S., 994 F.2d 518 (8th Cir. 1993)

Trial counsel's failure to object to errors in the presentence report can constitute ineffective assistance. **See also** _U.S. v. Bartholomew_, 974 F.2d 39 (5th Cir. 1992); _United States v. Stevens_, 851 F.2d 140, 145 (6th Cir. 1988); _Jordan v. Housewright_, 620 F.Supp. 47 (D.C. Nev. 1985); _Ryder v. Morris_, 752 F.2d 327, 332-33 (8th Cir.)

Smith v. United States, 871 F.Supp. 251, 255 (E.D. Va. 1994)

Defense counsel's failure to lodge objections to clear and indisputable error in presentence report is not within the wide range of professional performance Remanded by the Sixth Amendment.

Haase v. United States, 800 F.2d 123 (7th Cir. 1986)

Defense counsel ill-advised Haase to decline to submit his "version of the offense" to the probation officer. The Court found this to be inadequate representation but refused to resentence Haase because the Court mistakenly believed that Haase could still bring a Rule 35 motion. The Seventh Circuit remanded for resentencing.

UNITED STATES SENTENCING GUIDELINES

Failed to Argue Applicability of Guideline Provisions:

Acceptance of Responsibility

U.S. v. Gordon, 172 F.3d 753 (10th Cir. 1999)

Gordon alleged that his substitute counsel was ineffective for not discussing the Presentence Report (PSR) with him and by failing to bring to the court's attention factual inaccuracies in the PSR, which were relevant to determinations of relevant conduct and acceptance of responsibility. The district court held that these claims were procedurally barred because Gordon failed to raise them on direct appeal. The Tenth Circuit **REVERSED and REMANDED** to the district court to consider the merits of these claims.

Brown v. U.S., 42 F.Supp. 2d 122 (D. Puerto Rico 1998)

Defense counsel's failure to move the court for a three level downward adjustment for acceptance of responsibility pursuant to _U.S.S.G. §3E1.1 (a, b)_, constituted ineffective assistance of counsel.

U.S. v. Mohammad, 999 F. Supp. 1198 (N.D. Ill. 1998)

Trial counsel's failure to explore possibilities of plea agreement which would have probably resulted in at least a two (2) level adjustment in defendant's base offense level for acceptance of responsibility and possibly a different adjustment relating to the defendant's role in the offense constituted ineffective assistance of counsel.

U.S. v. Garrett, 90 F.3d 210 (7th Cir. 1996)

The Court held that "defendant was entitled to three-level decrease in his sentencing score for acceptance of responsibility despite uncounseled motion to withdraw guilty plea." The defendant's first attorney died after he entered his plea, and he did not have counsel when he filed his motion to withdraw guilty plea.

U.S. v. Ford, 918 F.2d 1343 (8th Cir. 1990)

Trial counsel's failure to object to the probation officer's failure to reduce Ford's base offense level for accepting responsibility, in accordance to the Sentencing Guidelines constituted performance below an objective standard, and there existed a reasonable probability that Ford's sentence would have been reduced by over three (3) years, absent counsel's unprofessional errors and omissions. This claim was raised on direct appeal.

Booker Applies to Restitution

United States v. Holland, 380 F.Supp.2d 1264, 1273-75 (N.D. Ala. 2005)

Trial and appellate counsel was constitutionally ineffective where they failed to test the constitutionality of restitution award procedure because court imposed a penal sanction of restitution that was never charged in the indictment, nor proved beyond a reasonable doubt by the government as required by *Booker*.

Career Offender

United States v. Horney, 333 F.3d 1185, 1187-88 (10th Cir. 2003)

Counsel's failure to object to the use of Horey's prior conviction for possession of cocaine as a predicate offense for the Career Offender Enhancement, where possession of cocaine does not qualify as a predicate offense under §4B1.1, definition of a crime of violence, and constitutes ineffective assistance of counsel.

Stinson v. U.S., 102 F.Supp.2d 912 (M.D. Tenn. 2000)

Defense counsel's failure to move for a downward departure based on defendant's career offender designation overstated seriousness of defendant's criminal history constituted ineffective assistance of counsel. **See also *U.S. v. Hall*, 40 F.Supp. 2d 340 (D. Md. 1999)**

U.S. v. Williamson, 183 F.3d 458 (5th Cir. 1999)

Appellate counsel's failure to raise the ***Bellazerius* issue** which held that drug conspiracy conviction could not serve as trigger for **Career offender sentencing enhancement** constituted ineffective assistance of counsel and required resentencing without the use of the **Career Offender enhancement**.

U.S. v. Gaviria, 116 F.3d 1498 (D.C. Cir. 1997)

Defense counsel erroneously advised Gaviria that if he accepted the government's plea for conspiracy to distribute cocaine, a criminal forfeiture count, and a charge unlawful re-entry into the U.S. following deportation that he would be sentenced as a career offender to 360 months to life. Defense counsel's advice was erroneous because in

United States v. Price, 990 F.2d 1367, 1370 (D.C. Cir. 1993), the Court held that a defendant convicted of conspiracy could not be sentenced as a career offender because the statute under which the Guideline career offender provision was initially promulgated did not list conspiracy as a crime warranting career offender treatment. Gaviria proceeded to trial and was convicted and received a mandatory life. Had Gaviria been correctly advised by counsel, he would have received a Guideline range of 188-262 months. The Court of Appeals remanded for an evidentiary hearing to resolve the ineffective assistance claim.

U.S. v. Breckenridge, 93 F.3d 132 (4th Cir. 1996)
Trial counsel's failure to argue under the guidelines provisions §§4A1.2 and 4B1.1 that defendant's prior offense, which were consolidated for trial and "related" for sentencing purposes of career offender provisions, should be treated as a single sentence constitutes ineffective assistance of counsel.

U.S. v. Kissick, 69 F.3d 1048 (10th Cir. 1995)
Trial counsel's failure to object or challenge the use of a prior conviction which was insufficient to fit the definition of a controlled substance offense to place defendant in the status of a career offender under the Sentencing Guidelines constitutes ineffective assistance, and prejudice was shown because defendant received a harsher sentence.

Crack Cocaine Characterization

Ramirez v. U.S., 963 F. Supp. 329 (S.D.N.Y. 1997)
Counsel's failure to contest at sentencing the government's characterization of drugs involved in defendant's offense as "crack cocaine" was not ineffective assistance, when defendant made numerous statements during the guilty plea colloquy that he was involved with trafficking of crack cocaine.

U.S. v. Watts, 29 F.Supp. 2d 657 (E.D. Cal. 1998)
Counsel's failure to argue at sentencing the distinction in sentencing guidelines between "crack" cocaine and other forms of cocaine did not constitute-ineffective, absent any evidence suggesting that substance was form of cocaine other than crack.

Edawards v. United States, 523 U.S. 517, 140 L. Ed. 2d 703, 118 S.Ct. 1475 (1998)
"Federal Judge held… to determine for sentencing purposes whether crack as well as cocaine was involved in controlled-substances conspiracy."

Rice v. U.S., 971 F. Supp. 1297 (D. Minn. 1997)
Counsel's erroneously advised petitioner that cocaine base was crack which caused petitioner to plead guilty, entitled defendant to discovery on his ineffectiveness of counsel claim.

USSG §2D1.1 Drug Quantity

United States v. Stricklin, 290 F.3d 748, 751-52 (5th Cir. 2002)
Counsel's failure to object to the quantity of P2P, used to calculate Stricklin's base offense level constituted ineffective assistance. The Presentence Report used 2,500 milliliters of a mixture containing a detectable amount of P2P to determine Stricklin's base offense level. The 2,500 milliliters of a mixture containing a detectable amount

of P2P, contained a waste-by-product, which had to separated before the P2P could be used. Prejudice was shown under Strickland, because Amendment 484 of the Sentencing Guidelines required the Court to exclude the waste by-product before determining the defendant's base offense level. Had the waste-by-product been excluded, Stricklin's sentencing range would have been 63 to 78 months, as opposed to the 188 month sentence he received.

Johnson v. United States, 313 F.3d 815, 818 (3rd Cir. 2002)

Counsel was constitutionally ineffective for failing to object to Presentence Report's computation of Johnson's offense level pursuant to **U.S.S.G. §2D1.1 Application Note 12** "[i]n an offense involving an agreement to sell a controlled substance, the agreed upon quantity of the controlled substance shall be used to determine the offense level **unless the sale is completed and the amount delivered more accurately reflects the scale of the offense.**" Here, the sale was completed and there was no evidence that the **48.3** grams of crack actually sold did not represent the "scale of the offense," which would have produced a base offense level <u>30</u> as opposed to a level 32. Thus, defendant was prejudiced where he could have received a **121** month sentence as opposed to the **151** month sentence he received.

United States v. Rodriquez, 153 F.Supp.2d 590 (E.D. Pa 2001)

Counsel's failure to argue drug quantity assessed to defendant was improper required an evidentiary hearing to resolve ineffective assistance claim.

U.S. v. Mannino, 212 F.3d 835 (3rd Cir. 2000)

Appellate Counsel's failure to raise the issue that the district court's failure to apply the proper methodology in determining the amount heroin attributable to defendants in conspiracy to import and distribute heroin constituted ineffective assistance of counsel.

Arredondo v. U.S., 178 F.3d 778 (6th Cir. 1999)

Defense counsel's failure to object to drug quantity through relevant conduct of other codefendant's involved in the conspiracy required an evidentiary hearing to resolve ineffective assistance of counsel claim where defendant could have received eight-year difference in sentence.

Nichols v. U.S., 75 F.3d 1137 (7th Cir. 1996)

Trial counsel's failure to object or argue the amount of drugs attributed to defendant based on calculation of the Sentencing Guidelines, amounted to ineffective assistance of counsel where only witness' testimony gave wide range of amounts, and the court failed to make any findings of credibility of said witness' testimony.

United States v. Bounds, 943 F.2d 541 (1991)

For the first time on appeal, Bounds provides an impressive scientific explanation of precursor chemicals, theoretical yields, and the dramatic differences between phenylacetone and phenylacetic acid. He claims that the calculations of the government's expert witness were erroneous, that the government's expert witness was not qualified in forensic chemistry, and that the government failed to prove that the chemicals found could have been used to produce amphetamine. Evidence not produced at sentencing will not be considered on appeal. Bounds' only alternative at this stage is to show, if he can, that his attorney's failure to produce evidence, to challenge witnesses, and to assert a failure of proof constituted ineffective assistance of counsel.

Type of Methamphetamine

Welch v. United States, *134 F.Supp.2d 741 (W.D. N.C. 2001)*
 Counsel was constitutionally ineffective by failing to argue during sentencing that the government failed to prove the substance was d-methamphetamine; rather, than l-methamphetamine requiring resentencing.

U.S. v. Aguilar, *90 F.Supp.2d 1152 (D. Col. 2000)*
 Defense counsel's failure to object to the court's use of D- methamphetamine to determine sentence and to hold the government to the burden of proof at sentencing constitutes ineffective assistance of counsel.

U.S. v. Glover, *97 F.3d 1345 (10th Cir. 1996)*
 Counsel's failure to contest the fact that the government failed to prove that the alleged substance in the offense was D-methamphetamine constituted ineffective assistance where L-methamphetamine provided a significantly less harsh sentence.

Smith v. U.S., *945 F. Supp. 1439 (D. Col. 1996)*
 Trial counsel's failure to object to the presentence report regarding the type of methamphetamine involved constituted ineffective assistance.

U.S. v. Acklen, *47 F.3d 739 (5th Cir. 1995)*
 Trial counsel's failure to object to defendant's sentence being based on D-methamphetamine instead of the lower determination under l-methamphetamine, may constitute ineffective assistance of counsel.

U.S. v. Patrick, *983 F.2d 206,208 (11th Cir. 1993)*
 In order to determine whether Methamphetamine is D or L, the more sophisticated "plane polarized light" test or the "optically active column" test are required to distinguish the difference of D from L-Methamphetamine.

USSG §2D1.1(b)(1) Weapon Enhancement

Suggs v. United States, *513 F.3d 675, 679-680 (7th Cir. 2008)*
 Counsel's failure to challenge the sufficiency of evidence used to enhance Suggs' base offense level two levels pursuant to Sentencing Guideline Provision, **Section 2D1.1(b) (1)**, for possession of a dangerous weapon amounted to ineffective assistance.

USSG §5C1.2 Safety Value

Garcia v. United States, *301 F.Supp.2d 1275, 1282 (D.N.M. 2004)*
 Counsel was constitutionally ineffective for failing to object to the Presentence Report that increased petitioner's Criminal History Category Points by 2 points for a DWI, that occurred after the instant offense because those two points should not have been counted under **U.S.S.G. §4Al.l(b)**, and deprived petitioner of the benefits from the "safety value" pursuant to **18 U.S.C. §3553(f)** due to counsel's omissions.

Downward Departure Pursuant to *U.S.S.G. § 5K1.1*

U.S. v. De La Fuente, 8 F.3d 1333 (9th Cir. 1993)
> Trial counsel's failure to contest the government's breach of plea where the government failed to move for a downward departure below the mandatory minimum, pursuant to *U.S.S.G. § 5K1.1*, constitutes ineffective assistance and established cause for procedural default.

Diminished Mental Capacity

U.S. v Zedner, 401 F.3d 36, 52-53 (2d Cir. 2005)
> District Court erroneously concluded that it could not depart downward for diminished mental capacity in light of the jury verdict finding beyond a reasonable doubt that Zedner intended to defraud various financial institutions with counterfeit bonds. Contrary to the district court's conclusion, **Section 5K2.13** does not preclude a downward departure for diminished mental capacity because of a jury verdict and required a remand for resentencing under the advisory guidelines in accordance with ***Booker***. See also *U.S. v Milstein*, **401 F. 3d 53, 73 (2nd Cir. 2005)**.

Downward Departure Of Mandatory Sentence

U.S. v. Crawford, 407 F.3d 1174, 1182 (11th Cir. 2005)
> A sentencing court cannot depart downward under the advisory ***Booker*** guidelines for a defendant's substantial assistance, absent a government motion pursuant to **U.S.S.G. §5Kl.1**.

Dantzler v. U.S., 696 A.2d 1349 (D.C.App. 1997)
> Counsel's failure to present critical evidence qualifying defendant for addict exception to mandatory minimum sentence for distribution of controlled substance constituted ineffective assistance of counsel and warranted an evidentiary hearing to resolve claim.

U.S. v. Shorter, 54 F.3d 1248 (7th Cir. 1995)
> Counsel's failure to argue for a downward departure from the mandatory sentencing range because of a conflict of interest deprived defendant of opportunity to have district court impose a lesser term of imprisonment and warranted a new sentencing.

Ex Post Facto Application of Guidelines

United States v. Harmon, 409 F.3d 701, 706 (6th Cir. 2005)
> The district court must use the Guidelines Manual in effect at the time of sentencing. **See U.S.S.G. §1B1.11(a).** However, when the use of that Edition violates the ex post facto clause of the United States Constitution by producing a greater sentence than the earlier Edition, the earlier version must be used. **See U.S.S.G. §1B1.11(b).** The Court of Appeals remanded for resentencing with the use of the correct Guideline Manual in light of the advisory Guidelines under ***Booker***.

Illegal Reentry 16-Level Enhancement

Rios-Delgado v. U.S., 117 F.Supp. 2d 581 (W.D. Tex. 2000)
Defense counsel's failure to object, in illegal reentry case, to the imposition of a 16-level enhancement based on the classification of his prior felony conviction of Commercial Burglary as an aggravated felony constituted ineffective assistance of counsel.

United States v. Jaimes-Jaimes, 406 F.3d 845, 851 (7th Cir. 2005)
The district court made factual findings and enhanced Jaimes base offense 16 levels under the erroneous assumption that he had a prior "crime of violence" pursuant to **U.S.S.G. §2L1.2(b)(1)(A)(ii)**. The Jaimes Court, however, concluded that Jaimes' prior conviction did not qualify as a predicate offense under **§2L1.2(b)(1)(A)(ii)** and vacated his sentence with instructions for the district court to consider the guidelines as advisory in light of ***Booker*** upon resentencing.

Failed to Inform Defendant that Government Could
Appeal Downward Departure

Wogan v. United States, 846 F.Supp. 135 (D.Me. 1994)
Defense counsel's failure to inform defendant that government could appeal downward departure from the Guidelines constituted ineffective assistance of counsel.

USSG §4A1.1 Criminal History Category

Buford v. United States, 532 U.S. 59, 149 L.Ed.2d 197, 121 S.Ct. 1276 (2001)
Deferential review is appropriate when a United States Court of Appeals reviews a trial court's sentencing Guidelines determination as to whether defendant's prior convictions were consolidated or related for sentencing purposes under **U.S.S.G. §4A1.2 comment., n. 3** (prior offenses are "related" if "consolidated for trial or sentencing")

U.S.. v Olson, 408 F3d 366,373 (7th Cir. 2005)
If the prior conviction stems from relevant conduct, then the defendant's Criminal History Score cannot be increased based on that prior conviction; however, if that conviction was not based on relevant conduct, then the Criminal History Score may be increased based on that prior conviction. See **U.S.S.G. §4A1.1** and **4A1.2 (2)**. The sentencing Court failed to make factual findings as to why such prior offense did not constitute relevant conduct, therefore, resentencing was required under the advisory guidelines in accordance with ***Booker***.

Garcia v. United States, 301 F.Supp.2d 1275, 1282 (D.N.M. 2004)
Counsel was constitutionally ineffective for failing to object to the Presentence Report that increased petitioner's Criminal History Category Points by 2 points for a DWI, that occurred after the instant offense because those two points should not have been counted under **U.S.S.G. §4A1.1(b)**, and deprived petitioner of the benefits from the "safety value" pursuant to **18 U.S.C. §3553(f)** due to counsel's omissions.

U.S. v. Allen, 88 F.3d 769 (9th Cir. 1996)
Defendant was entitled to sentencing hearing on claim that he was denied his Sixth

Amendment Right to counsel, at time of prior convictions, which were used to calculate guideline criminal history.

Defendant Had a Minimal or Minor Role

U.S. v. Harst, 168 F.3d 398 (10th Cir. 1999)
> Defense counsel's failure to argue that defendant was a minor or minimal participant in drug distribution case required an evidentiary hearing to resolve claim of ineffective assistance of counsel.

U.S. v. Soto, 132 F.3d 56 (D.C. Cir. 1997)
> Trial counsel's performance fell below an objective standard of reasonableness where counsel failed to request a downward adjustment under Guideline provision §3B1.2 for minimal or minor participation, where defendant was specifically the type of person covered by provision and defendant, was prejudiced by counsel's errors where defendant could have received less harsh sentence, absent counsel's unprofessional errors.

United States v. Headley, 923 F.2d 1079 (3rd Cir. 1991)
> Trial counsel's failure to argue for a downward adjustment under the Federal Sentencing Guidelines due to *Headley's* minimal or minor role in the drug conspiracy fell below the requirements of the Sixth Amendment and, there exist a reasonable probability that *Headley's* sentence would have been reduced had it not been for counsel's unprofessional errors and omissions. The Court found there was simply no rational basis to believe that counsel's failure to argue for a downward adjustment under the Sentencing Guidelines was a strategic decision.

Defendant's Legitimate Income

Lee v. U.S., 939 F.2d 503 (7th Cir. 1991)
> The Court held that: "Defendant was prejudiced by trial counsel's failure at sentencing hearing to present evidence regarding defendant's legitimate income during period of his criminal activity, and remand was warranted for determination of whether default brought counsel beneath constitution minimum for effective representation". *Id.*

Improper Aggregation of Different Drugs to Trigger Higher Statutory Penalty

Alaniz v. United States, 351 F.3d 365, 368 (8th Cir. 2003)
> Counsel's failure to object to the district court's improper aggregation of marijuana and the methamphetamine to trigger a higher statutory penalty range, which exceeded the statutory maximum twenty (20) year sentence under **21 U.S.C. §841(b)(1)(C)**, constitutes ineffective assistance of counsel.

Relevant Conduct

United States v. Reinhart, 357 F.3d 521, 530-31 (5th Cir. 2004)
> Counsel was constitutionally ineffective by failing to object to the use of "relevant conduct" under **USSG §1B1.3** that occurred prior to petitioner joining the conspiracy

to increase petitioner's base offense level and sentencing range during sentencing and on direct appeal.

Jansen v. United States, 369 F.3d 237,243-48 (3rd Cir. 2004)
Counsel was constitutionally ineffective for failing to object and present arguments that the 34.2 grams of cocaine and 16.3 grams of crack cocaine seized in defendant's pants were for personal use and could not be used as "relevant conduct" pursuant to **U.S.S.G. §1B1.2** to determine defendant's base offense level.

U.S. v. Granados, 168 F.3d 343 (8th Cir. 1999)
Defense counsel's failure to challenge the prosecution's breach of plea agreement in which the government agreed that defendant's **relevant conduct** would not exceed five kilograms of cocaine and counsel's unfamiliarity with the Sentencing Guidelines constitutes ineffective assistance of counsel.

Arredondo v. U.S., 178 F.3d 778 (6th Cir. 1999)
Defense counsel's failure to object to drug quantity through relevant conduct of other codefendant's involved in the conspiracy required an evidentiary hearing to resolve ineffective assistance of counsel claim where defendant could have received eight-year difference in sentence.

U.S. v. Gordon, 172 F.3d 753 (10th Cir. 1999)
Gordon alleged that his substitute counsel was ineffective for not discussing the Presentence Report (PSR) with him, and by failing to bring to the court's attention factual inaccuracies in the PSR which were relevant to determinations of relevant conduct and acceptance of responsibility. The district court held that these claims were procedurally barred because Gordon failed to raise them on direct appeal. The Tenth Circuit **REVERSED and REMANDED** to the district court to consider the merits of these claims.

Ristagno v. U.S., 32 F.Supp. 2d 184 (M.D. Pa. 1998)
Defendant's personal drugs for use were relevant conduct.

United States v. Wyes, 147 F.3d 631, 632 (7th Cir. 1998)
The government is entitled to only one opportunity to present evidence on the issue of relevant conduct. **See also *United States v. Olson*, 408 F.3d 366, 374 (7th Cir. 2005).**

Nichols v. U.S., 75 F.3d 1137 (7th Cir. 1996)
Trial counsel's failure to object or argue the amount of drugs attributed to defendant, based on calculation of the Sentencing Guidelines, amounted to ineffective assistance of counsel where only witness' testimony gave wide range of amounts, and the court failed to make any findings of credibility of said witness' testimony.

U.S. v. De Alba Pagan, 33 F.3d 125 (1st Cir. 1994)
Counsel's failure to advise defendant that the court could use relevant conduct to determine sentence may constitute ineffective assistance of counsel and require a remand for an evidentiary hearing.

Relevant Conduct Doesn't Trigger Mandatory Minimums

**U.S. v. Santos,** _195 F.3d 549, 553 (10th Cir. 1999)_
>The mandatory minimum sentencing directives in 21 U.S.C. §841 (b) are governed solely by the drug quantities involved in the offense of conviction. "[O]ther drug quantities, which would qualify as 'relevant conduct' for calculating the sentencing range under the [Guidelines] ... may [not] be included in an aggregate to trigger the statutory directives. _Id. At 550._

**U.S. v. Tayman,** _885 F.Supp. 832 (E.D.Va. 1995),_
>The Court held that: (1) Irvin decision, that mandatory minimum sentence applied only to quantity of drugs reasonably foreseeable to conspiracy defendant, was retroactively applicable, and (2) defendant, whose mandatory minimum sentence was based upon amount of drugs involved in conspiracy rather than amount reasonably foreseeable to him, was entitled to collateral relief in form of hearing to determine amount reasonably foreseeable. Relief granted.

USSG §3A1.2 Victim's Status Enhancement

**Cirilo-Munoz v. U.S.,** _404 F.3d 527, 530-535 (1st Cir. 2005)_
>Appellate counsel was constitutionally ineffective for failing to challenge the sentencing enhancement pursuant to **U.S.S.G. §3A1.2(a)**(offense motivated by victim's status as an officer), which increased Cirilo's sentencing range from 27 to 34 years, to life imprisonment, where there was no evidence to support the enhancement in the record, and the district court erroneously relied in part upon the jury verdict for a finding that the jury did not visibly make.

USSG §3C1.1 Obstruction of Justice

**U.S. v. Phillips,** _210 F.3d 345 (5th Cir. 2000)_
>Appellate counsel's failure to challenge the enhancement for obstruction of justice where the district court failed to make proper factual findings on the record on direct appeal constituted ineffective assistance of counsel.

**Nearly v. U.S.,** _998 F.2d 563 (8th Cir. 1993)_
>Trial counsel objected to enhancement of defendant's sentence for "obstruction of justice" under the Guidelines but failed to raise the issue on appeal which constituted performance below an objective standard of reasonableness and required an evidentiary hearing to resolve ineffective assistance of counsel claim.

**U.S. v. Greig,** _967 F.2d 1018 (5th Cir. 1992)_
>Defense counsel and defendant's unethical meeting with co-defendant created conflict of interest, which resulted in defendant's sentence being enhanced for obstructing of justice.

USSG §3D1.2 Grouping

**Glover v. United States,** _531 U.S. 198, 148 L.Ed.2d 607, 611, 121 S.Ct. 696 (2001)_
>Defense counsel was constitutionally ineffective for failing to argue at sentencing and on direct appeal that Glover's conviction for federal labor racketeering, money

laundering, and tax evasion should be grouped under **USSG §3D1.2**, which allows the grouping of counts involving substantially the same harm. As a result of counsel's ineffectiveness Glover's offense level was increased two levels, resulting in an increased sentence of between 6 and 21 months. The ***Glover*** Court held that any amount of actual jail time has Sixth Amendment significance under ***Strickland***.

USSG §1B1.8 Prohibiting use of Statements

U. S v. Baird, *218 F.3d 221, 232 (3rd Cir. 2000)*
Defense counsel's failure to challenge the presentence report or sentence under U.S.S.G. §1B1.8 prohibiting the prosecutors assurance that defendant's statements will in no way be used against them, warranted an evidentiary hearing to resolve the ineffectiveness of counsel claim.

21 U.S.C. §846 Applicability of Mandatory Minimums

Soto v. U.S., *37 F.3d 252, 254-56 (7th Cir. 1994) (per curiam)*
Trial counsel's failure to contest defendant's opening date of a conspiracy which occurred in 1986 and end date which occurred in 1987, prior to the November 18, 1988 enactment date of mandatory minimums into conspiracy pursuant to *21 U.S.C. § 846*, can constitute ineffective assistance of counsel.

Sentence Exceeds Statutory Maximum

United States v. Conley, *349 F.3d 837, 840-842 (5th Cir. 2003)*
Counsel failed to object to the imposition of the **120** month sentence for conspiracy to commit money laundering, where the indictment charged two separate statutes and the Court used a general verdict form making it impossible to tell which statute the jury convicted petitioner by the verdict, and **18 U.S.C. §371** charged in the indictment carried a five year maximum penalty, and constituted ineffective assistance of counsel.

Illegal Sentence

Jones v. United States, *224 F.3d 1251, 1259 (11th Cir. 2000)*
Counsel was constitutionally ineffective for failing to object to the district court imposing a general sentence of 360 months imprisonment for all four counts. A general sentence is an undivided sentence for more than one count that does not exceed the maximum possible aggregate sentence for all counts, but does exceed the maximum allowable sentence on anyone count. Since a general sentence is per se illegal in the Eleventh Circuit the case would have been remanded on direct appeal for resentencing, absent counsel's unprofessional errors and omissions.

United States v. Macedo, *406 F.3d 778, 790 (7th Cir. 2005)*
It is a miscarriage of justice to give a person an illegal sentence that increases his punishment, just as it is to convict an innocent person.

Armed Career Criminal

Begay v. United States, 170 L.Ed.2d 490, 497 (2008)

Mr. Begay pled to felony in possession of a firearm, in violation of **18 U.S.C. Section 922(g) (1)**. Mr. Begay had twelve New Mexico convictions for Driving under the Influence of alcohol. Under New Mexico state law the fourth (DUI), and over is a felony. The sentencing court after reviewing the Presentence Report found that Mr. Begay was an "Armed Career Criminal" as defined by **18 U.S.C. Section 924(e) (2) (B) (ii)**, and sentenced him to 15 years imprisonment. The Tenth Circuit affirmed the sentence. The Supreme Court reversed the judgment and remanded for further proceeding. The Supreme Court found that DUI was unlike the crimes listed in **924(e) (B) (ii)**. The listed examples include: burglary, arson, extortion, or crimes involving the use of explosives, which illustrated the kind of crimes that fell with the statutes scope. DUI a strict liability crime is different form those listed and does not qualify as a violent felony.

Shepard v. United States, 544 U.S. 13, 161 L.Ed.2d 205, 125 S.Ct. 1254 (2005)

Shepard pleaded guilty to being a felon in possession of a firearm under 18 U.S.C. §922(g) (1) and the government sought to use ACCA to enhance his sentence. The text of the Massachusetts statute under which Shepard previously had been convicted did not meet the requirements of ACCA that the conviction be a "violent felony." The government offered documents like the police reports to show that even if some convictions under the state statute might not be violent felonies, Shepard's own convictions were. **Id. at 1257-58**. The Supreme Court rejected this approach. It prohibited judges from resolving a disputed fact about a prior conviction at sentencing by relying on documents such as police reports. The Shepard court approved sources including, the prior court's jury instructions, charging documents, guilty plea transcripts, terms of plea agreement, verdicts and factual basis for the plea.

U.S. v. Williams, 403 F.3d 1188, 1199-1200 (10th Cir. 2005)

A 210 month sentence under the A.C.C.A. for being a felon in possession of a firearm required a remand for resentencing in light of _**Booker**_ under the advisory guidelines where the sentencing judge indicated that he did not want to impose such sentence and that he was disgusted with the sentence.

U.S. v. Sanders, 404 F.3d 980, 988-989 (6th Cir. 2005)

In order for the district court to sentence Sanders under the ACCA it must establish in light of _**Booker**_ and _**Shepard v. United States**_, **125 S.Ct. 1254, 161 L.Ed.2d (2005)**, that Sanders has three violent felonies by virtue of statutory elements, charging documents, jury instructions, plea agreement and plea colloquy or explicit factual findings by trial judge to which defendant assented. The Sanders Court remanded for resentencing in light of _**Booker**_ and _**Shepard**_ with instructions that the district court must explain basis for its decision to sentence Sanders as ACCA under the guidelines.

U.S. v. Washington, 404 F.3d 834, 841-42 (4th Cir. 2005)

District court's factual findings that Washington's prior state conviction for breaking and entering into a Drug and violent Crime task Force Office constituted a "crime of violence" which went beyond the charging documents and the like, were in violation of the Sixth Amendment in light of *Booker* and required resentencing. **See also** *Shepard*, **125 S.Ct. 1254, 161 L.Ed.2d (2005).**

DeRoo v. United States, 223 F.3d 919, 926-27 (8th Cir. 2000)
Defendant's Minnesota conviction for a fifth degree sales of controlled substance was not a "serious drug offense" under the Armed Career Criminal Act.

Hill v. U.S., 118 F.Supp. 2d 910, 915-16 (E.D. Wis. 2000)
Defense counsel's failure to investigate predicate offenses used for armed career criminal sentence enhancement, where predicate offenses showed through receipt of discharge certificates that previous felonies contained no firearm restrictions constituted ineffective assistance of counsel.

Sanders v. U.S., 8 F. Supp. 2d 674 (N.D. Ohio 1998)
Petitioner collaterally attacked his state prior conviction used to enhance his current federal sentence under the **Armed Career Criminal Act** pursuant to *28 U.S.C.§2255* motion to vacate even through state prior conviction had expired decades ago. The Court held that the Armed Career Criminal Act sentence enhancement could not be applied where said prior conviction was the result of ineffectiveness of counsel where counsel failed to object to an inadequate jury instructions on self-defense state assault case.

$50.00 Special Assessment Fee

United States v. Bass, 310 F.3d 321, 329-330 (5th Cir. 2002)
Counsel was ineffective by failing to raise sufficiency of evidence claim on direct appeal in continuing criminal enterprise (CCE) case. Defendant was prejudiced by counsel's omission because he received a $50.00 special assessment fee on the CCE offense.

Discretion of Court to Reduce Sentence

United States v. Ryals, 512 F.3d 416, 419-420 (7th Cir. 2008)
Defense counsel's motion to withdraw and for appointment of new counsel was timely where said motion was filed three weeks before sentencing. *Ryals* is entitled to resentencing, if he can meet the prejudice prong of Strickland and show the district court erred denying the motion to withdraw. The Seventh Circuit concluded that *Ryals* is entitled to resentencing because a more vigorous presentation at the end of the sentencing hearing could have swayed the Court to impose sentence below the advisory guideline range of 360 to life.

U.S. v. Castro, 26 F.3d 557, 560 (5th Cir. 1994)
Defense counsel's failure to provide district court with an opportunity to have sentencing court exercise its discretion in defendant's favor to reduce sentence can constitute ineffective assistance of counsel.

OTHER INEFFECTIVE ASSISTANCE CLAIMS AT SENTENCING:

Failed to Provide Assistance at Sentencing

Groseclose v. Bell, 130 F.3d 1161 (6th Cir. 1997)
Counsel's failure to put on any meaningful mitigating evidence at sentencing was ineffective assistance.

Patrasso v. Nelson, 121 F.3d 297 (7th Cir. 1997)
Defense counsel at sentencing made no effort to contradict prosecution's case, or to present mitigating factors, thus, leaving defendant without a defense at sentencing or an opportunity to argue for a sentence less than statutory maximum, which he received. The Seventh Circuit found under these circumstance counsel failed to subject the prosecution's case to a meaningful adversarial testing and applied the *Cronic* standard where prejudice was presumed.

Tucker v. Day, 969 F.2d 155 (5th Cir. 1992)
Counsel's failure to provide the defendant with any assistance at the resentencing hearing amounted to a constructive denial of the right to counsel which warranted relief.

Standing Silent at Sentencing

Miller v. Martin, 481 F.3d 468, 473-474 (7th Cir. 2007)
Counsel provided constitutionally ineffective assistance for standing silent at sentencing, failed to object to the Presentence Report, and present mitigating evidence that would have probably resulted in a lesser sentence.

Counsel Misadvised Court of Terms of Plea

Davis v. Grigas, 443 F.3d 1155, 1158 (9th Cir. 2006)
Counsel was ineffective for erroneously advising the sentencing court that petitioner stipulated to two fifteen year terms, when petitioner stipulated to two six-to-fifteen year sentencing caps, and the Nevada Supreme Court relied an unreasonable determination of facts to deny petitioner's ineffective assistance of counsel claim. Thus, requiring a remand for an evidentiary hearing.

Failed to Inform Court of Youth Act

Burley v. Cabana, 818 F.2d 414 (5th Cir. 1987)
Trial counsel's failure to inform trial court of Mississippi Youth Court Act for sentencing purposes constitutes ineffective assistance of counsel.

Right to Testify in Capital Sentencing

Canaan v. McBride, 395 F. 3d 376, 386 (7th Cir. 2005)
Counsel's failure to inform/advise petitioner of his right to testify in capital murder trial penalty phase constituted ineffective assistance of counsel.

Fifth Amendment Privilege Claim

Estelle v. Smith, *451 U. S. 454, 463, 101 S.Ct. 1866, 1874, 68 L.Ed.2d 359 (1981)*
> At sentencing the prosecutor used statements made without warning during a competency examination that infringed upon the defendant's Fifth Amendment rights.

Counsel Attacked Defendant's Character and Seperated Himself From Defendant

Horton v. Zant, *941 F.2d 1449 (11th Cir. 1991)*
> Defense counsel rendered ineffective assistance of counsel at sentencing, where counsel attacked defendant's character and sought to separate himself from defendant.

Counsel Sought to Withdraw and Failed to Act as an Advocate

U.S. v. Mateo, *950 F.2d 44 (1st Cir. 1991)*
> Defendant was entitled to resentencing where counsel sought to withdraw as counsel and failed to act as an advocate for defendant at sentencing.

Failed to Argue Other Individuals had Motive and Opportunity to Commit Crime

Henderson v. Sargent, *926 F.2d 706 (8th Cir. 1991)*
> Trial counsel's failure to argue at guilt phase of murder trial that several other individuals, including victim's husband, had opportunity and motive to kill victim, constituted ineffective assistance of counsel. The district court found that trial counsel could have reasonably presented evidence implicating O'Neal in the murder, and presenting such a theory would have been entirely consistent with Henderson's alibi defense, and the evidence against Bob O'Neal was substantial.

Failed to Educate Jury

Waters v. Zant, *979 F.2d 1473 (11th Cir. 1992)*
> Trial counsel's failure to educate jury as to role of aggravating and mitigating circumstances during penalty phase amounted to ineffective assistance.

Failed to Seek Judicial Recommendation Against Deportation

United States v. Kwan, *407 F.3d 1005, 1015-17 (9th Cir. 2005)*
> Counsel misled Kwan that by pleading guilty to bank fraud he would not be deported and such advice was deficient performance. Counsel failure to inform the sentencing judge that a sentence only two days lighter would enable Kwan to avoid deportation and remain united with his family constitutes ineffective assistance of counsel and warranted granting the coram nobis petition.

Mandarino v. Ashcroft, *290 F.Supp.2d 253, 261-263 (D. Conn. 2002)*
> Counsel was constitutionally ineffective during sentence to move for a downward departure and inform the sentencing court of relevant immigration law, i.e., the relevant sentence ceiling of five years for seeking a waiver from deportation pursuant to **8 U.S.C. §212(c)**.

U.S. v. Castro, 26 F.3d 557 (5th Cir. 1994)
> Trial counsel's failure to seek judicial recommendation against deportation where defendant played only minor role in conspiracy, had strong ties to the United States, and judge's apparent leniency in sentencing may constitute ineffective assistance of counsel.

Failed to Aid or Speak for Defendant

Gardiner v. U.S., 679 F.Supp. 1143 (D. Me. 1988)
> Failure to speak in defendant's behalf at sentencing may constitute ineffective assistance of counsel.

Failed To Request Bond

United States v. Hammonds, 425 F.2d 597 (D.C. Cir. 1970)
> Trial counsel's failure to request bond after conviction and to speak on defendant's behalf after sentencing, constituted ineffective assistance of counsel.

Failed to Contest Breach of Plea Agreement

Santobello v. New York, 92 S.Ct. 495, 404 U.S. 257, 30 L.Ed.2d 427(1971)
> The Supreme Court found where state's breach of plea agreement concerning sentence recommendation on a guilty plea required the Court to remand the case to state courts to decide whether there be specific performance of the plea agreement on guilty plea or whether circumstances required that petitioner be granted an opportunity to withdraw his plea of guilty.

U.S. v. Granados, 168 F.3d 343 (8th Cir. 1999)
> Defense counsel's failure to challenge the prosecution's breach of plea agreement in which the government agreed that defendant's **relevant conduct** would not exceed five kilograms of cocaine, and counsel's unfamiliarity with the Sentencing Guidelines constitutes ineffective assistance of counsel.

U.S. v. De La Fuente, 8 F.3d 1333 (9th Cir. 1993)
> Trial counsel's failure to contest the government breach of plea, where the government failed to move for a downward departure below the mandatory minimum, pursuant to *U.S.S.G. § 5K1.1*, constitutes ineffective assistance and established cause for procedural default.

U.S. v. Flowers, 934 F. Supp. 853, 855 (E.D. Mich. 1996)
> Bureau of Prisons effectively breached plea agreement by refusing to deem defendant's concurrent sentence as commencing on date he began serving his earlier sentence.

Failed to Contact Defendant to Prepare for Capital Sentencing

Hall v. Washington, 106 F.3d 742 (7th Cir. 1997)
> Trial counsel's failure to contact defendant for preparation of capital sentencing constituted ineffective assistance of counsel.

Unfamiliar With Capital Sentencing Statute

Hardwich v. Crosby, 320 F.3d 1127, 1167-1182 (11th Cir. 2003)
Counsel misunderstood the mitigation laws relevant to capital sentencing; failed to present evidence of defendant's substantial alcohol and drug consumption and lack of sleep before the murder; and the defendant's dysfunctional upbringing that included mental and physical abuse constituted ineffective assistance of counsel.

House v. Balkcom, 725 F.2d 608 (11th Cir. 1984)
Trial counsel who is unfamiliar with capital sentencing statute is ineffective.

Erroneous Legal Advice About Unanimous Decision on Death Penalty

Hall v. Washington, 106 F.3d 742 (7th Cir. 1997)
Trial counsel's failure to inform/advise defendant that jury had to reach a unanimous decision on death penalty before it could be imposed resulted in prejudice where defendant's waiver of sentencing jury resulted from incorrect advice from counsel and state judge imposed death sentence constitutes ineffective assistance.

Stand-by Counsel Ineffectiveness Claims

U.S. v. Taylor, 933 F.2d 307 (5th Cir. 1991)
The trial court's denial of Petitioner's request to withdraw his waiver of right to counsel and to have standby counsel represent him during sentencing phase of trial was prejudicial per se and constituted a denial of the right to counsel.

Prosecutions Misleading Arguments

Christy v. Horn, 28 F. Supp. 2d 307 (W.D. Pa. 1998)
The Court held that prosecutor's misleading arguments to jury during penalty phase concerning petitioner's future dangerousness to society unconstitutionally tainted jury's death finding and warranted habeas corpus relief.

Jail Credits

United States v. Wilson, 503 US 329, 117 L.Ed.2d 593, 112 S.Ct. 1351, (1992)
Attorney General or Bureau of Prisons Credit computed time spent in official detention before defendant's sentence begins pursuant to *18 USCS §3585 (b)*.

Reno v. Koray, 515 U.S. 50, 132 L.Ed.2d 46, 115 S.Ct. 2021 (1995)
A federal prisoner is not entitled to jail credit time for time spent in a "halfway house" awaiting sentencing.

U.S.. v. Crozier, 259 F.3d 503, 520 (6th Cir. 2001)
Whether a district court has power to award jail credit for time served is a question of law reviewed de novo on appeal.

Romandine v. U.S., 206 F.3d 731 (7th Cir. 2000)
The district court may not require its sentence to be served consecutively to a state sentence that may be imposed in the future.

U.S. v. Hernandez, 234 F.3d 252 (5th Cir. 2000)

Trial court does not have to warn defendant during the guilty plea colloquy that his federal sentence would run consecutively to his anticipated state sentence. **But, see** *U.S. v. Neely,* **38 F.3d 458 (9th Cir. 1994)**(district court was required before accepting guilty plea, to advise defendant that his federal sentence could be served consecutively to his state sentence).

Rosemond v. Menifee, 137 F. Supp. 2d 271, 272-73 (S.D. N.Y. 2000)

The sovereignty which first arrests the individual acquires the right to prior and exclusive jurisdiction over him, and this plenary jurisdiction is not exhausted until there has been a compliance with the terms and service of any judgment imposed by the court of that first sovereignty.

U.S. v. Dorsey, 166 F.3d 558 (3rd Cir. 1999)

District court has authority pursuant to *USSG §5G1.3 comment (n.2), and 18 U.S.C.A. §3584 (a),* to grant sentencing credit against federal sentence that was imposed concurrently with state sentence arising from same conduct.

Rios v. Wiley, 34 F. Supp. 2d 265 (M.D. Pa. 1999)

Twenty-two (22) months spent in federal detention pursuant to a writ of habeas corpus ad prosequendum was sufficiently long enough to constitute "federal custody," and properly credited to federal sentence.

U.S. v. Mahmood, 19 F. Supp. 2d 33 (E.D. N.Y. 1998)

Prisoner was entitled to appointment of counsel in proceedings to determine whether the Bureau of Prisons correctly credited his sentence with time spent in official detention.

U.S. v. D.H. (A Juvenile), 12 F. Supp. 2d 472 (D. Virgin Island 1998)

A juvenile was not a "person entitled to credit for presentence time served," as calculated by the Federal Bureau of Prisons.

Taylor v. Reno, 164 F.3d 440 (9th Cir. 1998)

Releasing defendant on federal bail relinquished federal primary jurisdiction, so that state obtained primary jurisdiction over defendant when it arrested him on state murder charges.

U.S. v. Payton, 159 F.3d 49 (2nd Cir. 1998)

The Bureau of Prisons may award credit for time spent in state detention pending trial on state charges which were subsequently dismissed, that arose out of the same incident for which prisoner was convicted of in federal court.

U.S. v. Sanchez-Rodriguez, 161 F.3d 556 (9th Cir. 1998)

Downward departure under Sentencing Guidelines, based on time already served in state custody was warranted due to delay in indicting and sentencing defendant on federal charge, where defendant lost opportunity to serve a greater portion of his state sentence concurrently with his federal sentence.

Sentencing Ineffectiveness

U.S. v. Daily, 970 F. Supp. 628 (N.D. Ill. 1997)
>Defense counsel's failure to file a motion for credit for time served on home confinement did **not** constitute ineffective assistance of counsel, since the district court did not have power to determine jail credits.

Luther v. Vanyur, 14 F. Supp. 2d 773 (E.D. N.Y. 1997)
>Federal sentence began on the date prisoner was initially received into custody by the United States Marshal, even though he was subsequently released to the custody of state officials. His federal sentence continued to run during the 3½ months when he was in state custody because the period away from federal custody was not caused by any activity of the prisoner.

U.S. v. Flowers, 934 F. Supp. 853, 855 (E.D. Mich. 1996)
>Bureau of Prisons effectively breached plea agreement by refusing to deem defendant's concurrent sentence as commencing on date he began serving his earlier sentence.

Chambers v. Holland, 920 F. Supp. 618, 622 (M.D. Pa. 1996)
>A federal prisoner's sentence may commence when and if the Attorney General or Bureau of Prisons agrees to designate a state facility for service of federal sentence.

Brown v. Perrill, 28 F.3d 1073 (10th Cir. 1994)
>The Court held that: (1) petitioner who was detained by federal authorities pursuant to writ of habeas corpus ad prosequendum for 19 months was not merely "on loan" from state authorities, and (2) statute providing for credit does not permit Attorney General unilaterally to eliminate credit by administrative action and increase term once it has been provided expressly by sentencing court.

U.S. v. Drake, 49 F.3d 1439 (9th Cir. 1995)
>District court was required to reduce defendant's mandatory minimum sentence, pursuant to **U.S.S.G. §5G1.3(b)** for time served in state prison for robbery sentence on the ground that the robbery had been taken into account in determination of the offense level for weapons in federal case.

United States v. Kiefer, 20 F.3d 874 (8th Cir. 1994)
>A sentencing court has authority pursuant *USSG §5G1.3 (b)* to grant a defendant credit on federal sentence for all the time defendant served, before sentencing, in state custody on related charge.

Martinez v. U.S., 19 F.3d 97 (2d Cir. 1994)
>A prisoner is not entitled to sentencing credit for time spent during his release on bond/bail towards his sentence.

Fraley v. United States Bureau of Prisons, 1 F.3d 924, 925-26 (9th Cir. 1993)
>A prisoner is not entitled to be credited to his sentence for time spent during home confinement detention.

Kayfez v. Gasele, 993 F.2d 1288 (7th Cir. 1993)
>Petitioner was entitled to credit against federal sentence, even though time had already been credited against concurrent state sentence.

McClain v. Bureau of Prisons, 9 F.3d 503 (6th Cir. 1993)
> The federal authorities took custody from the state by virtue of the writ of habeas corpus ad prosequendum. Subsequently, petitioner was paroled on the state charges. His release on parole from state charges essentially put him in exclusive federal custody. The district court should have directed the Attorney General or (BOP) to credit petitioner with the additional time spent in custody after he was paroled. Petitioner was released from federal custody before the Sixth Circuit decided this case. The Sixth Circuit held the claim was not moot and **REVERSED and REMANDED because petitioner's term of supervised release dates were affected by the** *erroneous computation.*

U.S. v. Moore, 978 F.2d 1029 (8th Cir. 1992)
> Petitioner entitled to credit on federal sentence, for time served in state custody on dismissed state charges arising out of the same incident.

Randall v. Whelan, 938 F.2d 522, 525 (4th Cir. 1991)
> A prisoner who is "detained" or "sentenced" and subject to the control of the BOP is entitled to that time credited towards his sentence.

United States v. Winter, 730 F.2d 825 (1st Cir. 1984)
> A federal prisoner may be entitled to credit for time spent in state prison on unrelated charge, if continued state confinement was exclusively the product of such action by federal law enforcement officials that would respectfully justify treating state jail as the practical equivalent of federal jail.

United States v. Blankenship, 733 F.2d 433, 434 (6th Cir. 1984)
> Credit against the federal sentence attaches only when the federal detainer is the exclusive reason for the prisoner's failure to obtain his release on bail. See also ***Ballard v. Blackwell***, **449 F.2d 868 (5th Cir. 1971).**

Shaw v. Smith, 680 F.2d 1104, 1106 (5th Cir. 1982)
> Time spent in state custody, even if for an unrelated offense, must be credited toward time served on a federal sentence if the continued state confinement was exclusively the product of such action by federal law-enforcement officials so as to justify treating the state jail as the practical equivalent of a federal one. For example, a state defendant is denied bail solely because of a federal detainer issued against him, the time spent in state custody awaiting trial must be credited to his federal sentence.

In re Liberatore, 574 F.2d 78, 79 (2nd Cir. 1978)
> The Court held that "any loan" to the second sovereignty in compliance with such a writ or any other temporary transfer of custody from the sovereignty having the prior jurisdiction, cannot affect in any way whatever any final judgment of conviction already entered against the petitioner there or affect the running of the sentence imposed pursuant to that judgment.

Polakoff v. United States, 489 F.2d 727, 730 (5th Cir. 1974)
> Time spend on bail or bond, regardless of how "highly restricted bond," is **not** creditable as "custody" for jail credits.

United States v. Eidum, 474 F.2d 579 (9th Cir. 1973)
    A federal prisoner was entitled to credit against federal sentence for the portion of time spent in state custody when release was prevented by a federal detainer.

Willis v. United States, 438 F.2d 923, 925 (5th Cir. 1971)
    Prisoner was entitled to evidentiary hearing where federal detainer prevented prisoner from making bond on state charges to determine whether he was entitled to credit for time spent on his state charges, which were run concurrently with his federal sentence.

Davis v. Attorney General, 425 F.2d 238 (5th Cir. 1970)
    A federal prisoner is entitled to credit towards his federal sentence for time spent in presentence custody, where a federal detainer was responsible for his confinement by state authorities because state officials relied on detainer warrant in refusing to release him on bail on state charges.

Brown v. United States, 311 F.Supp. 325 (N.D. Ga. 1970)
    Federal prisoner who was not permitted to make bail on state charges because of a federal detainer/holds and therefore remained in state custody without bail, time spent in state custody without bond was custody "in connection with" federal offense and petitioner was entitled to credit on federal sentences for time federal detainers forced him to spend in state custody.

21 U.S.C. § 851 Sentencing Enhancement Notice

Prou v. U.S., 199 F.3d 37 (1st Cir. 1999)
    Trial counsel's failure to object to the prosecutions untimeless in filling its 21U.S.C. §851 information seeking to enhance defendant's sentence because of higher conviction, which shall be filed before trial, constituted ineffective assistance of counsel.

State Conviction Used To Enhance Federal Sentence

U.S. v. Clark, 203 F.3d 358 (5th Cir. 2000)
    State expired conviction used to enhance federal sentence may be challenged pursuant to 28 U.S.C. §2255 motion to vacate sentence as long as relief sought is framed as an attack on present sentence which prisoner is still in custody.

APPELLATE INEFFECTIVENESS

STANDARDS

The *Strickland* Standard Applies to Appellate Counsel Ineffectiveness Claims

<u>*Gray v. Greer,*</u> *800 F.2d 644 (7th Cir. 1986)*
> The <u>***Strickland***</u> two-part test, which governs ineffective assistance of counsel claims, applies to appellate counsel.

<u>*Mayo v. Henderson,*</u> *13 F.3d 528 (2nd Cir. 1994)*
> Appellate counsel's failure to raise Rosario claim for prosecution's failure to disclose police officer's memo constitutes ineffective assistance of counsel. This case presents a clear evaluation of the prejudice prong of <u>***Strickland***</u>.

Invalid Waiver Of Counsel

<u>*Snook v. Wood,*</u> *89 F.3d 605 (9th Cir. 1996)*
> Waiver of right to counsel on appeal was not valid where court failed to advise defendant of dangers and disadvantages of self-representation, which required reinstatement of appeal with appointment of counsel.

FAILED TO FILE OR . . .

Notice of Appeal/An Appeal

<u>*Becker v. Montgomery,*</u> *532 U.S. 757, 149 L.Ed.2d 983, 121 S.Ct. 1801 (2001)*
> Party's failure to sign timely notice of appeal did not require Court of Appeals to dismiss appeal.

<u>*United States v. Poindexter,*</u> *492 F. 3d 263, 268-270 (4th Cir. 2007)*
> Counsel provided constitutionally ineffective assistance for failing to file Poindexter's requested notice of appeal, despite Poindexter's waiver of appeal as part of his plea agreement.

<u>*Watson v. United States,*</u> *493 F.3d 960, 963-964 (8th Cir. 2007)*
> Evidentiary hearing warranted to resolve ineffective assistance of counsel claim related to failure to file notice of appeal.

<u>*United States v Sandoval-Lopez,*</u> *409 F.3d 1193, 1199 (9th Cir. 2005)*
> Evidentiary hearing required to determine whether Sandoval-Lopez requested his lawyer to file a notice of appeal and his lawyer refused.

<u>*United States v. Garrett,*</u> *402 F.3d 1262, 1267 (10th Cir. 2005)*
> Claim of ineffective assistance of counsel for failing to file defendant's requested notice of appeal required an evidentiary hearing to resolve factual disputes.

Appellate Ineffectiveness

Lozada v. Deeds, 488 U.S. 430, 112 L.Ed.2d 956, 111 S.Ct. 860(1991)
Defense counsel's failure to inform petitioner of his right to appeal constitutes ineffective assistance of counsel.

Peguero v. United States, 526 U.S. 23, 143 L.Ed.2d 18, 119 S.Ct. 961 (1999)
District court's failure to advise defendant of his appellate rights, in accordance to Federal Rules of Criminal Procedure *Rule 32 (a) (2)*, held to be harmless error where defendant knew of right to appeal. **See also** *Ristagno v. U.S., 32 F.Supp. 2d 184 (M.D. Pa. 1998)*

Houston v. Lack, 487 U.S. 266, 275, 108 S.Ct. 2379. 101 L.Ed.2d 245 (1988)
Pro se prisoner's notice of appeal is considered to be filed on the date that prisoner delivers the notice to prison authorities for mailing. This became known as the **"Mailbox Rule."**

Hernandez v. U.S., 202 F.3d 486 (2nd Cir. 2000)
Defense counsel's failure to file timely notice of appeal to perfect defendant's direct appeal constitutes ineffective assistance of counsel without necessity of showing of prejudice. **See also** *Hayes v. Morgan, 58 F.Supp.2d 817 (N.D. Ohio 1999); Stinson v. U.S., 102 F.Supp.2d 912 (M.D. Tenn. 2000); Restrepo v. Kelly, 178 F.3d 634 (2nd Cir. 1999); Ortego v. Roe, 160 F.3d 534 (9th Cir. 1998)*

U.S. v. Beers, 76 F.3d 204 (8th Cir. 1996)
Counsel's failure to file notice of appeal constitutes ineffective assistance of counsel and, required vacating judgment of conviction and sentence and entering a new judgment, thereby enabling defendant to appeal within ten days. **See also** *Slater v. U.S., 38 F.Supp. 2d 587 (M.D. Tenn. 1999); U.S. v. McKenzie, 99 F.3d 813 (7th Cir. 1996); U.S. v. NAGIB, 56 F.3d 798 (7th Cir. 1995)*

Blaik v. U.S., 117 F.3d 1289 (11th Cir. 1997)
Defense counsel failed to file a timely notice of appeal on the denial of Blaik's, rule 35 motion to reduce sentence and, as such, constituted ineffective assistance.

Montemdino v. U.S., 68 F.3d 416 (11th Cir. 1995)
Where defendant requested counsel to appeal his guideline sentence in a guilty plea case and counsel fails to do so, such failure constitutes ineffective assistance of counsel and requires an evidentiary hearing to resolve the claim.

Martin v. U.S., 81 F.3d 1083 (11th Cir. 1996)
Counsel's failure to file an appeal when requested to do so by defendant, even though defendant pled guilty, constituted ineffective assistance of counsel and required the defendant to be able to file an out-of-time appeal. **See also** *U.S. v. Ruth, 768 F.Supp. 1428 (D. Kan. 1991); U.S. v. Peak, 992 F.2d 39 (4th Cir. 1992); U.S. v. Gipson, 985 F.2d 212 (5th Cir. 1993); U.S. v. Stearns, 68 F.3d 328 (9th Cir. 1995)*

Abels v. Kaiser, 913 F.2d 821 (10th Cir. 1990)
Retained counsel's failure to file a motion to withdraw as counsel before defendant's time to file appeal constitutes ineffective assistance of counsel.

Consult With Defendant About Appeal

***Roe v. Flores-Ortega*, 528 U.S. 470, 120 S.Ct. 1029, 145 L.Ed.2d 985 (2000)**

Counsel has a constitutional duty to consult with the defendant about an appeal and failure to do so when the defendant would have appealed constitutes prejudice under *Strickland*.

***Frazer v. South Carolina*, 430 F.3d 696, (4th Cir. 2005)**

Counsel's failure to consult with Frazer regarding a direct appeal following the imposition of consecutive sentences on state trafficking and possession of a weapons charges in 1994, which resulted in Frazer's loss of his right to appeal constitutes ineffective assistance of counsel warranting a new appeal. **See also *Galviz-Zapata v. United States*, 431 F.3d 395, 399 (2nd Cir. 2005); *Gomez-Diaz v. United States*, 433 F.3d 788 (11th Cir. 2005)** (evidentiary hearing required); ***Campusano v. United States*, 442 F.3d 770, 774 (2nd Cir. 2006).**

***Thompson v. United States*, 481 F.3d 1297, 1302 (11th Cir. 2007)**

Counsel provided constitutionally ineffective assistance for failing to consult with Thompson regarding appealing his sentence or his right to an appeal.

***United States v. Shedrick*, 493 F.3d 292, 301 (3rd Cir. 2007)**

Counsel provided constitutionally ineffective assistance for failing to discuss or consult with Shedrick about appealing his sentence because he specifically claimed he was not pleading to the shooting incident which was used to enhance his sentence. Shedrick wrote the judge a letter stating that he requested his lawyer to file an appeal. The Judge's chambers left a message on counsel's answering machine that Shedrick wanted to appeal. Counsel took no action to effect Shedrick's appeal.

***Thompson v. United States*, 504 F.3d 1203, 108 (11th Cir. 2007)**

Counsel's failure to consult with Thompson about appealing his sentence constituted ineffective assistance and required granting an out-of-time appeal. **See also *Parson v. United States*, 505 F.3d 797 (8th Cir. 2007)**(Counsel's failure to file notice of appeal ineffective).

An Appeal

***United States v. Snitz*, 342 F.3d 1154, 1156 (10th Cir. 2003)**

Counsel's failure to perfect defendant's requested notice of appeal amounted to ineffective assistance.

***Benoit v. Bock*, 237 F.Supp. 2d 804, 810 (E.D. Mich. 2003)**

Counsel was constitutionally ineffective for failing to pursue petitioner's requested appeal.

***Edwards v. United States*, 246 F.Supp. 2d 911, 915 (E.D. Tenn. 2003)**

Counsel was ineffective for failing to prosecute petitioner's requested direct appeal due to money dispute and prejudiced was presumed.

Appellate Ineffectiveness

Johnson v. Champion, 288 F.3d 1215, 1229 (10th Cir. 2002)
    Appellate counsel's failure to file a timely appellate's brief constitutes ineffective assistance and required remanding the case with instructions to grant a writ ordering the petitioner's release unless State authorities afford him an appeal out of time.

Hudson v. Hunt, 235 F.3d 892, 896 (4th Cir. 2000)
    Counsel's failure to consult with petitioner regarding appeal required a remand to determine whether prejudiced by counsel's deficient performance.

Miller v. U.S., 150 F.Supp. 2d 871, 881-82 (E.D.N.C. 2001)
    Defense counsel's failure to properly consult with petitioner about an appeal, where petitioner was convicted by plea agreement that waived his right to appeal except in a situation where the sentence exceeded 160 months and petitioner received a 240 month sentence, and specifically requested counsel to file an appeal constituted ineffective assistance of counsel.

U.S. v. Soto, 159 F.Supp.2d 39, 50 (E.D. Pa. 2001)
    Defense counsel's failure to comply with defendant's expressed desire to file an appeal constituted ineffective assistance of counsel and required resentencing to afford the defendant an opportunity to file a timely notice of appeal.

Ludwig v. U.S., 162 F.3d 456 (6th Cir. 1998)
    Counsel's failure to perfect a direct appeal, when defendant requested counsel to file an appeal is a per se violation of the Sixth amendment and constitutes ineffective assistance of counsel. **See also _Batista Zabala v. U.S._, 962 F. Supp. 244 (D. Puerto Rico 1997)**; **_Sincox v. United States_, 571 F.2d 876 (5th Cir. 1978)**; **_Castellanos v. U.S._, 26 F.3d 717 (7th Cir. 1994)**; **_Dumer v. Berge_, 975 F. Supp. 1165 (E.D. Wis. 1997)**; **_Abels v. Kaiser_, 913 F.2d 821 (10th Cir. 1990)**; **_Becton v. Barnett_, 920 F.2d 1190 (4th Cir. 1990)**; **_U.S. v. Davis_, 929 F.2d 554 (10 Cir. 1991)**; **_Mack v. Smith_, 659 F.2d 23 (5th Cir. 1981)**

Saba v.I.N.S., 52 F.Supp. 2d 1117 (N.D. Cal. 1999)
    Counsel's failure to file an appeal to the Board of Immigration Appeals deprived aliens' of due process and constitutes ineffective assistance of counsel.

Turner v. U.S., 961 F. Supp. 189 (E.D. Mich. 1997)
    Defense counsel's failure to file direct appeal due to some miscommunication or misunderstanding was a direct per se violation of defendant's Sixth Amendment Right to counsel where appeal was never filed.

Griffin v. U.S., 109 F.3d 1217 (7th Cir. 1997)
    Counsel filed a notice of appeal, but the took no action to prosecute that appeal and then ignores court orders to show "cause" for failure to prosecute and constitutes ineffective assistance.

Martin v. U.S., 81 F.3d 1083 (11th Cir. 1996)
    Counsel's failure to file an appeal when requested to do so by defendant, even though defendant pled guilty, constituted ineffective assistance of counsel and required the defendant to be able to file an out-of-time appeal.

Williams v. Lockhart, 849 F.2d 1134 (8th Cir. 1988)
> Counsel's failure to perfect appeal required evidentiary hearing on claim of ineffective assistance of counsel, where dispute existed between petitioner and his attorney as to whether petitioner requested counsel to file an appeal. **See also** *Page v. U.S., 884 F.2d 300 (7th Cir. 1989)*; *Perez v. Wainwright, 640 F.2d 596 (5th Cir. 1981)*; *Hannon v. Maschner, 781 F.Supp. 1547 (D. Kan. 1992)*; *Brady v. Ponte, 705 F.Supp. 52 (D. Mass. 1988)*; *Estes v. U.S., 883 F.2d 645 (8th Cir. 1989)*; *Hannon v. Maschner, 845 F.2d 1553 (10th Cir. 1988)*; *Becton v. Barnett, 920 F.2d 1190 (4th Cir. 1990)*

Apprendi Issue

Ballard v. U.S., 400 F.3d 404, 408-09 (6th Cir. 2005)
> Appellate counsel was constitutionally ineffective for failing to raise Ballard's *Apprendi* and *Dale* claims where the indictment charged two drugs in one count and where the jury **never** determined which drug it used to convict Ballard because the trial court used a general verdict form, and then imposed sentence based on cocaine which carries a greater sentence than marijuana.

Baston Claim

Grate v. Stinson, 224 F.Supp.2d 496, 511-520 (E.D.N.Y. 2002)
> Appellate counsel was constitutionally ineffective for failing to raise the issue that the government's exercise of peremptory challenges during jury selection was impermissibly based on race, in direct violation of *Baston*, and there was a reasonable probability that the outcome of the appellate proceedings would have been different, absent counsel's errors.

Eagle v Linahan, 268 F.3d 1306, 1322 (11th Cir. 2001)
> Appellate counsel's failure to raise *Batson* claim on direct appeal based on trial judge's failure to require prosecution to produce neutral explanation for challenging black venire persons amounted to ineffective assistance of counsel.

Eagle v. Linahan, 279 F.3d 926, 943 (11th Cir. 2001)
> Appellate counsel's failure to raise an obvious *Batson* claim, where the trial judge stated reason for rejecting the *Batson* claim that he believed that both sides were using their strikes in a discriminatory manner constituted ineffective assistance of counsel.

Consolidate Appeals

Bishawi v. United States, 292 F.Supp. 2d 1122, 1127-1128 (S.D. Ill. 2003)
> Appellate counsel was constitutionally ineffective for failing to file a consolidated appeal to include both issues arising from denial of motion for new trial and issues related to conviction and sentencing. The appropriate remedy was vacate judgment and reimposed judgment to permit a new direct appeal.

Counsel Abandoned Appeal

McHale v. U.S., 175 F.3d 115 (2nd Cir. 1999)
> Appellate counsel's abandonment of filed appeal and allowed the appeal to be dismissed for failure to perfect the appeal constituted ineffective assistance of counsel and required reinstatement of said appeal.

Significant Portion Of Record

__Moore v. Carlton__, *74 F.3d 689 (6th Cir. 1996)*
> Counsel's failure to file significant portion of record on direct appeal rendered his performance deficient when sufficiency of evidence was issue at trial, but <u>no</u> prejudice was shown under *Strickland.*

Motion to Withdraw as Counsel *Anders* REQUIREMENTS

__Anders v. California__, *386 U.S. 738, 18 L.Ed.2d 493, 87 S.Ct. 1396, reh den 388 U.S. 924, 18 L.Ed.2d 1377, 87 S.Ct. 2094 (1967)*
> The Supreme Court held "that the Constitutional right to counsel requires that on an indigent's first appeal from his conviction, court-appointed counsel support the appeal to the best of his ability, requesting permission to withdraw only if he finds the case to be wholly frivolous, in which event he must file a brief referring to anything in the record that might arguably support the appeal."

__Page v. Frank__, *343 F.3d 901, 907-911 (7th Cir. 2003)*
> Appellate counsel's failure to raise issue of trial counsel's ineffectiveness in __*Anders*__ brief; petitioner's failure to raise trial counsel's ineffectiveness in response to __*Anders*__ brief did not constitute a waiver of the claim; it was error to reject the claim based on res judicata grounds in habeas proceedings.

__United States v. Skurdal__, *341 F.3d 921, 927-928 (9th Cir. 2003)*
> Appellate counsel was constitutionally ineffective by failing to comply with __*Anders*__ and __*Griffy*__ when seeking to withdraw as counsel on appeal. Counsel failed to brief the issue that the trial court erred denying petitioner self-representation, by holding that petitioner was not competent to represent himself because he lacked the "technical legal knowledge" and deprived petitioner of his Fifth Amendment right to effective assistance of counsel on appeal.

__Delgado v. Lewis__, *168 F.3d 1148 (9th Cir. 1999)*
> Appellate counsel ignored trial counsel's ineffective assistance of counsel claims which were legitimate, specific and compelling appellate issues and choose to inform the court that there were no arguable issues. Appellate counsel deliberately elected to ignore the requirements of __*Anders*__, and, as such, deprived Delgado completely of his right to counsel on appeal. **See also __Davis v. Kramer__, *167 F.3d 494 (9th Cir. 1999)* ; __Grubbs v. Singletary__, *900 F.Supp. 425 (M.D. Fla. 1995)*; __Allen v. U.S.__, *938 F.2d 664 (6th Cir. 1991)***

__Robbins v. Smith__, *152 F.3d 1062 (9th Cir. 1997)*
> Appellate counsel's failure to comply with the __*Anders*__ requirement for filing a no-merit briefs where there were two arguable issues. Defendant was entitled that new counsel to be appointed by state appellate court to argue whether defendant's attempt to withdraw waiver of his right to counsel was error and whether the inadequacy of the jails law library deprived him of a meaningful opportunity to prepare his defense.

__Lofton v. Whitley__, *905 F.2d 885 (5th Cir. 1990)*
> Appellate counsel who filed a two-page brief requesting review of the record for errors failed to follow the __*Anders*__ procedures for withdrawal and constituted

ineffective assistance of counsel where defendant raised one claim warranting habeas relief by asserting that he had been illegally detained while police took a photograph that was later used in a photographic array.

Evans v. Clarke, 868 F.2d 267 (8th Cir. 1989)
Appellate counsel has a duty when counsel files an *Anders* brief under the Supreme Court's decision in *Anders v. California, 386 U.S. 738, 743, [87 S.Ct. 1396, 1399, 18 L.Ed.2d 493] (1967)*, to refer to anything in writing that is in the record that could possibly be arguably to support the appeal. Appellate counsel's failure to point to issues of arguable merit warrants reinstatement of direct appeal for consideration of those issues when raised in a pro se post-conviction proceeding.

Penson v. Ohio, (1988) 488 U.S. 75, 102 L.Ed.2d 300, 109 S.Ct. 346
The Supreme Court found that the lower court of appeals erred allowing counsel to withdraw as appellate counsel after it determined that there were several arguable claims of error and, that such a complete denial of counsel on appeal can never be harmless error and prejudice is automatically presumed.

Jones v. Berge, 246 F.Supp. 2d 1045, 1058 (E.D. Wis. 2003)
Counsel abandoned petitioner by failing to file his requested notice of appeal; failed to file an *Anders* brief, and file a motion to withdraw as counsel.

Fields v. Bagely, 275 F.3d 478, 483 (6th Cir. 2001)
Defense counsel failed to represent petitioner at all on appeal, failed to notify petitioner that the state was appealing the suppression order by interlocutory appeal, failed to file a motion to withdraw as counsel, and left petitioner without counsel on appeal which amounted to ineffective assistance of counsel. Prejudiced was found because Fields was unable to point out that the appellate court did not have the full record of the suppression proceeding before it. The missing part of the record was where the district Judge stated in open court that I'm granting the suppression motion because I did not find the police officer's testimony credible.

Hughes v. Booker, 220 F.3d 346, 349-51 (5th Cir. 2000)
Appellate counsel filed a brief in compliance with the Mississippi, "*Killingsworth procedure*," for withdrawal of counsel, which did not afford adequate and effective appellate review and amounted to a constructive denial of appellate counsel. Thus, prejudice is presumed under the discrete facts of this case.

Morse v. Trippett, 102 F.Supp. 392, 410-11 (E.D. Mich. 2000)
Appellate counsel filed a motion to withdraw while the appeal was still pending and the Court of Appeals granted the motion. There is no indication that Petitioner knowingly waived his right to counsel or concurred in the attorney's withdrawal from the appeal. No substitution counsel was appointed and the Court held that petitioner was consecutively denied his right to counsel on appeal.

Abels v. Kaiser, 913 F.2d 821 (10th Cir. 1990)
Retained counsel's failure to file a motion to withdraw as counsel before defendant's time to file appeal constitutes ineffective assistance of counsel.

Appellate Ineffectiveness

Right To Proceed Pro se On Appeal

Vega v. Johnson, 149 F. 3d 354 (5th Cir. 1998)

Defendant has a Sixth Amendment right to file a pro se Appellant's brief on direct appeal.

Myers v. Johnson, 76 F.3d 1330 (5th Cir. 1996)

The district court's denial of defendant's right to file pro se briefs on direct appeal was not subject to harmless error remedy was to afford defendant an opportunity to present out-of-time pro se appellate brief to State Court of Appeals.

Greene v. Brigano, 123 F.3d 917 (6th Cir. 1997)

Defendant who exercises his Sixth Amendment Right to pro se representation on appeal is entitled as a matter of due process and equal protection to be provided with a copy of the trial transcripts.

Appear at Oral Arguments

U.S. v. Birtle, 792 F.2d 846 (9th Cir. 1986)

The Court held that: "(1) Appellate counsel's performance is evaluated under the *Strickland* test, and (2) petitioner failed to show prejudice from failure of counsel to appear at oral argument or file a reply brief."

A Reply Brief

U.S. v. Birtle, 792 F.2d 846 (9th Cir. 1986)

The Court held that: "(1) Appellate counsel's performance is evaluated under the *Strickland* test, and (2) petitioner failed to show prejudice from failure of counsel to appear at oral argument or file a reply brief."

Jurisdictional Statement

Griffin v. U.S., 109 F.3d 1217 (7th Cir. 1997)

Appellate counsel failed to file brief or a jurisdictional statement and advised Griffin to dismiss his appeal to file a rule 35 (b) motion which was non-existence, for the defense, constituted ineffective assistance of counsel.

Obtain Grand Jury Testimony Transcripts

Miller v. Wainwright, 798 F.2d 426 (11th Cir. 1986)

The Court held that: "(1) Ineffective assistance of counsel claims had to be re-examined by district court under correct *Strickland* standard where federal district court had improperly accorded presumption of correctness to State court's mixed law-fact determination of absence of ineffective assistance; (2) it was incumbent upon some court to review grand jury testimony of eye witnesses to determine whether petitioner had particularized need sufficient to overcome need for secrecy of grand jury proceedings, where witnesses had testified to two different versions, both under oath."

Transcripts For Appeal

Miller v. Smith, 99 F.3d 120 (4th Cir. 1996)
> The Court held that Maryland's interpretation of state rule as requiring indigent defendant to be represented by state public defender's office in order to receive at state expense the transcripts necessary for appeal violated constitutional rights of defendant with pro bono legal representation.

Greene v. Brigano, 123 F.3d 917 (6th Cir. 1997)
> Defendant who exercises his Sixth Amendment Right to pro se representation on appeal is entitled as a matter of due process and equal protection to be provided with a copy of the trial transcripts.

Reconstruct Trial Transcripts

Terry v. Cross, 112 F.Supp. 2d 543 (E.D. Va. 2000)
> Petitioner had a right to be present at post-sentencing hearing to correct trial transcripts.

U.S. v. Medina, 90 F.3d 459, 463 (11th Cir. 1996)
> When a defendant is represented by a new attorney on appeal, the defendant need only show that "there is a substantial and significant omission from the trial transcripts" for a new trial.

U.S. v. Preciado-Cordobas, 923 F.2d 159, 160-61 (11th Cir. 1991)
> The Court of appeals remanded for reconstruction of trial transcripts closing arguments.

United States v. Taylor, 607 F.2d 153, 154 (5th Cir. 1979)
> The Court of Appeals remanded for the district court to reconstruct the trial transcripts.

State Withheld Transcripts

Boyko v. Parke, 259 F.3d 781 (7th Cir. 2001)
> Habeas petitioner would be entitled to evidentiary hearing if state withheld transcripts of hearing held before his case was waived from juvenile court.

State Must Furnish Transcript of Mistrial

Kennedy v. Lockyer, 379 F. 3d 1041, (9th Cir. 2004)
> The state is required to provide an indigent defendant with the transcripts of the proceedings of a prior mistrial in order to aid him in preparing for a second trial. This includes pretrial motions, opening statements, closing arguments, and jury instructions.

Accepted Change to Trial Transcript

Terry v. Cross, 112 F.Supp.2d 543, 553-54 (E.D. Va. 2000)
Trial and appellate counsel erred accepting the change in the trial transcript relating to the age of a victim in a statutory rape case, without specific evidence or consulting with the defendant constituted ineffective assistance of counsel.

Missing Trial Exhibits

U.S. v. Novation, 271 F.3d 968, 993 (11th Cir. 2001)
The Court of Appeals remanded the case for the district court to reconstruct the trial transcripts based on the missing trial exhibits that contained co-conspirator statements relating to Reynaldo Rodriquez' **Federal Rules of Evidence, Rule 806 argument**.

Unseal Jury Verdict

United States v. Lane, 624 F.2d 1336, 1338 n. 4 (5th Cir.) cert. denied, 499 U.S. 956 (1980)
The first jury verdict was sealed because the district court had omitted part of its instructions. The Court of Appeals ordered the sealed jury verdict to be unsealed and be made part of the record.

Unseal Secret Proceedings

United States v. Tashman, 478 F.2d 129, 130 n. 1 (5th Cir. 1973)
The Court of Appeals ordered that the transcripts of the "secret" proceedings to be unsealed.

A Two Page Appellant's Brief

Lofton v. Whitley, 905 F.2d 885 (5th Cir. 1990)
Appellate counsel who filed a two-page brief requesting review of the record for errors, failed to follow the *Anders* procedures for withdrawal, and constituted ineffective assistance of counsel where defendant raised one claim warranting habeas relief by asserting that he had been illegally detained while police took a photograph that was later used in a photographic array.

A Brief in Opposition Where the State Appealed

U.S. Ex Rel. Thomas v. O'Leary, 856 F.2d 1011 (7th Cir. 1988)
The Court held that: (1) Failure of trial counsel to file opposition brief during State's appeal of trial court's suppression order was ineffective assistance of counsel; (2) counsel's ineffectiveness was presumptuously prejudicial; and (3) State appellate court's consideration of State's appeal knowing defendant was not properly represented was unfair.

Appellant Brief Ineffectiveness

Hendricks v. Lock, 238 F.3d 985, 988-89 (8th Cir. 2001)
Appellate counsel prepared petitioner's appellant's brief in a manner that resulted in the court's refusal to consider issue on the merits, which amounted to a constructive denial of counsel and prejudice was presumed.

Assign Order Declining to Suppress Confession as Error

Claudio v. Scully, 982 F.2d 798 (2d Cir. 1992)
Appellate counsel's failure to assign order declining to suppress confession as error, constitutes ineffective assistance of counsel.

Notify Petitioner That Appeal Was Denied

Shiloh-Bryant v. Director, TDCJ-ID, 104 F. Supp. 2d 696, 704 (E.D. Tex. 2000)
Appellate counsel's failure to timely notify petitioner that his appeal had been denied and advise him of his right to file for discretionary review, which prevented petitioner from pursuing his right for discretionary review and constituted ineffective assistance of counsel.

File for Discretionary Review

Shiloh-Bryant v. Director, TDCJ-ID, 104 F. Supp. 2d 696, 704 (E.D. Tex. 2000)
Appellate counsel's failure to timely notify petitioner that his appeal had been denied and advise him of his right to file for discretionary review, which prevented petitioner from pursuing his right for discretionary review and constituted ineffective assistance of counsel.

Petition for Writ of Certiorari

Freeman v. Lane, 962 F.2d 1252 (7th Cir. 1992)
Appellate counsel's failure to present issue, on direct appeal, based on prosecutor's improper comments that defendant refused to testify, prejudiced defendant where counsel's failure prevented defendant from presenting issue for discretionary review to the United States Supreme Court.

Miller v. Keeney, 882 F.2d 1428 (9th Cir. 1989)
Appellate counsel's incorrect advice to not file a petition for writ of certiorari to the United States Supreme Court held not to violated defendant's constitutional rights to effective assistance of counsel.

FAILED TO RAISE

Acceptance of Responsibility

Brown v. U.S., 42 F.Supp. 2d 122 (D. Puerto Rico 1998)
Appellate counsel's failure to argue that the district court abused its discretion for not giving the defendant a three level reduction in sentence for acceptance of responsibility pursuant to *U.S.S.G. §3E1.1 (a, b)*, constituted ineffective assistance of counsel.

Aggravating Factor to Support Death Penalty

Lawrence v. Branker, 517 F.3d 700, 704 (4th Cir. 2008)
> Appellate counsel provided constitutionally ineffective assistance for failing to appeal the submission of Lawrence's burglary conviction as an aggravating factor to support death sentence.

Biased Juror Claim

Franklin v. Anderson, 267 F.Supp. 2d 768, 793-794 (S.D. Ohio 2003)
> Appellate counsel was constitutionally ineffective by failing to raise the issue that petitioner's conviction was unconstitutional because a biased juror deprived petitioner of the right to a fair and impartial trial as guaranteed by the due process clause.

Confrontation Clause Claim

Clemmons v. Delo, 124 F.3d 944 (8th Cir. 1997)
> Appellate counsels failure to raise confrontation clause claim on direct appeal, constitutes ineffective assistance of counsel and provided "cause" for procedural default.

Double Jeopardy Issue

Jackson v. Leonard, 162 F. 3d 81 (2nd Cir. 1998)
> Appellate counsel's failure to raise issue that the prosecution was barred by double jeopardy constituted ineffective assistance of counsel.

U.S. v. McDonald, 981 F.Supp. 942 (D,Md. 1997)
> Counsel's failure to object to defendant being sentenced to bank robbery which was lesser included offense of armed robbery required the sentence to be vacated on the lesser included offense and constituted ineffective assistance.

Griffin v. U.S., 598 A.2d 1174 (D.C. App. 1991)
> Appellate counsel's failure to raise a double jeopardy claim on appeal constituted ineffective assistance of counsel which warranted recalling the previously issued mandate.

"Dead Bang" Winner

U.S. v. Cook, 45 F.3d 388 (10th Cir. 1995)
> Appellate counsel's failure to raise a dead-bang winner, constitutes ineffective assistance and establishes "cause" for failure to raise the error.

Denial of Motion for Continuance

Kane v. Kyler, 201 F.Supp. 2d 392, 398-399 (E.D. Pa. 2001)
> Appellant counsel was constitutionally ineffective for failing to appeal the district court's denial of defendant's motion for continuance for purposes of obtaining alibi testimony from defendant's nonambulatory father.

Drug Quantity

U.S. v. Mannino, 212 F.3d 835 (3rd Cir. 2000)
Appellate Counsel's failure to raise the issue that the district court's failure to apply the proper methodology in determining the amount heroin attributable to defendants in conspiracy to import and distribute heroin constituted ineffective assistance of counsel.

General Verdict Form

Ballard v. U.S., 400 F.3d 404, 408-09 (6th Cir. 2005)
Appellate counsel was constitutionally ineffective for failing to raise Ballard's _Apprendi_ and _Dale_ claims where the indictment charged two drugs in one count and where the jury **never** determined which drug it used to convict Ballard because the trial court used a general verdict form, and then imposed sentence based on cocaine which carries a greater sentence than marijuana.

Meritorious Issues

Banks v. Reynolds, 54 F.3d 1508, 1515-16 (10th Cir. 1995)
Appellate court's failure to raise clearly meritorious issues on direct appeal constitutes ineffective assistance.

Douglas v. Wainwright, 714 F.2d 1532 (11th Cir. 1983)
Trial and appellate counsel's failure to raise fact that defendant's prior conviction used was invalid constitutes ineffective assistance of counsel.

Inadmissible Hearsay

Mason v. Hanks, 97 F.3d 887 (7th Cir. 1996)
Appellate counsel's failure to raise issue of inadmissible hearsay evidence of informants' tips to officer that defendant was drug dealer constituted ineffective assistance of counsel.

Prosecutor Misconduct

Freeman v. Lane, 962 F.2d 1252 (7th Cir. 1992)
Appellate counsel's failure to present issue, on direct appeal, based on prosecutor's improper comments that defendant refused to testify prejudiced defendant where counsel's failure prevented defendant from presenting issue for discretionary review to the United States Supreme Court.

Reynolds v. Ellingsworth, 843 F.2d 712 (3rd Cir. 1988)
Appellate counsel's failure to raise prosecutor's improper remarks during opening arguments may constitute ineffective assistance of counsel.

Appellate Ineffectiveness

Robison v. Maynard, 829 F.2d 1501 (10th Cir. 1987)
> Appellant's counsel's failure to raise issue of prosecutorial misconduct in state appeal required an evidentiary hearing, where Oklahoma court granted other defendants relief from same kind of conduct by same prosecutor, to resolve ineffective assistance of counsel claim.

Martire v. Wainwright, 811 F.2d 1430 (11th Cir. 1987)
> Appellant counsel's failure to raise issue of improper admission of evidence, which amounted to comments of defendant's post-arrest silence, fell below the wide range of competent counsel in criminal case and was prejudicial in light of state court rule of automatic reversal.

Improper Consecutive Sentences

Beavers v. Lockhart, 755 F.2d 657 (8th Cir. 1985)
> Appellate counsel was ineffective and required an evidentiary hearing where counsel failed to raise the issue of the trial court's imposition of consecutive sentence.

Keep Appeal Alive Waiting Supreme Court Decision

Perez v. Dept. of Corrections, 227 F.Supp. 2d 1298, 1304-07 (S.D. Fla. 2002)
> Appellate counsel was constitutionally ineffective by failing to keep petitioner's appeal alive while the Florida Supreme Court heard a case determining the validity of the attempted felony murder doctrine; petitioner was prejudiced by counsel's errors because the Florida Supreme Court ultimately eliminated the attempted felony murder offense.

Obvious Issues on Appeal

Daniel v. Thigpen, 742 F.Supp. 1535 (M.D. Ala. 1990)
> Appellate counsel's failure to raise obvious issue in the record, such as whether the trial court erred in failing to conduct a competency hearing, and trial counsel's failure to raise adequacy of lesser included offense jury instruction on direct appeal constituted ineffective assistance of counsel.

Gray v. Greer, 778 F.2d 350 (7th Cir. 1985)
> Appellate counsel's ineffective assistance in failing to raise an issue on appeal, can constitute "cause" even if counsel's ineffectiveness did not violate the constitution under the requirements of *Wainwright*. See also *Gray v. Greer, 800 F.2d 644 (7th Cir. 1986).*

Inadmissible Hearsay

Mason v. Hanks, 97 F.3d 887 (7th Cir. 1996)
> Appellate counsel's failure to raise issue of inadmissible hearsay of informant's out-of-court statements that defendant was dealing heroin, where issue was preserved for review, constitutes ineffective assistance of counsel.

Instructional Error

Carter v. Bowerson, 265 F.3d 705, 715-717 (8th Cir. 2001)
>   Appellate counsel was constitutionally ineffective for failing to raise the instructional error in penalty phase of capital sentencing, where one juror had attempted to change her vote during sentencing required setting aside the death sentence.

Court's Refusal to Grant Funds for a Psychiatric Expert

Holland v. Horn, 150 F.Supp. 2d 706 (E.D. Pa. 2001)
>   Appellant counsel was ineffective for failing to raise issue that petitioner was denied his Fifth Amendment right to court-appointed defense expert during penalty phase of capital trial to help develop defense in support of mitigating evidence.

Boliek v. Delo, 912 F.Supp. 1199 (W.D. Mo. 1995)
>   Appellate counsel's failure to raise issue that trial court committed reversible error in denying defendant's motion for funds and appointment of psychiatric expert, constituted ineffective assistance.

Ineffective Assistance of Counsel

Koras v. Robinson, 257 F.Supp. 2d 941, 950-954 (E.D. Mich. 2003)
>   Appellate counsel's failure to raise trial counsel's deficient performance by failing to move to suppress petitioner's statement to police, after he had invoked his right to counsel under *Miranda* and *Edwards*; petitioner's statement was the key evidence against petitioner that would have been suppressed, absent counsel's errors.

Greer v. Mitchell, 264 F.3d 663 (6th Cir. 2001)
>   Appellate counsel's failure to raise trial counsel's ineffectiveness on direct appeal for failure to investigate and present mitigating evidence during penalty phase required an evidentiary hearing.

Ramirez v. Attorney General of State of New York, 280 F.3d 87, 95 (2d Cir. 2001)
>   Appellate counsel's letter application to state's highest court for leave to appeal conviction sufficiently exhausted federal claim of ineffective assistance of counsel at the state level. The Second Circuit remanded with instructions for the district court to entertain Ramirez' ineffective assistance of counsel claims.

White v. Schotten, 201 F.3d 743 (6th Cir. 2000)
>   Appellate counsel's failure to file application, under Ohio law, to reopen direct appeal to permit defendant's assertion of ineffectiveness of counsel claims constituted ineffective assistance of counsel.

Matthews v. Abramajtys, 92 F.Supp.2d 615 (E.D. Mich. 2000)
>   Appellate counsel was ineffective in failing to raise a valid claim of trial ineffectiveness of counsel for failure to investigate witness before trial, to cross-examine witnesses, and to present alibi witness as theory of defense.

Mapes v. Coyle, 171 F.3d 408 (6th Cir. 1999)
>   Evidentiary hearing required to determine whether appellate counsel's failure to raise on

direct appeal trial counsel's failure to investigate mitigating evidence in reference to a prior murder conviction supporting petitioner's death specification, and the trial court's errors in precluding jury from considering mitigating evidence during penalty phase constitutes ineffective assistance of counsel.

Delgardo v. Lewis, 181 F.3d 1087 (9th Cir. 1999)
Appellate counsel's failure to argue issues in appellate brief constructively left defendant without counsel on appeal and counsel did not file a motion to withdraw as counsel on appeal. **See also** *Delgado v. Lewis, 168 F.3d 1148 (9th Cir. 1999)*; *Lombard v. Lynaugh, 868 F.2d 1475 (5th Cir. 1989)*

Grubbs v. Singletary, 900 F.Supp. 425 (M.D. Fla. 1995)
Appellate counsel's failure to raise trial counsel's ineffectiveness on direct appeal may constitute ineffective assistance of counsel where the claim could be resolved on the record.

Daniel v. Thigpen, 742 F.Supp. 1535 (M.D. Ala. 1990)
Appellate counsel's failure to raise obvious issue in the record, such as whether the trial court erred in failing to conduct a competency hearing, and trial counsel's failure to raise adequacy of lesser included offense jury instruction on direct appeal, constituted ineffective assistance of counsel.

U.S. Ex Rel. Barnard v. Lane, 819 F.2d 798 (7th Cir. 1987)
Appellate counsel's failure to raise ineffective assistance of counsel claim against trial counsel on direct appeal constituted "cause" for procedural default for trial counsel's deliberate withholding of manslaughter jury instruction.

Allen v. U.S., 938 F.2d 664 (6th Cir. 1991)
Reinstatement of appeal is appropriate remedy of ineffective assistance of appellate counsel where counsel failed to litigate defendant's claims.

Insufficient Factual Basis for Guilty Plea

Coddington v. Langley, 202 F.Supp. 2d 687, 702 (E.D. Mich. 2002)
Appellate counsel was constitutionally ineffective by failing to raise that there was insufficient factual basis for the guilty plea on direct appeal, where petitioner did not admit to touching his daughter for the purpose of sexual contact under Michigan law.

Insufficiency of Evidence

Wilson v. Vaughn, 304 F.Supp.2d 652, 658-659 (E.D. Pa. 2004)
Appellate counsel was constitutionally ineffective for failing to raise the issue that there was insufficient evidence to support a conviction, that petitioner was a member of legitimate organization, as required under Pennsylvania Corrupt Organization Act.

Carpenter v. Mohr, 163 F.3d 938 (6th Cir. 1998)
Appellate counsel's failure to challenge sufficiency of evidence supporting conditional guilty plea constituted ineffective assistance of counsel.

Holsclaw v. Smith, 822 F.2d 1041 (11th Cir. 1987)

Trial counsel's failure to raise issue of insufficient evidence at the end of trial or move for dismissal based on insufficient evidence, constituted ineffective assistance of counsel.

Court's Denial of Pro Se Representation

United States v. Skurdal, 341 F.3d 921, 927-928 (9th Cir. 2003)

Appellate counsel was constitutionally ineffective by failing to comply with *Anders* and *Griffy* when seeking to withdraw as counsel on appeal. Counsel failed to brief the issue that the trial court erred denying petitioner self-representation, by holding that petitioner was not competent to represent himself because he lacked the "technical legal knowledge" and deprived petitioner of his Fifth Amendment right to effective assistance of counsel on appeal.

Orazio v. Dugger, 876 F.2d 1508 (11th Cir. 1989)

Appellate counsels failure to raise trial counsel's denial of defendant's request to proceed pro se on direct appeal, constitutes ineffective assistance of counsel.

Court's Failure to Conduct Competency Hearing

Daniel v. Thigpen, 742 F.Supp. 1535 (M.D. Ala. 1990)

Appellate counsel's failure to raise obvious issue in the record, such as whether the trial court erred in failing to conduct a competency hearing, and trial counsel's failure to raise adequacy of lesser included offense jury instruction on direct appeal constituted ineffective assistance of counsel.

Improper Advice from Court During Plea Proceedings

Rogers v. U.S., 990 F.2d 1008 (8th Cir. 1993)

Appellate counsel's failure to raise, on direct appeal, district court's failure to advise defendant that, if the district court refused to accept prosecutor's sentence recommendation, defendant had no right to withdraw guilty plea, stated a sufficient claim of ineffective assistance of counsel and warranted an evidentiary hearing.

Reasonable Doubt Instruction

McKee v. U.S., 167 F.3d 103 (2nd Cir. 1999)

Appellate counsel's failure to challenge reasonable doubt jury instruction constituted ineffective assistance of counsel and required a remand for an evidentiary hearing.

Jackson v. Leonard, 162 F.3d 81 (2nd Cir. 1998)

Appellate counsel's failure to raise double jeopardy claim where it was apparent that Jackson's two charges of first degree robbery and criminal use of a firearm in the first degree rested on the same factual predicated constitutes ineffective assistance of counsel.

Defective Jury Instruction

U.S. Ex Rel. Barnard v. Lane, 819 F.2d 798 (7th Cir. 1987)
> Appellate counsel's failure to raise ineffective assistance of counsel claim against trial counsel on direct appeal constituted "cause" for procedural default for trial counsel's deliberate withholding of manslaughter jury instruction.

Smith v. Wainwright, 741 F.2d 1248 (11th Cir. 1984)
> Appellate counsel's failure to challenge defective jury instruction constituted ineffective assistance of counsel.

Plain Error Review on Jury Instruction

Roe v. Delo, 160 F.3d 416 (8th Cir. 1998)
> Appellate counsel's failure to request, a plain error review of an erroneous first degree murder jury instruction which lightened the prosecutions burden of proof constituted ineffective assistance of counsel.

Court's Failure to Suppress Evidence

Joshua v. Dewitt, 341 F.3d 430, 441-443 (6th Cir. 2003)
> Appellate counsel was ineffective for failing to argue on appeal that the continuing detention of petitioner following traffic stop based on a police flyer; absent any proof that officer who issued flyer had reasonable suspicion to link petitioner to criminal activity, violated the Supreme Court's decision in *Hensley*.

Claudio v. Scully, 982 F.2d 798 (2nd Cir. 1992)
> Failure to raise trial court's refusal to suppress confession on appeal constituted ineffective assistance of counsel.

Lofton v. Whitley, 905 F.2d 885 (5th Cir. 1990)
> Failure to raise on appeal that defendant's photograph was obtained in violation of the Fourth Amendment, which was used in a photographic array, constituted ineffective assistance of counsel.

Improper Sentencing Enhancement for Obstruction of Justice

Nearly v. U.S., 998 F.2d 563 (8th Cir. 1993)
> Trial counsel objected to enhancement of defendant's sentence for "obstruction of justice" under the Guidelines, but failed to raise the issue on appeal, which constituted performance below an objective standard of reasonableness and required an evidentiary hearing to resolve ineffective assistance of counsel claim.

Failed to Request Voir Dire Transcripts

Smith v. Wainwright, 741 F.2d 1248 (11th Cir. 1984)
> Appellate counsel's failure to request transcripts of entire voir dire proceedings was ineffective assistance.

Failed to Discuss Merits of Appeal

Baker v. Kaiser, 929 F.2d 1495, 1499-1500 (10th Cir. 1991)
>   Defense counsel's failure to ask defendant whether he wanted to appeal and failed to discuss the merits of an appeal constituted ineffective assistance.

Peoples v. Bowen, 791 F.2d 861 (11th Cir. 1986)
>   Appellate counsel's failure to advise defendant that if he appealed the twenty (20) year sentence, that the Court of Appeals may remand for resentencing, at which time defendant would receive life under the mandatory habitual felony offender statute, constituted ineffective assistance of counsel.

Appeal Dismissed Over Two Years

Mack v. Smith, 659 F.2d 23 (5th Cir. 1981)
>   Appellate counsel hiding the fact that defendant's appeal had been dismissed for more than a year and assuring defendant that counsel was still waiting for a copy of the trial transcripts was sufficient allegation for an evidentiary hearing.

Exposed Defendant to Additional Punishment

Peoples v. Bowen, 791 F.2d 861 (11th Cir. 1986)
>   Appellate counsel's failure to advise defendant that if he appealed the twenty (20) year sentence, that the Court of Appeals may remand for resentencing, at which time defendant would receive life under the mandatory habitual felony offender statute, constituted ineffective assistance of counsel.

Defendant Waived Appeal

Childs v. Collins, 995 F.2d 67 (5th Cir. 1993)
>   Defendant waived his right to appeal where he failed to inform counsel or the trial court of his desire to appeal.

Johnson v. U.S., 838 F.2d 201 (7th Cir. 1988)
>   A waiver of an appeal, if done intentionally, is a relinquishment of a known right and is effective unless involuntary. *Federal Rules of Criminal Procedure, Rule 51(d)* is designed to ensure that no criminal appeal is dismissed unless the defendant files a formal waiver. The defendant must demonstrate that he knows about his right to appeal and deliberately forswears it. Such a declaration is as binding as any other waiver.

Counsel's Failure to Raise His Own Ineffectiveness Created a Conflict of Interest

Whiting v. Burt, 266 F.Supp. 2d 640, 644 (E.D. Mich. 2003)
>   Appellate counsel labored under a conflict of interest because he was petitioner's trial counsel and refused to raise claim of ineffectiveness of counsel against himself on direct appeal. The appropriate remedy was to grant a new appeal.

Counsel Not Required to Raise His Own Ineffective Assistance of Counsel

Page v. U.S., 884 F.2d 300 (7th Cir. 1989)
>   Appellate counsel is not required to raise his own ineffectiveness on appeal in order to preserve claim for *28 U.S.C. §2255* motion.

Denial of the Right to Counsel

Wisconsin Ex Rel. Toliver v. McCaughtry, 72 F.Supp.2d 960 (E.D. Wis. 1999)
>   Denial of the right to counsel on the first direct appeal warranted conditionally granting the writ and ordering that Toliver be released within 120 days unless the state reinstates the direct appeal and providing Toliver with appointed counsel within 120 days.

Walker v. McCaughtry, 72 F.Supp.2d 1025 (E.D. Wis. 1999)
>   Denial of appellate counsel resulted in automatic prejudice and required reinstatement of state appeal.

Due Process Requires Effective Assistance on Appeal

Evitts v. Lucey, 469 U.S. 387, 83 L.Ed.2d 821, 105 S.Ct. 830 (1985)
>   Due Process guarantees defendant the right to effective assistance of counsel on first direct appeal.

Lane v. Brown, 372 U.S. 477, 9 L.Ed.2d 892, 83 S.Ct. 768 (1963)
>   Due process requires appointment of counsel and free transcripts for appellate purposes of an indigent defendant.

Lofton v. Whitley, 905 F.2d 885 (5th Cir. 1990)
>   The Due Process Clause of the Constitution guarantees defendant effective assistance of counsel on first appeal.

Eight and One-Half Year Delay in Appeal

Elcock v. Henderson, 947 F.2d 1004 (2nd Cir. 1991)
>   An eight and one-half year delay in appeal from conviction violated due process.

Panel is Bound by Other Panel of Judges Decision

U.S v. Short, 181 F.3d 620 (5th Cir. 1999)
>   Fifth Circuit panel is bound by precedent of previous Fifth circuit panel absent an intervening Supreme Court case overruling that prior precedent.

Ramsey v. Johnson, 149 F. 3d 749 (8th Cir. 1998)
>   One panel of the Court of Appeals is bound by the decisions of the other panels of judges.

Application To Re-open Direct Appeal

White v. Schotten, 201 F.3d 743 (6th Cir. 2000)
>   Appellate counsel's failure to file application, under Ohio law to reopen direct appeal to permit defendant's assertion of ineffectiveness of counsel claims constituted ineffective assistance of counsel.

POST-VERDICT INEFFECTIVENESS

FAILED TO FILE MOTION FOR NEW TRIAL

Enoch v. Gramley, 70 F.3d 1490 (7th Cir. 1995)
> Trial counsel's failure to file a motion for new trial can constitute representation below an objective standard of reasonableness, but the defendant must be able to establish prejudice.

Robinson v. Norris, 60 F.3d 457 (8th Cir. 1995)
> Defendant is entitled to counsel in motion for new trial proceeding, a critical stage of the proceedings, which constitutional right to counsel attaches.

U.S. v. Kladouris, 739 F.Supp. 1221 (N.D. Ill. 1990)
> Facts forming a basis of defendant's defense not presented at trial can constitute newly discovered evidence and form a basis for ineffective assistance of counsel claim for a new trial under *Federal Rules of Criminal Procedure Rule 33.* **See also** *House v. Balkcom, 725 F.2d 608 (11th Cir. 1984)*; *Rummel v. Estelle, 498 F.Supp. 793 (W.D. Tex 1980)*; *Johnson v. United States, 328 F.2d 605 (5th Cir. 1964)*

Holsclaw v. Smith, 822 F.2d 1041 (11th Cir. 1987)
> Trial counsel's failure to raise issue of insufficient evidence at the end of trial or move for dismissal based on insufficient evidence, constituted ineffective assistance of counsel.

Summit v. Blackburn, 795 F.2d 1237 (5th Cir. 1986)
> Trial counsel's failure to move for a post-verdict judgment of acquittal or a modification of the verdict for a conviction on a lesser included charge constitutes ineffective assistance of counsel.

FAILED TO ADVISE DEFENDANT OF TIME LIMITS AND APPELLATE PROCEDURE

White v. Johnson, 180 F.3d 648 (5th Cir. 1999)
> Trial counsel's failure to advise defendant that he had only 30 days under Texas State law to file state appeal constituted ineffective assistance of counsel.

U.S. v. Gipson, 985 F.2d 212 (5th Cir. 1993)
> Trial counsel's failure to inform defendant of time limits for filing of an appeal constitutes ineffective assistance of counsel.

FAULTY OR INCORRECT LEGAL ADVICE

Wogan v. United States, 846 F.Supp. 135 (D.Me. 1994)
> Defense counsel's failure to inform defendant that government could appeal downward departure from the Guidelines constituted ineffective assistance of counsel.

Bell v. Lockhart, 795 F.2d 655 (8th Cir. 1986)

Counsel erroneously advised defendant that if he appealed, that he would be subjecting himself to the death penalty, if he was successful on appeal, based on this advice, defendant did not appeal. Counsel's advice constituted ineffective assistance of counsel, and required granting a new appeal.

Peoples v. Bowen, 791 F.2d 861 (11th Cir. 1986)

Appellate counsel's failure to advise defendant that if he appealed the twenty (20) year sentence that the Court of Appeals may remand for resentencing at which time defendant would receive life, under the mandatory habitual felony offender statute, constituted ineffective assistance of counsel.

MOTION TO COMPEL UNITED STATES TO FILE RULE 35(b) MOTON TO REDUCE SENTENCE

United States v. Wilson, 390 F.3d 1003, 1009-1010 (7th Cir. 2004)

Wilson filed a motion to compel the United States to file a **Rule 35(b)** motion to reduce his sentence based on his substantial assistance to the government. Wilson showed bad faith on behalf of the United States. The district court failed to address Wilson's claims and denied relief. The Seventh Circuit reversed and remanded for further proceedings.

FAILED TO FILE MOTION TO REDUCE SENTENCE (Rule 35)

Blaik v. U.S., 117 F.3d 1289 (11th Cir. 1997)

Defense counsel failed to file a timely notice of appeal on the denial of Blaik's, rule 35 motion to reduce sentence and, as such, constituted ineffective assistance.

Griffin v. U.S., 109 F.3d 1217 (7th Cir. 1997)

Counsel file a rule 35 (b) motion to reduce sentence, under Federal Rules of Criminal Procedure, a motion that only the government could file, which is a non-existent motion for the defense under federal practice and constitutes deficient performance under Strickland.

U.S. v. Golden, 854 F.2d 31 (3rd Cir. 1988)

Trial counsel's failure to file a motion for reduction of sentence within time limits, after denial of certiorari, at the defendant's request constituted a denial of counsel and deprived defendant of opportunity to have sentencing judge to exercise discretion over the reduction of sentence.

FAILED TO ADVISE DEFENDANT OF HIS APPELLATE RIGHTS

Lozada v. Deeds, 488 U.S. 430, 112 L.Ed.2d 956, 111 S.Ct. 860(1991

Defense counsel's failure to inform petitioner of his right to appeal constitutes ineffective assistance of counsel.

**Brady v. Ponte, 705 F.Supp. 52 (D. Mass. 1988)**

Trial counsel's failure to file an appeal or to inform defendant of appellate procedures constitutes ineffective assistance of counsel

FAILED TO REQUEST BOND AFTER CONVICTION

**United States v. Hammonds, 425 F.2d 597 (D.C. Cir. 1970)**

Trial counsel's failure to request bond after conviction and to speak on defendant's behalf after sentencing, constituted ineffective assistance of counsel.

MOTION FOR WRIT OF ERROR CORAM NOBIS

**United States v. Morgan, 346 U.S. 502, 512, 74 S.Ct. 247, 253, 98 L.Ed.2d 248(1954)**

The United States Supreme Court has held that the writ of error _coram nobis_ is available to correct errors "of the most fundamental character." _**(quoting United States v. Mayer, 235 U.S. 55, 69, 35 S.Ct. 16, 19-20, 59 L.Ed. 129 (1912)). Morgan**_ held the district court had power, under the _**All-Writs Act, 28 U.S.C. §1651 (a)**_, to issue a writ of error coram nobis to vacate a conviction on the ground that the defendant had been deprived of counsel without his knowing waiver of his constitutional right to counsel. Although this writ is an "extraordinary remedy [available] only under circumstances compelling such action to achieve justice." _**346 U.S. at 511.**_

**United States v. Kwan, 407 F.3d 1005, 1015-17 (9th Cir. 2005)**

Counsel misled Kwan that by pleading guilty to bank fraud he would not be deported and such advice was deficient performance. Counsel failure to inform the sentencing judge that a sentence only two days lighter would enable Kwan to avoid deportation and remain united with his family constitutes ineffective assistance of counsel and warranted granting the coram nobis petition.

**U.S. v. Castro, 26 F.3d 557 (5th Cir. 1994)**

Defendant was entitled to **coram nobis relief** based on ineffective assistance of counsel where counsel failed to advise him of availability of judicial recommendation against deportation.

**United States v. Drobny, 955 F.2d 990, 996 (5th Cir. 1992)**

The Fifth Circuit noted that the standard for coram nobis relief was more "demanding" than the cause and prejudice standard for habeas corpus relief under _**28 U.S.C. §2255.**_

**U.S. v. Dawes, 895 F.2d 1581 (10th Cir. 1990)**

The Tenth Circuit held that despite the fact that defendants **were currently in custody** that they were entitled to reversal under motion for writ of error coram nobis.

**United States v. Walgren, 885 F.2d 1417 (9th Cir. 1989)**

The Ninth Circuit set forth the standards for coram nobis relief if the petitioner can demonstrate: "'(1) a more usual remedy is not available; (2) valid reasons exist for not attacking the conviction earlier; (3) adverse consequences exist from conviction sufficient to satisfy the case or controversy requirement of Article III; and (4) the error is of the most fundamental character.'" _**Id at 1420.**_

Post Verdict Ineffectiveness

U.S. v. Golden, 854 F.2d 31 (3rd Cir. 1988)

Golden complained that even through his conviction was affirmed, that his counsel was ineffective where he failed to file a requested timely **Rule 35 motion to reduce sentence** and that his counsel abandonment deprived him of significant substantive right to have the sentencing judge exercise the discretion, which **Rule 35** confers, to reduce his sentence. The government, in defense of the district court's ruling, characterized Golden's motion as one pursuant to *28 U.S.C. §2255 (1982)*. That section, according to the government, affords relief only from the underlying judgment of sentence. The Third Circuit in *Golden* found "While the government may be right about the kinds of relief available under section *2255, see United States v. Hill, 826 F.2d 507 (7th Cir. 1987)*, it fails to take into account relief which may be available under the All Writs Act. *28 U.S.C. §1651 (1982).* It is settled that by virtue of the All Writs Act the writ of **coram nobis** is available with respect to judgments in criminal matters in the federal courts. *E.g., United States, 346 U.S. 502, 74 S.Ct. 247, 98 L.Ed. 248 (1954); United States ex. rel. Bogish v. Tees, 211 F.2d 69 (3rd Cir. 1954); Casias v. United States, 421 F.2d 1233 (10th Cir. 1970).*

United States v. Mandel, 862 F.2d 1067, 1075 (4th Cir. 1988), cert. Denied, 491 U.S. 906, 109 S.Ct. 3190, 105 L.Ed.2d 699 (1989)

Writ of error coram nobis properly granted where defendants were convicted of conduct that was not criminal.

CAUSE FOR PROCEDURAL DEFAULT

This section of the book deals with establishing "cause" for procedural default, which

the government, as a general rule, argues. *See*, *Frady v. United States, 456 U.S. 152 (1982).*

FACTORS WHICH CONSTITUTES "CAUSE"

Murray v. Carrier, 477 U.S. 478, 488, 106 S.Ct. 2639, 2645, 91 L.Ed.2d 297 (1986)
> The Supreme Court observed that "cause" would be established by a showing that (1) the factual or legal basis for a claim was not reasonably available to counsel; (2) that some interference by officials made compliance impracticable; or (3) the procedural default was the result of constitutionally ineffective assistance.

COURT IS NOT REQUIRED TO RAISE PROCEDURAL BAR

Trest v.Cain, 522 U.S. 87, 139 L.Ed.2d 444, 118 S.Ct. 478 (1997)
> A court of appeals is not required to raise the issue of procedural default **sua sponte.**

INEFFECTIVE ASSISTANCE OF COUNSEL CONSTITUTES "CAUSE" FOR PROCEDURAL DEFAULT

Massaro v. United States, 538 U.S. 500, 155, L.Ed.2d 714, 123 S.Ct. 1690 (2003)
> A federal prisoner's failure to raise claim of ineffective assistance of counsel on direct appeal does not bar review on **28 U.S.C. §2255** motion.

Edwards v. Carpenter, 529 U.S.446, 146 LEd.2d 518, 120 S.Ct. 1587 (2000)
> The Supreme Court held that "A procedurally defaulted ineffective- assistance – of- counsel claim could serve as cause to excuse the procedural default of another claim only if the petitioner could satisfy the "cause and prejudice" standard with the respect to the ineffective- assistance- of- counsel claim where – as in the case at hand- there was not at issue the cause- and- prejudice standard's exception for a fundamental miscarriage of justice," Id.

Kimmelman v. Morrison, 477 U.S. 365, 91 L.Ed.2d 305, 106 S.Ct. 2574 (1986)
> Where the court held that "[t]he Constitution constrains our ability to allocate as we see fit the cost of ineffective assistance. The Sixth Amendment mandates that the State [or the government] bears the risk of constitutionally deficient assistance of counsel". *Id.*

Ege v. Yukins, 485 F.3d 364, 378-380 (6th Cir. 2007)
> Counsel's failure to object to expert testimony establishes <u>cause</u> for procedural default.

Mickens v. Taylor, 227 F.3d 203, 209 (4th Cir. 2000)
> A federal habeas petitioner can establish "cause" that overcomes both the exhaustion and procedural default bars by showing that the factual basis of the claim was

unavailable to him when he filed his state habeas petition and establishes actual prejudice.

***Hooks v. Ward*, 184 F.3d 1206 (10th Cir. 1999)**
The Court remanded for determination whether Oklahoma's procedural bar on ineffective assistance of trial counsel claims barred relief as to claims not raised on direct appeal.

***U.S. v. Gordon*, 172 F.3d 753 (10th Cir. 1999)**
Ineffective assistance of counsel and due process claims which were not raised on direct appeal were not procedurally barred and required a Certificate of Appealability.

***U.S. v. Galloway*, 56 F.3d 1239 (10th Cir. 1995)**
Ineffective assistance of counsel claims raised on direct appeal does not procedural bar ineffective assistance claims on §2255 motion if new claims are based on different grounds.

***U.S. v. Cook*, 45 F.3d 388 (10th Cir. 1995)**
Appellate counsel's failure to raise a dead-bang winner constitutes ineffective assistance and establishes "cause" for failure to raise the error.

***Medina v. Barnes*, 71 F.3d 363 (10th Cir. 1995)**
Trial counsel's failure to investigate prosecution's key witness in murder case, where key witness lied about his criminal activity with victim at the time he called police constituted "cause" for procedure default and required an evidentiary hearing under the fundamental miscarriage of justice standard to resolve ineffective assistance of counsel claims.

***Gray v. Lynn*, 6 F.3d 265 (5th Cir. 1993)**
Trial counsel's ineffectiveness for failure to object to erroneous jury instruction that expanded elements of crime, constitutes "cause" for procedural default.

***U.S. v. De La Fuente*, 8 F.3d 1333 (9th Cir. 1993)**
Trial counsel's failure to contest the government breach of plea where the government failed to move for a downward departure below the mandatory minimum, pursuant to *U.S.S.G. §5K1.1*, constitutes ineffective assistance and established cause for procedural default.

***U.S. v. Davenport*, 986 F.2d 1047 (7th Cir. 1993)**
Trial counsel's failure to move to suppress confession may constitute "cause" under ineffective assistance of counsel for procedural default rule.

***Thomas v. Harrelson*, 942 F.2d 1530 (11th Cir. 1991)**
Trial counsel's ineffectiveness in failing to object to the constructive amendment to the indictment constituted "cause" for procedural bar.

***Smelcher v. Attorney General of Alabama*, 947 F.2d 1472 (11th Cir. 1991)**
Trial counsel's failure to object to the state court's exclusion of evidence of sexual relations between defendant and raped victim constitutes "cause" for procedural default.

Daniel v. Thigpen, 742 F.Supp. 1535 (M.D. Ala. 1990)
> Trial counsel's failure to object to jury instruction or request an instruction for a lesser included offense constituted ineffective assistance of counsel and established "cause" for procedural default.

United States ex.rel. Caruso v. Zelinsky, 689 F.2d 435 (3rd Cir. 1982)
> Counsel's ineffectiveness in failing to inform defendant of state's plea offer constitutes "cause" for procedural default and requires an evidentiary hearing.

Osborn v. Shillinger, 861 F.2d 612 (10th Cir. 1988)
> Ineffective assistance of counsel claims may be properly brought for the first time in collateral proceedings, which constitutes "cause" for procedural default.

Conflict of Interest Constitutes "Cause" For Procedural Default

Dawan v. Lockhart, 980 F.2d 470 (8th Cir. 1992)
> Trial counsel's conflict of interest constituted "cause" for failure to present ineffective assistance of counsel claim. See also ***Bliss v. Lockhart, 891 F.2d 1335 (8th Cir. 1989)***.

Jamison v. Lockhart, 975 F.2d 1377 (8th Cir. 1992)
> Defendant's trial counsel, who was also City Attorney, created a conflict of interest and constitutes "cause" for procedural default.

Rosenwald v. U.S., 898 F.2d 585 (7th Cir. 1990)
> Rosenwald's §2255 motion alleged ineffective assistance of counsel due to attorney simultaneous representation, on unrelated civil matter, of government's key witness, and if established, constitutes "cause" under the Frady Rule.

Actual Innocence/Fundamental Miscarriage of Justice is an Exception to "Cause" for Procedural Default

Murray v. Carrier, 477 U.S. 478, 496, 106 S.Ct. 2639, 2649-50, 91 L.Ed.2d 397 (1985)
> The Supreme Court, although cautioning that it would not always be true, instructed that "where a constitutional violation has probably resulted in the conviction of one who is actually innocent, a federal habeas court may grant the writ even in the absence of a showing of cause for the procedural default". The Supreme Court in ***Smith v. Murray, 477 U.S. 527, 537, 106 S.Ct. 2661, 2667-68, 91 L.Ed.2d 434 (1986)***, did imply that the actual innocence exception may apply to non-capital sentencing cases: We reject the suggestion that the principles of ***Wainwright v. Sykes*** [cause and prejudice requirements in cases of procedural default] apply differently **depending on the nature of the penalty** a State imposes for the violation of its criminal laws. We similarly reject the suggestion that there is anything "fundamentally unfair" about enforcing procedural default rules in cases devoid of any substantial claim that the alleged error undermined the accuracy of the guilt or **sentencing determination**. (Emphasis added)

Schlup v. Delo, 513 U.S. 298,130LEd.2d 808,115 S.Ct. 851 (1995)
> A credible claim of actual innocence involves the petitioner's supporting his constitutional claims with "new reliable evidence-whether it be exculpatory scientific evidence, trustworthy, eyewitnesses accounts, or critical physical evidence-that was

not presented at trial." Id. The court "is not bound by the rules of admissibility that would govern at trial." And should" consider the probative force of relevant evidence that was either excluded or unavailable at trial." Id. "[A] petitioner does not meet the threshold requirement unless he persuades the district court that, in light of the new evidence, no juror, acting reasonably, would have voted to find him guilty beyond a reasonable doubt." Id., Also see*, McCoy v. Norris, 958 F.Supp. 420 (E.D.Ark. 1996)*

Sawyer v. Whitley, 505 U.S. 333, 120 L.Ed.2d 269, 112 S.Ct. 2514 (1992)
The ***Sawyer*** Court found that Sawyer had not satisfied the "actual innocence" exception in order for consideration of his claims in a successive petition. Sawyer failed to present "clear and convincing evidence."

Selvage v. Collins, 494 U.S. 108, L.Ed.2d 93, 110 S.Ct. 974 (1990)
The Supreme Court remanded this case for the Court of Appeals to reconsider whether there was "cause" for not raising a claim based upon arguments later accepted in ***Perry v. Lynaugh, 492 U.S. 302, 106 L.Ed.2d 256, 109 S.Ct. 2934 (1989)***, and whether failure to consider the claim would result in a fundamental miscarriage of justice.

Bouseley v. United States, 523 U.S. 614, 140 L. Ed. 2d 828, 118 S.Ct. 1604 (1998)
"Actual innocence" means factual innocence, not mere legal insufficiency.

Dugger v. Adams, 489 U.S. at 401, 411 n.6, 109 S.Ct. 1211, 1217 n.6, 103 L.Ed.2d 435 (1989)
If one is "actually innocent" of the sentence imposed, a federal habeas court can excuse the procedural default to correct a fundamentally unjust incarceration.

Majoy v. Roe, 296 F.3d 770, 776 (9th Cir. 2002)
Majoy filed a habeas petition and the district court dismissed the petition as untimely. Majoy appealed and the Ninth Circuit remanded to the district court for determination whether Majoy could pass through the actual innocence gateway to review otherwise time-barred claims. Majoy need not show that he is actually innocent of the crime. Rather, he must show that a court cannot have confidence in the outcome of his trial.

U.S. v. McKie, 73 F.3d 1149 (D.C. Cir. 1996)
The Court held that a remand would be required to determine whether procedural bar, arising from defendant's failure to raise claim on direct appeal, would be set aside to avoid miscarriage of justice, as there was evidence that defendant was innocent of crime in question.

U.S. v. Yizar, 956 F.2d 230 (11th Cir. 1992)
The Court found that the defendant was entitled to evidentiary hearing on claim that ***Brady*** required prosecutor to volunteer statements made by co-defendant that defendant was innocent on the arson charge.

Barden v. Keohane, 921 F.2d 476 (3rd Cir. 1990),
The Court found that the Bureau of Prison's failure even to consider Barden's claim for relief from possible mistake or inadvertence in failing to designate the state prison as a place of federal confinement carries a serious potential for a miscarriage of justice. Accordingly, the Bureau's error is fundamental and can be corrected through

habeas. See ***Murray v. Carrier*** (citation omitted) (habeas available to avoid potentially serious miscarriage of justice). The ***Barden*** Court Vacated and Remanded.

U.S. v. Shaid, 916 F.2d 984 (5th Cir. 1990)

The Court held in pertinent part that: (3) if inmate were convicted of recklessly disregarding interest of the bank, rather than knowingly misapplying funds, his conviction could not stand. The defective jury instruction could have resulted in the conviction of an actual innocent person, which is an exception to the actual "cause" standard.

Actual Innocence Consideration Applies To Sentence Imposed

Dretke v. Haley, 541 U. S. 386, 158 L.Ed.2d 659, 124 S.Ct. 1847 (2004)

The Supreme Court refused to apply the "actual innocence" exception to the noncapital sentencing error, but instead remanded with instruction to address the merits of Haley's ineffective assistance of counsel claims related to the sentencing error which would grant the same relief.

Dugger v. Adams, 489 U.S. at 401, 411 n.6, 109 S.Ct. 1211, 1217 n.6, 103 L.Ed.2d 435 (1989)

If one is "actually innocent" of the sentence imposed, a federal habeas court can excuse the procedural default to correct a fundamentally unjust incarceration.

Borrego v. U.S., 975 F. Supp. 520 (S.D.N.Y. 1997)

Petitioner demonstrated facts that he was actual innocent in order to establish "cause" for procedural default, to the court's imposition of a second term of supervised release which was not permitted under applicable statute and the imposition of second term of supervised release violated ex post facto clause.

U.S. v. Maybeck, 23 F.3d 888 (4th Cir. 1994)

The Court found that: "actual innocence" exception to "cause and prejudice" requirement for consideration of issue despite procedural default extends to non-capital sentencing enhancement cases; and defendant was prejudiced by career offender sentencing designation for which he was actually innocent and, therefore, was entitled to relief despite procedural default.

Jones v. Arkansas, 929 F.2d 375, 381 (8th Cir. 1991)

The Court found that the defendant's claim that he was sentenced under Arkansas habitual offender statute which did not apply to him by its very terms, to which came within actual innocence exception to general rule that federal habeas petitioner must show cause and prejudice to excuse default in raising his claim in state court. The Court then found that Jones presented a compelling case where manifest injustice would occur were we to adhere rigidly to the procedural default rule.

Henderson v. Sargent, 926 F.2d 706 (8th Cir. 1991)

The Court of Appeals held that: (1) petitioner's counsel was ineffective during the guilty phase of the trial for failure to investigate and develop the possibility that the victim's husband, rather than the petitioner, committed the murder; (2) ineffective assistance of state post-conviction counsel provided cause for the procedural default that occurred when the ineffective assistance of trial counsel claim was not included in the state post-conviction petition; and (3) even if cause and prejudice did not exist, the actual innocence exception permitted habeas corpus review. The district court granted relief. The state of Arkansas appealed. *Id.*

Grooms v. Lockhart, 919 F.2d 505 (8th Cir. 1990)

The Court considered question of whether habeas petitioner is actually innocent of being a habitual offender under Arkansas sentencing law. The Court found Grooms admitted to three prior felonies and denied the "actual innocence claim".

Factual Innocence

Kuhlmann v. Wilson, 477 U.S. 436, 91 L.Ed.2d 364, 106 S.Ct. 2616 (1986)

A four-justice plurality of the Supreme Court suggested that the ends of justice will demand consideration of the merits of claims only where there is "a colorable showing of factual innocence. *Id. at 2627.*

Jones v. Henderson, 809 F.2d 946 (2d Cir. 1987)

This case was remanded for determination of whether the district court should review the merits of the challenge to closure of the courtroom following Officer DeSaro's testimony. Upon a determination by the district court that the "ends of justice" would be served and in making such a determination the district court may consider whether changes in the law have occurred and the petitioner made a colorable showing of factual innocence.

Moore v. Kemp, 824 F.2d 847 (11th Cir. 1987)

The Eleventh Circuit found that a "colorable showing of factual innocence" is the test, or the test is whether the alleged error precluded the development of true facts or resulted in the admission of false ones, on a material question involving the sentence, the result is the same. The Court then held that at, a minimum, the ends of justice will demand consideration of the merits of a claim on a successive petition where there is a colorable showing of factual innocence. The *Moore* Court was guided by *Smith v. Murray*. In consideration of whether "the alleged constitutional error [either] precluded the development of facts [or] resulted in the admission of false ones". *Id.*

Legal Innocence Claims

Chambers v. U.S., 22 F.3d 939 (9th Cir. 1994)

The Court found that even if defendant's conduct in receiving child pornography fell with core of child pornography exception to First Amendment where statute under which he was convicted was later declared unconstitutional in its decision in *U.S. v. X-Citement Video Inc.*, 982 F.2d 1285 (9th Cir. 1992) and where there was no valid statute on the books prohibiting such conduct, defendant was entitled to collateral relief; while perhaps morally "guilty", defendant was legally innocent.

U.S. v. Yizar, 956 F.2d 230 (11th Cir. 1992)

The Court found that the defendant was entitled to evidentiary hearing on claim that *Brady* required prosecutor to volunteer statements made by co-defendant that defendant was innocent on the arson charge.

Ewing v. McMackin, 799 F.2d 1143 (6th Cir. 1986)

The Court found that the "record was insufficient for the Court of Appeals to evaluate effect of multiple errors alleged by habeas corpus petitioner on his "actual" as opposed to "legal" innocence requiring the Court to remand for further proceeding.

External Factor Can Constitute "Cause" For Procedural Default

Murray v. Carrier, 477 U.S. 478, 91 L.Ed.2d 397, 106 S.Ct. 2639 (1986)

The Supreme Court stated, "the existence of cause for a procedural default must ordinarily turn on whether the prisoner can show that some objective factor external ⅄ to the defense impeded counsel's efforts to comply with the state's procedural rule, such as where the factual or legal basis for a claim was not reasonably available to counsel or interference by officials made compliance impracticable." *Id.* This language can provide a successful argument. See *Amadeo v. Zant*, 486 U.S. 214, 100 L.Ed.2d 249, 108 S.Ct. 1771 (1988).

Amadeo v. Zant, 486 U.S. 214, 100 L.Ed.2d 249, 108 S.Ct. 1771 (1988)

Holding that facts found by Federal District Court in federal habeas corpus case - including concealment of key memorandum by county officials - were sufficient as matter of law to permit district court to conclude that accused had established "cause" to excuse prior procedural default in raising jury-composition challenge in state court.

Dulin v. Cook, 957 F.2d 758 (10th Cir. 1992)

Dulin, a state prisoner housed in a Nevada prison, failed to file a petition for writ of certiorari in a Utah Supreme Court on another conviction. Dulin alleged, because he was in a Nevada prison, he had no access to or notice of Utah appellate rules and, thus, had no way of knowing that further state appeal was required or available. In effect, Dulin contended that this lack of access to rules or notice regarding his right to appeal constitutes "cause" for his procedural default. The Court concluded Dulin sufficiently alleges "cause" when he claimed that, due to his incarceration in Nevada, he had no reasonable access to or notice of Utah appellate rules. The Court, however, stressed that it was not deciding that "cause" actually exists in this case, but merely determined that the complaint on its face states a claim for cause under the cause and prejudice standards. The case was remanded for further consideration and to develop the record on the cause and prejudice standard.

Fernandez v. Leonardo, 742 F.Supp 55 (E.D. N.Y. 1990)

The Court found that the new ruling regarding Confrontation Clause articulated in the Supreme Court's decision in *Cruz*, that co-defendant's confession that implicated defendant may not be introduced unless defendant is given opportunity to cross-examine co-defendant. Thus, the ruling in *Cruz* may be applied retroactively in this habeas corpus proceeding. As it comes within the second *Teague* exception, it goes to the fundamental fairness. The Court expressed belief that the right of confrontation and cross-examination is an essential and fundamental requirement for the kind of fair trial, which is this country's constitutional goal.

Bliss v. Lockhart, 891 F.2d 1335 (8th Cir. 1989)

The Eighth Circuit found that Ms. Bliss established "cause" where the prosecutorial interference with failure to disclose the full evidence about Charles Bliss' dominating influence over Ms. Bliss and through ineffective assistance of counsel for failure to investigate which would have shown petitioner's defense based on coercion or duress.

Buffalo v. Sunn, 854 F.2d 1158 (9th Cir. 1988)

Buffalo established "cause" due to Hawaii prison officials had placed Buffalo in lock down, which amounted to official impediment. *See*, *Amadeo v. Zant*, 486 U.S. 214, 100 L.Ed.2d 249, 108 S.Ct. at 1776-77 (1988) (procedural default excused if caused by some external, objective impediment). *Murray*, 477 U.S. at 488, 106 S.Ct. at 2645.

Alcorn v. Smith, 647 F.Supp. 1402 (E.D. Ky. 1986)

The Court held that evidentiary hearing was required to permit magistrate to determine whether petitioner could demonstrate cause for procedural default, either by showing objective, external factor or by showing ineffective assistance of counsel.

Hamilton v. McCotter, 772 F.2d 171 (5th Cir. 1985)

The Court held, in pertinent part, that the petitioner's claim that the indictment was forged and, thus, that the petitioner was never properly before the state trial court's jurisdiction should not have been dismissed. Hamilton argued that the Dallas district attorney's office was "manufacturing" fraudulent indictments during the period of time relevant to his indictment. Due to the nature of this claim, counsel could not be faulted for not raising this claim and the abuse of the writ did not apply under this type of circumstance which would have been concealed by the State.

Novelty Issue of Constitutional Law

Reed v. Ross, 468 U.S. 1, 16, 104 S.Ct. 2901, 2910, 82 L.Ed.2d 1 (1984)

The Supreme Court in held "that where a constitutional claim is so novel that its legal basis is not reasonably available to counsel, a defendant has cause for his failure to raise the claim in accordance with acceptable state procedures". In order to establish the novelty of a constitutional claim sufficient to provide cause, a defendant must initially demonstrate that his situation is one where a court has "articulated a constitutional principle that has not been previously recognized but which has been held to have retractive application". *Id. at 17, 104 S.Ct. at 2911*.

U.S. v. Tayman, 885 F.Supp. 832 (E.D.Va. 1995)

The Court found that the Irvin rule was substantive rather than procedural. Irvin involved the scope of a criminal penalty provision, especially, the question presented in Irving was what conduct triggers the penalties set forth in *21 U.S.C. '841(b)* do not apply to defendants who participated in conspiracies that trafficked in the stated quantities was reasonably foreseeable to the defendant. Thus, Irvin did not "prescribe procedural rules that govern the conduct of a trial". It did not relate to the processes by which the processes by which criminal judgments are obtained obtain criminal judgments. Instead, it recognized that the "trial court lacked authority" to impose a mandatory minimum sentence on Irvin based on amounts that were not reasonably foreseeable to him. In other words, Irving "reinterpret[ed] a criminal statute so as to narrow it,, thus essentially repealing the statute as to other defendant". In short, Irvin is plainly a ruling concerning substantive criminal. The **Tayman** Court distinguished the **Teague** rule based on those facts and then applied the *Reed v. Ross*, 468 U.S. 1, 82 L.Ed.2d 1, 104 S.Ct. 2901 (1984) analysis finding that Tayman's claim was sufficiently novel at the time of his sentencing in May, 1992 to excuse his counsel's failure to raise it, which established "cause" for failure to raise the issue.

Lowe v. U.S., 727 F.Supp. 1241 (C.D. Ill. 1989)

The Court found "cause" other than ineffective assistance is presented in this case. The *Lowe* Court relying on *Ross v. Reed*, found the "cause" prong to be satisfied because the legal question at issue was novel and counsel had no reasonable basis for asserting it on appeal. *Lowe* received the enhancement provision of the Armed Career Criminal Statute based on his prior Illinois conviction for witness intimidation under statute allowing conviction based on inflicting or threatening physical harm to property, a subsequent decision found that this crime does not constitute a violent felony for the purposes of armed career criminal statute.

Dutton v. Brown, 812 F.2d 593 (10th Cir. 1987)

The Court found that "cause" existed for the procedural default because trial counsel, at the time of trial in 1979, could not have known that the prosecutor's remarks in closing argument which suggested to jury that it was not responsible for imposition of death penalty, might have raised constitutional questions. The law petitioner relied on did not become established until the Supreme Court decision in *Caldwell* in 1985. The Court could not expect trial counsel "to exercise extraordinary vision or to object to every aspect of the proceeding in hope that some aspect might mask a latent constitutional claim.

Hargrave v. Dugger, 832 F.2d 1528 (11th Cir. 1987)

The Court found that a retroactive decision of the United States Supreme Court required consideration of non-statutory mitigating factors in capital sentencing was "clear break with the past" and thus, habeas petitioner lacked tools to construct constitutional challenge to death sentence before Supreme Court decision and had cause for failure to object to consideration only of statutory mitigating circumstances at sentencing hearing and on appeal to State Supreme Court.

Singleton v. Lockhart, 653 F.Supp. 1114 (E.D. Ark. 1986)

The Court found that "cause" existed where there was no reasonable basis upon which defense counsel could have been expected to predicate pecuniary gain argument which duplicated element of capital murder based upon robbery and violated the Eighth Amendment. Thus, defendant was actually "acquitted" by reviewing court based on insufficient evidence for the death penalty barred the state from seeking the death penalty upon resentencing.

Intervening Change in Law; or Retroactive Application of the Law

Horn v. Banks, 536 U.S. 266, 153 L.Ed.2d 301, 122 S.Ct. 2147 (2002)

The Supreme Court held that the court of appeals committed clear error by failing to consider prisoner's claim under *Mills v. Maryland*, **486 u.s. 367, 100 L.Ed.2d 384, 108 S.Ct. 1860 (1988)**, that holds the Federal Constitution prohibits state from requiring jurors to unanimously agree that a particular mitigating circumstances exist before jury were permitted to consider that circumstance in capital sentencing determination applies retroactively under *Teague v. Lane*, **489 U.S. 288, 103 L.Ed.2d 334, 109 S.Ct. 1060 (1989)**.

Cause For Procedural Default

***Stringer v. Black*, 503 U.S. 222, 117 L.Ed.2d 367, 112 S.Ct. 1130 (1992)**
 The Supreme Court held that the rule of its decision in ***Maryland v. Cartwright*, 486 U.S. 356, 100 L.Ed.2d 372, 108 S.Ct. 1854 (1988)**, and ***Clemons v. Mississippi*, 494 U.S. 738, 108 L.Ed.2d 725, 110 S.Ct. 1441 (1990)**, holding aggravating circumstances unconstitutionally vague in capital sentencing was retroactively available to support federal habeas relief.

***Davis v. United States*, 417 U.S. 333, 346, 94 S.Ct. 2298, 41 L.Ed.2d 109 (1974)**
 The Supreme Court held that to determine whether a change in the substantive criminal law was to be applied retroactively, "the appropriate inquiry [is] whether the claimed error of law was a 'fundamental defect which inherently results in a complete miscarriage of justice'". ***Davis*, 417 U.S. at 346, 94 S.Ct. at 2305** (citations omitted). For Justice Stewart and a majority of the ***Davis*** Court, a conviction arising from acts that the law no longer made criminal left "no room for no doubt", ***id.***, that the failure to apply the law retroactively would "inherently result in a miscarriage of justice. ***Id.***

***Bailey v. United States*, 516 U.S. 137, 133 L.Ed.2d 472, 116 S.Ct. 501 (1995)**
 The United States Supreme Court held that (1) A conviction for use of a firearm for purposes of *'924(c)(1)* requires evidence sufficient to show an active employment of the firearm by the accused, a use that makes the firearm an operative factor in relation to the predicate offense; (2) the *'924(c)(1)* convictions in question were not supported by sufficient evidence that the firearms were actively employed in anyway; and (3) because the accused were charged under both the "use" and "carry" prongs of *'924(c)(1)* and because the Court of Appeals did not consider liability under the "carry" prong of the statute, a remand would be ordered for consideration of that basis for upholding the convictions. ***Id.***

***Bell v. U.S.*, 917 F.Supp. 681 (E.D. Mo. 1996)**
 The Court explained that the ***Bailey*** decision does not announce a new constitutional rule of criminal procedure. On the contrary, the ***Bailey*** decision rests on tenets of statutory construction and announces a reading of *18 U.S.C. § 924(c)* which is more narrow than the interpretations of the statute by lower courts. ***Bailey*, 516 U.S. 137, at 144, 116 S.Ct. at 506-508**. Because ***Bailey*** operates to expose the errors made by lower courts in interpreting the substance of *18 U.S.C. § 924(c)*, this Court finds that ***Davis v. United States*, 417 U.S. 333, 346, 94 S.Ct. 2298, 2305, 41 L.Ed.2d 109 (1974)**, and not ***Teague v. Lane***, is applicable to Bell's case.

 In ***Davis***, the Supreme Court held that collateral relief from a federal criminal conviction is available under §2255 such that petitioner's conviction and punishment are for conduct, which the law does not criminalize. ***Davis* 417 U.S. at 346, 94 S.Ct. at 2305**. To allow the conviction and punishment to stand "Results in a 'complete miscarriage of justice' and 'present[s] exceptional circumstances' that justify collateral relief under §2255". ***Id.* at 346-47, 94 S.Ct. at 2305**. ***Teague*** does not disturb the validity of the ***Davis*** decision. See generally ***United States v. McKie*, 73 F.3d 1149, 1153 (D.C. Cir. 1996)**. Thereafter, the ***Bell*** Court found Bell's guilty plea was not voluntary and that Bell showed "cause" based on the recent announcement of the Supreme Court's ***Bailey*** decision. Bell also has show prejudice, in light of ***Bailey*** the facts underlying his criminal conviction do not constitute a violation of *§924(c)(1)* and therefore, in a since, Bell is "innocent" of the crime to which he plead guilty. The ***Bell*** Court granted the §2255 motion and ORDERED Bell released from federal custody.

U.S. v. Hansen, 906 F.Supp. 668 (D.C. Cir. 1995)
> The Court found the United States Supreme Court's *Hubbard* decision, which "dramatically" limited reach of False States Act, constituted intervening change of law under *Davis*, and applied retroactively to former Congressman, who, filed a petition for writ of error coram nobis to set-aside his conviction under Act for making false statements to the House of Representatives; based upon the Supreme Court's *Hubbard* interpretation of False Statements Act upon which Hansen's conviction was based was always invalid. This type of claim stands for the proposition of an actual innocence claim, which would result in a miscarriage of justice if the conviction was allowed to stand.

Hamilton v. McCotter, 772 F.2d 171 (5th Cir. 1985)
> The Court explained that if petitioner provides a legal excuse for failure to raise claim in a prior habeas petition, after previous proceeding, such as a change in the law or petitioner becomes aware of new facts which claim is based, then the petitioner did not abuse the writ.

The "Ends of Justice"

Sanders v. United States, 373 U.S. 1, 10 L.Ed.2d 148, 83 S.Ct. 1068 (1963)
> The Supreme Court stated that "even if the same ground was rejected on the merits on a prior application, it is open to the applicant to show that the ends of justice would be served by permitting the redetermination of the ground. If factual issues are involved, the applicant is entitled to a new hearing upon showing that the evidentiary hearing on the prior application was not full and fair". If purely legal questions are involved, the applicant may be entitled to a new hearing upon showing an intervening change in the law or some other justification for having failed to raise a crucial point or argument in the prior application. Two further points should be noted. First, the foregoing enumeration is not intended to be exhaustive; the test is "the ends of justice" and it cannot be too finely particularized. Second, the burden is on the applicant to show that, although the ground of the new application to show that, although the ground of the new application was determined against him on the merits on a prior application, the ends of justice would be served by a redetermination of the ground.

Kuhlmann v. Wilson, 477 U.S. 436, 91 L.Ed.2d 364, 106 S.Ct. 2616 (1986)
> A four-justice plurality of the Supreme Court suggested that the ends of justice will demand consideration of the merits of claims only where there is "a colorable showing of factual innocence. *Id. at 2627*.

McCoy v. Norris, 958 F. Supp. 420 (E.D.Ark. 1996)
> The "ends of justice" require federal courts to entertain successive petitions only where the petitioner makes a colorable showing of factual innocence.

Byrd v. Delo, 917 F.2d 1037 (8th Cir. 1990)
> The Court explained that it may reconsider habeas claims previously denied on the merits if the "ends of justice" so require. *Sanders v. United States, 373 U.S. 1, 10 L.Ed.2d 148, 83 S.Ct. 1068 (1963) (Sanders)*. For instance, reconsideration is appropriate if the petitioner has shown "change in the law or some other justification for having failed to raise a crucial point or argument in the prior application". *id. at 17, 83 S.Ct. at 1078*, quoted in *Williams v. Lockhart, 862 F.2d 155 (8th Cir. 1988)*, or

if there are "new facts or legal developments warranting relitigation of the claim". *Williams v. Lockhart, 862 F.2d 155, 158*.

In addition, a petitioner must supplement his claim with a "colorable showing of factual innocence". *Id. at 1039, 1040*.

Witt v. Wainwright, 755 F.2d 1396, 1397 (11th Cir. 1985)
The Court explained that the "ends of justice" which requires reconsideration is determined by objective factors such as "whether there was a full and fair hearing on the original petition or whether there was an intervening change in the facts of the case or the applicable law".

False or Misleading Facts

Moore v. Kemp, 824 F.2d 847 (11th Cir. 1987)
The Eleventh Circuit found that a "colorable showing of factual innocence" is the test, or the test is whether the alleged error precluded the development of true facts or resulted in the admission of false ones, on a material question involving the sentence, the result is the same. The Court then held that, at a minimum, the ends of justice will demand consideration of the merits of a claim on a successive petition, where there is a colorable showing of factual innocence. The *Moore* Court was guided by *Smith v. Murray*. In consideration of whether "the alleged constitutional error [either] precluded the development of facts [or] resulted in the admission of false ones". *Id.*

Mills v. Scully, 653 F.Supp. 885 (S.D. N.Y. 1987)
Defense counsel's failure to move to correct testimony, which he knew was false or misleading, may constitute ineffective assistance of counsel.

HABEAS CORPUS MISCELLANEOUS

28 U.S.C. §2255 ONE-YEAR PERIOD OF LIMITATION ON FILING §2255 MOTIONS

The Antiterrorism and Effective Death Penalty Act of 1996, Pub. L. No. 104-132, 110 Stat. 1214, ("AEDPA"), established a one-year period of limitation for the filing of §2255 motion. The limitations period being from the latest of: (1) the date on which the judgment of conviction becomes final; (2) the date on which the impediment to making a motion created by government action in violation of the Constitution or laws of the United States is removed, if the movant was prevented from making a motion by such government action; (3) the date on which the right asserted was initially recognized by the Supreme Court, if that right has been newly recognized by the Supreme Court and made retroactively applicable on collateral review; or (4) the date on which the facts supporting the claim or claims presented could have been discovered through the exercise of due diligence. 28 U.S.C. §2255 (west Supp. 1997).

28 U.S.C. §2255(f)(1)

Clay v. United States, 537 U.S. 522, 155 L.Ed.2d 88, 123 S.Ct. 1072 (2003)
Clays **28 U.S.C. §2255** motion to vacate, set aside or correct sentence, was timely filed; the time limitations for **§2255(f)(1)** begun to run when the time for filing a petition for writ of certiorari expired.

Spotville v. Cain, 149 F.3d 374, 378 (5th Cir. 1998)
A pro se habeas corpus is filed for purposes of determining the applicability of the Antiterrorism and Effective Death Penalty Act of 1996, when prisoner delivers the papers to prison authorities for mailing.

U.S. v. Smith, 215 F. 3d 1338 (10th Cir. 2000)
Dismissing a 2255 motion as time barred and rejecting argument that the limitations period did not begin to run until the appellate Court denied defendant's untimely direct appeal.

Robinson v. United States, 416 F.3d 645, 647 (7th Cir. 2005)
The one-year limitations period of Section 2255(f)(1) attaches when the Supreme Court affirms on the merits on direct review or denies petition for writ of certiorari, or the time for filing a certiorari petition expires, not when the Court denies petition for rehearing a denial of certiorari.

------------------------------*------------------------------

Griffth v. Kentucky, 479 U.S. 314, 93 LEd. 2d 649, 107 S. Ct. 708 (1987)
The Supreme Court stated that by "final," we mean a case in which a judgment of conviction has been rendered, the availability of appeal exhausted and the time for a petition for certiorari finally denied. Also see, *United States v. Johnson, 457 U.S. 537, 73 Led. 2d 202, 102 S.Ct. 2579 (1982) footnote 8.*

28 U.S.C. §2255(f)(3)

Dodd v. United States, 545 U.S. 343, 162, L.Ed.2d 343, 345, 125 S.Ct. 2478 (2005)
The one-year limitation period for a federal prisoner's motion for relief from a sentence under **28 U.S.C. §§2255¶6(3)& ¶8(2)**, on the basis of a newly recognized right begins to run when the right asserted was initial recognized, rather than when the right is made retroactive. This time limitation period applies to all §2255 motions, the initial as well as second of successive petitions.

United States v. Swinton, 333 F.3d 481, 486 (3rd Cir. 2003)
The **Apprendi** Court created a "newly recognized" constitutional right within the meaning of **28 U.S.C. §2255¶6(3)**, governing the "one-year limitations period;" the court of appeals and district court's have the authority to determine the issue of retroactivity applicable to cases on collateral review under §2255¶6(3). **See also *United States v. Lopez*, 248 F.3d 427, 432 (5th Cir.), cert. denied 534 U.S. 898, 122 S.Ct. 222, 151 L.Ed.2d 158 (2001); *Garcia v. United States*, 278 F.3d 1210, 1212-13 (11th Cir.), cert. denied, 537 U.S. 895, 123 S.Ct. 180, 154 L.Ed.2d 163 (2002).**

U.S. v. Lloyd, 188 F.3d 184 (3rd Cir. 1999)
Lloyd's *§2255* petition was timely filed within the meaning of *§2255 (3)* when filed within one-year of the Supreme Court's determination in ***Bousely*** of retroactive applicability of the new right it earlier recognized in ***Bailey***, requiring active employment of firearm to support a conviction of carrying firearm during drug trafficking crime pursuant to *18 U.S.C. §924(c)*, and ***Lloyd's*** demonstrated an actual innocence claim.

28 U.S.C. §2255(f)(4)

Johnson v. United States, 544 U.S. 295, 302, 161 L.Ed.2d 542, 125 S. Ct. 1571 (205)
28 U.S.C. Section 2255(f)(4) provides that: "the date on which the facts supporting the claim or claims presented could have been discovered through the exercise of due diligence." The Johnson Court, held that the state-court vacatur of a predicate offense used to enhance a federal sentence can trigger the limitation period under Section 2255(f)(4). The Johnson Court, then concluded that Johnson failed to act diligently to obtain the state court order vacating his predicate offense and rejected his claim under 2255(f)(4). The due diligence requirement of 2255(f)(4), in light of Johnson require a federal prisoner to commence collateral attack on a state predicate offense used to enhance his/her federal sentence within one-year of the imposition of the federal sentence.

§2255 Miscellaneous

Davis v. United States, 417 U.S. 333, 342, 41 L.Ed.2d 109, 116, 94 S.Ct. 2298 (1974)
The prior determination made on a claim of law can be re-raised in a **§2255** motion, "if new law has been made since the trial and appeal." **See also *Sanders v. United States*, 373 U.S. 1, 10 L.Ed.2d 148, 83 S.Ct. 1068 (1963); *Kaufman v. United States*, 394 U.S. 217, 230, 22 L.Ed.2d 227, 89 S.Ct. 1068 (1969).**

Romandine v. United States, *206 F.3d 731, 736 (7th Cir. 2000)*

The limitations on successive motions do not apply to statute governing writs of habeas or the Administrative Procedural Act. **See** *Felker v. Turpin*, **518 U.S. 651, 116 S.ct. 2333, 135 L.Ed.2d 837 (1996).**

United States v. Addonizio, *442 U.S. 178, 60 L.Ed.2d 805, 99 S.Ct. 2235 (1979)*

An error of law does not provide a basis for collateral attack under §2255 unless the claimed error constitute "a fundamental defect which inherently results in a complete miscarriage of justice." **See also** *Hill v. United States*, **368 U.S. 424, 428, 7 L.Ed.2d 417,82 S.Ct. 468 (1962).**

Hill v. United States, *368 U.S. 424, 7 L.Ed.2d 417, 82 S.Ct. 468, reh. den. 369 U.S. 808, 7 L.Ed.2d 556, 82 S.Ct. 640 (1962)*

A Section **2255** petitioner cannot raise the district court's failure to afford the defendant an opportunity personally to speak in his own behalf at sentencing in violation of the Federal Rules of Criminal Procedure, **Rule 32**, in a **§2255** motion or a **Rule 35** motion.

Kafo v. United States, *467 F.3d 1063, 1070 (7th Cir. 2006)*

28 U.S.C. §2255 motions must be verified under oath or an affidavit must be submitted with the motion detailing the facts supporting the motion in order to obtain an evidentiary hearing. The Seventh Circuit vacated the district court's denial of Kafo's §2255 motion and remanded with instructions to allow Kafo to amend his motion by submitting it under oath or by attaching an affidavit, rather than denying it without an evidentiary hearing.

Kingsberry v. United States, *202 F.3d 1030, 1032 (8th Cir.), cert. denied, 531 U.S. 829, 121 S.Ct. 81, 148 L.Ed.2d 43 (2000)*

An evidentiary hearing on a **28 U.S.C. §2255** motion must be granted unless the motion, files, and records of the case, establish conclusively that the petitioner is not entitled to relief.

COURT CANNOT RECHARACTERIZE PRO SE MOTION AS A §2255 MOTION WITHOUT WARNING DEFENDANT

Castro v. United States, *540 U.S. 375, 157 L.Ed.2d 778, 124 S.Ct. 786 (2003)*

A district court cannot recharacterize a pro se litigants motion as a first **28 U.S.C. §2255** motion, unless it first informs the litigant of its intent to recharacterize, warns the litigant that this recharacterization means that any subsequent **§2255** motion will be subject to the restrictions of a "second or successive" motions, and provides the litigant an opportunity to withdraw the motion or to amend it so that it contains all the **§2255** claims he believes he has. If these warnings are not given, the motion cannot be considered to have become a **§2255** motion for purposes of applying the "second or successive" restrictions to the later motions." **Id**

28 U.S.C. §2244(d)(1)(A)

Egerton v. Cockrell, *334 F. 3d 443 (5th Cir. 2003)*

Discussing application of **28 U.S.C. 2244(d)(1)**, which governs the limitations period for filing petitions under **28 U.S.C. 2254**, that is, nearly identical to the limitations period set forth in **28 U.S.C. 2255**.

Wilkinson v. Cockrell, 240 F. Supp. 2d 617 (N.D. Tex. 2002)
> Texas State Court's deferred adjudication of charge against petitioner commenced statutory period for filing for federal habeas relief.

Brannigan v. United States, 249 F.3d 584 (7th Cir. 2001)
> 28 U.S.C. §2244(b)(1) provides that a "claim" presented in a prior application is forever closed. Defining what a "claim" is, as §2244(b)(1) uses the word. The Court held that a single set of facts producing a single injury is one "claim" regardless of how many legal theories can be invoked in support of relief.

Hill v. Braxton, 277 F.3d 701, 707 (4th Cir. 2002)
> When a federal habeas court perceives a pro se, **28 U.S.C. §2254**, petition to be untimely and the state has not filed a motion to dismiss based on the one-year statute of limitations periods under **28 U.S.C. §2244(d) (1) (A)**, the court must warn the petitioner that the case is subject to dismissal pursuant to **§2244(d)**, absent a sufficient explanation. The *Hill* Court vacated the district court's dismissal and remanded with instructions to afford the petitioner an opportunity to respond to the untimely issue. **See also** *Herbst v. Cook*, **260 F.3d 1039, 1042 (9th Cir. 2001)**; *Acosta v. Artuz*, **221 F.3d 117, 125-26 (2d Cir. 2000)**.

28 U.S.C. §2244(d)(1)(B)

Lloyd v. Miller, 152 F.Supp.2d 1119, 1122 (N.D. Ind. 2001)
> State's failure to provide Lloyd with a copy of his opening and closing arguments transcript did not constitute an "impediment" to filing habeas application under **28 U.S.C. §2244(d) (1) (B)**. Lloyd eventually filed his habeas application without the opening and closing arguments transcript, which indicated that he could have easily filed a timely habeas application.

U.S. ex rel. Willhite v. Walls, 241 F.Supp.2d 882, 886-87 (N.D. Ill. 2003)
> **28 U.S.C. §2244 (d) (1) (B)** expressly pertains only to state-imposed impediments that prevent a prisoner from filing federal habeas petition, not a state action that prevented Willhite from filing a timely petition to state Supreme Court of Illinois.

Egerton v. Cockrell, 334 F.3d 433, 437-38 (5th Cir. 2003)
> Prison law library's failure to provide a copy of AEDPA constituted "impediment . . . created by state action, " under 28 U.S.C. §2244(d) (1) (B), which tolled limitations period, unless evidence that petitioner had actual knowledge of the AEDPA and its limitation period exist. Cf. *Whalem-Hunt v. Early*, **233 F.3d 1146, 1148 (9th Cir. 2000) (en banc)** (finding that the unavailability of the AEDPA in prison library may create an "impediment" for purposes of §2244(d) (1) (B)).

Wyzykowski v. Department of Corrections, 226 F.3d 1213, 1216 (11th Cir. 2000)
> In the event of illegal state action that prevents the petitioner from filing habeas corpus application, the limitation period does begin until after the state impediment is removed pursuant to **§2244(d) (1) (B)**.

Valverde v. Stinson, 224 F.3d 129, 134, 136-37 (2d Cir. 2001)
> Correctional officers confiscation of Valverde's petition and legal papers that prevented him from filing a timely petition constitutes extraordinary circumstances to justify tolling of the one-year limitation period under **28 U.S.C. §2244 (d) (1) (B)**; and, required a

remand to develop the facts relevant to petitioner's claim that he was prevented from filing his petition on time by the wrongful confiscation of his petition and legal papers.

Minter v. Beck, 230 F.3d 663, 666 (4th Cir. 2000)
The Court defined the term "impediment" in §2244 (d) (l) (B), since the term "impediment" was not defined in the AEDPA. First, turning to the dictionary definition for its common meaning. **See *United States v. Lehman*, 225 F.3d 426, 428-29 (4th Cir. 2000)** (turning to dictionary definition of statutory term not defined in statute for term's common meaning), the Court found that, the Random House Webster's Unabridged Dictionary defines the term "limpediment" as "obstruction; hindrance; [or] obstacle." **959 (2d ed. 1998).**

Whalem/Hunt v. Early, 233 F.3d 1146, 1148 (9th Cir. 2000)
The court of appeals remanded for determination of whether there was an "impediment" to filing a timely habeas petition because of lack of knowledge of limitations period, and the unavailability of legal material describing the Antiterrorism and Effective Death Penalty Act time limitations.

Lott v. Mueller, 304 F.3d 918, 925-26 (9th Cir. 2002)
Prisoner is entitled to equitable tolling of the statute of limitations under **28 U.S.C. §2244(d) (2)**, for pro se habeas petition based on petitioner's claim that he was denied access to legal material files during transfer to another district court on an unrelated matter under the "impediment" clause pursuant to **§2244 (d) (1) (B)**.

Moore v. Battaglia, 476 F.3d 504, 506-508 (7th Cir. 2007)
Inadequate prison law library may amount to a state-created impediment to timely filing of a habeas petition requiring a factual findings related to equitable tolling.

28 U.S.C. §2244(d)(1)(C)

Peterson v. Cain, 302 F. 3d 508, 510 (5th Cir. 2002)
A prisoner may collaterally attack a judgment within one year of the date in which the claimed constitutional right was newly recognized by the United States Supreme Court and made retroactive to cases on collateral review, pursuant to 28 U.S.C. 2244(d)(1)(c).

Wyzykowski v. Department of Corrections, 226 F. 3d 1213, 1216 (11th Cir. 2000)
In the event the Supreme Court recognizes a constitutional right and makes it retroactivity applicable to cases on collateral review, the limitations period of **28 U.S.C. §2244(d) (1) (C)**, permits filing a petition asserting that right within one-year after the initial recognition of the right by the Supreme.

28 U.S.C. §2244(d)(1)(D)

Ybanez v. Johnson, 204 F.3d 645, 646 (5th Cir. 2000)
The Court held that "Section **2244 (d) (1) (D)** provides for "equitable" tolling when the facts on which a federal habeas claim is based could not have been discovered by a duly diligent petitioner.

Hasan v. Galaza, 254 F.3d 1150, 1154-55 (9th Cir. 2001)

The statute of limitation period under **28 U.S.C. §2244(d)(1)(D),** "the date on which the factual predicate of the claim or claims presented could have been discovered through the exercise of due diligence" for filing habeas claim alleging ineffective assistance of counsel did not begin to run until petitioner knew, or should have known, of relationship between prosecution witness and person who engaged in witnesses tampering.

Wyzykowski v. Department of Corrections, 226 F. 3d 1213, (11th Cir. 2000)

The one-year limitation period of 28 U.S.C. §2244(b) (1) (D), does not begin until the "factual predicate of the claim or claims presented could have been discovered through the exercise of due diligence."

McCray v. Vasbinder, 499 F.3d 568, 571-577 (6th Cir. 2007)

Petitioner's new evidence, along with the evidence presented at trial failed to establish that it was more likely than not, that no reasonable juror would have found petitioner not guilty beyond a reasonable doubt as required to excuse petitioner's late filing of his habeas petition.

28 U.S.C. §2244(d)(1)

Ege v. Yukins, 485 F.3d 364, 313 (6th Cir. 2007)

The Wayne County prosecutor's letter concerning the unreliability of its expert witness, Dr. Warnick, who testified in Ege's trial was a factual predicate for habeas petition pursuant to **28 U.S.C. §2244(d) (l)** limitation period.

28 U.S.C. §2244(d)(2)

Garcia v. United States, 301 F.Supp.2d 1275, 1282 (D.N.M. 2004)

Counsel was constitutionally ineffective for failing to object to the Presentence Report that increased petitioner's Criminal History Category Points by 2 points for a DWI, that occurred after the instant offense because those two points should not have been counted under **U.S.S.G. §4Al.l(b)**, and deprived petitioner of the benefits from the "safety value" pursuant to **18 U.S.C. §3553(f)** due to counsel's omissions.

Tillema v. Long, 253 F.3d 494, 498 (9th Cir. 2001)

The State court collateral proceeding tolled period for filing federal habeas petition pursuant to **28 U.S.C. §2244 (d) (2)**; the district court's failure to afford petitioner an opportunity to abandon his sole unexhausted claim as alternative to dismissal of first habeas petition equitably tolled period of limitations.

Swartz v. Meyers, 204 F.3d 417, 424 (3rd Cir. 2000)

Habeas limitations period was tolled pursuant to **28 U.S.C. §2244(d)(2)**, until expiration of time that petitioner could seek an appeal from denial of post-conviction relief petition.

Miller v. Collins, 305 F.3d 491, 495-96 (6th Cir. 2002)

Habeas statute of limitations was equitable tolled from the date of decision of the Ohio Court of Appeals regarding petitioner's application to reopen appeal, until the date petitioner received notice of the decision rejecting application.

Equitable Tolling of One Year Limitations

Carey v. Saffold,*536 U.S.214, 122 S.Ct. 2134, 153 L.Ed.2d 260 (2002)*

The Supreme Court provided guidance as to how to analyze the "AEDPA's" limitations period with its accompanying tolling provision, which promotes the exhaustion of state remedies while respecting the interest in the finality of the state court's judgments.

Phillips v. Hust, 477 F.3d 1070, 1076 (9th Cir. 2007)

The Prison librarian's refusal to allow the prisoner to combine his petition for writ of certiorari for the United States Supreme Court, violated prisoner's right to access to courts.

Laws v. Lamarque, 351 F.3d 919, 924 (9th Cir. 2003)

Laws was entitled to further factual development, discovery, expansion of the record or, an evidentiary hearing on issue of whether his mental illness prevented him from timely filing his habeas petition as to warrant equitable tolling of the limitation period. Equitable tolling of the one-year limitations period in **28 U.S.C. §2244** is available where "extraordinary circumstance beyond a prisoner's control make it impossible to file a petition on time" and "the extraordinary circumstances were the cause of his untimeliness." **See also *Spitsyn v. Moore*, 345 F.3d 796, 799 (9th Cir. 2003); *Nara v. Frank*, 264 F.3d 310, 319-20 (3rd Cir. 2001).**

Miller v. Collins, 305 F.3d 491, 495-96 (6th Cir. 2002)

Habeas statute of limitations was equitable tolled from the date of decision of the Ohio Court of Appeals regarding petitioner's application to reopen appeal, until the date petitioner received notice of the decision rejecting application.

Majoy v. Roe, 296 F.3d 770, 776 (9th Cir. 2002)

Majoy filed a habeas petition and the district court dismissed the petition as untimely. Majoy appealed and the Ninth Circuit remanded to the district court for determination whether Majoy could pass through the actual innocence gateway to review otherwise time-barred claims. Majoy need not show that he is actually innocent of the crime. Rather, he must show that a court cannot have confidence in the outcome of his trial.

Neverson v. Bissonnette, 261 F.3d 120, 127 (1st Cir. 2001)

Neverson presented an equitable tolling argument in the district court. The district court dismissed Neverson's habeas petition as untimely without addressing his equitable tolling claim. The First Circuit remanded for adjudication of Neverson's equitable tolling claim.

Clark v. Stinson, 214 F.3d 315 (2nd Cir. 2000)

A petition for writ of error coram nobis pending in state court would not be counted towards the tolling provision of the **AEDPA** statute of limitations period for habeas corpus purposes.

Loveland v. Hatches, 231 F.3d 640, 645 (9th Cir. 2000)

An evidentiary hearing required before district court to determine whether trial counsel's failure to file a direct appeal excused habeas petitioner's default in failing to file a timely state post-conviction petition or prejudiced petitioner.

Phillips v. Donnelly, 216 F.3d 508, 510-11 (5th Cir. 2000)
>A four-month delay in a petitioner's receipt of notice that his state habeas corpus application had been denied could warrant equitable tolling.

U.S. v. Patterson, 211 F.3d 927, 930-31 (5th Cir. 2000)
>A federal district court's issuance of several Orders misleading the Section **2255** petitioner as to the deadline for filing of his motion to vacate warranted equitable tolling of the limitations period.

Felder v. Johnson, 204 F.3d 168, 170-71 (5th Cir. 2000)
>Neither the petitioner's pro se status, incarceration, claims of actual innocence, nor complaints of an inadequate prison law library warranted equitable tolling.

Turner v. Johnson, 177 F.3d 390, 391-92 (5th Cir. 1999)
>Petitioner's unfamiliarity with the legal process nor his lack of representation during applicable filing period does **not** merit equitable tolling, regardless of whether the unfamiliarity is due to illiteracy or some other reason.

Loveland v. Hatcher, 231 F.3d 640, 644 (9th Cir. 2000)
>Loveland's reliance on counsel to file direct appeal is sufficient cause for federal habeas purposes to excuse Loveland's procedural default in failing to file a <u>timely</u> state post-conviction relief petition, if he establishes: (1) he actually believed his counsel was pursuing his direct appeal, (2) his belief was objective reasonable, and (3) he filed his state post-conviction habeas petition within a reasonable time after he should have known that his counsel was not pursuing his direct appeal.

Coleman v. Johnson, 184 F.3d 398, 403 (5th Cir. 1999)
>Holding that "equity is not for those who sleep on their rights."

Davis v. Johnson 158 F.3d 806, 811 (5th Cir. 1998)
>Equitable tolling was appropriate where the federal district court granted the petitioner's court-appointed counsel several extensions of time within which to file a federal habeas corpus petition.

Helton v. Singletary, 85 F.Supp.2d 1323 (S.D. Fla. 1999)
>Trial counsel incorrectly informed defendant as to when the one year limitations period for federal habeas petitions under the Antiterrorism and Effective Death Penalty Act began to run constituted an "Extraordinary circumstances" warranting equitable tolling of such period.

COURT MUST AFFORD PETITIONER AN OPPORTUNITY TO RESPOND TO UNTIMELINESS

Herbst v. Cook, 260 F.3d 1039, 1043 (9th Cir. 2001)
>The district court erred sua sponte dismissing petitioner's habeas petition as untimely based on statute of limitations grounds, without first, providing petitioner with notice, and an opportunity to respond, so that he could plead facts that would prevent the running of limitations period.

Hill v. Braxton, 277 F.3d 701,706-08 (4th Cir. 2002)
    Habeas court should not dismiss petition for untimeliness before giving petitioner notice and an opportunity to respond to the statute of limitation affirmative defense.

Hill v. Braxton, 277 F.3d 701, 707 (4th Cir. 2002)
    When a federal habeas court perceives a pro se, **28 U.S.C. §2254**, petition to be untimely and the state has not filed a motion to dismiss based on the one-year statute of limitations periods under **28 U.S.C. §2244(d) (1) (A)**, the court must warn the petitioner that the case is subject to dismissal pursuant to **§2244(d)**, absent a sufficient explanation. The *Hill* Court vacated the district court's dismissal and remanded with instructions to afford the petitioner an opportunity to respond to the untimely issue. **See also** *Herbst v. Cook*, **260 F.3d 1039, 1042 (9th Cir. 2001);** *Acosta v. Artuz*, **221 F.3d 117, 125-26 (2d Cir. 2000).**

State Waived Statute of Limitation Defense

Scott v. Collins, 268 F.Supp.2d 923, 928 (6th Cir. 2002)
    State waived statute of limitations defense by failing to assert it in response to petitioner's habeas petition. **See also** *Miller v. Collins*, **305 F.3d 491, 497 (6th Cir. 2002).**

SECOND OR SUCCESSIVE 28 U.S.C.A. §2255 MOTION UNDER THE AEDPA

Under the AEDPA, of 1996, before a second or successive §2255 motion may be considered by the district court, it must be certified by a three-judge panel of the court of appeals to contain;
   (1) newly discovered evidence that if proven and viewed in light of the evidence as a whole, would be sufficient to establish by clear and convincing evidence that no reasonable factfinder would have found the movant guilty of the offense ; or
   (2) a new rule of constitutional law, made retroactive to cases on collateral review by the Supreme Court, that was previously unavailable. *28 U.S.C. §2255 (Apr. 24, 1996).*

§2255 Saving Clause Provision

Christopher v. Miles, 342 F. 3d 378, 382 (5th Cir. 2003)
    A petitioner seeking relief under the 2255 savings clause must demonstrate three things: (1) his claim is based on a retroactively applicable Supreme Court decision; (2) the Supreme Court decision establishes that he was "actually innocent" of the charges against him because the decision decriminalized the conduct for which he was convicted; and (3) his claim would have been foreclosed by existing Circuit precedent had he raised it at trial, on direct appeal, or in his original 2255 petition. *Id.* **See also** *Reyes-Requena v. United States*, **243 F. 3d 893, 904 (5th Cir. 2001);** *Jeffers v. Chandler*, **253 F. 3d 827, 830 (5th Cir. 2001).** "[T]he core idea is that the petitioner may have been imprisoned for conduct that was not prohibited by law." *Reyes-Requena*, **243 F.3d at 903-04;** *Jeffers*, **253 F. 3d at 831.**

Habeas Corpus Miscellaneous

MOTION FOR LEAVE TO FILE A SECOND PETITION FOR WRIT OF HABEAS CORPUS "GRANTED"

***Nevius v. Summer*, 105 F.3d 453 (9th Cir. 1996).**
Nevius argued that he was entitled to file a second petition for writ of habeas corpus pursuant to 28 U.S.C. §2244 (b) (2) (A), because the reasonable doubt instruction given at his trial was unconstitutional and, he has made a **prima facie** showing that the claim "relies on a new rule of constitutional law, made retroactive to cases on collateral review by the Supreme Court, that was previously unavailable." Id. Nevius asserted the new rule in ***Cage v. Louisiana*, 489 U.S. 39, 111 S.Ct. 328, 112 L.Ed.2d 339 (1990),** where the Court held that due process did not permit a reasonable-doubt instruction that "suggest[s] a higher degree of doubt than is required for acquittal under the reasonable-doubt standard. Nevius asserted that this rule was made retroactive by the Supreme Court in ***Adams v. Evatt*, 114 S.Ct. 1365, 128 L.Ed. 2d 42 (1994),** where the Court vacated a decision of the Eleventh Circuit holding <u>Cage</u>, super, not to be retroactive; the opinion was vacated for reconsideration in light of ***Sullivan v. Louisiana*, 508 U.S. 275, 113 S.Ct. 2078, 124 L.Ed. 2d 182 (1993).** The Ninth Circuit concluded that Nevius made "a prima facie showing that the application satisfies the requirements of 28 U.S.C. §2244 (b) (3) (c), and granted Nevius leave to file a second petition for habeas corpus. Also see, ***Nevius v. McDaniel*, 104 F.3d 1120 (9th Cir. 1996).**

SECOND HABEAS PETITION IS ACTUALLY FIRST

***Slack v. McDaniel*, 529 U.S. 473, 120 S. Ct. 1595, 146 LEd.2d 542 (2000)**
The Supreme Court held that "A federal habeas corpus petition which was filed by a state prisoner after an initial petition was dismissed without adjudication on the merits for failure to exhaust state remedies – and was further dismissed without condition and without prejudice – was not a second or successive petition within the meaning of Rule 9 (b)."

***Shepeck v. United States*, 150 F.3d 800 (7th Cir. 1998)**
Appellate court approval not required to commence what would be first substantive collateral challenge, pursuant to **28 U.S.C. §2255,** upon reimposition of sentence after petitioner was abandoned by his first counsel prior to direct appeal reset to zero the counter of collateral attacks pursuant to **28 U.S.C. §2255 motion.**

***Petrocelli v. Angelone*, 248 F.3d 877, 884-85 (9th Cir. 2001)**
Habeas petition filed after first petition was dismissed without prejudice because it contained unexhausted claims, was not a "second or successive" petition for abuse of writ under ***Slack***.

***Sacco v. Cooksey*, 214 F.3d 270 (2nd Cir. 2000)**
Habeas petition did not constitute a "second or successive" petition within the meaning of the **AEDPA** because Sacco's prior petition was dismissed for failure to exhaust all of the claims presented in the state court's and not on the merits. **See *Slack*, 120 S.Ct. at 1605.**

***Stewart v. Martinez-Villareal*, 523 U.S. 637, 140 L. Ed. 2d 849, 118 S.Ct. 1618 (1998)**
The Supreme Court held that: "the accused's 1997 request for federal habeas corpus relief on the basis of reopening his Ford claim was not subject to the restrictions in **§2244 (b),** as amended by ***AEDPA***, on second or successive applications, for (1) even though the

accused's 1997 request may have been the second time that he asked the federal courts to provide relief on his Ford claim, (a) there was only one application for federal habeas corpus relief, and (b) the accused was entitled to an adjudication of all the claims presented in his 1993 application for relief and (2) if the accused's 1997 request were to be considered a second or successive application, then the implications for federal habeas corpus practice would be far reaching and seemingly perverse." *Id.*

FEDERAL HABEAS CORPUS DISCOVERY

Rule 6 of the Rules governing 28 U.S.C. §§2254 and 2255 proceedings entitles litigants to request the discovery process available under the Federal Rules of Civil Procedure if good cause shown and the court exercises its discretion allowing discovery. Federal Rules of Civil Procedure, Rules 26(a) through 36 provides a wide range of discovery devices available which includes but not limited to: "depositions, production of documents or other physical materials, physical and mental examinations, request for admission and interrogatories, permission to enter upon land or other property for inspection or other purposes. The Court may appoint counsel for indigent prisoners if necessary for effective utilization of discovery." See, *18 U.S.C. §3006A(g).*

Cherrix v. Braxton, 131 F.Supp. 2d 756 (E.D. Va. 2000)
Petitioner showed good cause for new DNA testing on semen found in murder victim following his conviction for sodomy and capital murder based on advancement in DNA technology which could demonstrate a viable claim of his actual innocence.

Payne v. Bell, 89 F.Supp.2d 967 (W.D. Tenn. 2000)
Good cause for discovery exists under Rule 6(a) governing Section §2254 cases ("Habeas Rule") where specific allegations before the court showed reason to believe that the petitioner may, if the facts are fully developed be able to demonstrate that he is entitled to relief. Also see *Harris v. Nelson, 394 U.S. 286, 89 S.Ct. 1082, 22 LEd. 1082, 22 LEd.2d 281 (1969).*

Jones v. Wood, 114 F.3d 1002 (9th Cir. 1997)
Petitioner demonstrated "good cause" for conducting discovery to obtain notes for trial counsel implicating another suspect and to conduct test on blood samples from both him and his wife's as well as hair found in murdered wife's hands, where test might establish prejudice on his ineffectiveness of counsel claims.

Toney v. Gammon, 79 F.3d 693 (8th Cir. 1996)
Habeas petitioner was entitled through <u>discovery</u> to access to state's evidence to conduct DNA and other scientific testing; court's denial of discovery is an abuse of discretion if discovery is indispensable to a fair, rounded development of material facts.

Rice v. Clarke, 923 F.2d 117 (8th Cir. 1991).
Habeas Petitioner was granted discovery to ascertain whether the "FBI" performed a voice print analysis of the telephone caller's voice because of the statement by the assistant chief of police.

Rice v. Clarke, 923 F.2d 117 (8th Cir. 1991).
State's failure to provide defense counsel with tape of emergency 911-phone call, which lured police officer to his death, did not violate due process.

Warden Kentucky State Penitentiary v. Gall, 865 F.2d 786 (6th Cir. 1989).
> Petitioner entitled to have independent testing done by laboratory of his choice of various items of evidence to support his ineffective assistance of counsel claims.

Mckenzie v. Risley, 915 F.2d 1396 (9th Cir. 1990).
> Petitioner entitled to discovery in habeas proceeding concerning the possibility of reliance by the sentencing judge on ex parte materials submitted by prosecutor.

Ross v. Kemp, 785 F.2d 1467 (11th Cir. 1986).
> Habeas petitioner claiming systematic discrimination in formulation of juries was entitled to supplement record... with deposition of official custodian of county's jury lists.

EXPANSION OF THE RECORD

Sacco v. Cooksey, 214 F.3d 270 (2nd Cir. 2000)
> Habeas petition did not constitute a "second or successive" petition within the meaning of the **AEDPA** because Sacco's prior petition was dismissed for failure to exhaust all of the claims presented in the state court's and not on the merits. See *Slack*, 120 S.Ct. at 1605.

McDonald v. Johnson, 139 F.3d 1056, 1060 (5th Cir. 1999)
> The expansion of the record in a habeas proceeding is appropriate to determine whether an evidentiary hearing is proper.

Laws v. Lamarque, 351 F.3d 919, 924 (9th Cir. 2003)
> Laws was entitled to further factual development, discovery, expansion of the record or, an evidentiary hearing on issue of whether his mental illness prevented him from timely filing his habeas petition as to warrant equitable tolling of the limitation period. Equitable tolling of the one-year limitations period in **28 U.S.C. §2244** is available where "extraordinary circumstance beyond a prisoner's control make it impossible to file a petition on time" and "the extraordinary circumstances were the cause of his untimeliness." **See also** *Spitsyn v. Moore*, **345 F.3d 796, 799 (9th Cir. 2003);** *Nara v. Frank*, **264 F.3d 310, 319-20 (3rd Cir. 2001)**

Garner v. Mitchell, 502 F.3d 394, 406 (6th Cir. 2007)
> The district court did not abuse its discretion granting Garner's motion for expansion of the record pursuant to **Rule 7** governing **28 U.S.C. Section 2254** proceeding. The expansion of the record included expert psychological test results and expert opinions related to the "Instruments for Assessing Understanding & Appreciation of Miranda Rights" test referred to as the "Grisso Test," because the court determined that Garner was not at fault for failing to develop the evidence in state court because his requests for discovery, expert funds, and an evidentiary hearing were summarily denied by the state court.

CHAPTER 153-HABEAS CORPUS-AEDPA

State-Federal Habeas Corpus 28 U.S.C. §2254 (d) (1) (2) and (e) (1) shall not be granted
> unless-

(d)   An application for a writ of habeas corpus on behalf of a person in custody pursuant to the judgment of a State court shall not be granted with respect to any claim that was adjudication of the claim-

(1)   resulted in a decision that was contrary to or involved an unreasonable application of, clearly established Federal law, as determined by the Supreme Court of the United States; or

(2)   resulted in a decision that was based on an unreasonable determination of the facts in light of the evidence presented in the state court proceeding.

(e) (1) In a proceeding instituted by an application for a writ of habeas corpus by a person in custody pursuant to the judgment of a State Court, a determination of a factual issue made by a State Court shall be presumed to be correct. The application shall have the burden of rebutting the presumption of correctness by clear and convincing evidence.

PRESUMPTION OF CORRECTNESS

O'Rourke v. Endell, 153 F,3d 560 (8th Cir. 1998)
> The State Court deprived Petitioner of due process of law where it failed to appoint counsel to argue during competency hearing that Petitioner lacked capacity to waive his appeal in a post-conviction proceedings. Additionaly, the state court's findings that petitioner was competent was not entitled to presumption of correctness.

Dyer v. Calderon, 151 F.3d 970 (9th Cir. 1998)
> State court's finding on habeas petition are presumed to be correct on federal habeas review, but facts left undeveloped by state court and habeas court may set them aside only in limited circumstances under *Title 28 U.S.C. §2254 (d) (1-8).*

Salazar v. Johnson, 96 F.3d 789 (5th Cir. 1996)
> A ineffective assistance of counsel claim based on counsel's failure to advise defendant of his appellate rights, which is denied by the district court based solely on a paper record is not entitled to an automatic presumption of correctness in habeas corpus proceedings.

UNREASONABLE APPLICATION OF FEDERAL LAW

Holland v. Jackson, 542 U.S. 649, 159 L.Ed.2d 683, 124 S.Ct. 2736 (2004)
> The Sixth Circuit erred holding that the state-court decision concerning ineffective assistance of counsel claim was an unreasonable application of *Strickland*.

Woodford v. Visciotti, 537 U.S. 19, 154 L.Ed.2d 279, 123 S.Ct. 357 (2002)
> The United States Court of Appeals for the Ninth Circuit exceeded **28 U.S.C. §2254(d)** 's limits on federal habeas corpus review in rejecting the state court's determination that capital defendant had not been prejudiced by ineffective assistance of counsel in the penalty phase. Under **§2254(d)(1)**, it is not enough to convince a federal habeas court that, in its independent judgment, the state court decision applied *Strickland* incorrectly. The Court found that the federal habeas scheme leaves primary responsibility with the state courts for these judgments and authorizes federal habeas court intervention only when a state court decision is objectively unreasonable application of clearly established federal law.

Bell v. Cone, 535 U.S. 685, 694, 122 S. Ct. 1843, 152 L. Ed 2d 914 (2002)
> A state Court's merit determination is "contrary to" the United States Supreme Court clearly established law if it applies a rule "different from the governing law set forth in Supreme Court cases," or if it "confronts a set of facts that are materially indistinguishable from a decision of the Supreme Court and nevertheless arrives at a result different from Supreme Court precedent." See also *Price v. Vincent*, **538 U.S. 634, 123 S. Ct. 1848, 1853, 155 L. Ed. 2d 877 (2003).**

Mitchell v. Mason, 325 F.3d 732, 741-744 (6th Cir. 2003)
> Counsel who spent approximately six minutes spanning over three separate meetings with petitioner prior to trial and was suspended from practice a month before trial resulted in a complete denial of counsel. The state court's application of *Strickland* standard was an unreasonable application of clearly established Supreme Court law in *Cronic*.

Mitchell v. Mason, 257 F.3d 554, 565 (6th Cir. 2001)
> The state court's analysis of murder defendants claim of complete denial of counsel before trial, as claim of ineffective assistance under *Strickland* standards, was

unreasonable application of clearly established Supreme Court precedent established in *United States v. Cronic*.

Plaskowski v. Casperson, 126 F.Supp. 1149 (E.D. Wis. 2001)
The Court held that there was insufficient evidence to support defendant's conviction and the Wisconsin appellate court's decision holding to the contrary was an unreasonable application of the constitutional standard set forth by the Supreme Court in *Jackson v.Virginia*, 443 U.S. 307, 319, 99 S.Ct. 2781, 61 L.Ed.2d 560 (1979).

Koste v. Dormire, 260 F.3d 872, 879-80 (8th Cir. 2001)
The State Court's decision that Koste could only obtain post-conviction relief on claim that his defense counsel was ineffective due to a conflict of interest if he showed prejudiced was "contrary" to clearly established federal law by Supreme Court precedent in *Holloway V. Arkansas*, 435 U.S. 475, 98 S.Ct. 1173, 55 L.Ed.2d 426 (1976), because Koste had raised a timely objection, and the trial court failed to adequately inquiry into the conflict of interest.

Wanatee v. Ault, 259 F.3d 700, 703-04 (8th Cir. 2001)
The State Court's decision was an unreasonable application of clearly established federal law by Supreme Court precedent, that petitioner was not prejudiced by ineffective assistance of counsel during plea bargaining stage because he subsequently received a fair trial.

Herrera v. Lemaster, 225 F.3d 1176, 1178 (10th Cir. 2000)
The New Mexico state court determination that admission of evidence seized in violation of the Fourth Amendment was harmless error and was contrary to clearly established Supreme Court precedent; the state court did not utilize the *Chapman* standard of harmless beyond a reasonable doubt.

Williams v. Talor, 529 U.S. 420, 120 S. Ct. 1495, 146 LEd.2d 435 (2000)
Under the "unreasonable application" clause, a federal habeas court may grant the writ if the state court identifies the correct governing legal principle from the court's decisions but unreasonably applies that legal principle to the facts of the prisoner's case. *120 S. Ct. at 1522-1523.*

Barker v. Yukins, 199 F.3d 867, 872-73 (6th Cir. 1999)
Petitioner met §2254(d) (1)' s "unreasonable application" standard by showing that the trial court failed to give a proper jury instruction which had a substantial and injurious effect on the jury's verdict.

Atley v. Ault, 191 F.3d 865 (8th Cir. 1999)
The State Appellate Court's holding that the district court made constitutionally adequate *Holloway* inquiry into conflict of interest was an "unreasonable application" of clearly established federal law.

French v. Jones, 41 F.Supp. 2d 726 (E.D. Mich. 1999)
The State Court of Appeals decision that counsel's absence during time when the trial court reinstructed deadlock jury was contrary to federal law and could be set aside under the **AEDPA**.

THE ANTITERRORISM AND EFFECTIVE DEATH PENALTY ACT (AEDPA) AMENDMENTS TO CHAPTER 153 APPLIES ONLY TO CASES FILED AFTER ENACTMENT.

Lindh v. Murphy, 521 U.S. 320, 117 S.Ct. 2059, 138 L.Ed. 2d 481 (1997).
The Supreme Court noted that, in contrast to the provisions concerning <u>non-capital</u> cases, Congress included a section in the AEDPA regarding capital cases that stated that it applied "to cases pending on or after the date of enactment of this act." Id. 117 S.Ct. at 2063. (quoting AEDPA §107(c)). Reading the AEDPA as a whole, the Court concluded that the Act "reveals Congress's intent to apply the amendments to chapter 153 [regarding the habeas corpus statutes for non-capital cases] only to such cases as were filed after the Statutes Enactment." Id. At 117 S.Ct. at 2063. As a result, the Court held that "the new provisions of chapter 153 generally apply only to cases filed after the AEDPA became effective." Id. At 117 S.Ct. at 2063.

CERTIFICATE OF

Appealability/Probable Cause

Henry v. Cockrell, 327 F.3d 429, 431 (5th Cir. 2003)
Under the Antiterrorism and Effective Death Penalty Act (AEDPA) , a petitioner must obtain a <u>certificate</u> <u>of</u> <u>appealability</u> (COA) before he can appeal the district court's decision. **28 U.S.C. §2253(c) (1)**. A COA will be granted only if the petitioner makes "a substantial showing of the denial of a constitutional right." **28 U.S.C. §2253 (c) (2)**. In order to make a substantial showing, a petitioner must demonstrate that a "reasonable jurists would find the district court's assessment of the constitutional claim debatable or wrong." ***Slack v. McDaniel*, 529 U.S. 473, 484, 120 S.Ct. 1595, 146 L.Ed.2d 542 (2000)** . When the district court has denied a claim on procedural grounds, then the petitioner must demonstrate that a "jurists of reason would find it debatable whether the district court was correct in its procedural ruling." **id.** As the Supreme made clear in its decision in ***Miller-El v. Cockrell*, 537 U.S. 322, 123 S.Ct. 1029, 1039, 154 L.Ed.2d 931 (2003)**, a COA is "jurisdictional prerequisite," and "until a COA has been issued, the federal courts of appeals lacks jurisdiction to rule on the merits of appeals from habeas petitioners." When considering a request for a COA, "[t]he question is the debatability of the underlying constitutional claim, not the resolution of that debate." **id. at 1042.**

Roberts v. Dretke, 356 F.3d 632, 640 (5th Cir. 2004)
Counsel's failure to develop evidence of petitioner's mental illness and suicide intentions and make adequate use of court-appointed psychiatrist stated a valid claim of ineffective assistance and warranted a certificate of appealability (COA).

Love v. McCray, 413 F.3d 192, 195 (2nd Cir. 2005)
Counsel's failure to produce or make use of a composite sketch developed from the victim's physical description of the burglar that does not resemble Love stated a valid claim of ineffective assistance of counsel and warranted a COA.

**United States v. Kwan**, 407 F.3d 1005, 1009 (9th Cir. 2005)
> Certificate of Appealability requirements does not apply to motion for writ of error coram nobis proceedings where Kwan has already served his sentence and is no longer in custody.

**Slack v. McDaniel**, 529 U.S. 473, 146 L.Ed.2d 542, 120 S.Ct. 1595 (2000)
> A notice of appeal in a habeas corpus case should be application for Certificate of Appealability.

**Hohn v. United States**, 524 U.S. 236 , 141 L.Ed.2d 242, 118 S.Ct. 1969 , (1998)
> The Supreme Court held to have jurisdiction to review Federal Court of Appeals' denial of **certificate of Appealability** concerning Federal District Court's denial of accused motion under _28 USCS §2255_ to vacate federal conviction.

**U.S. v. Gordon**, 172 F.3d 753 (10th Cir. 1999)
> Ineffective assistance of counsel and due process claims which were not raised on direct appeal were not procedurally barred and required a Certificate of Appealability.

**U.S. v. Kimler**, 150 F. 3d 429 (5th Cir. 1998)
> A notice of appeal is not a constructive request for review of issues refused certification by the district court where the district court certified some, but not all issues. Petitioner **must specifically request** certifications on issues denied by the district court.

**U.S. v. Allen**, 157 F.3d 661 (9th Cir. 1998)
> The Ninth Circuit held that "where a district court has issued a Certificate of Appealability on some issues but not all issues, we treat the briefing of an uncertified issues as a request for a COA and first decide whether one should issue." _**Allen**, 157 F.3d at 665._

**U.S. v. Gobert**, 139 F.3d 436 (5th Cir. 1998)
> _**Gobert's**_ claim that his due process rights were violated where there was insufficient evidence under _**Bailey**_ to establish a factual basis for his guilty plea for "using" a firearm during a drug trafficking offense pursuant to _18 U.S.C. §924 (c)_, required granting a _**Certificate of Appealability**_. _**Gobert's**_ claim basically stated an actual innocence claim where his conduct which he was convicted of was beyond the scope of a criminal statute and would result in a complete miscarriage of justice if the court refused to grant relief.

**Morales v. U.S.**, 25 F. Supp. 2d 246 (S.D.N.Y. 1998)
> Certificate of appealability granted with respect to question whether _**Morales**_ was deprived of the effective assistance of counsel by his trial counsel's failure to more diligently pursue the possibility of testimony favorable to _**Morales**_ from women who had been at the brothel.

**Tokar v. Bowersox**, 1 F. Supp.2d 986 (E.D. Mo. 1998)
> Certificate of Appealability was granted where the court believed a reasonable jurists might disagree with the state trial court's penalty phase jury instructions determination that did not violate petitioner's due process rights.

**Story v. Kindt**, 970 F. Supp. 435,465 (W.D. Pa. 1997)
> Certificate of appealability issued with respect to whether petitioner was deprived of his Sixth Amendment Right to be tried by an impartial jury, by reason of the fact that his jury was death qualified which was not applicable to case.

COA On Procedural Issues

***Slack v. McDaniel*, 529 U.S. 473, 120 S.Ct. 1595, 1600, 146 L.Ed.2d 542 (2000)**
The Supreme Court found when considering whether a COA should be issued where the petition was dismissed on procedural grounds has two components, one directed at the underlying constitutional claims and one directed at the district court's procedural holding. The procedural issues must be resolved first under, ***Ashwander v. TVA*, 297 U.S. 288, 347, 80 L.Ed 688, 56 S.Ct. 466 (1936) (Brandeis, J., concurring)**, allows and encourages the Court to first resolve procedural issues. **Id.**

THE MAILBOX RULE

***Houston v. Lack*, 487 U.S. 266, 275, 108 S.Ct. 2379. 101 L.Ed.2d 245 (1988)**
Pro se prisoner's notice of appeal is considered to be filed on the date that prisoner delivers the notice to prison authorities for mailing. This became known as the "Mailbox Rule."

***Ivy v. Caspari*, 173 F.3d 1136 (8th Cir. 1999)**
Defendant placing his post-conviction motion in the prison mail box on certain date which would meet the deadline rendered the motion timely filed.

***Adams v. U.S.*, 173 F.3d 1339 (11th Cir. 1999)**
"Mailbox rule" on prisoner's filing motions does not extend to a "photocopying rule."

***U.S. v. Gray*, 182 F.3d 762 (10th Cir. 1999)**
The filing date under the "prison mail box rule," is the date the prisoner delivers legal mail "Motion to vacate" to prison authorities for forwarding to the court clerk.

***Spotville v. Cain*, 149 F.3d 374, 378 (5th Cir. 1998)**
Date inmate places his federal habeas petition in prison official hands for mailing is filing date for limitations period under the **AEDPA**.

***Libby v. Magnusson*, 177 F.3d 43, 48 (1st Cir. 1999)**
A second or successive **28 U.S.C. §2254** petition is timely filed, if it is filed within one year of any of the specific events that triggers the **AEDPA's** statute of limitations pursuant to **28 U.S.C. §2244(d) (1) (B)-(D)**.

State Law Procedural Default Rule

***Smith v. Stewart*, 241 F.3d 1191 (9th Cir. 2001)**
Arizona state's procedural default ruling did not rest on independent state law ground so as to bar federal habeas review; state procedural default rule recognized exception for errors of constitutional dimension.

***LA Crosse v. Kernan*, 211 F.3d 468 (9th Cir. 2000)**
A denial for petition for state habeas relief pursuant to untimeliness rule was not based on adequate and independent state-law ground, and thus did not bar federal habeas corpus review of petitioner's claims.

Magistrate Judge's Finding's

Cullen v. U.S., 194 F.3d 401 (2nd Cir. 1999)
> District court was not entitled to reject magistrate Judge's proposed findings of prejudice in §2255 proceeding without conducting a hearing to determine Movant's credibility.

Jailhouse Lawyer's Incompetency

U.S. v. Prince, 167 F.Supp.2d 1296, 1301-02 (D.Kan. 2001)
> Federal prisoner was not entitled to reconsideration of the denial of his **28 U.S.C. §2255** motion to vacate, set aside or correct sentence because jailhouse lawyer failed to properly prepare and argue motion where prisoner adopted the motion by signing the document.

HABEAS MISCELLANEOUS

Estelle v. McGuire, 502 U.S. 62, 67-68, 112 S.Ct. 475, 116 L.Ed.2d 385 (1991)
> Where a state law violation is also a violation of federal law a petitioner may obtain federal habeas relief.

Romandine v. United States, 206 F.3d 731, 736 (7th Cir. 2000)
> The limitation period on successive motions do not apply to statute governing writs of habeas corpus **(28 U.S.C. §2241)** or the Administrative Procedural Act. **See also *Felker v. Turpin*, 518 U.S. 651, 116 S.Ct. 2333, 135 L.Ed.2d 837 (1996)**.

Dismissal of 1st Habeas Petition Is a Serious Matter

Lonchar v. Thomas, 517 U.S. 314, 324, 134 L.Ed.2d 440, 116 S.Ct. 1293 (1996)
> "Dismissal of a first federal habeas petition is a particularly serious matter for that dismissal denies the petitioner the protections of the Great Writ entirely, risking injury to an important interest in human liberty."

Improper Dismissal of Habeas for Failure to Exhaust State Remedies

Reese v. Baldwin, 282 F.3d 1184, 1194 (9th Cir. 2002)
> The district court dismissed petitioner's ineffective assistance of counsel claims for failure to exhaust state remedies. The Ninth Circuit reversed and remanded finding that the petitioner had fairly present his claims to the Oregon Court of Appeals, and to Oregon Supreme Court with instructions to consider petitioner's ineffective assistance of counsel claims.

District Court Must Address All Claims in a Habeas Petition

Clisby v. Jones, 960 F.2d 925, 935-936 (11th Cir. 1992) (en banc)
> The Court held, under the court's supervisory power, that the district courts in this Circuit must address all claims presented in a habeas petition regardless of whether relief is granted or denied. **See also *Rose v. Lundy*, 455 U.S. 509, 102 S .Ct. 1198, 1204, 71 L.Ed.2d 379 (1982)** ("To the extent that the ['total exhaustion'] requirement reduces piecemeal litigation, both the courts and the prisoner should benefit, for as a result the district court will be more likely to review all of the prisoner's claims in a single

proceeding, thus providing for a more focused and thorough review."); *Galtieri v. Wainwright*, 582 F.2d 348, 356 (5th Cir. 1978) (en banc). The *Clisby* Court held that "[t]he havoc a district court's failure to address all claims in a habeas petition may wreak in the federal and state court systems compels us to require all district court to address all such claims. Accordingly, this court, from now on, will vacate the district court's judgment without prejudice and remand the case for consideration of all remaining claims whenever the district court has not resolved all such claims." **Id. at 960 F.2d 938.**

Catlin v. United States, 324 U.S. 229-244, 89 L.ed 911, 916 (1921)
A "final decision" generally is one which ends the litigation on the merits and leaves nothing for the court to do but execute the judgment.

Laffey v. Northwest Airlines, Inc., 642 F.2d 578, 584 (D.C. Cir. 1980)
An order is final only when the court has resolved all disputed matters before it and need take no further action save to execute the judgment. The 1974 order did not meet this standard of finality because it left unadjudicated the calculations essential to ascertainment of the amount of back pay NWA owed each employee who was victimized by its Equal Pay Act and Title VII transgressions. **Id. at 642 F.2d at 584. See also** *Johnson v. Combs*, **471 F.2d 84, 87 (5th Cir. 1972), cert. denied, 413 U.S. 922, 93 S.Ct. 3063, 37 L.Ed.2d 1044 (1973).**

In Re Gerry, 670 F.Supp. 276, 277 (ND. Cal. 1987)
An order is final only when the court has resolved all disputed matters before it and no further action is required except the execution of the judgment."

In "Custody" Requirement

Garlotte v. Fordice, 515 U.S. 29, 115 S.Ct. 1948, 132 L.Ed. 36 (1995)
A prisoner serving consecutive sentences is "in custody" under any one of them for purposes of habeas statute requirements for being in custody.***

Federal Rules of Civil Procedure, Rule 59

Rule 59. New Trials; Amendment of Judgments provides that:

(a) **Grounds.** A new trial may be granted to all or any of the parties and on all or part of the issues (1) in an action in which there has been a trial by jury, for any of the reasons for which new trials have heretofore been granted in actions at law in the courts of the United States; and (2) in an action tried without a jury, for any of the reasons for which rehearings have heretofore been granted in suits in equity in the courts of the United States. On a motion for a new trial in an action tried without a jury, the court may open the judgment if one has been entered, take additional testimony, amend findings of fact and conclusions of law or make new findings and conclusions, and direct the entry of a new judgment.

(b) **Time for Motion.** A motion for a new trial shall be served not later than 10 days after the entry of the judgment.

(c) **Time for Serving affidavits.** When a motion for new trial is based upon affidavits, they shall be served with the motion. The opposing party has 10 days after such service within which to serve opposing affidavits, but that period may be extended for an additional period not exceeding 20 days, either by the court for good cause or by the parties' written stipulation. The court may permit reply affidavits.

(d)   On Initiative of Court. Not later than 10 days after entry of judgment the court, of its own initiative, may order a new trial for any reason for which it might have granted a new trial on motion of a party. After giving the parties notice and an opportunity to be heard on the matter, the court may grant a motion for new trial, timely served, for a reason not stated in the motion. In either case, the court shall specify in the order the grounds therefor.

(e)   Motion to Alter or Amend a Judgment. A motion to alter or amend the judgment shall be served not later than 10 days after entry of the judgment.

Browder v. Director, Ill. Dept. Of Corrections, 434 U. S. 257, 54 L.Ed.2d 521, 98 S.Ct. 556 (1978)
> Rule 52 through Rule 59 which have strict time limits, are applicable to habeas corpus proceedings and any timely Rule 52, & 59 motion for reconsiderations tolls the time for filing notice of appeal.

Browder v. Director, Ill. Dept. Of Corrections, 434 U.S. 257, 54 L.Ed.2d 521, 98 S.Ct. 556 (1978)
> A motion under Fed. R. Civil Proc. Rule 59, which is *not* filed within the 10 day period as required by the Rule, does not toll the time for filing a notice of appeal.

Fabian v. Reed, 707 F.2d 147, 148 & n.l (5th Cir. 1983)
> Motion for reconsideration filed within 10 days of entry of judgment is treated as a motion to alter or amend the judgment under Federal Rules of Civil Procedure, Rule 59(e), which effectively tolls the period for filing a notice of appeal.

389 Orange St. Partners v. Arnold, 179 F.3d 656, 665 (9th Cir. 1999)
> A Rule 59(e) motion for reconsideration should not be granted, absent highly unusual circumstances, unless the district court is presented with newly discovered evidence, committed clear error, or if there is an intervening change in law.

Parkus v. Delo, 985 F.2d 425, 426 (8th Cir. 1993)
> Federal Rules of Civil Procedure, Rule 6(a), governs the computation of time period for filing timely **Rule 59(e)** motions. Under Rule 6(a), intermediate Saturdays, Sundays, and legal holidays (State and Federal), are excluded from the computation for filing timely Rule 59(e) motions.

York v. Tate, 858 F.2d 322, 326 (6th Cir. 1988), cert. denied, 490 U.S. 1049 (1989)
> A timely Rule 59(e) rehearing petition seeking reconsideration of petition tolls time for appeal.

United States v. Davis, 924 F.2d 501, 506 (3rd Cir. 1991)
> A timely Rule 59 motion to alter or amend a district judgment strips the appellate court of jurisdiction, regardless of whether the Rule 59 motion was filed before or after the notice of appeal.

Federal Rules of Civil Procedure, Rule 60

Rule 60. Relief from Judgment or Order provides that:

(a) Clerical Mistakes. Clerical mistakes in judgments, orders or other parts of the record and errors therein arising from oversight or omission may be corrected by the court at any time of its initiative or on the motion of any party and after such notice, if any, as the court orders. During the pendency of an appeal, such mistakes may be so corrected before the appeal is docketed in the appellate court, and thereafter while the appeal is pending may be so corrected with leave of the appellate court.

(b) Mistakes, Inadvertence; Excusable Neglect; Newly Discovered evidence, Fraud, Etc. On motion and upon such terms as are just, the court may relieve a party or a party's legal representative from a final judgment, order, or proceeding for the following reasons; (1) mistake, inadvertence, surprise, or excusable neglect; (2) newly discovered evidence which by due diligence could not have been discovered in time to move for a new trial under Rule 59(b); (3) fraud (whether heretofore denominated intrinsic or extrinsic), misrepresentation, or other misconduct of an adverse party; (4) the judgment is void; (5) the judgment has been satisfied, released, or discharged, or a prior judgment upon which it is based has been reversed or otherwise vacated, or it is no longer equitable that the judgment should have prospective application; or (6) any other reason justifying relief from the operation of the judgment. The motion shall be made within reasonable time, and for reasons (1), (2), and (3) not more than one year after the judgment, order or proceedings was entered or taken. A motion under this subdivision (b) does not affect the finality of a judgment or suspend its operation. This rule does not limit the power of a court to entertain an independent action to relieve a party from a judgment, order, or proceedings, or to grant relief to a defendant not actually personally notified as provided in Title 28 U.S.C. §1651, or to set aside a judgment for fraud upon the court. Writs of coram nobis, coram vobis. audita querela, and bills of review and bills in obtaining any relief from a judgment shall be by motion as prescribed in these rules or by an independent action.

Fierro v. Johnson, 197 F.3d 147, 150 (5th Cir. 1999)
Fierro filed a motion requesting that the district court vacate its earlier judgment denying his first habeas petition. Fierro argued in his motion that the district had authority to vacate its earlier judgment under (1) its "inherent equitable powers"; (2) Fed. R. Civ. P. 60(b)(5); and (3) Fed. R. Civ. P. 60(b) (6). The district court denied the motion, relying on Fifth Circuit precedent holding that Rule 60(b) motions are treated as successive habeas petitions. The district court then concluded that it had no jurisdiction to consider the arguments in the motion because the Fifth Circuit had not authorized a successive habeas petition on grounds stated in the motion. After having his motion denied, Fierro sought to obtain a Certificate of Appealability ("COA') in the Fifth Circuit, hoping to obtain authorization for an appeal of the denial of his motion for relief from judgment. The Fifth Circuit denied the ("COA") as being unnecessary and instructed Fierro that he did not need to seek a COA to appeal the denial of his motion based on his equitable claims.

Pasatiempo v. Aizawa, 103 F.3d 796, 801 (9th Cir. 1996)
The denial of a motion for reconsideration under Fed. R. Civ. P. Rule 59(e) is construed as a denial of relief under Rule 60(b).

Cooter & Gell v. Hartmarx Corp., 496 U.S. 384, 405, 110 S.Ct., 2447, 2461, ,110 L.Ed.2d 359 (1990)
A court abuses its discretion when its ruling is based on an erroneous view of the law or on a clearly erroneous assessment of the evidence.

Floyd v. Laws, 929 F.2d 1390, 1400 (9th Cir. 1991)
An appeal from a denial of a Rule 60(b) motion brings up only the denial of the motion for review, not the merits of the underlying judgment.

Faile v. Upjohn Co., 988 F.2d 985 (9th Cir. 1993)
The Court reversed a denial of Rule 60(b) motion to vacate dismissal, where the district court had failed to apply provision of **Fed. R. Civ. P Rule 5(b)**, that service is complete upon mailing.

Banks v. U.S., *167 F.3d 1082, 1083-84 (7th Cir. 1999)*
> Fed. R. Civil Proc. Rule 60(b) motion for relief from judgment in initial post-conviction proceedings is appropriate means to bring claim that conduct of counsel affected the integrity the post-conviction proceeding.

Meadows v. Gohen, *409 F.2d 750 (5th Cir. 1969)*
> The Court of appeals held that the district court abused its discretion in not granting a Rule 60(b) motion for relief from a judgment, "which was clearly at variance with the plain wording" of a federal statute." **Id. at 753**.

Ames v. Miller, *184 F.Supp.2d 566, 578 (N.D. Tex. 2002)*
> The "law of the case" doctrine does not prevent relief under **Rule 60(b)**. The fact that the judgment sought to be set aside had been affirmed on appeal does not impair the trial court's ability to grant **Rule 60(b)** relief *Standard Oil Co. v. United States*, **429 U.S. 17, 97 S.Ct. 31, 50 L.Ed.2d 21 (1976)**.

United States v. Eisen, *974 F.2d 246, 253 (2nd Cir. 1992)*
> Misrepresentations in pleadings and pretrial submissions were made in the hope of fraudulently inducing a settlement before trial.

United States v. Rodolitz, *786 F.2d 77 (2nd Cir.) cert. denied, 479 U.S. 826,107 S.Ct. 102, 93 L.Ed.2d 52 (1986)*
> The defendant had brought a fraudulent civil action against his insurance company and recovered a money judgment from the company at trial. In affirming the defendant's conviction for mail fraud, the Court explicitly recognized that false evidence at a civil trial works not only on the jury but on the opposing party as well. **Id. at 80-81. See also** ***Averbach v. Rival Manufacturing Co.*, 809 F.2d 1016 (3d Cir.), cert. denied, 482 U.S. 915, 107 S.Ct. 3187, 96 L.Ed.2d 675 (1987).**

Metcalf v. Williams, *104 S.Ct. 93, 26 L.Ed 665 (1881)*
> Courts of equity may set aside judgments obtained by fraud, accident or mistake, where there is no remedy at law.

Outen v. Balitmore County, *177 FDR 346 (DC Md. 1998), aff'd without op (4th Cir. 1998), 164 F.3d 625, reported in full (1998), CA4 Md) 1998 US App. LEXIS 26289:*
> One year limitations period of FRCP 60(b) (3) does not limit court's power to set aside judgment under "fraud on the court" doctrine.

Averbach v. Rival MFG. Co., *809 F.2d 1016, 1021-22 (3rd Cir. 1987)*
> Time limit in Fed. R. Civ. P. 60 permitting relief from final judgment, on motion made within one year, for fraud, misrepresentation, or other misconduct of adverse party did not apply to independent actions also permitted by Rule 60.

Harris v. United States, *367 F.3d 74, 82 (2nd Cir. 2004)*
> Motion for relief from judgment pursuant to **Rule 60 (b)(6)** attacking the integrity of a previous habeas proceedings based on ineffective assistance of counsel must be so egregious and profound that they amount to the abandonment of the clients case altogether, either through physical disappearance or constructive disappearance and deprived movant of any opportunity to be heard. **See *United States v. Cirami*, 563 F.2d 26, 34-35 (2nd Cir. 1977); *Vindigni v. Meyer*, 441 F.2d 376 (2nd Cir. 1995). See also *Baldayague v. United States*, 338 F.3d 145, 154 (2nd Cir. 2003)** (Jacobs, J., concurring)

(habeas lawyer does not act as client's agent when he takes a fee to file a case and then deliberately fails to do so, depriving his client of an opportunity to be heard).

Ritter v. Smith, 811 F.2d 1398, 1401 (11th Cir. 1987)

The *Riiter* court held that a supervening change in the law could, but, would not always, constitute sufficiently extraordinary circumstances to warrant relief from a final judgment under Rule 60(b)(6). See id. at 1401. There the supervening change in the law was in the form of a final and definitive ruling by the Supreme Court of the United States. Several additional factors convinced this court that Rule 60(b)(6) relief was appropriate; the judgment from which relief was sought became final; there was a close relationship between the two cases; and consideration of comity. Id. at 1401-03.

Lopez v. Douglas, 141 F.3d 974 (10th Cir. 1998)

Federal Rules of Civil Procedure, Rule 60(b)(6) motion for relief from judgment cannot be used to circumvent restraints on successive habeas petitions.

U.S. v. Rich, 141 F.3d 550, 551-52 (5th Cir. 1998)

A motion for reconsideration under Fed. R. Civ. P. Rule 60(b)(6), which essentially seeks to set aside the criminal conviction constitutes a second or successive motion to vacate, set aside or correct sentence, and cannot be used to circumvent the restrictions under the Antiterrorism and Effective Death Penalty Act.

Community Dental Services v. Tani, 282 F.3d 1164, 1168 (9th Cir. 2002)

"To obtain relief from . . . judgment under 'catch-all' clause of rule, on ground of 'extraordinary circumstances' which prevented or rendered a party unable to prosecute or defend his case, the party must demonstrate both injury and circumstances beyond his control that prevented him proceeding with the prosecution or defense of the action in a proper fashion."

Gray v. Estelle, 574 F.2d 209, 214 (5th Cir. 1978)

District Court abused its discretion refusing to grant a full evidentiary hearing under the provisions of **Rule 60 (b) (6)** to resolve the conflict of interest and waiver issues.